THE MARK TWAIN PAPERS

Edited from manuscripts chiefly in the
Mark Twain Papers at the University of California, Berkeley,
and the Henry W. and Albert A. Berg Collection
of The New York Public Library.

From Your friend
Saml L. Clemens.

MARK TWAIN'S
LETTERS
TO
HIS
PUBLISHERS

1867–1894

Edited with an Introduction by Hamlin Hill

Mark Twain

UNIVERSITY OF CALIFORNIA PRESS
Berkeley and Los Angeles **1967**

CENTER FOR EDITIONS OF
AMERICAN AUTHORS
AN APPROVED TEXT
MODERN LANGUAGE
ASSOCIATION OF AMERICA

UNIVERSITY OF CALIFORNIA PRESS
Berkeley and Los Angeles, California

CAMBRIDGE UNIVERSITY PRESS
London, England

© 1967 The Mark Twain Company
Library of Congress Catalog Number: 66–16422

Designed by Adrian Wilson

Manufactured in the United States of America

Editor's Preface

THE PRESENT volume includes the texts of 290 letters by Mark Twain to his publishers. Twenty-three letters have been included from texts in *Mark Twain, Business Man* in order to provide a complete perspective on Mark Twain's career; the originals of these letters are presently inaccessible for scholarly research. Another five are reprinted from *Mark Twain's Letters*, since the location of the originals is not now known.

A few letters not addressed to Mark Twain's official publishers—letters to Orion Clemens, Charles Dudley Warner, T. B. Pugh, Thomas Bailey Aldrich, and Moncure Conway, for example—are included because their major substance concerns publishing.

All letters except those reprinted from *Mark Twain's Letters* and *Mark Twain, Business Man* are previously unpublished and are transcribed wherever possible from originals or photocopy duplicates. For a number of years, however, the editors of the Mark Twain Estate have been collecting typescripts of letters from book dealers' catalogs, auction records, and private collectors. Whenever a letter depends upon a typescript rather than the original, the "Calendar of Letters" at the end of the volume indicates this.

Locations and dates of letters have been regularized, with those places and parts of dates supplied by the editor included in square brackets. Complimentary closes and signatures are transcribed as they were written.

Postscripts have been placed at the end of the text of a letter, regardless of where Mark Twain may have written them. Interlineations and marginal comments have been placed at the appropriate place in the text without editorial comment.

No attempt has been made to include all Mark Twain's deletions Only those which can be accurately read and which change the substantive meaning of a letter are revived, and enclosed in the text with angle brackets. Editorial comment and intrusions are indicated, as are conjectural dates and locations, by square brackets; Mark Twain's square brackets have been rendered as parentheses.

Silent editing and normalization have been kept to an absolute minimum. Obvious typographical errors have been corrected and Mark Twain's slips of the pen revised, but consistent spelling and punctuation peculiarities have been retained—the spelling *envelop,* for example. The only significant exception to this rule is that Mark Twain's usual ampersands have been spelled out as *and,* except in the titles of organizations (Chatto & Windus, Charles L. Webster & Co.).

Complete texts of letters are always included, except when a substantial portion (always about non-business matters) will be published in another volume in the present series.

Acknowledgments

T HE COLLECTING of the materials included in this volume has depended in great measure upon the generosity of curators of libraries and owners of letters. The following persons have earned my deep thanks for their assistance: Mr. John D. Gordan, Chief of the Henry W. and Albert A. Berg Collection, New York Public Library; Mr. Edwin Sy, Curator of Special Collections, Lockwood Memorial Library, State University of New York at Buffalo; Mr. Kenneth A. Lohf, Columbia University Libraries; Mr. Clifton Waller Barrett and Miss Anne Freudenberg, Acting Curator of Manuscripts, University of Virginia Libraries; Mr. W. H. Bond, Librarian, Harvard College Libraries, and Mr. Richard Jenness and Miss Priscilla Smith, Houghton Mifflin Company; Mr. Robert O. Dougan, Henry E. Huntington Library (for holdings HM 7251 and HM 7252); Mr. Frederick B. Adams, Director, and Mr. Herbert Cahoon, Curator of Autograph Manuscripts, Pierpont Morgan Library; Mr. Matt. P. Lowman, Curator of Rare Books, Newberry Library; and Mr. Donald Gallup, Curator, American Literature Collections, Yale University Library.

Professors Walter Blair and Henry Nash Smith both read the manuscript and made valuable suggestions. Mrs. Ellen Ballou, Providence, R.I., and Mr. Charles Gold, St. Louis, provided helpful information.

The American Council of Learned Societies, the University of New Mexico's Alumni Organization and Research Allocations

Committee all provided funds for clerical aid in preparing the manuscript.

Frederick Anderson, literary editor of the Mark Twain Papers, added to his reputation for patient assistance; he suggested, advised, and cajoled the manuscript along its way during my seven-month siege of the Mark Twain Papers with avuncular concern.

Finally, there is the monumental debt of gratitude to a family which endures a near-nomadic existence with minimal complaint. My wife Arlette and my children Cynthia, Scott, and Sondra would each have been, in different times and circumstances, a gold-leaf, kid-glove, diamond-breastpin pilot.

Contents

Abbreviations

THE FOLLOWING abbreviations and location symbols have been used in the annotation. (For the location of the textual authority for the letters, see the "Calendar of Letters.") Unless otherwise indicated, all letters to Mark Twain quoted in the documentation are transcribed from the originals in the Mark Twain Papers.

RECIPIENTS OF LETTERS

EB	Elisha Bliss
FJH	Fred J. Hall
JRO	James R. Osgood
CLW	Charles L. Webster

PREVIOUSLY PUBLISHED TEXTS

BMT (*1935*)	Merle Johnson, *A Bibliography of the Works of Mark Twain* (New York: Harper and Brothers, 1935).
LE	*Letters from the Earth,* ed. Bernard DeVoto (New York: Harper and Row, 1962).
LLMT	*The Love Letters of Mark Twain,* ed. Dixon Wecter (New York: Harper and Brothers, 1949).
MT&BH	Margaret Duckett, *Mark Twain and Bret Harte* (Norman: University of Oklahoma Press, 1964).
MT&EB	Hamlin Hill, *Mark Twain and Elisha Bliss* (Columbia: University of Missouri Press, 1964).
MT&GA	Bryant M. French, *Mark Twain and The Gilded Age* (Dallas: Southern Methodist University Press, 1965).
MT&H	Walter Francis Frear, *Mark Twain and Hawaii* (Chicago: Lakeside Press, 1947).
MT&HF	Walter Blair, *Mark Twain and Huck Finn* (Berkeley and Los Angeles: University of California Press, 1960).

MTB   Albert Bigelow Paine, *Mark Twain: A Biography* (New York: Harper and Brothers, 1912).

MTBus   *Mark Twain, Business Man,* ed. Samuel C. Webster (Boston: Little, Brown, 1946).

MTE   *Mark Twain in Eruption,* ed. Bernard DeVoto (New York: Harper and Brothers, 1940).

MTHL   *Mark Twain-Howells Letters,* ed. Henry Nash Smith and William M. Gibson (Cambridge: Harvard University Press, 1960).

MTL   *Mark Twain's Letters,* ed. Albert Bigelow Paine (New York: Harper and Brothers, 1917).

MTLC   Paul Fatout, *Mark Twain on the Lecture Circuit* (Bloomington: University of Indiana Press, 1960).

MTLM   *Mark Twain's Letters to Mary,* ed. Lewis Leary (New York: Columbia University Press, 1961).

MTMF   *Mark Twain to Mrs. Fairbanks,* ed. Dixon Wecter (San Marino, Calif.: Huntington Library, 1949).

MTSFC   *Mark Twain: San Francisco Correspondent,* ed. Henry Nash Smith and Frederick Anderson (San Francisco: Book Club of California, 1957).

MTTB   *Mark Twain's Travels with Mr. Brown,* ed. Franklin Walker and G. Ezra Dane (New York: Alfred A. Knopf, 1940).

MTW   Bernard DeVoto, *Mark Twain at Work* (Cambridge: Harvard University Press, 1942).

TG   Guy Cardwell, *Twins of Genius* (East Lansing: Michigan State University Press, 1954).

Weber   Carl J. Weber, *The Rise and Fall of James Ripley Osgood* (Waterville, Maine: Colby College Press, 1959).

COLLECTIONS IN LIBRARIES

Berg   Henry W. and Albert A. Berg Collection
                   New York Public Library

Columbia   Columbia University Library
                   New York City

CWB   Clifton Waller Barrett Library
                   University of Virginia Library

Hartford   Mark Twain Memorial
   Memorial   Hartford, Connecticut

Harvard	Rogers Theater Collection Harvard University Library
MTP	Mark Twain Papers University of California Library Berkeley
Yale	Mark Twain Collections Yale University Library

INTRODUCTION

"The Bastard Monkey and the Human Louse"

"I have never hated any creature with a hundred thou-
sandth fraction of the hatred which I bear that human
louse, Webster."

(MT to Orion Clemens, [Elmira], 1 July, 1889)

Elisha Bliss "was a tall, lean, skinny, yellow, toothless
bald-headed, rat-eyed professional liar and scoundrel.
. . . He was a most repulsive creature. When he was
after dollars he showed the intense earnestness and eager-
ness of a circular-saw. In a small, mean, peanut-stand
fashion, he was sharp and shrewd. But above that level
he was destitute of intelligence; his brain was a loblolly,
and he had the gibbering laugh of an idiot. It is my belief
that Bliss never did an honest thing in his life, when he
had a chance to do a dishonest one. I have had contact
with several conspicuously mean men, but they were
noble compared to this bastard monkey."

(Unpublished autobiographical dictation,
21 February 1906 [TS²])

1

I T WAS a dangerously dehumanizing experience to be Mark Twain's publisher; Charles L. Webster also became "not a man, but a hog" (MT to Pamela Moffett, Elmira, 1 July 1889), and Webster's successor, Fred J. Hall, was transformed into a tadpole (*LLMT*, p. 300). Although the most feverish portion of the author's energies went into the composing, publishing, and marketing of his books, the most vitriolic of his hatreds were reserved for the very men who helped guide his literary work through its production and presentation to an audience.

After publishing *The Jumping Frog* with Charles H. Webb in 1867, the humorist published his next six volumes with the American Publishing Company of Hartford, directed by Elisha Bliss, from 1869 through 1880. In 1881, James R. Osgood published *The Prince and the Pauper,* followed by *Life on the Mississippi* and several small trade books—to be sold in bookstores. In 1884, Clemens provided the capital to found Charles L. Webster & Co., with his niece's husband as titular head. And from 1888 until Charles L. Webster & Co. went bankrupt in 1894, the organization was run by Fred J. Hall. None of these five major publishers escaped Clemens's wrath.

As a businessman whose commitment to the successful marketing of his books was of paramount importance, this author had serious difficulties reconciling his commercial ambitions with his literary judgment. The standards by which he gauged his success— 40,000 advance orders and impressive royalty checks—unfortunately often served as substitutes for literary or aesthetic values. Coming to "literature" from the commercial background of newspaper work and journalism, he tended much of the time to look upon his travel books as merchandise whose worth was its market value.

The world of subscription book publishing into which Clemens moved in 1867 could only have strengthened his commercial approach to "literature." It was a world of cynical and dishonest practices aimed at amassing the largest possible profit from material all too often of dubious value. Publishers betrayed not only their customers but their authors, their general agents and their canvassers as well. Prospectuses—sample pages in a sample binding carried by the door-to-door canvassers—were contrived to distort and misrepresent the volumes they described. Instructions to agents contained advice that could only insult whatever integrity they possessed. Charles L. Webster & Co.'s grisly decision to publish Sheridan's and Sherman's volumes to coincide with the deaths of those ailing generals epitomized the shrewdness with which subscription publishers could search for extra profit. It is small wonder that James R. Osgood, following the principles of respectable New England trade publication, went bankrupt trying to sell books by subscription.

But in the record that survives, there is not a single indication that Clemens disapproved of or deplored the methods his publishers used, or declined the tangible rewards of their work. The author "Mark Twain" was dragged into this world by businessman Samuel L. Clemens; and there were some obvious internal conflicts with resulting rages (whose blasts frequently singed the publisher who happened to be standing by). Although the author condemned aggressive materialism in narratives written during a wide span of years—*The Gilded Age, A Connecticut Yankee,* and *The £1,000,000 Bank-Note,* for example—there was still more than a hint of public confession in his portrayal of schemers, inventors, and entrepreneurs. One of Mark Twain's aquiline eyes was on the cash box, while the other focused on the almost ascetically high-minded world of the New England literary Brahmins.

In part, then, Clemens's antagonism toward his publishers was merely an antagonism toward the commercial aspect of his own personality. In flush times, when they could report impressive sales or mail royalty checks for several thousand dollars, Bliss, Osgood, Webster, and Hall were astute businessmen rather than monkeys or lice. But having sacrificed genteel approval by stubbornly choosing subscription publication, Clemens blamed his publishers (in arduously intemperate language) when a volume failed or a promotion scheme fell through. He blamed Bliss for the relative commercial failure of *Tom Sawyer* when in fact it was Twain who authorized the premature publication of the English edition which resulted in a flood of cheap Canadian reprints. He blamed Osgood for overprinting *Life on the Mississippi* when he had himself authorized the binding of an unneeded 10,000 copies. And he complained to Fred Hall that publishing costs had absorbed all the profits for *A Connecticut Yankee* when it was Clemens who insisted on expensive illustrations.

The letters collected in the present volume depict both Mark Twain, the author fussing with his manuscripts and correcting proof, and Samuel L. Clemens, the businessman suggesting illustrators and promotion plans, examining bindings and prospectuses. The novice, overwhelmed at the mechanics of publishing *The Innocents Abroad,* became a director of the American Publishing Company, concerned with those mercantile aspects of bookmaking which would insure his dividends as well as his royalties. Success and a decade's experience with Bliss led businessman Clemens to desire to reap the publisher's share of the profits as well as the author's. And after the abortive experiment with Osgood, author Mark Twain created the Frankenstein's monster, Charles L. Webster & Co.—only to discover that Clemens's obligations as a publisher were contrary to Twain's interests as an author. For the Company created with his capital abandoned one of his books (the *Library of Humor*) in order to follow the subscription-book rule of capitalizing on topical material. The impracticable, often self-contradictory advice and commands became even more confused when Mark Twain's literary interests had to compete with other authors' business interests in addition to his own.

If Mark Twain speaks for himself here, what does he say about the major publishers of his writing career? In the parts of his autobiography published under the title *Mark Twain in Eruption,* an embittered old man recorded his recollections of the bastard monkey, the human louse, and the tadpole. These reminiscences have been generally dismissed as a product of faulty memory and rancor; yet, beneath the vitriol, Mark Twain remembered his facts with amazing accuracy. In addition, Bliss, Osgood, Webster, and Hall speak for themselves here in the annotation (though the documentation during the Charles L. Webster period is much more thorough, simply because Mark Twain retained many more letters from his own Company than he did from Bliss or Osgood).

Bliss and Osgood were both older men than the humorist (thirteen and eleven years older), and neither tended to look upon him with any significant awe. When Bliss, whose scruples and business ethics required constant scrutiny, began his association with the writer, he was not only the older man but also much wiser in subscription-book mechanics and technique. Cannily aware of Mark Twain's potential, Bliss obtained the writer's signature on four book contracts by 1871, and whenever Clemens showed signs of bolting or insisting on his own way, Bliss could provide the legal pressure necessary to bring him back. In a sense, Bliss was too successful for the author's ultimate welfare; for it was those sales which Bliss led him to expect that made all his publishing ventures after the 1870's anticlimactic.

If Bliss was too successful, Clemens believed (correctly) that honesty was not one of his publisher's most impressive virtues. But James R. Osgood proved that an honest man had no place in the subscription-book business. Equipped with an impressive publishing heritage and an equally impressive list of authors, Osgood was as naive about subscription-book business as the humorist had been a dozen years earlier. And Clemens should have been astute enough by 1881 to know that *The Prince and the Pauper* was unpalatable fare for subscription publication. In a much quieter way than Bliss, Osgood defended his own judgments and refused to retreat before the writer's onslaughts.

Webster was sixteen years younger than Mark Twain, and his nephew as well. He had spent a three-year apprenticeship catering to his uncle's whims, running his errands, and learning his weaknesses. In response to the statements published in *Mark Twain in Eruption,* Samuel C. Webster edited *Mark Twain, Business Man* as an apologia for his father's management of the Company. His convincing portrayal has been accepted too readily by unwary students who frequently have echoed his representation. The present editor, for example, has written, "Twain's overwhelming, and occasionally overbearing, personality was a juggernaut under which Webster threw himself for eight years . . . quietly patient, docile, and self-effacing" (*MT&EB,* p. 158). The fact is that Charles L. Webster's letters to his uncle, which Samuel Webster unfortunately did not examine while editing his volume, become increasingly dictatorial, overweening, and almost hysterical as a result of the Company's early success. Unlike Bliss, who carried on an open conflict with Mark Twain, Webster overwhelmed and confused his uncle with elaborate monetary statistics. An accurate portrait of Charley Webster lies somewhere between the one in *Mark Twain in Eruption* and the one in *Mark Twain, Business Man;* the present volume should prove that it is considerably closer to the former than has been generally recognized.

Whatever the reasons (and the following record shows that they were significantly Webster's responsibility), by the time Fred Hall took command of Charles L. Webster & Co. in 1888 it was a gasping, moribund organization. Hall was even younger than Webster; he was 27—25 years younger than Clemens. The letters show that the *Library of American Literature* required such staggering operating expenses that the Company could not afford to subsidize it. They show it is untrue that Clemens drained badly needed capital from the Company to finance the Paige typesetter, although such a statement has often been accepted. After 1888, when he received his share of the profits from the sale of Grant's *Memoirs,* Clemens took only a very small percentage of his accrued royalties from the organization and none of his working capital of $75,000. Instead he allowed this money to remain in the Company, together with its interest, and supplied more than $60,000 in additional loans from his wife.

The pre-panic years of the early nineties undoubtedly made themselves felt in the pocketbooks of the very class of rural buyers upon whom subscription volumes depended. Increasing urbanization made trade bookstores more easily available, and increasing education may have elevated the general reading public's taste above the typical subscription offering. Whatever the reasons, the subscription market disappeared in the early 1890's, and Hall attempted to transform the Company by converting to trade publication. By 1893 Webster's entire subscription machinery except for the *Library of American Literature* was supplanted by dollar trade books.

But the $200,000 indebtedness from the subscription years could not be overcome—and certainly not by the sale of the jejune volumes Fred Hall chose to publish. His special tactic, promising Clemens flush times "next year"—and borrowing another $5000—at least kept the Company afloat another few years; but it made the crash even more audible.

The quarter-century which these letters span were the most productive years of Mark Twain's life. With the exception of the fragments of *The Mysterious Stranger,* they produced all of the significant literature upon which his reputation rests. Before 1867, he was an apprentice; after 1894, his world was one of unfinished manuscripts, personal tragedy, and increasing misanthropy. In a very real sense, he equated subscription success with the happier years of the 1870's and 1880's. As two letters to Henry Rogers suggest, the subscription book *Following the Equator* became his "objective correlative" with a past for which he wistfully hoped:

> [Frank Bliss] offers a guaranty of $10,000 on a round-the-world book. . . . I can write the *very book* for the subscription trade, and do it without difficulty. . . . I can write a book that Bliss can sell 60,000 copies of in 6 months and pay me $30,000—or, as he suggests, a possible $40,000. (Elmira, 11 June 1895)

> I think my reason for wanting my travel-book in Bliss's hands is sound. Harper publishes very high-class books and they go to people who are accustomed to read. That class are surfeited with travel-books. But there is a vast class that isn't—the factory hands and the farmers. *They* never go to a bookstore; they have to be hunted down by the canvasser. When a subscription book of mine sells 60,000, I always think I know whither 50,000 of them went. They went to people who don't visit bookstores.

> I planned this book, from the beginning, for the *subscription* market. I am writing it according to that plan. If it doesn't pay me $30,000 in the first six months, it will be because the new Bliss's lack their old father's push and efficiency. (London, November [1896])

If he yearned for a world that no longer existed, that same world and that part of his experience became his excuse for failure as well. The day after Clemens received the telegram informing him of the death of his daughter Susy, he wrote his wife from London: "I have spent the day alone—thinking; sometimes bitter thoughts, sometimes only sad ones. Reproaching myself for laying the foundation of all our troubles and this final disaster in opposing Pamela when she did not want Annie to marry that Webster adventurer." Whatever else such pathetic illogic tells about Mark Twain, it underscores the fact that in these letters there is something more than mere business detail. Mark Twain reveals here a part of himself and a part of his life that was essential both to his view of himself and to any reader's comprehension of his complex personality.

I

"I Abhor . . . Business"

(1867–1871)

"I abhor everything in the nature of business and don't even attend to my own."
Mark Twain to Mollie Clemens,
MTBus, p. 90

A s a jour printer, correspondent, and newspaper reporter, Mark Twain had had an extensive background in the mechanics of publishing before he became a full-fledged author. But, his attitude toward his first book, *The Jumping Frog,* was indifferent at best. There are no indications he read proof or paid very much attention to the marketing of that volume. And the casualness of his appointment of Frank Fuller as his "business agent" suggests that there were many things on Mark Twain's mind other than becoming a writer of books.

When Elisha Bliss wrote him in 1867 proposing a volume on the subscription plan, Twain replied that the question of probable profit from such a book "has a degree of importance for me which is almost beyond my own comprehension" (letter 3 below). Throughout the first four years of their relationship, Mark Twain was a

9

neophyte and Elisha Bliss was his mentor in the tactics of subscription publishing. The question of whether book writing could be as profitable as newspaper writing was not answered until after the publication of *The Innocents Abroad* and *Roughing It.*

With the success of those two books, Mark Twain was swept up into the current of the American Publishing Company's operations. And the increasing stream of letters to Elisha Bliss and his son Frank, Treasurer of the Company, his purchase of stock in the Company and eventual election to a directorship, and his securing a place for his brother Orion in the operation of the firm all attest to the fact that Mark Twain was becoming incurably smitten with the methods of high-power salesmanship and the complexities of book production.

1. To CHARLES H. WEBB

St. Louis
19 March [1867]

Friend Webb—

Everything is going well here, with the pilots, and I shall see that the same is the case with the New Orleans river men.[1]

Telegraph me what date you expect to publish, and if it is to be more than ten days hence, I had better lecture here. I have been invited, and I have promised to give the committee an answer just as soon as you can telegraph me from N.Y. about the book. If you are to publish before March is out, though, I will preach in N.Y. first.

Yrs Truly

Mark

[1] MT was on a lecture tour of the Midwest during March 1867 (see *MTTB*, pp. 122–148); perhaps he had attempted to gain publicity for *The Jumping Frog* from the river pilots.

2. To FRANK FULLER

New York
1 June 1867

Gov. Frank Fuller—

Dear Sir:

Please take charge of my affairs while I am gone to Europe, (as per previous understanding,) and in the absence of a better, let this note be full and sufficient authority. Collect the ten cents a copy due me on all sales of my book ("The Jumping Frog and Other

11

Sketches—by Mark Twain,") from my publisher, C. H. Webb, from time to time, and remit all such moneys to my mother, Mrs. Jane Clemens, 1312 Chestnut street, St. Louis, Mo.

        and Oblige

Yrs Very Truly

Sam. L. Clemens

P.S.—On board Quaker City, N.Y. harbor, June 8.—I forgot to forward this to you several days ago. I thought I had done so.

Sam L. Clemens

3. To Elisha Bliss

Washington
2 December 1867

Dear Sir:

I only received your favor of Nov. 21st [1] last night, at the rooms of the Tribune Bureau here. It was forwarded from the Tribune office, New York, where it had lain eight or ten days. This will be a sufficient apology for the seeming discourtesy of my silence.

I wrote fifty-two letters for the San Francisco "Alta California" during the Quaker City excursion, about half of which number have been printed, thus far. The "Alta" has few exchanges in the east, and I suppose scarcely any of these letters have been copied on this side of the Rocky Mountains. I could weed them of their chief faults of construction and inelegancies of expression, and make a volume that would be more acceptable in many respects than any I could now write. When those letters were written my impressions were fresh, but now they have lost that freshness; they were warm then—they are cold, now. I could strike out certain letters, and write new ones wherewith to supply their places. If you think such a book would suit your purpose, please drop me a line, specifying the size and general style of the volume; *when* the matter ought to be ready; whether it should have pictures in it or not; and particularly what your terms with me would be, and what amount of money I might possibly make out of it. The latter clause has a degree of importance for me which is almost beyond my own comprehension. But you understand that, of course.

I have other propositions for a book, but have doubted the propriety of interfering with good newspaper engagements except my way as an author could be demonstrated to be plain before me. But I know Richardson,[2] and learned from him, some months ago, something of an idea of the subscription plan of publishing. If that is your plan invariably, it looks safe.

I am on the N.Y. Tribune staff here as an "occasional," among other things, and a note from you addressed to

> Very Truly etc.
>
> Sam. L. Clemens

New York Tribune Bureau, Washington, will find me, without fail.

---

[1] EB's letter is published in *MTB*, pp. 349–350.

[2] Albert D. Richardson, EB's "star" author before MT began to publish with him. Richardson was the author of *The Secret Service, Beyond the Mississippi,* and *The Personal History of U. S. Grant.*

4. To Elisha Bliss

[New York]
27 January 1868

Dear Sir:

Your favor of Jan. 25th is received,[1] and in reply, I will say that I accede to your several propositions, viz: That I furnish to the American Publishing Company, through you, with MSS sufficient for a volume of 500 to 600 pages, the subject to be the trip of the Quaker City, the voyage, description of places, etc., and also embodying the substance of the letters written by me during that trip, said MSS to be ready about the first of August, next, I to give all

the usual and necessary attention in preparing said MSS for the
press, and in preparation of illustrations, in correction of proofs—
no use to be made by me of the material for this work in any way
which will conflict with its interest—the book to be sold by the
American Publishing Company by subscription—and for said MSS
and labor on my part, said Company to pay me a copyright of 5
per cent. upon the subscription price of the book for all copies
sold.

As further proposed by you, this understanding, herein set forth,
shall be considered a binding contract upon all parties concerned,
all minor details to be arranged between us hereafter.

> Very Truly Yours,
>
> Sam. L. Clemens.

(Private and general.)
I was to have gone to Washington tonight, but have held over, a
day, to attend a dinner given by a lot of newspaper Editors and
literary scalliwags, at the Westminster Hotel. Shall go down
tomorrow, if I survive the banquet.

> Yrs Truly
>
> Sam. Clemens

---

[1] EB's letter is not extant, though this reply makes its terms obvious.

5. To Elisha Bliss

> Washington
> 4 February 1868

Dear Sir:
If you ever do such a thing as give an author an advance, I wish
you would advance me a thousand dollars. I have cut my newspaper correspondence down a good deal, but I believe that in order to
give to the book the amount of attention it really requires I shall

have to cut loose from everything but one, and sometimes two, newspaper letters a week. One of our Senators suggested that I apply for the San Francisco postmastership, because, in case I got it I could perform its duties by Deputy, and then, in receipt of a large salary and perquisites, I could give myself up exclusively to scribbling. So I went to work and have eternally ruined the chances of the most prominent of the swarm of candidates. But upon looking further into the matter I believe I have *created* work for myself instead of lightening prospective duties. It is a mistaken idea that the postmaster of San Francisco, an office which wields a vast political power throughout the Pacific Coast, can be an idle man. I have made a stupid blunder. A Justice of the Supreme Court has pledged himself to secure my nomination without difficulty; the Pacific Senatorial delegations pledge themselves to secure its confirmation beyond a peradventure.

FEB. 6.—I have thrown away that office, when I had it in my grasp, because it was plain enough that I could not be postmaster and write the book, too. I can get another office when I want it, maybe. But it was worth from ten to twelve thousand a year. In consideration whereof, if you can stand an advance, I wish you *would,* and relieve me of this newspaper corresponding until July. I think the book will be largely the gainer by it. I am satisfied of it, for the correspondence has a constant tendency to snatch me out of the Excursion just as I am getting well interested in it.

If I can stand the *loss,* on the correspondence, of $300 a month for three months, don't you think you can stand the *loan* of it, you being capitalists and I being considerably otherwise? I am not making a demand—I am only making a request.

If you have any curiosity as to that notable post office sacrifice, a note from you to Mr. Justice Field, of the Supreme Bench, and another to Senator Conness of California, will satisfy you. I perceive that I have a good deal of work before me. As nearly as I can figure it, my printed letters will fall considerably short of making *one-half* the book.

Yrs Very Truly

Sam L. Clemens

6. To Elisha Bliss

San Francisco
28 May [1868]

Dr Sir—

H. H. Bancroft and Co, Publishers,[1] here, are anxious to have the agency for my book for this coast and Japan and China. Their subscription department is entirely separate from their other departments, and is superintended by a man who has no other duty to perform. They say they have sold 2,500 copies of Richardson's Mississippi, and will sell about as many more. But the winter has been severe, and they would not let the agents go out and spoil the field for spring labor. They say they have an energetic corps of canvassers, and one which has been sifted of inefficient material; and that their subscription business is ciphered down to a careful system.

I said I would write you, because I have a large number of personal friends in Japan and China, and Mr. Burlingame[2] told me not to overlook that trade. Bancroft has agencies there, and is establishing more. The paper I correspond for here (the *Alta,*) is taken by all the mercantile houses in that part of the Orient.

I shall have the MSS finished in twenty days and shall start east in the steamer of the 1st July. If delayed beyond that time I shall go overland. I have the R. R. Co's invitation to do so.

Very Truly etc

Sam. L. Clemens

[1] Bancroft was awarded the general agency for *Innocents,* but refused to send a review copy of the volume to Bret Harte for the *Overland Monthly* and was refused the agency for *Roughing It.* He was succeeded by A. Roman, publisher of the *Overland,* who remained West Coast general agent for all of MT's American Publishing Company books through *A Tramp Abroad.*

[2] Anson Burlingame, Minister to China, whom MT had first met in Hawaii in 1866 (see *MT&H,* pp. 109–112).

7. To FRANK BLISS

[Chicago]
7 January 1869

Dear Frank—

I am glad to hear that you are progressing well with the book.[1] It will have a great sale in the West—and the East too. Why don't you issue prospectuses and startling advertisements now while I am stirring the bowels of these communities?[2] I have big houses—and more invitations to lecture than I can fill.

Pay for the shaving-paper and keep it till I come. Send me the bill, or keep that till I come, also, just as is most convenient.

Kind regards to all.

Yrs

His ‖ mark

⟨Mark⟩ Twain

Mark 2—two marks.

His = Mark.

[1] The long blank between letters was filled with MT's trip to San Francisco to secure the rights to his *Quaker City* letters from the *Alta California* and by his courtship of Olivia Langdon. On 29 July 1868, EB had suggested that MT "send your manuscript up by express to me, let me look it over and see you on Monday in N.Y., and arrange things there." The manuscript had been turned over to the American Publishing Company, and the present letter was in response to a report (apparently not extant) from Frank Bliss, EB's son, and treasurer of the American Publishing Company.
[2] MT was on a forty-lecture tour of the Midwest during the winter of 1868–1869 (see *MTLC*, pp. 105–118).

8. To ELISHA BLISS

Elmira
30 March [1869]

Friend Bliss—

I sent the proofs to-day.[1] I could have sent them sooner, but was lazy. I will not delay you next time. I was glad Frank telegraphed.

I have concluded that if you will print the following titles on slips you will like one or the other of them:

"The Innocents Abroad;

or,

(*New*)

The Modern Pilgrim's Progress."

Or this:

"The Exodus of the Innocents;

or,

The New Pilgrim's Progress."

I like "The Innocents Abroad" rather the best.[2]

Trot your proofs along as fast as you please—and the sooner the book is out, the better for us, no doubt.

Yrs Truly

Mark.

---

[1] On 1 February 1869, MT had written Frank Bliss from Jacksonville, Illinois, asking him to send *Innocents* proof to Elmira between 3 February and 11 February, and stating that he wanted "to leave for California on a lecturing trip the middle of March." EB replied on 10 February that there were "no proofs as yet to send. . . . We are about ready to begin to Electrotype. We are *filling it with Engravings.*" He proposed hiring a professional proofreader to "expedite business" and invited MT to "come up and spend a week or two if you can do so." MT accepted the invitation, arrived in Hartford on 5 March, and read proof (see *MTMF*, pp. 83–85). Then he proofread in Elmira, and refers in the present letter to the proofs he returned to Bliss.

[2] On the perplexing problems of a title for the book, see *MT&EB*, pp. 29–31.

9. To Elisha Bliss

Elmira

12 April 1869

Friend Bliss—

I think St Mark and the others "by the Old Masters" are the very funniest pictures I ever saw. I cut them out of the proof to send to Mrs. Fairbanks of Cleveland who always pleaded that the Old Masters might be spared from a blackguarding.[1] I think *all* the engravings are handsome and attractive. I *did* "copper" that fountain, but since it looks like the one you got in Paris (Ky.)

yourself, I haven't another word to say. You see *I* thought it looked like a lot of niggers and horses adrift in a freshet—but I don't say a word, now, Bliss. I guess it will look well when it is neatly printed.[2]

Your idea about the "Echo" diagram is correct—glad it is to be engraved. What is become of the beautiful view of Spires (Milan Cathedral)? [3]

How is the name business? *Crusade of the Innocents*—Or, Pil. Prog., etc. *The Innocents Abroad*—Or, etc. *The Exodus of the Innocents*—Or etc.[4]

I'm pushing the proofs. Hereafter, they will return to you by the very next mail after reception.

> Yrs,
>
> Mark.

[1] See *MTMF*, pp. 84–85, for MT's teasing of Mrs. Fairbanks.

[2] The illustration of the "fountain at Versailles" (p. 154 of the first edition) was apparently appropriated from an illustration of a fountain in Paris, Kentucky. EB wrote MT on 14 April, "You get my *idea exactly* of the fountain, when I saw it (but don't tell anyone about that Paris of mine being in KY) some may think I have been Abr——rrod . . . nevertheless, it is good; and will do, particularly the *lamps*.")

[3] The "echo diagram" and the "Spires" illustrations appear on pp. 197 and 172 of the first edition.

[4] EB replied that either *The Innocents Abroad* or *Crusade of the Innocents* "will do" if MT could not "get something better" (Hartford, 14 April 1869).

10. To Elisha Bliss

> Elmira
> 20 April [1869]

Friend Bliss—

I wish you would have *my* revises revised again and look over them *yourself* and see that my marks have been corrected. A proof-reader who *persists* in making *two* words (and sometimes even *compound* words) of "anywhere" and "everything;" and who spells villainy "villiany" and liquefies "liquifies" etc., etc. is infernally unreliable—and so I don't like to trust your man. He never yet has

acceded to a request of mine made in the margin, in the matter of
spelling and punctuation, as I know of. He shows spite—don't trust
him, but revise my revises yourself. I have long ago given up trying
to get him to spell those first-mentioned words properly. I begin to
be afraid there is too much MSS. It don't seem to me that I ought
to be only just getting to Pompeii at the 326th page—ought to be a
heap further along than that, I should think. Half of the book is
finished, now, but I feel almost sure that it is going to crowd things
to get the rest of the MSS into 326 pages more. Please run over and
measure the remaining MSS and see how much more it is going to
make than what you want. I shall hate like everything to leave here,
(*even for forty minutes*—tell Mrs. Bliss that) but still, if the MSS
must be cut down, and it *can't* be helped, telegraph me and I will
dart for Hartford instantaneously.

"The Innocents Abroad;

or

The New Pilgrim's Progress"

seems to be the neatest and the easiest understood—by farmers and
everybody—suppose we adopt it—and you suggest to the artist an
idea for a title-page—you are good at it—remember your idea about
it before?—What they *expected* to see—and what they *did* see?

Yrs

Mark.

I think my next proof will include the chapter on *Pompeii*—
please send me TWO copies of that chapter. Instruct your foreman
about it, now while you think of it.

11. To ELISHA BLISS

Elmira
April Something 1869

Friend Bliss:—

All the names were correct, I think, except Masserano. Jam the
Queen of Greece in anywhere. She is the daughter of the Emperor

of Russia, and can stand it. *No*—put her in the Grecian chapter—that will be better.

You will find *Scylla and Charybdis* mentioned *before* you come to Athens—perhaps the cut you speak of comes in there. (If it is a picture of Acropolis, though, put it in along with the description of the Acropolis in the Chapter on Greece.)

I think the "suppositions" I dealt in about the oyster shells were not funny, but foolish—and so, being disgusted I marked them out and was sorry I had ever printed them—so I think it much better to let them stay out.[1] But you are always accommodating and I wish to be accommodating too—so if you prefer it, let the "suppositions" go in. (I don't say that reluctantly, but cordially and heartily, and *meaning* it.)

Your printers are doing well. I will hurry the proofs.

Always, etc.,

Mark.

[1] The "suppositions" were included in Chapter XXXIX of *Innocents*.

12. To Elisha Bliss

Elmira
29 April [1869]

Friend Bliss—

All right. I hope there won't be a necessity to cut much, but when you say you are only to the 800 or 900th page you don't comfort me entirely, because so much of the 400 or 500 pages still left are reprint, and so will string out a heap.

Certainly—snatch out *Sampson*—it isn't even necessary to mention him. Yes, snatch out the *Jaffa Colony*, too. Also, snatch out my *Temperance Society experience*. (I will re-inclose your letter, so that you can see in detail what you have suggested—then just follow your own written suggestions—they suit me.)

I suppose I put Ab (Abdel Kader) in by mistake among the

pictures. I don't mention him anywhere. I simply bought his photograph in Constantinople because his father and mine were about of an age and might have been twins if they had had the same mother. Of course this thought touched me, and made Ab seem near and dear to me—made him seem a sort of jack-legged uncle to me, as I may say—and so I bought his picture, with many tears. I wish to have it buried with me. Preserve it. But if you have got a picture of the old Agitator made, don't waste it—put it in, and call it "Specimen of how the Innocents usually appeared, in the Orient"—or *something*, no matter what. You can add the above as explanatory foot-note.

As to the rest of your letter, Good, good, good.

Tell me just about when our proofs will reach ⟨the Jaffa Colony⟩ the beginning of Egypt. It is time I was thinking about packing my trunk.

Yrs Truly
Mark Twain

13. To Elisha Bliss

Elmira
22 July [1869]

[No Salutation]

Mr. Bliss, are you not making a mistake about publishing this year? The book was to have been ready peremptorily just a year ago exactly. Then as it was necessary to make room and a market for Grant's biography, it was judged much better to delay this book of mine a month or two. Then to be up with a rival publisher and make capital out of a rival book, it was thought best to make a *spring* book of mine, in order to give the "Metropolis" a chance. And *then* in order once more to fight a rival book and a rival house, it was considered best to make mine a *summer* book, and give the "Mississippi" a fresh boost. And now that the further delay of my book will encourage agents to continue to labor for the "Mississippi" (I only just barely suppose this from hearing you tell a new agent he could have my book when issued *if* he would work on the "Mississippi" until that vague and uncertain event transpired) it is deemed best to hold it back and make a *fall* book of it. Do not misunderstand. I am not complaining. I am not contending that there is any occasion for you to comply with that portion of a contract which stipulates that the book shall be issued "early in the spring." I am not pretending that there is a *community* of interest here which would make it improper for you to take the liberty and the responsibility of departing from the letter of a contract in order to subserve your interest without first inquiring for form's sake whether it will be satisfactory all round—or whether it will be equally profitable all round. I am not contending that I am hurt unto death simply because the delay for "Grant" damaged my interests; or because the delay for the "Metropolis" damaged my interests, likewise, or because the delay necessary to make me a spring vegetable damaged my interests, or because the delay in order to open up the "Mississippi" again damaged my interests; or because the further delay to bail the "Mississippi" dry is *still* damaging my interests. *No.* All *I* want to know is,—viz;—to-wit— as follows:

After it is done being a fall book upon what argument shall you perceive that it will be best to make a winter book of it? And—

After it is done being a winter book, upon what argument shall you perceive that it will be best to make another spring book of it again? And—

When it is done being another spring book again, upon what argument shall you perceive that it will be best to-to-to—

Are you going to publish it *before* Junius Henri Brown's Travels in Italy and Germany, or after?

All I desire is to be informed from time to time what future season of the year the publication is postponed to and why—so that I can go on informing my friends intelligently—I mean that infatuated baker's dozen of them who, faithful unto death, still believe that I *am* going to publish a book. But, seriously, I object to any further delay and hereby enter my protest against it. These delays are too one-sided. Every one of them has had for its object the furthering of the Am Pub Co's interest and to compass this *my* interests have been entirely disregarded. We both know what

figure the sales were expected to reach if due and proper diligence
were exerted in behalf of the publication. If that result is not
achieved shall you be prepared to show that your tardiness was not
the cause? And failing this, shall you be prepared to recompense
me for the damage sustained? These are grave questions. I have
ceased to expect a large sale for a book whose success depended in
a great measure upon its publication while the public were as yet
interested in its subject, but I shall feel entirely justified in holding
the Publishing Company responsible in case the sales fall short or
reasonably short of what we originally expected them to reach. I
think you will do me the justice to say that I have borne these
annoying and damaging delays as patiently as any man whose
bread and butter and reputation were at stake could have borne
them. I cannot think that I have been treated just right.[1]

Yrs truly

Saml L. Clemens.

[1] This is the letter to which MT referred in *MTE,* p. 148, as a telegram, and
which was prompted by EB's mention that *"unavoidably* we propose to make a
fall book of it with every advantage of full preparation and an early start"
(Hartford, 17 July 1869). The books to which this letter refers are Junius H.
Brown's *The Great Metropolis,* A. D. Richardson's biography of U. S. Grant,
Richardson's *Beyond the Mississippi,* and Brown's *Sights and Sensations in
Europe.* Actually, the earliest expectation MT had for publication was December
1868 (MT to Frank Fuller, San Francisco, 12 May [1868]).

14. To ELISHA BLISS

Elmira

1 August [1869]

Friend Bliss—

I had some notion of running up to Hartford, but I believe I
shall not be able to do it. I suppose you are right about sending the
books to the newspapers the first thing,—you are old in the
business and ought to know best—though I thought maybe it
would have been better to get all your machinery in trim first.
However, after so long a time to get ready in, you must surely be

about as ready as it is possible to be in *this* world, anyhow. I wrote you a wicked letter, and was sorry afterward that I did it, for it occurred to me that perhaps you had very good reasons for delaying the book till fall which I did not know anything about. But you didn't state any reasons, you know—and I have been out of humor for a week.[1] I had a bargain about concluded for the purchase of an interest in a daily paper and when everything seemed to be going smoothly, the owner *raised* on me.[2] I *think* I have got it all straightened up again, now, and therefore am in a reasonably good humor again. If I made you mad, I forgive you.

The 3 books you speak of have not come. How did you direct them?—to Twain or Clemens?—and by what express did you send them?

I have received a jolly good letter from Henry Clay Trumbull, which I enclose. You had better go and tell him *this* is a plenty good enough notice, if he will let it be printed with his name signed to it.

> Yrs Truly
>
> Saml L. Clemens.

[1] EB had written MT on 30 or 31 July, sending three copies of *Innocents* and explaining that he had not released the book "for valid reasons."
[2] MT refers to his unsuccessful attempt to buy into the Cleveland *Herald;* see *MTMF,* pp. 100–102.

15. To Elisha Bliss

> Buffalo
> 12 August [1869]

Friend Bliss—

Your splendid letter has arrived,[1] and I confess I owe you one. I was in an awful sweat when I wrote you, for everything seemed going wrong end foremost with me. I had just got mad with the Cleveland Herald folks—broken off all further negotiations for a purchase, and so I let you and some others have the benefit of my ill nature.—But that is all gone by, and now we will smoke the pipe of peace and bury the hatchet. I have bought one-third of the Buffalo "Express," and it is an exceedingly thriving newspaper. We propose to make it more so. I expect I shall have to buckle right down to it and give up lecturing until next year.

I was at Elmira yesterday and saw the book, and my faith in it has all come back again. It is the very handsomest book of the season and you ought to be proud of your work. It will sell. Between us we will *make* it sell.—Miss Langdon has a very flattering letter about it from young Mrs. Perkins of Hartford. I will get a copy and send to you. They live in that big place at the foot of the street that starts from the front of the Episcopal Church.—Send Henry Ward Beecher a copy. However, I believe I put his name in that list. I will send you the Elmira notices when they appear. I gave that handsome gilt-edged copy to my sweetheart—I wish you would send one like it to Charley J. Langdon, Elmira, and one to my mother, Mrs. Jane Clemens, 203 South 16th street, St. Louis, Mo. I have no copy myself, but I can get along without, having already perused it. I think it would be a good idea to send both bound and unbound copies to the Buffalo *Express*, the Buffalo *Courier*, and the Buffalo *Commercial*, but that is for you to judge of.

Well, I believe I haven't anything more to say, except that I like the circulars, I like the book, I like you and your style and your business vim, and believe the chebang will be a success.

Heartily and sincerely

Saml. L. Clemens.

"Buffalo Express" is my address hereafter—shall marry and come to anchor here during the winter.

---

[1] Portions of EB's "splendid letter" are in *MT&EB*, p. 34. EB also explained, "I only proposed delaying the opening of the Ball for a week or two until haying and harvesting was over. To show you how absolutely dull July is, I will add that we shipped but *1003 Books* all told last month. . . . I have held back . . . solely with a view to the interest of the book, on which I personally have risked almost my reputation for judgment and sagacity—for knowing what will sell."

16. To Elisha Bliss

Buffalo
15 August 1869

Friend Bliss—

There is a literary weekly of trifling circulation and influence in Elmira called the *Saturday Review*—I mention it so that you can send it a book if you think it worth while. Don't send it through me, because I have reasons. The Review is handsome and right well edited, I am obliged to say that. I enclose letters to Reed of the Tribune and *Wm. H. Chase* of the Herald, to be sent with the books. Maybe you had better envelop and mark them "Personal" and deliver them through your agent.

I can't write to the Boston men, for I am not well acquainted with any of them and, moreover I have forgotten their names. Redfield [Redpath?] would be just the man to attend to it handsomely—but then a while ago I conceived that the book was going to issue too late to give me a large lecture list in New England, and so I canceled my engagements and withdrew from the field. Their courses are pretty much filled, now. Since purchasing here I have shut off all my engagements outside of N. England and withdrawn from the talking ring wholly for this season. You know when I got to counting up the irons I had in the fire (marriage, editing a newspaper, and lecturing,) I said it was most too many, for the subscriber.

I like the "puffs." I will attend to the Buffalo books for the press —send them along as soon as you please—did I tell you that I took dinner with the whole press gang yesterday?—Good fellows they are too.

Yrs in haste

Clemens

17. To Elisha Bliss

[Buffalo]
3 September 1869

Friend Bliss—

I "cave." You are right, and I was not. But I am only impatient about things once or twice a day—and then I sit down and write letters. The rest of the time I am serene.

Yes the Herald's is a good notice and will help the book along. The irreverence of the volume appears to be a tip-top good feature of it, ⟨financially⟩ diplomatically speaking, though I wish with all my heart there wasn't an irreverent passage in it.

The books will arrive to-day, no doubt, and we'll turn the papers loose on them at once, if you say so, ⟨or would you rather we waited till you have an agent here?⟩

Ys Truly

Clemens

18. To Elisha Bliss

[Buffalo]
27 September 1869

Friend Bliss—

Arnold called on me two days ago, and introduced his two Buffalo canvassers. I don't know anything about him. He said he was going to rush things right along. I told him we were going to publish a supplement of notices of the book next Saturday, ⟨a page or more⟩ and he asked that the type be kept standing till Saturday afternoon, when he would arrive and see if he could make a trade for 5 or 10,000 copies for distribution. I gave him to understand that we would furnish them at cost, or even less. He said nothing about advertising in the Buffalo papers.

I like newspapering very well, as far as I have got—but I adjourn, a week hence, to commence preparing my lecture, and shall not be here again till the middle of February. After a few days, now, I shall be *in Elmira till Nov. 1. Recollect.*

Yes, our paper is a good one to advertise in, and so is the "Commercial-Advertiser" and the "Courier." (Latter is Democratic, but good boys.)

None of us have noticed the book yet—shall, this week, maybe. Regards to Mrs. B. and the longest half of Frank.

Yrs

Clemens.

I think the book is making more stir than other people's books, and I guess you are pushing it for all it is worth.

19. To ELISHA BLISS

Elmira
22 January 1870

Friend Bliss—

Our boys in Buffalo wrote you something about a ratio of prices for clubs and books, etc., and they are anxious to get an answer—been waiting 2 or 3 weeks. Tell them about it. They are much pleased with your sending their bills and circulars to your agents.

I don't copyright the "Round the World" [1] letters because it don't hurt anything to be well advertised—and these are getting pretty well advertised—but you see out of 50 letters not more than 6 or 10 will be copied into any *one* newspaper—and *that* don't hurt.

I mean to take plenty of time and pains with the Noah's Ark book [2]—maybe it will be several years before it is *all* written—but it will be a perfect lightning-striker when it *is* done.

You can have the *first say*—that is plain enough—on that or *any other* book I may prepare for the press. As long as you deal in a fair, open and honorable way with *me*, I do not think you will ever find me doing otherwise with *you*.

I wish Fairbanks would keep still about that Noah's Ark book—somebody will steal the idea from me. I had no business ever mentioning it to a man of his limitless gab.

I am prosecuting Webb in the N.Y. Courts—think the result will be that he will yield up the copyright and plates of the Jumping Frog, if I let him off from paying me money. Then I shall break up those plates, and prepare a new vol. of Sketches, but on a different and more "taking" model.[3]

I can get a book ready for you any time you want it—but you *can't* want one before this time next year—so I have plenty of time.

I wish you could have the quarterly statement here *by Feb. 1*—because we are to be married *Feb. 2,* and would like to know what we are doing it on, and whether we can afford it or not. But no matter—if it isn't ready then, forward it to Buffalo. We leave for Buffalo at noon, Feb. 3. You may *telegraph the amount* to us here, Feb. 1st or 2d—that is what I chiefly want to know.[4] I have been keeping fine large stories afloat about our sales.

Miss Nellie did no harm, in opening the letter.

Yrs Truly

Saml. L. Clemens.

[1] On the "Round the World" series in the Buffalo *Express,* see *BMT* (1935), pp. 169–176. The letters were an abortive collaboration with Professor D. R. Ford, who was escorting Charles Langdon on a *Wanderjahr.*
[2] On the "Noah's Ark Book," see *MTMF,* pp. 117–118.
[3] For MT's troubles with Webb over *The Jumping Frog,* see *MT&EB,* pp. 85–87, and *MTMF,* pp. 143–144.
[4] On 11 March 1870, MT wrote EB that he discovered he did not need the royalty check after all, and had turned it over to Olivia's father to draw interest (Berg).

20. To Elisha Bliss

Elmira
28 January [1870]

Friend Bliss—

I want you to do just as you please with that Evans.[1] I wash my hands of him. I guess he is just as likely to be a "beat" as anything else—though fools are so cheap and so plenty that I had placed him in that catalogue, for charity's sake.

I re-enclose the Express letter, as you desire. I only meant you to correspond with our people about it. I never bother or meddle with the concern's *business* matters—and ought to have told *them* to write you, and not shove it off on to *my* shoulders. I don't care two cents about the concern's business. And what I want *you* there for, is because I want a man who can *run* the business department without boring anybody else with it. I hate business.

Yes, I *am* satisfied with the way you are running the book. You are running it in staving, tip-top, first-class style. I never wander into any corner of the country but I find that an agent has been there before me, and many of that community have read the book. And on an average about ten people a day come and hunt me up to thank me and tell me I'm a benefactor!! I guess that is a part of the programme we didn't expect in the first place.

Indeed *I* don't want to bother with booksellers or anybody else. That chap in Buffalo wanted me to speak a word to you for him, and I said I was too lazy—and if he would make Larned [2] write the letter, I would endorse it, whether it were true or false. And I did. But when I saw a great stack of "Innocents" in his bookstore, an hour or so afterward, I was rather sorry I did.

January and November didn't pan out as well as December—for you remember you had sold 12,000 copies in December when Twichell and I were there on the 27th or 28th. But $4,000 is pretty gorgeous. One don't pick that up often, with a book. It is the next best thing to lecturing.

I think you are rushing this book in a manner to be proud of; and you will make the finest success of it that has ever been made with a subscription book, I believe. What with advertising, establishing agencies, etc., you have got an enormous lot of machinery under way and hard at work in a wonderfully short space of time. It is easy to see, when one travels around, that one must be endowed with a deal of genuine generalship in order to maneuvre a publication whose line of battle stretches from end to end of a great continent, and whose foragers and skirmishers invest every hamlet and besiege every village hidden away in all the vast space between.

I'll back you against any publisher in America, Bliss—or elsewhere.

Yrs as Ever

Clemens.

¹ Albert S. Evans, MT's antagonist "Fitz Smythe" in the San Francisco days
(see *MTSFC*, pp. 18–47), was attempting to peddle a manuscript to EB, which
eventually appeared under the imprint of the Columbian Book Company in 1870
with the title, *Our Sister Republic.*
    ² J. L. Larned was MT's coeditor on the Buffalo *Express.*

21. To ELISHA BLISS

[Buffalo]
23 February [1870]

Friend Bliss—

Why bless your soul, I never have time to write letters these days
—takes all my time to carry on the honey-moon. I would like to
talk to Mrs. Bliss two or three or four hours about my wife now, if
she could stand it—she *used* to stand it very well when I was at
your house.

Express gets along well. I have a strong notion to write a—

Well, never mind, I'll tell you about it another time.

I am glad Mrs. Barstow has retrieved her credit—I was about to
write you to charge her $150.00 to me, when your second letter
came. I am very glad, simply for her own sake, that she has kept up
her credit.[1]

6,000 and upwards, in 16 days, is splendid—*Splendid,* isn't it?

I don't go near the Express office more than twice a week—and
then only for an hour. I am just as good [as] other men—and other
men take honey-moons I reckon.

Hello!—there's the bell—my wife is taking a nap and I am receiving calls.

Yrs Ever.

Mark

¹ Mrs. Kate Barstow of Alexandria, Virginia, received MT's recommendation to canvass *Innocents* (*LLMT*, p. 131), and on 15 February 1870, EB advised that she "suddenly disappeared from our sky, owing $157.40." Apparently, in a letter no longer extant, EB advised MT of her reappearance.

22. To ELISHA BLISS

Buffalo
23 April [1870]

Friend Bliss—

All right—the quarterly statement will arrive in a good time. For I shall pay a debt or two then, and I shall be paying a thousand dollars and some other money toward buying a beautiful home for my mother in a village near here—my sister paying the other five or six thousand.

When you come we'll talk books and business. I wish my wife wanted to spend the summer in England, but I'm afraid she don't. But we shall soon know, now, whether Mr. Langdon will try Europe or not.

I shall watch this Galaxy business pretty closely, and whenever I seem to be "letting down," I shall withdraw from literature and recuperate.—But this month's "Memoranda" hasn't hurt my reputation, and next month's won't—I want to bet something on that.¹

Will you let some neat-handed and artistic person, like Miss Nellie, for instance, paste the enclosed in the fly-leaf of the nicest copy of the Innocents you have got, and send it *Express paid* (and charged to me,) to

Mrs. Bart. Bowen,[2]
Columbia,
Mo.

and oblige

Yrs

Clemens.

---

[1] On 2 May, EB, enclosing a quarterly royalty statement for $3,914.65, replied, "Don't think your *Galaxy articles* hurt your reputation at all. It was good. *Capital. Capital.*"
[2] Mrs. Bart Bowen was the wife (possibly the widow) of Bart Bowen, the childhood and piloting friend of MT.

23. To ELISHA BLISS

[Elmira]
7 May 1870

Private.

Friend Bliss—

I have just been stricken with an idea, in the shape of a scheme to secure a wide-spread advertisement. Whenever our sales reach 100,000—no matter when that may be—you or the Directors call me to Hartford to an oyster supper in celebration of the Event— the Hartford Editors to be present—and I will either come there and make a speech that will travel well in the papers, or I will send one to be read there that will travel. If you can think of something simpler and just as effectual, let's have it—for suppers are sometimes a nuisance, and besides, the object of this one might be too glaringly apparent. Set your invention to work.[1]

I sent you dispatch yesterday to acknowledge rec'pt of your check for $3,914.62, and also to express my eminent satisfaction at the way the book is selling.

Mr. Langdon has been dangerously ill for some days, and it is plain that he cannot travel a mile this year. So we shall not move out of reach of sudden call. That closes out all notion of crossing the ocean—though we expect to go to the Adirondacks with the Twichells.

Yrs Ever

Mark.

[1] Presumably Bliss replied that sales would not reach 100,000 for some time, since on 18 [May], MT lowered his sights: "Whenever you are ready for a 'blow' on the 75th thousand, send me a brief note to *inquire* if I could attend a dinner to celebrate it—and I will answer no as affably and felicitously as possible and thus we'll save the dinner and yet compass the advertisement" (Berg). From Buffalo on 30 May, he explained further: "About the dinner—I cannot go on to Hartford very well for the dinner and I have a plan which seems to me a good one. *Write a dinner invitation* to me and let me write a speech (for the dinner and publish it as a speech made at a dinner in honor of our having worked [?] 70,000 copies of the book) *in answer* and you publish it. That will answer the same purpose as if we had a dinner, and I should have to send the speech to the dinner any way instead of going myself—what do you think of that plan?" (Yale).

24. To Elisha Bliss

Buffalo

20 May 1870

Confidential

Friend Bliss—

Appleton wants me to furnish a few lines of letter-press for a humorous picture book—that is, two lines of remarks under each picture. I have intimated that if the pictures and the pay are both good, I will do it. What do you think of it? [1] I thought that in as much as half the public would think I made the engravings as well as did the letter-press, it would be a unique and splendid advertisement wherewith to boost the "Innocents." I am to see proofs of the pictures before I contract.

Yrs

Mark

[1] No further information about the Appleton's scheme is known to have survived.

25. To Elisha Bliss

Elmira
4 July 1870

Friend Bliss

Mr. Langdon is ever so much better and we have every reason to believe that he is going to get well and that speedily. I fancy the book you speak of must be the Appleton book. I cannot think of any other and have no knowledge of any other.[1] But I shall probably never have to do the Appleton book. They asked me to name a price. I named a pretty stiff one. And at the same time, I said that *if it were a subscription book* I could afford easier terms. They misunderstood me and thought that I was *suggesting* that it be made a subscription work and so they *accepted* my suggestion and offered *higher* pay than I spoke of. But I wrote them immediately that they had misconstrued me and that I could not do a *subscription* book for them *at any price whatever*. And moreover that I could do *nothing* more than the original proposition called for. And that I could not even do that unless I could do it either before or immediately after my Adirondack trip. They have had ample time to have written me half a dozen times since, and haven't done it. Therefore it is *far* from likely that any "humorous book" will issue from my pen shortly.

If Mr. Langdon gets thoroughly well in time my wife and I will go straight from Buffalo to Vergennes, Vt. at the end of July and be joined there by the Twichells. It is our shortest and straightest route to the woods.

We shall be here 10 days or 2 weeks yet. Come—come either here or to Buffalo.

Yrs

Mark

[1] Actually, MT had written EB from Elmira, on 5 May, "I have a bid for a book from a Philada subscription house offering unlimitedly."

26. To Elisha Bliss

[Elmira]

2 August 1870

Friend Bliss—

You know I already had an offer of *ten* per cent from those same parties in my pocket when I stipulated for 7½ with you.[1] I simply promised to *give them a chance to bid;* I never said I would publish with them if theirs was the best bid. If their *first* offer had been 12½ I would merely have asked you to climb along up *as near that figure as you could and make money,* but I wouldn't have asked anything more. Whenever you said that you had got up to what was a fair divide between us (there being no *risk,* now, in publishing for me, while there was, before,) I should have closed with you on those terms. I never have had the slightest idea of publishing with anybody but you. (I was careful to make no promises to those folks about their bid.)

You see you can't get it out of your head that I am a sort of a rascal, but I ain't. I can stick to you just as long as you can stick to me, and give you odds. I made that contract with all my senses about me, and it suits me and I am satisfied with it. If I get only half a chance I will write a book that will sell like fury provided you put pictures enough in it.

Yes, we'll put the portrait in the new book.

Say—when does Frank's wedding come off?

Ask Frank if he is going to get up the *annual* account of sales for me which you spoke of?

We still sit up with Mr. L. He is somewhat worse again.

Yrs

Mark.

---

[1] MT and EB had signed the contract for what would become *Roughing It* on 15 July 1870, and in letters which apparently do not survive EB justified his own lower royalty and took MT to task for his lack of loyalty.

27. To ELISHA BLISS

Elmira

11 August [1870]

Friend Bliss—

I meant to telegraph Mr. Langdon's death to you, but was kept too busy.

This is a house of mourning, now. My wife is nearly broken down with grief and watching.

However, I believe I did telegraph you.

I wrote that publisher that your bid was lower than his, but not enough lower to justify me in deserting you. He wrote back a hot answer, saying "he was surprised to hear me confess that his bid was the highest, and in the same letter say that I had awarded the book to you." I sent him back a warm one in which I said *I* was surprised at his infernal impertinence—and then I talked sassy to him for a page or so and wound up by saying I judged he would be able from the foregoing to form a sort of shadow of an idea of my private opinion of him and his kind. If he don't go mighty slow I will print something personal about him.

Say—I learn from Constantinople that the celebrated guide, "Far-Away Moses" goes to the American Consulate and borrows my book to read the chapter about himself to English and Americans, and he sends me a beseeching request that I will forward a copy of *that chapter* to him—he don't want the whole book, but only just that to use as an advertisement. Can't you take the loose sheets of that form and send them to him with my compliments (You or Frank can write the autograph,) care of the American Consulate?

Ys

Mark.

28. To ELISHA BLISS

Buffalo
4 September [1870]

Friend Bliss—

During past week have written first four chapters of the book,[1] and I tell you the "Innocents Abroad" will have to get up early to beat it.—It will be a book that will jump right strait into a continental celebrity the first month it is issued. Now I want it illustrated lavishly. We shall sell 90,000 copies the first 12 months. I haven't even a shadow of a doubt of that. I see the capabilities of my subject.

Got Frank's ac/. All right.

Yrs

Clemens.

[1] *Roughing It.*

29. To ELISHA BLISS

Buffalo
22 [September 1870]

Friend Bliss—

My map is attracting a deal of attention.[1] We get letters requesting copies from everywhere. Now what you need is something to make the postmasters and the public *preserve* your posters about "Innocents" and stick them up and if you would put that map and accompanying testimonials right in the centre of the poster and the thing is accomplished, *sure,*

If you want to do this, write or telegraph me at once, and I will have a stereotype made and send to you.

Ys

Clemens.

---

¹ The Map of Paris had appeared in the Buffalo *Express* on 17 September, and was frequently reprinted, though not as a part of *Innocents* advertising matter.

30. To Elisha Bliss

Buffalo
13 October 1870

Friend Bliss:

I have a notion to let the Galaxy publishers have a volume of old sketches for a "Mark Twains Annual——1871"—provided they will pay me about 25 per cent. That is what they offered once, I believe. I believe a Christmas volume will outpay Josh Billings' Allminax. What do you think? Write me at once—and don't discourage me.¹ Did that scalawag of a boy of yours trot through here the other day? We found a card of the firm, with his name underscored, and guessed he had stopped at the office. However, we were at Fredonia N.Y. all the week and so if he *was* here we couldn't have seen him. I never once thought of Frank's being absurd enough to take upon himself one of those ghastly tortures called a "bridal trip," else we would have grieved to think we couldn't entertain the couple a few days—for the young lady was very low then and we couldn't have made room—(she died on the 29th in our bedroom—perhaps I wrote you).²

I am driveling along tolerably fairly on the book—getting off from 12 to 20 pages, (M.S.) a day. I am writing it so carefully that I'll never have to alter a sentence I guess but it is *very* slow work.³ I like it well, as far as I have got. The people will read it.

Yrs in haste

Mark.

[1] EB's reply was apparently discouraging, for on 26 November 1870, MT wrote Charles H. Webb (CWB):

> Business first. I could not consent to a new edition of the J. F. any time within two or three years without vitiating my contracts with my present publishers and creating dissatisfaction. I would have issued the Galaxy (they belong wholly to me) and other sketches, in a couple of volumes, before this, but for the reason abovementioned. But when I go down to New York in the spring I want to look the whole J. F. matter over, and whatever is fair and right, I am perfectly willing to do.

The contract for *Roughing It* had stipulated that MT would publish no other books until that volume was issued.

[2] Emma Nye, a friend of Olivia Clemens's, who died of typhoid fever.

[3] On 19 September 1870, MT reported, "Finished 7th or 8th chapter of book today. Forget which—am up to page 180—only about 1500 more to write."

31. To Elisha Bliss

Buffalo
5 November [1870]

Friend Bliss:

It is a splendid idea![1] He will make a tip-top editor—a better than I, because he is full of talent and besides is perfectly faithful, honest, straightforward and reliable. There isn't money enough in America to get him to do a dishonest act—whereas I am different. You just take him in hand and laugh with him and talk with him and keep him jolly, and I will answer for his editorial ability. I don't fancy that you will have much trouble keeping him jolly, either, though he is not quite so sprightly and idiotic as I am. I find he is getting $1,300 a year where he is, but if you can't stand the extra hundred, I'll pay it. He gets $25 a week = $1,300 a year.

I have written him to let me know how soon he can come on, and have advised him to leave his wife here or at Fredonia with my sister till he goes to Hartford and arranges for board or house-rent.

I guess that after you have had him a year you will find that he is really worth a deal of money to you—I am well enough satisfied of it to bet money on it.

Well I thank you very much, Bliss, and I hope that results will in every way justify your kindness and leave you nothing to regret in the matter.

Yrs

Clemens.

¹ EB had proposed making Orion Clemens the editor of his new paper, *The American Publisher,* after first offering the job to MT (see *MTBus,* p. 116). EB had written MT on 2 November:

> Paper will be out last of the month.
>
> How would your brother do for an editor of it?
>
> Would he be satisfied with $100 a month for present, until we could do better by him.
>
> You see we have no real place just now for him, but would like for *your sake to create a position* for him, if possible. Would this do?

Orion required some persuasion to accept the editorship, for MT wrote on at least two occasions, with increasing exasperation, about the possibilities of the job (undated fragment and 11 November 1870). EB may have had the idea of a paper or journal as early as 1 November 1869, when he wrote MT, "Why don't you order the Buffalo Ex. sent us? . . . Don't want to be *immodest* in *asking,* but will exchange with you and send our paper when we print one."

32. To ELISHA BLISS

Buffalo

28 November [1870]

Private and Conf.

Friend Bliss:

My brother expects to start east in about 6 or 8 days.

I have put my greedy hands on the best man in America for my purpose and shall *start him to the diamond fields of South Africa within a fortnight, at my expense.*¹

I shall write a book of his experiences for next spring, (600 pp 8vo.,) spring of '72 and write it just as if I had been through it all myself, but will explain in the preface that this is done merely to give it life and reality.

That book will have a perfectly beautiful sale.

1. Now WILL YOU PAY ME 10 PER CENT COPYRIGHT ON IT?

2. Will you advance me a thousand dollars, (or $1,500 if it should be necessary,) now, for this purpose, with this distinct understanding, viz: That if the thing works and I manage to write the book on the diamond adventures, you are to deduct all of that thousand or $1,500 from the first sales of said book; but if the project fails and I can't get a book out of it, then you to lose half of the thousand or fifteen hundred dollars and I to lose the other half.

Say yes or no quick, Bliss, for this thing is brim-full of fame and fortune for both author and publisher.[2] Expedition's the word, and I don't want any timidity or hesitancy now.

But whether my project and my terms find favor in your eyes or not, *I* am perfectly satisfied with the scheme, and my man will be packing his trunk by this time tomorrow. And in another 24 hours he will be full-freighted with my minute instructions and will have his name to the contract and off for Africa within a fortnight, as I said.

Yrs Truly

S. L. Clemens.

Keep all this a secret, even from Frank himself, now and henceforth—for I don't want to furnish some other Hartford publisher with an idea, though I would really care no more than about 2 figs for his opposition. But keep it a secret. It is best to do it.

Mrs. Fairbanks (my best critic) likes my new book WELL, as far as I have got.

P.S. I don't care two cents whether there is a diamond in all Africa or not—the adventurous narrative and its wild, new fascination is what I want.

---

[1] James H. Riley had been a close friend and fellow correspondent of MT's during the winter in Washington in 1867. He was now in Washington as a clerk, but as he told MT in his letter of 30 November, "I am somewhat of an

expert in precious stones, thanks to that poor old Brazillian Diamond Hunter whom I befriended in the Cal. mines, years ago; have a taste that way and thanks to my early experience in the gold fields and in Mexico and Centro-America am a good campaigner and know to take [care] of myself and others."

² The major part of EB's reply (Hartford, 30 November 1870) was as follows:

Yours just recd. Yes we will go in on that game. You don't think I am very timid do you. I never was called that.

But I want to tell you what I think is fair between us.

I shall be short and plain. First. I know well that people offer you big percentages, all right, but they can't afford to pay 10%—no man can. On your Book, had we paid 10% we should not have made $5000—this is true—I can show you figures. Now then I say this frankly to you and then leave it for you to say whether it shall be 7½ or 10%. Look at it a moment. We are paying agents, *all good ones, 50%*. We pay our general agents 55%, some 60%—to keep them—a book at 3.50 55% off gives us 1.57½—the book costs us about 1.00 without any copyright, cost of Plates, or any other expenses. 7½% copyright is about 25 cts—nearly $1.25 cost of Book, giving us a small profit. At 50% it gives us 50 cts profit, pay $10,000 for plates and engravings, to start, pay for adverts, offers, etc, and unless a man sells a pile he will lose money. This is a plain show, no matter how others figure. It is truth. Another point. Should the man not succeed and the book fail, why not have it understood some other subject agreed on by us shall take its place and a book come anyway if you like. Is this unfair? That is all. Shall we put it in this light? A *Book* to be *written* by you to follow the next, soon as possible and politic. Terms etc same as *next book* as agreed in contract. Subject Diamond Land or *some other mutually agreeable*—$1000 to $1500 advanced by us to come out of copyright on first sales (if this suits you).

Will this suit you? Ain't it fair? I am with you heart and hand, and want to go in of course—and give you my ideas—of right and wrong. If you don't *see it,* say where and how it should be, but please "put yourself in our place" and decide it.

If this basis seems fair to you telegraph *all right* and whatever else you want to say. If it doesn't telegraph where it is not, and I will reply. When do you need the Cash? *It will be ready.*

33. To ELISHA BLISS

Buffalo
2 December 1870

Dont overlook
the Post Scripts

Friend Bliss:
I'll tell you what I'll do, I'll not take advantage of your consent to

pay me 10 per cent, but I'll do this. You're to pay me 8½ *per cent,* and advance me another thousand dollars (in addition to the fifteen hundred,) any time I demand it during 1871, this thousand *also* to come out of my first earnings on the African book. (I have been looking into the matter, and my man *might* need more ⟨money⟩ than the $1500 though I'll not demand the extra $1000 from you unless he demands it of *me,* by and bye.) And further: If my man don't get back and I can't write the African book for you, I'll write you a 600 page 8 vo. book *in place of it,* which you are to pay me 8½ per cent copyright on and you to subtract all that $1500 or $2500 from my first receipts on *that* book.

How's that?

1 Don't you see? you get a *book* in any event.

2 You pay me 8½ per cent copyright in any event.

3 I *alone* risk that advance money on my man. If nothing comes of it. I lose it *all* you *none* of it.

I would not publish a book through you (or any other person) at a copyright which I believed would preclude you getting your fair and full share of the profits of the enterprise.

Write or telegraph

Yrs

S. L. Clemens

P.S. Keep this whole thing a dead secret—else we'll have somebody standing ready to launch a book right on our big tidal wave and swim it into a *success* when it would otherwise fall still-born.

P.P.S. If this suits draw a written contract or else take proper measures to make this fully and legally binding on both of us in its present form.[1]

Clemens

[1] EB sent MT a contract for the book, stipulating an 8½ percent royalty, on 6 December.

34. To James H. Riley

Buffalo
2 December 1870

(Preserve this letter.)

Dear Riley:

Your letter has come, and I have "reflected." I had already done that a good deal and so my mind is not altered.

You know right well that I would not have you depart a hair from any obligation, for any money. The boundless confidence I have in you is *born* of a conviction of your integrity in small as well as great things. I know plenty of men whose integrity I would trust to *here,* but not off yonder in Africa.

I do not want you to dishonor any obligation, but I want you to write instantly to the Alta and the other papers saying, "I am offered a rare opportunity to permanently better my fortunes, and therefore I have appointed so and so to be your correspondent in my place, provided you approve; otherwise please instruct me by return mail how next to proceed." Of course you can elaborate this, but is the idea correct?—that is, providing there is nothing graver or more binding than usually exists between publisher and correspondent. If these publishers can *discharge* you when they please, just as they can discharge their local reporter when they please, you are doing nothing wrong if you give them a fortnight's warning and do all you can to leave your place satisfactorily supplied.[1]

But if your understandings are *stronger,* you cannot thus *give them notice,* but you can ask them as a perfectly reasonable favor, to *release you* with all convenient dispatch. None of these propositions of mine have in them any taint of dishonor.

As for Sutro, his big heart will simply jump up and say, "By —— Riley, don't stop a minute for my matters—if it's the best thing for you I won't stand in your way."

That Cole and Carter will "rely on your aid" is an obligation only this far: if they can *insure* you better results than some other field offers, then *in a business way* they are entitled to rely on your aid. If you are in debt to them for past favors predicated tacitly upon your aid in this session, then you are *morally* bound. But in any case your simple request with averment that you see an unusually promising chance for you ought to secure their instant and cordial acquiescence.

As to your committees. By a vote, your committees can discharge you. By a vote they can decline to re-elect you, after all your long service. If they could greatly better themselves, it would not only be their fair and just *policy* to do one of these things, but their official DUTY to do it. But if I engage you to go to Africa for 3 or 6 months, for wages, for me, I can *not* discharge you, till your time is up, no matter whether you suit me or not.

But take no snap judgment on the committees, either. Let them choose a clerk, and do you diligently instruct him while you get ready for Africa.

You have certain *moral* obligations resting upon you toward all these parties you have mentioned—and also some less strenuous *business* ones. But in both cases they are doubtless such as an earnest *request* from you would cheerfully cancel.

Now I come to business.

This thing is the pet scheme of my life. As follows:

1. I to pay your passage both *to and from* the South African diamond fields.

2. You to skirmish, prospect, work, travel, and take pretty minute notes, with hand and brain, for ⟨3 or 6 months⟩ 3 months ⟨⟨or 5 or 6 if necessary⟩⟩ I paying you a hundred dollars a month, for you to live on. (Not more, because sometimes I want you to have to shin like everything for a square meal—for *experiences* are the kind of book-material I want.)

3. If you *should* pick up $5,000 worth of diamonds, (within the specified time,) you to pocket that.

4. If you *should* make more, (in any way whatever,) before returning here ⟨⟨either during or subsequent to the specified 3 or 6 months,⟩⟩ you to send me *half* of that *surplus*—after first securing your $5,000 all right.

5. You to overstay the 3 months on no other condition than that you pay me $5,000 a month *in advance* for each month so overstaid, and divide earnings with me beside. (Oh, I guess you'd *better* come home for a while and persuade me to drop No. 5, at least.)

6. You to use these manifold-paper diaries so that you can every day or every few days write two journals at once, and mail one to me and preserve the other carefully yourself.

7. You are to write no newspaper letters while gone, and write no private letters without taking care that their contents shall be kept out of print.—(I want to lay all the ropes thoroughly and then *spring* this book on the public. I don't want other publishers to have a chance to come the usual pitiful game—i.e., come out with an opposition book which rides into grand prosperity on the tide of the other's success, instead of falling still-born, as it would if left to itself.) This to be a *secret* expedition while in progress, but to be a frightfully celebrated one 6 months afterward, not only here but in every language in civilized Europe.

8. You to come to my house at the end of your labors, and live with me, at $50 a month and board, (I to furnish the cigars,) from 4 to 12 months, till I have pumped you dry—for, the purpose of your diary is to keep *you* (as well as me,) bright and inspire your tongue every morning when you take a seat in my study. You are to talk one or two hours to me every day, and *tell* your story—and the rest of the day and night you can do what you please with—and at 3 P.M., I shall always quit work too. With your diary by me I shall be able to write without mistakes after you are gone out walking or driving.

9. At no time within five years are you to write or publish a book *about Africa or its diamond fields.* (This will fool rival publishers, too.)

All the above is for *my* benefit. But *some* shall enure to you, in case you follow my plan. Thus:

1. You see an interesting part of the world, and one upon which the eyes of the whole world are centred.

2. It don't cost you a cent to go or come, nor give you a chance to starve while there.

3. It *does* give you a chance to pick up a fortune in 3 months— the very same chance that thousands would be glad to take at their *own* expense.

4. I should write the book as if *I* went through all these

adventures myself—this in order to give it snap and freshness. But would begin the book by saying: "When Daniel de Foe wanted to know what life on a solitary island was like, and doubted whether he was hardy enough to stand it himself, he sent the ingenious Robinson W. Crusoe; and when I wanted to know all about wild life in the diamond fields and its fascinations, and could not go myself, I sent the ingenious Riley. Now Riley, having returned from his pilgrimage, sits down night after night and tells his story and when he has finished I set it down from memory—not caring so much about the exact language as about the *spirit* of the narration, of course [2]—but using his language when it suits me, and when it suits me putting words of my own to his ideas, fancies and adventures—and just as often the one as the other. In all cases it is Riley speaking, whether the children of his mind appear in the clothing wherein they issued from the door of their nursery, or have doffed a cap or changed a stocking here and there. And to begin, Riley says: 'I left New York on board, etc., etc., etc.' "

Do you see? And I'll hurl in a parenthesis of my own, occasionally, in brackets,—a comment on you or descriptive remark or anecdote about you, or fancy portrait of you in various circumstances of the voyage or adventures in the mines—and do these things so guilelessly that before the reader knows it he is perishing to see *Riley*.

Then my object is accomplished and my game's made! Because thus I can slam you into the lecture field for life and secure you ten thousand dollars a year as long as you live, and all the idle time you want, to loaf and travel in or raise a family. I mention lecturing without any fears because you were born for the platform —you were intended to stand before an audience, and not smile or make a gesture, but simply talk quietly along in a conversational voice and fashion and make them deal out laughter and applause in avalanches. And I mention lecturing with [no] misgivings that you may object, for the reason that I do not take you to be a man either afraid or ashamed to undertake a responsibility which another man would dare.

I would want to "coach" you, thoroughly, drill you completely (for it took me 3 or 4 years to learn the *dead sure* tricks of the platform, but I could teach them to you in 3 or 4 weeks so that when you stepped on a stage you would not be wondering within yourself whether you were going to vanquish the audience, but would absolutely *know* you would do it.)

When you got to Boston or Philadelphia, (either you pleased,) I would introduce you to the audience (provided you wished it,) or follow you with a paragraph, and if it wasn't a good advertisement I want to know why?

5. You should infallibly begin your lecture career at $75 to $150 a night, and in your second lecture season (with the same old lecture,) you should have engagements enough to keep you talking right along for seven months, if you wanted to.

6. In your "off" months you could travel to some quaint country and get up a new lecture about it, and issue a profitable book through my publisher, well aware that your celebrity would give it a great sale—but I'd *rather* that you went at my expense every time and let *me* have the book, old boy.[3]

7. If you never lecture, and never make anything in the diamond land (over $5,000) you'll not owe me anything. But if you *do* lecture, then you can pay me back your expenses, *in your second or third season*, provided your lecturing is the success I have promised it will be, but *not otherwise*.

Finally.—

1. You don't get a cent out of the book. But,

2. You *may* pick up $50,000 in the mines. And,

3. In 5 years of lecturing you *shall* receive $50,000 if you'll lecture.

Pull and all haul my scheme as you please—criticise as you will, it's as sound as a drum—there isn't a leak in it. I'm *bound* to make money out of it if you get back, and you are *bound* to make money lecturing if you *will*.

For the certain and assured prosperity of us both, there needs not to be a solitary (or solitaire) diamond in all Africa,—what we want is to tell in the book and on the platform how lively a time we had *hunting* for them.

But I *urge* upon you, "Expedition's the word!" Clear out *now*, and let us publish the FIRST book and take the richest cream and deliver the freshest and newest and most fascinating picture of this rush, and not come lagging in second or third or fourth, on a public whose appetite has begun to lose its grand ravenousness.—*Now* is the time to start—strike while the iron is hot. Sail hence, New Year's:—

10th Jan. arrive England.
30th "   "   Natal.
Feb. Mch. Apl. in Africa.
Sail May 1, reach here June 30.
July, Aug., Sept., Oct., you talk and I write.

Nov., Dec. and Jan., the book in press and printing 50,000 copies before one is issued; Agents taking 50,000 subscriptions in the meantime. And in the meantime let the publishers scratch for all the opposition books they want to—I'll launch the Riley book Feb. 1, 1872, and sweep the world like a besom of destruction (if you know what that is.)

⟨Feb. and March and April I'll⟩ During Feb., I'll drill you in your lecture. March, Apl., May, ⟨June, July⟩ send you traveling, if there's nothing better to do, and let you get me another book and return and fill me up.

June, July, Aug and Sept., you talk and I write.

Middle of October, you begin and lecture till first of next April or May and then go to Cal and talk in San F at $1200 or $1500 a night.

There isn't a solitary thing in this entire programme that cannot be carried out *to the very letter*, if you will *lecture*. I don't say if you *can*, but if you *will*. I'll make you make some of the "humorous" lecturers very sick.

But *hurry*, now. There is no single moment of time to lose. If you could start *now*, it would be splendid—we'd gain a month— but I know you'll have to have 2 or 3 weeks in which to fairly and honorably release yourself from your existing business ties.—Run up here as soon as you can, and let's talk it all over.

Commence, now, Riley, and post yourself as to expenses, and let me know. I say nothing about posting yourself about other matters needful to know, because I know your habits of mind.

Hang it, I'll have you so well known in 18 months that there will be no man so ignorant as to have to ask "Who is Riley?"—and that will stab Fitz Smythe to the heart!

Answer.

Yr Friend

Saml L. Clemens.

P.S. Mind you keep the secret absolutely. One don't have such a valuable one entrusted to him every day.

P.S. If *you* couldn't, I had my eye on Dan de Quille, but I sort of doubt if poor old Dan could [have] a right big interest in *any*thing, now.

---

¹ In his reply to MT's first proposal, Riley had pointed out that because of his clerkship for a number of senators in Washington "and my engagement with the *Alta*," "it would not be right for me to leave at this time." In response to the present letter, however, Riley telegraphed MT on 5 December, "Plan approved. Will get ready to go." An extensive collection of additional Riley letters is in MTP.

² The text of the original letter in MTP is interrupted here, but the missing fragment, not in MT's hand, of the following paragraphs is in Berg.

³ At this point, the Berg fragment ends and the MTP copy supplies the remainder of the text.

35. To Elisha Bliss

Buffalo

22 December 1870

Friend Bliss:

This is to acknowledge receipt of the fifteen hundred dollars for the foreign expedition. Thanks.

Saml L. Clemens

The contract has gone to you, approved and signed. Send me one.

You'd better go to canvassing for the vol. of sketches *now*, hadn't you? You must illustrate it—and mind you, the man to do the choicest of the pictures is Mullin—the Sisters are reforming him and he is sadly in need of work and money. Write to Launt Thompson the Sculptor, (Albemarle [remainder missing]

36. To ELISHA BLISS

Buffalo
3 January [1871]

Friend Bliss—

No, if this pamphlet pays,[1] I want you to issue Jumping Frog *illustrated*, along with 2 other sketches for the *holidays* next year. I've paid high for the Frog [2] and I want him to get his price back by himself. The Sketch Book will be good enough without him.[3]

Name the Sketch book *"Mark Twain's Sketches"* and go on canvassing like mad. Because if you don't hurry it will tread on the heels of the *big* book next August. In the course of a week I can have most of the matter ready for you I think. Am working like sin on it.

Yrs

Clemens

[1] The pamphlet was presumably Sheldon's publication of *Mark Twain's (Burlesque) Autobiography*. There is a series of letters in MTP from Isaac Sheldon, offering MT half-profits or a 15 percent royalty on the volume.
[2] As he explained in *MTE*, pp. 148–50, MT had lost $2,003.60, more or less, by publishing *The Jumping Frog* with Webb.
[3] EB obviously wanted to include "The Jumping Frog" in the proposed volume of sketches. As he explained in his letter of 27 December 1870, "Don't you think Jumping Frog would be a big thing in the sketch book? Seems to me it will do you as much good there as anywhere and pay you best. Think strongly of it and see if you don't think it will be best to put it in there. By the way where are the plates and don't you want the book sold as it is."

37. To ELISHA BLISS

Buffalo
24 [January 1871]

Friend Bliss

Orion says you hardly know whether it is good judgment to throw the Sketch Book on the market and interfere with the Innocents.[1] I believe you are more than half right—it is calculated to do more harm than good, no doubt. So if you like the idea, suppose we defer the Sketch Book till the *last*. That is, get out the big California and Plains book first of August, then the Diamond book first March or April 1872—and *then* the Sketch book the following fall. Does that strike you favorably? If so write out the contract in that way and forward it. By that time I can write a great many brand new sketches and they'll make the book sell handsomely—and by that time, too, some of the best of the *old* sketches will be forgotten and will read like new matter.

Drop me a line on it.

Yrs

Clemens

[1] In reply, Orion explained on 25 January: "About the sketch-book interfering with the Innocents—Bliss says he is going on with the sketch-book, and you will see which is right. The substance is that the new book will outsell the old one, and few people want to buy two books from the same author at the same time."

38. To ELISHA BLISS

Buffalo
27 January [1871]

Friend Bliss:

Tell you what I'll do, if you say so. Will write night and day and send you 200 pages of MS. every week (of the big book on

California, Nevada and the Plains) and finish it all up the 15th of April if you can without fail *issue* the book on the 15th of May—putting the Sketch book over till another time. For this reason: my popularity is booming, now, and we ought to take the very biggest advantage of it.

I have to go to Washington next Tuesday and stay a week, but will send you 150 MS pages before going, if you say so. It seems to me that I would much rather do this. *Telegraph* me now, right away—don't wait to write. Next Wednesday I'll meet you in N.Y. —and if you can't come there I'll run up and see *you.*

You could get a *cord* of subscriptions taken and advertising done between now and April 15. I have a splendid idea of the sagacity of this proposition.

Telegraph me right off.

Yrs

Mark

39. To Elisha Bliss

Buffalo
15 February 1871

Friend Bliss—

This is to acknowledge receipt of your check for $1,452.62—copyright on sales of Innocents Abroad for quarter ending Jan. 31. The sales keep up amazingly.[1]

Riley sailed finally from London Feb. 1.[2] It is a thirty-day voyage. He had plenty of company—every ship goes full. He sends me London papers which reveal to me that we are all asleep over here. But that is all the better for me. I mean to print *nothing* beforehand, but let the book be a booming surprise.

Tell Orion that we cannot tell what the result is going to be. Sometimes I have hope for my wife,—so I have at this moment—

but most of the time it seems to me impossible that she can get well.³ I cannot go into particulars—the subject is too dreadful. I thank him and Mollie for their kind offers.

Ys

Clemens

¹ The American Publishing Company's statement, dated 13 February 1871, and covering royalties on 8,024 copies of *Innocents*, is in MTP.

² Nineteen pages of Riley's notes are preserved in MTP, but he never did extensive work on the diamond mine volume. On 15 May 1872, MT explained the situation to Frank Bliss: "The simple fact is, that the cancer has fast hold of his vitals and he can live but a little while. Nine physicians have tried their hands on him, but the cancer has beaten the lot" (Elmira, Yale).

³ The death of Emma Nye and the premature birth of Langdon Clemens on 7 November 1870, had left Olivia Clemens in dangerously poor health all through the winter of 1870–1871. In a letter to his family from Buffalo, dated merely "17th," MT advised, "By means of opiates we have given Livy 2 nights' rest and sleep, and she seems better, but still is very low and very weak. She is in her right mind this morning, and has made hardly a single flighty remark" (TS, MTP).

40. To Orion Clemens

Buffalo
11 March 1871

Dear Brother:

Now why do you and Bliss go on urging me to make promises? I will not keep them. I have suffered damnation itself in the trammels of periodical writing, and I will *not* appear once a month, nor once in *three* months, in the Publisher, nor any other periodical.

You shall not advertise me as anything more than an *occasional* contributor—and I tell you I want you to let me choose my own occasions, too.—

You talk as if I am *responsible* for your newspaper venture.

If I am, I want it to stop right here—for I am not going to have another year of harassment about periodical writing.

There isn't money enough between hell and Hartford to hire me to write once a month, for *any* periodical.

I would do more to advance Bliss' interests than any other man's in the world, but the more I turn it over in my mind how your and Bliss' letters of yesterday are making the Publisher a paper which the people are to understand is Mark Twain's paper, and to sink or swim on his reputation, the more outrageous I get.

Why, confound it, when and how has this original little promise of mine (to "drop in an occasional screed along with the Company's *other* authors") grown into these formidable dimensions— whereby I am the *father and sustainer* of the paper and you have actually committed yourselves and me too with advertisements looking in that direction?

Let this cease. Say nothing more about my appearing in the paper, on any other footing than occasionally, like the other authors.

Curse it, man, I would not have had it published around that I was staking my reputation as the sponsor of a new journalistic experiment for $30,000 *cash*—and yet the thing is being done free gratis for nothing! I mean without any real and tangible contract.

Make me the very smallest among the contributors—the very seldomest, I mean—and in that way give me some *weight*.

Haven't I risked cheapening myself sufficiently by a year's periodical dancing before the public but must continue it?

I lay awake all last night aggravating myself with this prospect of seeing my hated nom de plume (for I do loathe the very sight of it) in print *again* every month.

I am plainly and *distinctly* committed by those shuffling gentlemen of the Galaxy for *Frequent* articles, and I tell you I wouldn't write them a single paragraph for $25.00 a word.

Keep that to yourself, but it is *so*.

I don't want to even see my *name* anywhere in print for three months to come.

As for being the high chief contributor and main card of the Publisher, I won't hear of it for a single moment. I'd rather break my pen and stop writing just where I am. Our income is plenty good enough without working for more: and sometimes I think I'm a sort of fool for going on working, anyhow.

Now whenever you mention my name in connection with the

paper, put *"occasional* contributor" after it and don't you intimate that I am anything more.

I must and will keep shady and quiet till Bret Harte simmers down a little and then I mean to go up head again and *stay* there until I have published the two books already contracted for and just one more beside, which latter shall make a ripping sensation or I have overestimated the possibilities of my subject.

Now write me something pleasant—and drop me back where I belong—as an *occasional* contributor. I can produce more than one letter from Bliss intimating that he would pay me $5,000 a year for regular *contributions*—and I *never took him up*—yet in your letter you say: "Put yourself in our place. A new enterprise in which Twain was to be a feature and so widely advertised. Are you going to kick the pail over?"

You had a perfect right to advertise me widely as an occasional contributor, but none to make me responsible for the life or death of the paper. Yet you say: "Squarely we *must* have something from you or we run the risk of going to the dickens"—

Simply puts the responsibility on my shoulders when I have tacitly refused to do the thing for $5,000 a year.

And in your next sentence you say "we must have something every month."

Clearly this is all wrong. Please to put yourself in *my* place.

The man who says the least about me in any paper for three months to come will do me the greatest favor. I tell you I mean to *go slow*. I will "top" Bret Harte again or bust. But I can't do it by dangling eternally in the public view.

Take all I have said kindly—impatiently, perhaps, but not ill-naturedly, toward either you or Bliss.

Yours,
Sam.

P.S. Shall ship some book M.S. next Wednesday.

I have left this letter two days "to cool"—in order to see if my mind remains the same about it.

I find that it *does* remain the same, only *stronger*. The more I think of it the more I feel wronged. After my Galaxy experience I would not *appear* (originally or otherwise) in any paper once a month for $7,000 a year.

Now *why* did you suppose I would appear *constantly* in the Publisher under a mere vague understanding that I was to be *paid* for it? (for I NEVER promised it.)

Is it because I am under obligations to the American Publishing Co.? To decide that, it will be necessary to *examine the accounts and see which of us has made the most money out of the other.*

When Bliss agreed, once, to *stand* a high royalty on a book contract we were making, I receded *voluntarily,* and put the percentage *a good deal lower.*

I have never tried to crowd the Co.—but here the Co. is trying very decidedly to crowd *me.*

I never will enter into even the most trifling business agreement hereafter without having it in writing, with a revenue stamp on it.

I want you to *right* me, now, as far as you can, and do it without any delay. Drop all advertisements about my writing *"exclusively"* for the Publisher, for I want no manacles on me. And put this paragraph in PROMINENTLY.

CORRECTION.

An item has appeared in several of the papers to the effect that I am to write *regularly* for *The Publisher.* It would be wrong to let this error go uncorrected. I only propose to write *occasionally,* nothing more—and shall doubtless *appear* less *frequently than any* other contributor.

MARK TWAIN.

If you alter or leave out that paragraph I shall publish it elsewhere.

Now I am heartily sick of this whole subject and do not want to hear another word about it. Write me on anything else you please, but drop this and drop it *entirely*—never to be touched upon **again.**

If you had not spread it abroad that I am to write, I would ask you to remove my name wholly from the list of contributors.[1]

Yours,

Sam.

[1] In reply, EB wrote on 15 March:
   Your brother has handed me your letter. I cannot conceive what we have done to draw your fire so strongly. I believe some misapprehension exists on your part of the position, and although you interdict the subject, I cannot let it drop without a reply. If I impressed you to write *monthly* for us, I am sorry. . . . Have you ever seen anything from us that has placed you in any difficult position, or thrust you prominently forward? In every advt. or card issued by us your name has appeared *with the others,* and nothing said specially about you. . . . *We have in no way intimated* that you were *sponsor* or *father* to the paper or that you had any connection with it, except as above *in common with other authors and contributors.*

41. To ELISHA BLISS

[Buffalo]
17 March [1871]

Friend Bliss:

Take my name clear out of the list of contributors, and never mention me again and then I shall feel that the fetters are off and I am free. I am to furnish an article for your next No. and I *will* furnish it—that is just the way I ruin myself—making promises. Do you know that for seven weeks I have not had my natural rest but have been a night-and-day sick-nurse to my wife? And am still —and shall be for two or three weeks longer—yet must turn in now and write a damned *humorous* article for The Publisher, because I have *promised* it—promised it when I thought that the vials of hellfire bottled up for my benefit *must* be about emptied. By the living God I don't believe they ever *will* be emptied.

The MS I sent to be copied is back but I find nothing in it that can be transferred to the Publisher—for the Chapter I intended to use I shall tear up, for it is simply an attempt to be funny, and a failure.[1]

When I get to Elmira I will look over the *next* chapters and send something—or, failing that, will write something—my own obituary I hope it will be.

As to where I got the idea, etc., etc., etc.—got it from Larned and Gray and other friends who got it from papers—never saw it myself—but you say truly that a newspaper rumor is binding on nobody. I see easily enough that your advertisements haven't anything in them that I can find any fault with—nothing at all. So I was wronging you—not you me. . . .

[1] On 10 March 1871, MT had written Orion from Buffalo, "Have just sent out 160 ms pages of my book to be copied—shall have it back next Tuesday. Then I will ship it to Bliss and mark a chapter to be transferred to the columns of the Publisher."

42. To Elisha Bliss

Elmira
20 [March 1871]

Friend Bliss:

We are all here, and my wife has grown weak, stopped eating, and dropped back to where she was two weeks ago. But we've all the *help* we want here.

Here is my contribution (I take it from the book,) and by all odds it is the finest piece of writing I ever did. Consequently I want the people to *know* that it is from the book:

Head it thus, and go on:

The Old-Time Pony-Express of the Great Plains. ⟨Having but little time to write volunteer contributions, now I offer this chapter from⟩

By Mark Twain.

⟨The following is a chapter from Mark Twain's forthcoming book and closes with a life-like picture of an incident of Overland stage travel on the Plains in the days before the Pacific railroad was built.—Ed. Publisher.

⟨From along about the 160th to 170th page of the MS.⟩ It begins thus:

"However, in a little while all interest was taken up in stretching our necks and watching for the pony-rider" etc.—Go on to end of chapter. Refer the marginal note to Orion, about postage. I feel *sure* I am wrong, and that it *was Four* Dollars an ounce instead of *Two*—make the correction, if necessary. *Read proof very carefully, Orion*—you need send none to me.

P.S. Before the book is printed I shall write that bull story over again (that precedes the pony) or else alter it till it is good—for it *can* be made good—and then you can put *that* in the Publisher too, if you want to.

Yrs

Clemens

You got the Book MS, of course?

43. To ORION CLEMENS

Elmira
4 April [1871]

Dear Bro:

In moving from Buffalo here I have lost certain notes and documents—among them what you wrote for me about the difficulties of opening up the Territorial government in Nevada and getting the machinery to running. And now, just at the moment that I want it, it is gone. I don't even know what it was you wrote, for I did not intend to read it until I was ready to use it. Have you time to scribble something again, to aid my memory. Little characteristic items like Whittlesey's refusing to allow for the knife,[1] etc are the most illuminating things—the difficulty of getting credit for the Gov't—and all that sort of thing. Incidents are better, any time, than dry history. Don't tax yourself—I can make a little go a great way.

Baby in splendid condition. Livy as feeble as ever—has not sat up but once or twice for a week.

Is Bliss doing anything with the MS I sent? Is he thinking of beginning on it shortly?

Ys

Sam

---

[1] See *Roughing It*, Chapter XXV.

44. To ORION CLEMENS

Elmira
8 April [1871]

Dear Bro:

If I don't add a postscript to this, tell Bliss to go ahead and set up the MSS and put the engravers to work. My copy is down at the house and I am up here at the farm, a mile and a half up a mountain, where I write every day.

I am to the 570th page and booming along. And what I am writing now is so much better than the opening chapters, or the Innocents Abroad either, that I do *wish* I could spare time to revamp the opening chapters, and even write some of them over again.

I will read the bull story when I go down, and see whether it will do or not. It don't altogether suit me, but I shall alter it *very little*, anyway. I don't want it to go in the same number of the paper with the pony sketch. Mind, I never want two articles of mine in the same number. Put it in the next if you choose.

Ys

Sam.

Tell Bliss to hatch up lots of pictures for the book—it is going to sell bully.

We carried Livy to the barouche, today, and she rode around the block twice.

P.S. *Leave out* the yarn about Jack and "Moses." It occurs about 117th page. Close the chapter with these words.

"and when they tried to teach a subordinate anything that subordinate generally 'got it through his head'—at least in time for the funeral."

Accompanying this, is the bull story, altered the way I want it. Don't put it in till about the fourth No. of the paper.

Tell Bliss to go ahead setting up the book just as it is, making the corrections *marked in purple ink,* in some 20 or 30 pages which I shall mail to-night.—possibly in this envelop.

Ys

Sam

P.S.—Monday—Am to 610th page, now.

45. To Orion Clemens

Elmira
18 April [1871]

My Dear Bro:

Since Knox [1] has printed a similar story (the same "situation" has been in print often—men have written it before Knox and I were born,)—let the Bull story alone until it appears in the book— or at least in the "specimen" chapters for canvassers.[2] That is to say, Do not put it in the paper, *at all.* I cannot alter it—too much trouble.

Joe Goodman is up here at the farm with me—will come up every day for 2 months and write a novel.

He is going to read my MSS critically.

Livy just the same—no better, no worse.

Yrs

Sam.

P.S. No—I won't print Jack and Moses. I may lecture next winter, and in that case shall want it.

Mind you, I must not appear in the paper oftener than bi-monthly, in *any* case.

[1] Presumably Thomas W. Knox, whose *Overland through Asia* was being published by The American Publishing Company at this time.

[2] EB was at work on the agents' prospectus and other aspects of the sales campaign for *Roughing It*, as his reply of 22 April indicated:

I have been going to drop you a line for some days, but am so busy, I hardly get time to write anything except what is absolutely necessary. I want to say to you that we go to work on a Pros. Monday, and shall get it out very quickly. I fear your brother has written in a manner to give you wrong impressions of my views. I have said to him that the first part of a book alone is not sufficient to make a proper prospectus of. I of course cannot get up full plate engravings until I know the subject. . . . I do not think there is as much of a desire to see another book from you as there was 3 months ago. Then anything offered would sell—people would subscribe to anything of yours without . . . looking at it much. Now they will inspect a Prospectus closer and buy more on the strength of *it*, than they would have done a few months ago.

Knowing this to be so, I feel particularly anxious to get out a *splendid Prospectus*. . . . Now this is my proposed plan to rush your next book. I did prefer to get out extracts of it, and get just as much notoriety for them as possible. I preferred to do this very soon—and whet the people's appetites for more of the same. Now then I supposed anything in our paper as coming from the book should be of a superior quality, and then would be largely copied. . . . I have made selections from MSS. here for Pros. and if you have any choice cuts further along in the book for it, send them on.

46. To Elisha Bliss

Elmira
3 May [1871]

Friend Bliss:

My friend Ned House,[1] of the N.Y. Tribune, is in Japan, and is writing a book that will read bully and sell ditto. His idea of illustrating it profusely with quaint Japanese wood cuts made by native artists is a splendid feature. If you want his book, let me know what royalty, etc, you will pay, and I will write him.[2] If your own hands should be full you might publish it through your brother's house.[3] I enclose the letter he wrote to David Gray [4] and me on the subject.

My book is half done. I mailed you the 12th, 13th, 14th and 15th chapters yesterday, and before that I had sent you the previous 11 chapters. Let me know if they all arrived safely.

This book will be pretty readable, after all; and if it is well and profusely illustrated it will crowd the "Innocents." [5]

Ys

Clemens.

[1] E. H. House, whose friendship with MT was to dissolve into insults and legal suits a decade later as a result of conflicting opinions about the right to dramatize *The Prince and the Pauper* (see Paul Fatout, "Mark Twain, Litigant," *American Literature*, XXXI [March, 1959], 30–45).

[2] On 17 May, EB replied, "Don't let anybody else get House's book!" But in spite of further references to it, the book was not published by the American Publishing Company; House's *Japanese Episodes* was issued by JRO & Co. in 1881.

[3] Several other subscription publishers, the Mutual Publishing Company and the Columbian Book Company among them, operated as subsidiaries of the American Publishing Company.

[4] David Gray was a poet, editor of the Buffalo *Courier*, and one of the few friends of the Clemens family in Buffalo.

[5] EB's letter of 17 May outlined his plans:

We intend to do *our part* towards making your book what it should be in illustrations. We shall try to have just the kind in that will suit, and think we shall succeed. I think it would be well to have Prospectus out *soon as practicable* as agents are anxious for it. . . . Suppose you do as you suggest. Send another batch on of *selected* chapters if you think best and I will get right to work.

47. To Elisha Bliss

Elmira
June 1871

Dear Bliss:

Here are three articles [1] which you may have if you'll pay $125 for the lot—and if you don't want them I'll sell them to "Galaxy," but not for a cent less than three times the money—have just sold them a short article (shorter than either of these,) for $100. If you take them, pay *one-tenth* of the $125 in weekly instalments to

Orion till he has received it all. Don't go over the one-tenth at a time—otherwise he will do no sort of good with it.

If you use the articles, print the Beecher one first, then let a whole edition go by before printing either of the others—then let the scientific articles appear one after the other in successive issues of the paper.

Yes, I would like to have you mention the lecture—and you can add this: "It is not a fight against Woman's rights or against any particular thing, but is only a pretentiously and ostentatiously supplicating appeal in behalf of the boys, which the *general tendency of the times* converts into a good-natured satire,—otherwise the lecture would hardly sound like a satire at all—at least to a careless listener." [2]

Have you heard anything from Routledge? Considering the large English sale he made of one of my other books (Jumping Frog,) I thought may be we might make something if I could give him a secure copyright.—There seems to be no convenient way to beat those Canadian re-publishers anyway—though I *can* go over the line and get out a copyright if you wish it and think it would hold water.

Yrs

Mark.

[1] On the three articles MT sent EB, see *MT&EB*, p. 193. EB agreed in a letter of 7 July to "pay O. as you say $12.50 per week."
[2] See *MTLC*, p. 151, for MT's lecture plans. Orion announced the lecture topics in *The American Publisher*, I (July 1871), 4.

48. To Orion Clemens

Elmira
2 July [1871]

Dear Bro—

My MSS? Shall bring it there myself before long. Say 2 to 4 weeks hence. Am just finishing Chapter 56. Have already nearly

MS enough, but am still writing—intend to cut and cull liber-
ally.[1]

Yrs

Sam

[1] Between the letter of 3 May, reporting the book "half done," and this report,
MT wrote Orion on 29 June, "Wrote 2 chapters of the book to-day—shall write
chapter 53 to-morrow." On 7 July, EB discussed his plans for the manuscript:
> Would like all the Mss. you have to be able to select subjects for *full page
> engravings*—want all I can of these to go in the Prospectus. And now another
> thing we have said nothing about. What is to be the title—this is a
> matter of some importance you know, and necessary for the Prospectus, unless
> we say we don't know it yet and call it the *"Unnamed"* and wait for
> developments to christen it. . . . Shall have prospectus ready early as possible
> to get the cuts ready, and make a sweep of the board this fall.

For other references concerning MT's composition, see *LLMT*, p. 159; *MTL*, pp.
185–188; and *MTMF*, pp. 153–154.

49. To Elisha Bliss

Wilkes-Barre

19 October 1871

Friend Bliss—

I brought the desert chapter away with me to write it up—but it
is no use. I am driven to death with travel, lecturing and
entertaining committees. It will be two weeks before I can get a
chance to write up this chapter.[1] I remember the heavy work it was
to write it before and I wish that man had the M.S. stuffed into his
bowels that lost it. If time presses, just leave the whole chapter out.[2]
It is all we can do.

In haste   Yrs

Mark

[1] MT refers to Chapter XX of *Roughing It,* which contains the Hank Monk-
Horace Greeley anecdote.

[2] Orion told his wife Mollie on 3 October that the manuscript was "just going
into the printer's hands." MT was engaged on a strenuous lecture campaign
during the autumn of 1871 (see *MTLC*, pp. 149–172), and presumably did
little proofreading for *Roughing It.* On 6 December, EB wrote, "We send you all
the parts of the book we have printed so far. We have set up to page 300—but
plates not finished up yet. . . . I could send you nothing except what I do
unless I send my set of proofs which I cannot possibly spare. We have started
presses and shall now have to finish up to keep them issuing."

II

"A Great Big Unpaying Thing"

(1872–1880)

"The business seems to be a great big unpaying thing."
MT to EB, 22 July 1876, TS in MTP

B Y 1872, Mark Twain was firmly committed to the American Publishing Company, subscription publication, and the world of high if slightly soiled finance. In his earliest letters to Elisha Bliss, he was the uncertain, overawed tyro watching the vast apparatus of the subscription-book machinery operate, with occasional suggestions but more frequent questions. As he became familiar with the process, however, his tone changed. He purchased $5,000 of stock in the American Publishing Company, became a Director, insisted —unsuccessfully—on having his contracts rewritten, and began making suggestions that had the distinct ring of command.

From 1872 to 1880, there was a steady progression in Mark Twain's confidence in his own abilities at running a subscription house. On 24 March 1874, for example, he told Thomas Bailey Aldrich, "Now I think seriously of *printing* my own next book and publishing it thro' this same subscription house." In 1876, he almost put the plan into effect with the English edition of *The Adventures of Tom Sawyer,* and in that same year attempted to start a palace revolution against Elisha Bliss with the help of the other directors of the American Publishing Company. Finally, he attempted to leave the Company to publish *A Tramp Abroad.* (Ultimately, with *The Prince and the Pauper* and *Life on the Mississippi,* he was to put into effect the scheme he mentioned to Aldrich, commissioning James R. Osgood to publish and market the volumes.)

Confidence in his own judgment had a definite corollary: suspicion of the judgments and motives of others. Charles H. Webb was the first to suffer through threats of prosecution; B. J. Such, Gilbert Densmore, and William F. Gill followed. Finally, even Elisha Bliss received treatment ranging from bad manners to open legal attack.

By 1880, when Elisha Bliss died and the year before Charles L. Webster took over as Mark Twain's general "troubleshooter," the stage was set for the period when everything Mark Twain touched "seemed to turn to gold." Not only was his thirst for investment, business, wild gambles and wilder schemes unquenched, but even more significant, the decade of the 1870's turned Twain's speculative interests toward aspects of publishing. There are many minor exceptions, but the major enterprises of Mark Twain's later career as a businessman were to be involved with publication (Charles L. Webster & Co.), printing (the Paige typesetter), and illustrating (the Kaolatype process).

50. To ELISHA BLISS

Elmira
20 March 1872

Friend Bliss—[1]

The more I think over our last Tuesday's talk about my copyright or royalty, the better I am satisfied. But I *was* troubled a good deal, when I went there, for I had worried myself pretty well into the impression that I was getting a smaller ratio of this book's profits than the spirit of our contract had authorized me to promise myself; indeed, I was so nearly convinced of it that if you had not been so patient with my perplexities, and taken the pains to show me by facts and figures and arguments that my present royalty gives me fully half and possibly even more than half the net profits of the book, I would probably have come to the settled conviction that such was not the case, and then I should have been dissatisfied.[2] I am glad you convinced me, for I would be sorry indeed to have come away from your house feeling that I had put such entire trust and confidence in you ⟨and the company⟩ to finally lose by it. ⟨And I am glad that you convinced me by good solid arguments and figures instead of mere plausible generalities, for that was just and business-like, and a conviction grounded in that way is satisfying and permanent.⟩ But everything is plain and open, now. And after thinking it over, I feel that, the result being the same, you will readily assent to the altering of our contract in such a way that it shall express that I am to receive half the profits. Any friend of mine can represent me in the matter. Charley Warner will do as well as another. ⟨Let Twichell attend to it. However, I suppose he has his hands about full; and perhaps he isn't much experienced in this sort of thing. Then let Charles Perkins do it. Contracts are in his line at any rate. It is too complicated for anybody but a lawyer to handle, anyhow; I could not even conduct it myself.⟩ I will ask him to do it.

I am at last easy and comfortable about the new book. I have sufficient testimony, derived through many people's statements to my friends, to about satisfy me that the general verdict gives "Roughing It" the preference over "Innocents Abroad." This is rather gratifying than otherwise. The *reason* given is, that they like a book about America because they understand it better. It is pleasant to believe this, because it isn't a great deal of trouble to write books about one's own country. Miss Anna Dickinson says the book is unprecedentedly popular—a strong term, but I believe that was it.[3]

We are all well and flourishing—all four of us.

Ys   `

Clemens.

---

[1] In addition to cancellations marked with angle brackets, the present letter shows an enormous amount of revision, intended to make its tone more

impersonal and businesslike. In the original draft, MT describes EB as "good
tempered" and describes the business conversation as "our long and pleasant
intercourse."

² Orion, who left his editorship of *The American Publisher* in March 1872
after a year of conflicts, wrote MT a letter (presumably not extant) claiming that
EB was cheating on statements about the manufacture of *Roughing It*. In a letter
of 7 March to Orion, MT had replied, "I cannot let you think I overlook or
underestimate the brotherly goodness and kindness of your motive in your assault
upon Bliss. I would have you feel and know that I fully appreciate *that,* and
value it. The fact that I contemn the *act* as being indefensible, does not in the
least blind me to the virtue of the *motive* underlying it." On 17 May 1872, Orion
apparently heard the rumor that MT was consulting with lawyers and wrote a
long letter to the humorist outlining his suggestions for legal action (quoted in
part in *MT & EB,* p. 66).

³ MT was attempting to arrange for Anna Dickinson to publish a subscription
book with the American Publishing Company. In a letter of 23 July, she told
MT, "I have just written Mr. Bliss to know if it is understood that I am to have a
guarantee of $10,000 at the rate of 7½ per ct. and a further payment—if the
book sells beyond that amount at 7½ per ct. . . . I won't write the book for less,
—nor, as I see the matter now, for any different terms whatever." On 23 June
1874, she wrote MT from Philadelphia, "I am slowly simmering over a book,
which must be done soon, and . . . will meet *Bliss's* approbation, and so that of
the public." Finally, on 24 March 1875, MT wrote EB, "Since Anna Dickinson
don't sign the contract, I think you are the lucky party—not she."

51. To Elisha Bliss

Elmira

21 March [1872]

Friend Bliss—

At last I have sat down in earnest and looked the new book ¹
through—and my verdict is, better a long sight *leave the Jumping
Frog out.* There is too much fun in the book as it is. For Heaven's
sake let us not *add* to it.—Don't hestitate about it but just *take the
Frog out.* What *we* want, is that the book should be *the best we can
make it.* We seriously injure it by putting in the Frog. Such is the
settled belief of

Ys

Clemens.

P.S. After all the preparations for putting this book ² on the market right you have let yourself get caught in a close place with a short edition. That wasn't like you.

---

[1] The "new book" was undoubtedly a Routledge edition of sketches—to which MT referred in the next letter. He was at work editing a collection of sketches to which he alluded in an 18 July letter to Redpath: "I am under contract to write a book and shall not get it done as soon as I desire, if I drift off to other things."
[2] *Roughing It.*

52. To JAMES R. OSGOOD

Elmira
Sunday, 1872

Dr. Sir:

Indeed I *would* like to publish a volume of sketches through your house, but unfortunately my contracts with my present publisher tie my hands and prevent me. I have just made up quite a portly volume of them for Routledge & Sons, London, but I have to leave my own countrymen to "suffer and be strong" without them. Much love to the boys.

Yr. Truly

Saml. L. Clemens.

53. To ELISHA BLISS

Saybrook
7 August 1872

Friend Bliss—

This is to acknowledge receipt of copyright to Aug. 1, $8,485.17, less $5,000 ⟨previously⟩ advanced to me by you before it was due.

I have written strongly to Anna Dickinson.

How about Harte's rooms? [1]

Hurry up your figuring on the volume of sketches, for I leave for England in 10 or 12 days to be gone several months.

Yrs

Clemens

[1] The idea of signing up Bret Harte—as well as Anna Dickinson—for a subscription book first occurred to MT in 1872. A letter from MT to EB dated merely "20th" said, "Been looking for Harte here. If he comes, will let you know." On 31 July, EB replied, "How about Harte's book—Can you give me any light on the subject? Has he been at Saybrook? He wrote me that after hearing from you I should probably hear from him, but no word yet. Am a little anxious to know, so as to shape my course for operations. Will rush at once to Holyoke Mt. for [to] prospect for rooms and report at once. Let me have a line from you if possible at once about the Book." Harte had visited MT during mid-June (see *MT&BH*, p. 77).

54. To ELISHA BLISS

Hartford
4 March 1873

Friend Bliss—

Statement rec'd for quarter ending Mch 1, and check for $1,656.69 for royalties on Innocents Abroad and Roughing It.

So Roughing It sells less than twice as many in a quarter as Innocents, a book which is getting gray with age. The fault is mainly in the engravings and paper, I think.—That, and the original lack of publicity. I believe have learned, now, that if one don't secure publicity and notoriety for a book the instant it is issued, no amount of hard work and faithful advertising can accomplish it later on. When we look at what Roughing It sold in the first 3 and 6 months, we naturally argue that it would have sold full 3 times as many if it had gotten the prompt and early journalistic boost and notoriety that the Innocents had.

Recognizing the importance, now, of this prompt notoriety (which I was *afraid* of and didn't want until we were dead sure of 50,000 subscriptions to R.I.—but which I am not afraid of now,) I have conceived a plan which will advertise the next book from Maine to the Marquesas free of expense before the proofsheets are all read. But I'll fix that, myself.[1]

Now Nast appears to be doing nothing in particular. I want him, solitary and alone, to illustrate this next book, it being an essentially *American* book, he will enjoy doing it. Nast only has just one *first-class* talent (caricature,) and no more—but this book will exercise that talent, I think. I think he will be glad to do this work below his usual terms. If you say so *I will write him*. Tell me what you think, and tell me about the total amount you think it best to put in the *drawing* of the illustrations.[2]

I wish you would say nothing about a new book from me for the spring (or rather next fall) issue, because as soon as I can get some more stock at easy figures, I want it. I want to be a Director, also.[3]

How [many] copies have been sold of Innocents? And how many of R.I.? Get it from the official figures.

Ys

Clemens.

[1] After a trip to England during the autumn of 1872, MT and Charles Dudley Warner were in the midst of composing *The Gilded Age,* no doubt the book to which this letter refers even though the contract for the volume was not yet signed. MT's plan for free advertising is obscure, but it sounds much more flamboyant than the ultimate announcements in the New York *Tribune* (see *MT&GA,* pp. 11–13).

[2] Thomas Nast did not, of course, illustrate *Gilded Age,* though EB claimed in his prospectus that the illustrations had cost $10,000. MT had written Nast the preceding December, "I do hope my publishers can make it pay you to illustrate my English book. Then I should have good pictures. They've got to improve on 'Roughing It' " (Albert Bigelow Paine, *Thomas Nast: His Period and His Pictures* [New York, 1904], p. 263). Nast replied on 15 December, "How much I should like to go with you and illustrate [a book of English travels]."

[3] On 7 January 1873, EB wrote MT, "You doubtless are aware that a chk for $500 is waiting for you here, being a dividend of 10% on your stock." MT was a Director of the American Publishing Company from 1873 through 1881.

55. To Elisha Bliss

[Hartford]
3 May 1873

Friend Bliss—

We shall doubtless be ready to talk business by about Tuesday,

Wednesday, or, at latest, Thursday—and we shall be in a hurry too
—shan't have long to talk. So, think it all over—Sheldon & Co
think we will make a serious and damaging mistake if we try to sell
a novel by subscription. Try and be ready, also to recommend to me
another Hartford subscription publisher to get out a telling book on
Japan,[1] for I suppose you have got your hands about full. I want
you to recommend a man who will appreciate a good thing, and
know how to push it.

Yrs

Clemens

[1] This may be a revival of MT's attempt to secure a publisher for E. H. House
(see letter 46, above). House visited MT during the spring of 1873 (see
MT&GA, pp. 14–15).

56. To CHARLES DUDLEY WARNER

Under Way
Sat. A.M. [May 1873]

Dear Warner—

Ask House to tell you about Whitelaw Reid. He is a contempt-
ible cur, and I want nothing more to do with him. I don't want the
Tribune to have the book at all. Please tell Bliss *not to send a copy
there under any circumstances.* If you feel at any time like
explaining, you may tell Reid or anyone that I desired this.[1]

I shall probably write some letters for Herald and possibly for
Advertiser.

We saw Boucicault, who, in some minor respects, is an ass. If
you describe the outside of your trunk to him he can tell you what
it's got in it.

I will not consent to his having more than one-third for
dramatising the book.

Yesterday I sued a New York fraud for $20,000 damages for
violating my copyright.[2]

We send love.

We are all well, and jolly.

Ys Ever

Saml. L. Clemens.

[1] Whitelaw Reid, editor of the New York *Tribune,* had made two announcements of *Gilded Age*—on 19 and 23 April. House offered to write a third notice of the book and Reid declined (see *MTHL,* p. 374).

[2] The "fraud" was B. J. Such, who published *A Book for an Hour* . . . in 1873. On 27 June 1879, Mr. Simon Sterne of the law firm of Sterne, Hudson & Straus wrote Dan Slote the particulars of the case: "I . . . at last determined that I would apply under the rule, that a man has a trademark in his articles published under a *nom de plume.* . . . After elaborate argument . . . an injunction absolute was issued. The defendant did not appeal from this injunction but allowed it to stand." No damages were paid, however.

57. To Elisha Bliss

London

16 July [1873]

Friend Bliss,

We shall issue a copyright edition of the novel here in fine style —three volumes; and in order that there shall be no mistakes I wish you would be particular to send sheets and duplicate casts of the pictures by successive steamers always. And send these casts and proofs along as fast as you get a signature done. Be sure to write on to Routledge and state as nearly as you can the exact day at which you can publish. Routledge will publish on that day or the day before. If you change the date of publication telegraph Routledge.

I told Joaquin Miller to write you proposing 7½ per cent for his book.[1]

Yours Truly,

Saml. L. Clemens.[2]

[1] EB published Miller's *Unwritten History* in 1874. See also *MTMF,* p. 174.

[2] Only the signature of this and the following letter are in MT's hand; Charles Warren Stoddard, who was serving as MT's personal secretary during the 1873 trip to England, transcribed the rest from dictation.

58. To Charles Dudley Warner

London
16 July [1873]

My Dear Warner,

I have just written Bliss asking him to send two sets of sheets and two casts of the pictures always by successive steamers, so that if one set is ever lost it need not stop the book. I wish you would see that this is done, and don't let a sheet be carelessly kept back for a week or two, scaring a body to death with the idea that it is lost; but have the sheets sent in their regular order faithfully. Don't wait for a quantity, but send it right along, signature by signature. And I have told Bliss to name the day of publication and to write Routledge about it; and that if he should change that date to telegraph to Routledge; because if Routledge makes a mistake in the publishing day of Bliss it may cost us our copy-right. Now you know what I have written Bliss, and you will know how to proceed.

Yours Truly,

Saml. L. Clemens.

59. To T. B. Pugh

Edinburgh
27 July [1873]

My Dear Pugh [1]—

I have got to remain in London till the 25th of October to see my book through the English press. As this is business and can't be avoided, I thought I had better let you know, so that you would be saved making any advertisements with my name in them of the great lecture-jubilee if it is to come off before I get back. I want to appear in that caravan, according to my promise, but it is now a fact beyond question that I shall have to remain in London till Oct. 25 and thus be able to secure English copyright.

Ys Truly

Saml. L. Clemens

[1] T. B. Pugh was the manager for "The Star Course of Lectures" in Philadelphia (Pugh to MT, Philadelphia, 7 February 1873). So far as is known, MT never lectured under his sponsorship.

60. To ELISHA BLISS

Edinburgh
27 July [1873]

Friend Bliss—

Confound it, I forgot to tell you not to advertise that pamphlet [1] (in case you publish it) or send a copy to any newspaper. Bother the luck, I wanted it to pass unnoticed.

Shall I look for Gilded Age sheets pretty soon?

Yrs

Clemens.

Care Routledge.

London

[1] On 1, 4, 9, 11, and 19 July, MT's letters describing the Shah of Persia appeared in the New York *Herald*. He intended to have EB reprint them as a pamphlet to forestall pirates, "along with the enclosed article about the Jumping Frog in French, (which is entirely new) and then add enough of my old sketches to make *a good fat 25 cent pamphlet* and let it slide—but don't charge *more* than 25¢ nor less" (MT to EB, London, 7 July [1873], CWB). His preface to the proposed book is extant:

To the Reader

It is not my desire to republish these New York Herald letters in this form; I only do it to forestall some small pirate or other in the book trade.

If I do not publish some such person may, and I then become tacitly accessory to a theft. I have had a recent unpleasant experience of this kind. I have copyrighted the letters here in London simply to prevent their republication in Great Britain in pamphlet form. My objection to such republication, either in America or England, is, that I think everybody has already had enough of the Shah of Persia. I am sure I have. To the letters I have added certain sketches of mine which are little known or not known at all in America, to the end that the purchaser of the pamphlet may get back a portion of his money and skip the chapters that refer to the Shah altogether.

With this brief apology, I am

Respectfully
Mark Twain

London, July 7

61. To Thomas Bailey Aldrich

[Hartford]
24 March 1874

Business

My Dear Aldrich:

All right, my boy, send along the proofs.[1]

Never mind Bliss. I don't feel around *him*. When you've a book ready, I'll only say, "I've the MS here, of a book by Aldrich. Can you pay him 10 per cent royalty, or shall I carry it over the way, to Worthington, Dustin & Co?" [2] The same with a book by Howells. Precious little tortuous diplomacy required when one names his price with a stiff upper lip and mentions the hated rival over the way. I'll attend to the *business* details, and the framing of the contract, if you'll let me.

Bliss had contracted to pay me 10 p.c. on my next book (contract made 18 months ago) so I made him pay that on Gilded Age. He paid 7½ p.c. on Roughing It and 5 p.c. on Innocents Abroad. I only made him pay 7½ p.c. on Joaquin Miller's Modoc book, because I don't think Miller much of a card in America.

There's an unknown cuss in N.Y. who wants to write a book on a purely commercial subject and make a reputation—but I reckon the lack of a publisher was rather a stumbling block in his way. So I have commissioned him to write the book for *me* and am to pay him $2,000 when he hands me the MS for said book—500 pages octavo—that is 1800 pages of note paper MS. He is to put his own name to it, and read the proofs.[3] I'll make $10,000 out of that book, but *not* by publishing it as you and Howells publish.

There is one discomfort which I fear a man must put up with when he publishes by subscription, and that is wretched paper and vile engravings. I fancy the publisher don't make a very large pile when he pays his author 10 p.c. You notice that the Gilded Age is rather a rubbishy looking book; well, the sale has now reached about 50,000 copies—so the royalty now due the authorship is about $18,000—yet the Company have declared only one ten per-cent dividend since the book was issued; they would have declared at least 25 per cent in dividends on 50,000 copies of a 7½ p.c. book.

Now I think seriously of *printing* my own next book and publishing it thro' this same subscription house. It will thus be a mighty starchy book, but I reckon I won't get so much money out of it. . . .

[1] MT had agreed to read proof of Chapter VII of Aldrich's *Prudence Palfrey* dealing with mining in Montana. On 28 June, Aldrich explained, "I didn't send you the revise of the Montana chapter, for I hadn't the face to impose any more on your kindness. I need not tell you how deeply I appreciate the trouble you took in the matter." On 25 March, MT made more specific suggestions:

You see (page 109) you've got that *ancient* river-bed in your head, and you've got the modern river-bed in your head, too, and you've gone and *mixed* the two together. But they *won't* mix, any more than oil and water. Nevins could see the stream down in the canyon, and that is what I allow him to see; and he could judge there was gold there (*in that stream*), by the look of things —and I allow him to do that; but he couldn't see one of those "ancient" river-beds, because it is *buried* in the very heart of the mountains; and if one little end of it *did* stick out of the mountain side that man couldn't see it a hundred yards (Harvard).

[2] Worthington, Dustin and Company was a subscription house which operated from 302 Asylum Street; the American Publishing Company's offices were at 149.

[3] It is not the Riley diamond mine book to which MT refers; Riley had died in 1872. Nor is it Captain Ned Wakeman, who was seeking a publisher for the manuscript of what was to become *The Log of an Ancient Mariner* (see Ray B. Browne, "Mark Twain and Captain Wakeman," *American Literature*, XXXIII [November, 1961], 320–329). On 18 March, MT wrote Orion, "I have written him [Wakeman] that *you* will edit his book and help him share the profits, and I will write the introduction and find a publisher."

62. To Charles Dudley Warner

Elmira
5 May [1874]

My Dear Warner:

Business. A San Francisco friend sends me a "Chronicle," whereby it appears that only my portions of the book are used in the play. It says "The story of Philip, Alice and all their friends is entirely left out." It is a one-character play, like Rip Van Winkle. The one character is Sellers.

Now what I want to propose is this: and it seems fair to me. You make over to me your ownership in our dramatic copyright (duly in writing,) so far as it concerns characters created by me in the Gilded Age, and I will convey to you my dramatic ownership in all the characters created by you. You can (then dramatize or permit to be) then use your characters in a drama, if you wish to, and I will buy this play of Densmore, re-write it if it is worth it—or burn it, and write one myself and enjoin D. from playing his.

I know Mr. D. mighty well and he shan't run any play on MY brains.—He is the chap who finished Bret Harte's story for him without Bret's asking it. Give me an early answer to my proposition. If you like it, please send me a copy of our printed dramatic copy-right page.[1]

Not Business.—We are packing trunks—we remove to the farm to-day. Livy ventured to sit through two acts of Rip Van Winkle last night, and got herself pretty full of back-aches; but she is tolerably well this morning again. If you and Susie will only give us a call at the farm presently, we would be a couple of entirely delighted people.

Ever Yrs

Mark.

[1] See *MTHL*, pp. 861–863, for a detailed account of the dramatization of *Gilded Age.*

63. To H. O. Houghton

[Hartford]
12 February [1875]

Gentlemen:

I like the whole plan except the money side of it.[1] I do not believe there would be much money in it, and I find that trying to support a family is a thing which compels one to look at all ventures with a mercenary eye. I hope to see a day when I can publish in a way which shall please my fancy best and not mind what the banking result may be—but that time has not come yet; and so I must not venture in this attractive case and in this goodly company, though I thank you all the same for the compliment you pay me in proposing it.

Yrs Truly

Saml. L. Clemens

P.S. I shall not mention your plan to any one.

[1] H. O. Houghton of Hurd & Houghton, Publishers, had written MT on 6 February, "We should like to ask your favorable consideration of a scheme which we have formed. . . . It is our wish . . . to make a specialty of the publication of bright, short American novels, giving them all the prominence which very careful attention to the printing and binding can secure, making them cheap, advertising them widely and securing this popularity for the several books and all possible reputation as well as profit for the authors. . . . Let us ask if we may not count on you for No. 1 in this series." Houghton wrote again after receiving the present letter, pointing out that "a novel small enough to go into a 16mo volume of 250 pp. would be too small for publication through a subscription house" (Cambridge, 20 February 1875).

64. To James R. Osgood

[Hartford]
12 February [1875]

My Dear Osgood:

Concerning that sketch-book. I went to Bliss yesterday and told him I had got all my old sketches culled and put together and a whole lot of new ones added, and that I had about made up my mind to put them in your hands. Whereupon he went to his safe and brought back a contract *four years old* to give him all my old sketches, with a lot of new ones added!—royalty 7½ per cent!

I had totally forgotten the existence of such a contract—*totally*. He said, "It wouldn't be *like* you to refuse to first fulfill *this* contract."

I said, "You flatter me; and moreover you have *got* me. But I won't fulfill it at 7½ per cent."

"We never have shown a disposition to be mean with you—state your terms," said Bliss.

I said, "Do you really mean that you will pay a higher royalty, with that contract at your back?"

"I mean that we will meet you in liberality half way and *more* than halfway."

"Very well," I said.—"The book shall be illustrated, and sell at $2.50. My royalty shall be 7½ per cent., if the sale does not exceed 50,000 copies. But the day it reaches 50,000 the royalty shall go up to 10 per cent, and the said 10 per cent shall also then be made good on the 50,000 already sold."

All of which Bliss agreed to with alacrity and put in writing without an objection.

So you see, that although I have not been able to furnish you the book, *you* have been able to raise an old contract up from 7½ to 10 per cent for me,[1] and I thank you very heartily and am glad, now, I paid your expenses on that Warwickshire excursion—a thing which I have been too prone to regret heretofore.

To tell the entire truth, I told Bliss I had a mind to send the sketches to you, the day after I came back from Boston; but the old fox (I don't say it disrespectfully, but admiringly) never said a word about the old contract, but only *argued* with me in favor of publishing with his company; but as soon as I had got the matter all ready for the press, (index, preface and everything,) out he comes with his blamed old document!

Osgood, Howells said (a month or so ago) he would take steamboat at St Louis with me, in March, and go to New Orleans and back.[2] He is not sure, now, whether he can go or not, but I hope he *will*. But in *any* case, don't you want to take a pleasure trip about that time? I wish you would go. Think of the gaudy times you and Howells and I would have on such a bender!

Ys Ever

Saml. L. Clemens

[1] JRO replied on 16 February, "I am more sorry than I can tell to lose the book, particularly as I came so near getting it." (See letters 35, 36, and 51, above, for earlier details on the volume of sketches.)

[2] MT looked for companions for a trip down the Mississippi, in order to gather material to expand his "Old Times" articles into a book-length manuscript. See *MTHL*, pp. 55–59.

65. To ELISHA BLISS

Hartford
26 February [1875]

Friend Bliss—

All right. Make it March 1—and then go back to the old system and make the next statement *May* 1. You see it was your delay that strung it out to Nov. 26; it *should* have been Nov. 1.

I inclose proxy.

Can get sketches ready any time, but shall wait awhile, as I have good hopes of finishing a book [1] which I am working like a dog on —a book which ought to outsell the sketches, and doubtless will. It will make a pretty lively sensation I bet you.

Yrs

Mark.

[1] MT refers either to the "Old Times" articles he was planning to develop (see *MTHL*, p. 62), or to the manuscript of *Tom Sawyer*, which he was also working on during the spring of 1875.

66. To CHARLES H. WEBB

[Hartford]
8 April [1875]

My Dear Webb: [1]

First—Bliss has never made a single reflection upon you in my hearing—not one.

Next—as to advising. I *could* have advised you, but you come so late. All I can advise now, is, do not go to law until you have tried all other ways and failed—and *then* don't—because you've nothing to fight with but a mere verbal contract, and that is the weakest of all weak weapons. If you had only come sooner I could have given you priceless advice, viz.,—Never make a verbal contract with any man. Under a *written* contract the author gets his money and his account of sales regularly, and there is no suspicion and no bad blood. Well, no *serious* bad blood, at any rate. There's always a remedy. But under a verbal one the author has none. *You* have none. None in the world. You can get a shyster of a lawyer to take your case—and lose it for you—at your expense. But a reputable lawyer will advise you to keep out of the law, make the best of a foolish bargain, and not get caught again.

I may not be much of a comforter, but I'm doing the best I can, when I advise you to worry through on friendly terms with the publisher and not go from the frying pan into the fire by appealing to the law and almost inevitable defeat. My contract on "Roughing It" was strongly drawn; but when 90,000 copies had been sold I came to the conclusion that an assertion of Bliss's which had induced me to submit to a lower royalty than I had at first demanded, was an untruth. I was going to law about it; but after my lawyer (an old personal friend and the best lawyer in Hartford) had heard me through, he remarked that Bliss's assertion being only verbal and not a part of a written understanding, my case was weak—so he advised me to leave the law alone—and charged me $250 for it.

I know how impulsive and belligerent your spirit used to be before you performed the wisest act of your life at the marriage altar; but as you have altered since then, I feel safe in suggesting that you consider well before you quarrel and appeal to the law. I don't know anything about the Columbian Co., but if Bliss is bossing it I am perfectly satisfied that your account of sales has been correctly rendered. It is a mighty tough year for books. But I think that the next 3 months will show a different state of things. Therefore I am venturing to bring out a new book—a thing I could not have been hired to do during any part of the past 12 months, for it would have been a sort of deliberate literary suicide.

So I've become Saml. *F.* Clemens to your waning memory! I'll just address this brief note to G. R. Webb, and see how *you* like it to have your name coldly mutilated!

Yrs

S. L. Clemens

P.S. It's a pretty long letter, and I proposed to mark out all the surplusage but found it too much trouble.

We've the diphtheria in the house and can't fool away much time in graceful and perspicuous composition.

---

[1] Webb, whose *John Paul's Book* had been published by EB's Columbian Book Company in 1874, wrote MT on 7 April 1875:

E.B. Jr. agreed to publish a Book for me in the fall of '73. Verbally he said he'd illustrate it as well as he did yours and give me the same copyright and sell—great Caesar, thousands!!!

Well it went on, and he slobbered and spit all over me, and fooled along without giving me a square contract, and turned me over to a little one horse concern (The Columbian). . . .

I don't believe the Columbian's statement of sales—and I don't want to have anything to do with such a breed of dogs.

On the envelope of Webb's letter MT wrote:

From Webb. (*Mem*—"The whirligig of time brings round its revenges." He swindled me on a verbal publishing contract on my first book (Sketches), (8 years ago) and now he has got caught himself and appealed to me for help.

I have advised him to do as I did—make the best of a bad bargain and be wiser next time.

67. To William F. Gill

Hartford

31 May 1875

My Dear Mr. Gill:

I see you announce your humble servant among your Treasure

Trove series. Don't do it any more. I've got burnt once (Lotos Leaves) [1]—that is enough. I shall be a very very old fool before I repeat the courtesy (i.e., folly) of giving my permission to print a sketch of mine in any book but mine.

Therefore, since I have endeavored to do you kindnesses before now please do one for me, inasmuch as your opportunity has come —to wit: Give notice *in print,* as quickly as you can, that in consequence of my publishers' unwillingness, nothing of mine will appear in your Treasure Trove. That will be sufficient without mentioning other reasons.

Truly Ys

S L Clemens

[1] Gill had published MT's "An Encounter with an Interviewer," possibly with the author's permission, in *Lotos Leaves* (1874).

68. To William F. Gill

Hartford

8 June 1875

My Dear Mr. Gill:

It is perhaps no more my publisher than it is myself that objects to the insertion of my matter in outside books.

I think that nothing of mine has ever so appeared (except in one case) without my permission being first asked and obtained. This permission I have time and time again refused, without speaking to my publisher. I almost *always* refuse it. I have granted it in the case of obscure books like "Readers," but never in the case of conspicuous works like your series.

It was hardly right of you to *announce* me and THEN propose to ask my permission. But I gather from your letter that your justification for this was that you felt free to take possession of any uncopyrighted matter of mine which might be lying around, and you meant to ask permission only in the case of copyrighted matter.

There was another publisher who allowed that queer sort of morality to fool him. He discovered, in a United States Court, to his serious pecuniary cost, that my sole ownership of my matter is perfect and impregnable—I mean *all* of my matter—every single page I ever wrote.

Now in giving you fair warning that if a single line of mine appears in one of your books I will assuredly stop that book with an injunction, I beg you to believe me when I say that I do not do this in any fractious or unamiable spirit toward you or your editor, but solely and only because I think it injurious to me to come prominently into print any oftener than I am professionally *obliged* to do.

Yours, in all kindness,
Saml. L. Clemens

69. To JAMES R. OSGOOD

Hartford
13 July [1875]

My Dear Osgood:

Do you see this puppy's drift? I enclose a couple of replies to his letter. Let the attorney send either or *neither* to Gill. If he thinks mine of June 8th (herewith enclosed) covers the whole ground,—all right—use his own judgment.

If Gill uses my matter without printing my name anywhere in his book he will do himself no good and me no serious harm—and neither will he be violating trademark, I suppose.

But what he is really up to, I imagine, is to use my name inside the book but not on the cover.

Say—the man is a natural deceiver. The title of his series shows it: Treasure *Trove* means treasure *found,* I think—whereas his is more properly Treasure *Stolen* and ought to be so styled. Damn a man who will lie so wantonly.

Ys Ever
S. L. Clemens

70. To James R. Osgood

Hartford
20 July [1875]

My Dear Osgood:

It seems a shame that a thief can go on and print 2000 copies of stolen goods and escape punishment through the weakness of the law; but still, since it is advised that we stop with the present result I am willing, provided the "public statement for moral effect" (and for Mr. Gill's exposure) be made.

We have gained everything, and established a strong point, useful in the future, if said public statement be made.

Yrs Truly
Saml. L. Clemens

71. To James R. Osgood

Hartford
23 July [1875]

My Dear Osgood:

My idea is, to let our lawyer show this[1] to Gill & Co. and ask them to sign it for publication (either this card or another containing the substance of it—to be drafted by Howells or some other of our unfortunates)—and Gill & Co. will refuse. Then show them our remarks beginning on page 7 (or other remarks to be furnished by Howells or some one else) and tell them we shall publish the card ourselves, with all our signatures appended to the remarks.

Then you must have every aggrieved author and publisher sign it (I would rather a greater name than mine should come first in the list—seems to me it would be better but I am not strenuous) —then you print it, making an agreement with all hands that we shall mutually pay the libel damages (if any—and it ain't likely there'll be any) out of our several pockets, each according to his financial ability.

By the way, I think Gill wrote me that Holmes and a lot more gave him permission to use copyright matter—which is probably a lie. Shall I hunt up that letter for you?

Yrs

Clemens

---

[1] The enclosure read as follows:

A Card.

Being under the impression that unwatched (that is to say, uncopyrighted) literary property was without protection in law, and could therefore be seized under the black flag and used with impunity, we recently laid hands upon a quantity of such goods and advertised that upon a certain date we would work the same up and deliver it to the public in a series of volumes. To make these volumes complete we were necessitated to use some of the *copyrighted* property of the same authors we were proposing to despoil—but *this* we honestly intended to ask for, since we could not get it in any other way. (We as good as said this, in a letter to one of these authors—which letter can be produced, in proof of this assertion, if required.) But certain of these authors not only declined to give us permission to use their copyrighted matter (as did also their publishers,) but even warned us to leave their uncopyrighted property alone, also, and threatened us with the heavy hand of the law if we disobeyed the warning. This had no effect upon us. We disobeyed. We published our book. But this present statement is to certify that in doing this we made a serious mistake; for the legal advisers of Messrs. J. R. Osgood (here insert the rest of the names, Osgood) and Mr. Mark Twain have proved to us a thing we never had dreamed of before, to-wit: *that an American author's right of property in his writings is absolutely perfect and indestructible,* EVEN WITHOUT THE PROTECTION OF A COPYRIGHT—

This fact being established to our satisfaction, we necessarily agreed to issue not another copy of our book with the forbidden names and matter in it. Two thousand copies of the book had already passed out of our hands, but no more will follow until the promised eliminations shall have been made.

(Signed)

We the undersigned sent the above card to Messrs. Wm. F. Gill & Co., publishers, with the request that they sign it, for publication. They have declined to do so. Why, one can not easily understand. The card states simply the truth, nothing more, nothing less. It is purposely couched in moderate and inoffensive language. It gives to writers and publishers a piece of information of the last importance and value. And finally it offered Messrs. Gill & Co an opportunity to perform an act of grace toward us whom they have ungently treated.

However, in simple justice to Messrs. Gill & Co., and to show that we harbor no harsh feeling toward them, we willingly publish the card ourselves.

(Signed)

Saml. L. Clemens (Mark Twain)

72. To Elisha Bliss

[Hartford]
5 November [1875]

Friend Bliss:

You may let Williams have all of Tom Sawyer that you have
received. He can of course make the pictures all the more
understandingly after reading the whole story. He wants it, and I
have not the least objection, because if he should lose any of it I
have got another complete MS. copy.[1]

I think you had better rush Dan's book into print, by New
Year's, if possible, and give Tom Sawyer the early spring market.[2] I
don't want to publish in the summer—don't want to wait till fall
—shall have a bigger book ready then.

What have you heard from England in the way of a proposition
for Tom Sawyer? I have an offer from the Routledges (which I
haven't answered), and if you have heard nothing from over there,
I propose to write the "Temple Bar" people.[3] Drop me a line about
this, will you?

Frank said he would send the infernal Type-Writer to Howells.
I hope he won't forget to afflict Howells with it.

I wish you would send me a couple of copies of the Sketch Book,
and also all the Sketches that were left out in making it up. I do
not want to lose them.

Didn't you make that correction of the paragraph smouched
from "Hospital Days?"[4] Twichell has an uncorrected copy.

Yrs

Clemens.

[1] MT had been at work on *Tom Sawyer* for over a year, and had had an
amanuensis copy (ultimately to be used for printing the English edition) made
for Howells to revise. True Williams was a Hartford artist who illustrated several
of MT's books. See *MT&EB*, pp. 101–112, for a more detailed description of the
composition of *Tom Sawyer*.

[2] On 24 March 1875, MT had written EB, suggesting William Wright ("Dan
DeQuille") should be signed up "to write a stirring and truthful book about the
'big bonanza', because he has been city editor on that paper [the *Territorial
Enterprise*] more than 14 years, and knows it *all*—and everybody." MT had

decided by this time to allow the American Publishing Company to issue *Tom Sawyer* in spite of H. O. Houghton's warning (see letter 63, note 1).

[3] Richard Bentley, editor of *Temple Bar,* had attempted to obtain material from MT in 1873, but the humorist decided ultimately not to send him the "Old Times" sketches (see *MTHL,* p. 60). Two months later—18 January 1876— Moncure Conway wrote his wife, "Mark Twain has written a remarkable book called 'Tom Sawyer,' a book which I wish you to try your hand in preparing the way for negotiations with Chatto Windus. He (Mark T.) would like to follow our plan—pay for the manufacture of his own book and pay the publisher for each copy sold." On 31 January, Chatto & Windus wrote Mrs. Conway, "We shall be happy to undertake the publication of Mark Twain's new work upon the terms suggested by you this morning—viz. that he should bear the entire cost of production, and pay us a royalty of 10 per cent upon the entire amount of sales." On 24 March, Conway reported to MT that "I have had two long sessions with the Routledges, father and son; found them very much opposed to publishing on 10 per cent commission, but finally willing to undertake it in a spirit that did not impress me as enthusiastic enough. I am disinclined to let them have Tom Sawyer." Conway apparently first met MT in England in 1873 (MT to Conway, London, 1 July [1873?], Columbia). Conway was invited to visit with the Clemenses in December 1875, and on 5 January 1876, MT wrote, "I want you to come here again before you sail. I want you to take my new book to England, and have it published there by some one (according to your plan) before it is issued here, if you will be so good" (TS, MTP).

[4] On the "Hospital Days" excerpt printed erroneously in *Sketches New and Old,* see *MTHL,* pp. 863–864.

73. To James R. Osgood

Hartford
17 January 1876

My Dear Osgood:

Yes, hand the check to the lawyers.

What I desire, *now,* is to go for Mr. Gill once more, at law—and this time, let us mean *"business."* Can you go in with me, and divide the expense? How would it do for us to go in together, but nobody appear in it but me; and if I win my case then we to join issue and try him on *your* case, I not appearing to be a party?

I want Gill tried—

1. Simply for *violating my trademark*—copyright not to be mentioned. (I suppose the lawyers have got the decision of the N.Y. court in my former case from Simon Sterne, attorney.) [1]

2.—*Damages* for said violation—say $1,000 or $⟨10,⟩3,000. (or more,⟩

3.—No compromise but on these terms: Gill to pay me $500 cash and sign a paper confessing in soft language that he is a detected liar and thief.

I think our lawyers will know how to handle Mr. Gill this time, after the experience they have had with him.

Keep the book you mention and don't mislay it.[2]

If you don't wish to go in with me, Osgood, I want you to put my case in our lawyers' hands at once, anyhow, and I'll play a "lone hand" (such as used to be too many for you at Warwick!)

Ys Ever

S. L. Clemens

P.S.—No—on second thoughts I don't want to compromise with Gill for less than *$1,000*—and a written confession that he is a liar and thief—and a promise to take my article and name out of his book at once—with a penalty of $5 per copy on every book issued afterward with name and article (or either) in it.

Yrs

S. L. Clemens

Sue for $1,000 to $10,000 damages,
and permanent injunction.

[1] See note 2. letter 56, above.
[2] Unidentifiable.

74. To James R. Osgood

Hartford
25 January [1876]

My Dear Osgood—

Yes I would like it if you would watch Mr. Gill and post me. But the lawyer says Gill has taken my *nom de plume* out of the book although he has left the article in it. Of course this destroys the

possibility of my suing him for violating trade-mark, and I don't
wish to sue him for anything else.

Now *wasn't* our lawyer a lame and impotent d———d fool to
compromise with Gill with Gill's mere *word* as the only security
that he would keep his promise? The more I see of lawyers, the
more I despise them. They seem to be natural, born *cowards,* and
on top of that they are God damned idiots. I suppose *our* law firm
are above average; and yet it would be base flattery to say that *their*
heads contain anything more valuable than can be found in a new
tripe.

Mind you keep your promise and stop off and see me.

Yrs
Clemens

75. To Elisha Bliss

[Hartford]
19 March 1876

Friend Bliss:

It is going to rush you too tight to do your canvassing and issue
"Tom" in the middle of April isn't it? If so you better clap on your
canvassers at once, but not publish till the middle of May. Drop me
a line about this at once—for if we don't issue in April I must
telegraph Howells to delay the *Atlantic* notice a month.[1]

Yrs
Clemens

---

[1] MT was in part responsible for delays which made it impossible to issue the
American edition of *Tom Sawyer* until December. Frank Bliss wrote him on 11
April, "Father says that he had an estimate all ready for the electros of 'Tom
Sawyer,' but as you changed the size it involves making a new estimate all
through, and he is fearful that reducing the size so much, of many of the cuts,
will interfere with their printing nicely." The change in size, whatever it
involved, was possibly prompted by a comment of Conway's to MT in his letter
of 24 March: "It will be positively necessary for the book to appear here in a difft
shape from the American—(which here is fatally unorthodox)." Part of MT's
concern over publishing dates involved Howells' premature *Atlantic Monthly*
review in the May issue; but, in addition, he was attempting to follow Conway's

instructions about coordinating the publication of the English and American editions. Conway's letters of 24 March, 11 April, and 18 April all warn that the English edition must appear before the American.

76. To Moncure D. Conway

Hartford
9 April [1876]

My Dear Conway:

Got your letter yesterday, and it seemed to me that the advantages of the two propositions were exactly evenly balanced.[1] It was so puzzling a question that I was sorry you hadn't decided it yourself, and commanded me accordingly. I finally submitted the matter to Mrs. Clemens, and she said, "Take the royalty; it simplifies everything; removes all risk; requires no outlay of capital; makes the labor easy for Mr. Conway; a gain of 25 per cent profit is hardly worth the trouble and risk of publishing on your own account."

I said "All right"—and so telegraphed you to take the royalty. If I could have *written,* I would simply have said, "Decide the question for yourself, and if you want the £500, telegraph me so."

Indeed it is not too late to say that *yet,* unless your contract is already closed. We certainly cannot issue here before May 1st, if we can even do it then. Hardly any of the pictures are finished yet. I have read only 2 chapters in proof, and they had blanks for the cuts. Perhaps, in view of this delay, it may be best to take the royalty and leave Chatto to take the risk—that is, if he is still willing.

A week from now the Atlantic will come out with a mighty handsome notice of the book, by Howells (which I will send to you,) but the book won't issue till 2 or even 4 weeks later. This notice says the book "gives *incomparably* the best picture of life in that (the West) region as yet known to fiction." "The story is a wonderful study of the boy-mind." "The tale is very dramatically wrought." "The worthless vagabond, Huck Finn, is entirely delightful throughout." "Tom Sawyer . . . was bred to fear God

and dread the Sunday-school"—etc. etc. etc. It's a jolly good
notice.

You can leave out the preface; or alter it so that it will not profess
to be a book for youth; or write a new preface and put your own
name or initials to it.—Fix it any way you want to, if as you say, it
will be best not to put it forth as a book for youth.[2]

(Before I forget it, let me remark that your 5-per centage is
entirely satisfactory to me, if it is to you, no matter which method
of publishing we adopt.)

My dear Conway, we *borrowed* our shape and style of book *from
England.*[3] We exactly copied the size, style, and get-up, of a half a
dozen of Cassel, Peter and Galpin's pretty books. But still, you and
Chatto must freely do as you like. If you still do not want to make
the book the size of ours and take a set of plates containing the cuts
and everything, telegraph thus:

"Twain—Hartford—pictures."

I will then send any and all pictures that can be cut down to
your size.—And send the original drawings of the rest.

If you *should* take a notion to have full plates, just telegraph
"Plates," instead of "Pictures."

Telegraph 20 or 30 words whenever necessary. It is no economy
to do business by mail.

Bliss can't give me price of full plates or pictures either, yet—but
says he will make it just as cheap as he possibly can—for
me. . . .

Ys Ever

S. L. Clemens

[1] In his letter of 24 March, Conway had explained the alternatives of accepting
a royalty from Chatto & Windus or paying them a commission. The contract
signed on 24 May 1876 by Conway was for the royalty method of payment.

[2] In his 24 March letter, Conway had commented, "I don't think it would be
doing justice to call it a boy's book and think it had better be left people to form
their own conclusions whether it is for young or old." Conway did not write a
new preface, however.

[3] On 6 May, Conway replied, "It is true that the shape of your sketchbook is
not unknown in this country, but only in connection with 'toybooks' or 2d class
things like Cassell's."

77. To Moncure D. Conway

Hartford

16 April [1876]

My Dear Conway:

Just as I feared, Tom Sawyer is not yet ready to issue. Would not be ready for 2 weeks or longer, yet. Therefore the spring trade is lost beyond redemption. Consequently I have told Bliss to issue in the autumn and make a Boy's Holiday Book of it. Another thing that has moved me to this course is the fact that whereas the Sketch Book sold 20,000 copies the first 3 months, it has only sold 3,700 the second 3 (ending March 30.) This distinctly means that this is no time to adventure a new book. I am determined that Tom shall outsell any previous book of mine, and so I mean that he shall have every possible advantage.

First publication in England cannot impair my American copyright (have telegraphed Spofford [1] and made sure on that point;) therefore I have just cabled you: "Hickson, Smithfield, London: We delay publication till fall, but you may publish as soon as you choose."

Now as to electros: Bliss will furnish *full set of plates,* (pictures, letter press and all,) at $2 per page—say total of about $600. Or, he will furnish the pictures alone, at 25 cents per inch square. Total, for picture-electros alone, $150 to $200. Write or telegraph me which you want and I will send them. [2] It is possible that Chatto may see *his* best market in waiting till fall and issuing as a holiday book. But he may do as he prefers.

Get the May Atlantic when it reaches London. You may be able to utilize Howells's notice of Tom.

In haste

Ys Ever

Saml L. Clemens

---

[1] A. R. Spofford, Librarian of Congress, telegraphed MT on 17 April, "No the first publication in England is essential to Copyright there but previous entry here will secure you in the United States."

[2] Conway wanted electrotypes of only the illustrations. His and Chatto's plan (outlined in his letter of 11 April) was to issue an expensive illustrated edition first, to be followed by a cheap, unillustrated one.

78. To Elisha Bliss

Elmira
24 June [1876]

Friend Bliss:

I am ready for the proofs, now, and shall be still better ready a week or ten days hence.

I hope those pictures have gone to Conway, as no doubt they have.

I have been thinking, and have arrived at the conclusion that if the Company will sell out two-thirds of its copyrights and electro-types, and also its printing office and presses, by auction, and move back into cheap quarters again and publish about one or two books at a time, it can declare some more dividends. I will lay the matter by letter before the other directors. They may object, but I hope not, for I think that the present extended business is a considerable detriment to my pocket. I think we publish books so fast that canvassers are likely to merely skim the cream of a district and then "lay" for the next new book. This is only human nature, and they are not to be blamed for it. I know you think differently from me; and perhaps we are both partly right and partly wrong. We will take the sense of the directors, and I shall have to abide by their decision, though I shall be mighty sorry to see Tom Sawyer issue when any other book of the firm is either being canvassed or within six months of *being* canvassed.

If the directors will cut the business down two-thirds, and the expenses one half, I think it will be an advantage to all concerned, and I feel persuaded that I shall sell more books.[1]

Please ask Frank to give me my July statement as promptly as he can conveniently, for I have a great curiosity to know what it is going to be.[2]

Yrs

S L Clemens

[1] On 18 July, EB, pleading illness as his excuse for delay, replied:
And now as respects the company business you mention. I would say, I shall certainly offer no personal objection or use any personal influence to prevent

the adoption of any plan deemed proper by the other directors. I do not know as you are aware of the condition of the Co or not. You have never been present at any of the meetings and have never asked for information of me. I am not ashamed to show my business up, for the past 10 or the past single year. It will compare well with anyone else's business, be it who it may. Still I think it might be run better and I thought so last Spring and I therefore preferred to give up my seat to some one more capable and also less costly. I urged this plan upon the Co. By this means the expenses can be cut down no doubt. I will be pleased to lay any proposition you have to make before the directors. I am sorry you found it necessary to talk against my management outside of our board as I have several times heard you have. Even the poor drunken Williams comes and boastingly taunts me with what you tell him— while another of my help gets letters from N.Y. stating what he says you told there. For myself I care nothing, but it seems poor policy to injure the stock this way, and our stock is too valuable to be made to suffer. As long as I stay in the Co. I will do my best for it and its authors as I have done, but when dissatisfaction arises, my usefulness here is over! Other avenues are open to me and I rather desire to tread them, as this business has its vexations and annoyances, and I hardly care to endure them much longer. The business can be cut down, and with a cheaper man at the helm, expenses can be made low and possibly larger profits made. The experiment can be tried and I will most cheerfully assist with all my might. . . .

What time do you wish Tom Sawyer to appear. We will bring him out when you say. Let us know.

[2] On 20 July 1876, Frank Bliss replied, forwarding a check for $746.38.

79. To ELISHA BLISS

Elmira
22 July 1876

PRIVATE.

Friend Bliss:

Of course I can neither confess nor deny your underlings' New York gossip without knowing what it is. But come—we are all a good deal alike, I judge. I listen to a director of the company and others, and under irritated impulse, talk and act unwisely, and get sorry at leisure. You tell hard things about me to entertain a group (the worst of it being that they are mainly true, although not pleasant things to remember,) and for a day I am angry and ready to do or say anything that comes handy; by that time I begin to imagine that I am fooling away time and tongue on a matter that is not very prodigious—so there an end for the time being. As regards

Williams, we will dismiss that with the single and simple remark that what I said to him occupied but short space and will bear repeating in any presence, since it was to no one's prejudice. But come—a truce to this—it is good matter to talk about together, but not to write about.

You write as if you supposed I was mightily concerned about the company and its expenses. I am concerned just this far, exactly: The business seems to be a great big unpaying thing, whereas the reverse would be the case if it were shrunk up, perhaps. I don't *know* it, I simply suggest it. And with the suggestion I stop. My duty as a director and stockholder ends there. I shall not lose any sleep about it one way or the other.

But there is a matter in which I am strongly interested. You told me, several times that a subscription house could not run two books at once and do justice to either of them. I saw no reason to disbelieve that, and I never have disbelieved it. Therefore I am solicitous about Tom Sawyer—more so than I would be about another book, because this is an experiment. I want it run by itself, if possible, and pushed like everything. Can this be done?—and when? Give me your ideas about it. What do you think of canvassing in September and October and issuing 1st Nov.? Shall you be canvassing any new book then?

You must not think that I never wanted to attend a director's meeting. It is a mistake. My notices always arrived too late. This is why I wrote twice requesting that my notice be mailed a day earlier.

I wouldn't have aggravated you if I had known you were going to be sick—I don't pick out such times purposely, but only by accident.

I think that if you offer a prize of $1000 (I to pay the money myself but not be known in it) for the canvasser who shall sell the largest number of Tom Sawyers in six months (putting it in the circulars but not in the newspapers,) it might have a good effect. Or make two $500. prizes of it—one for east of the east line of Ohio and the other for west of that line. What do you think of it?

I shall start the proofs back with this mail.

Confidentially, I shall have a business proposition to make to you individually in the fall when I return. I foresee advantage in it, and I think you will, also. I came near making it once before, but was restrained by a feeling which has well nigh ceased to exist, now, and seems likely to cease altogether and speedily.—I think I was unwise that I did not make it when I first thought of it. If I chance to have occasion to run to Hartford in the meantime, I can get my data together and make the proposition then. I have figured upon it for hours, to-day, and if I had had any wit I would have done the same thing long ago.[1]

Meantime I hope you will say nothing about the matter to anybody—and I shall not. I mark my letter "Private" for this reason.

Ys Truly

Saml. L. Clemens

Those chapters are a nice clean proof—please do it again.

[1] Since EB had announced his willingness to resign from the American Publishing Company, and since MT had examined the possibility of issuing the English *Tom Sawyer* at his own expense, it seems strongly probable that this proposition involved establishing a new publishing house with EB as titular head.

80. To Moncure D. Conway

Elmira
1 August 1876

My Dear Conway:

Your last just received. I sent you the price of the pictures entirely too late for your first edition (P.S.—No I didn't either; I sent the price in April or May 1st)—which was to be a cheap edition, as I understood it—but with ample time to let Chatto say he didn't want them for his fall high-priced edition, if he should not like the cost. I suppose the first edition was already in press before I received the order to forward the electros—and it was *printed* before the plates started from here; so the first edition was evidently not waiting for them. If Chatto did not want the pictures, why did he put me to all that bother about them. I could have earned their cost a couple of times with the running I did on their account.

I got Bliss's figures for the electros and forwarded them; (25 cents per square inch, I think it was;) I suppose, of course, Chatto ordered them upon that clear basis; he does not like their cost, now; who is to blame but himself? How am I to "do my best to favor him?" Bliss makes the plates—not me. It is no object to Bliss to favor Chatto; Bliss is in no wise concerned. If I ask Bliss to favor Chatto by reducing the contract price of the electros, what argument (not sentimental, but commercial,) am I to offer him to that end? I am sure I know of none which he would not smile a godless smile at.

Now in order to accomplish anything in this matter, I would have to go to work and correspond with Bliss every three days for a couple of weeks, before a comfortable and satisfactory result could be reached. Life is too short. Manuscript is too valuable. Let Chatto ship the electros back to Bliss and Bliss shall use them himself if he can, and if he can't he must charge them to me. This is the simplest way out of the tangle. You have already issued your high-priced edition—there is no money in another one.[1]

We are up here at the farm for the summer. You never have been here, I believe; therefore you don't know what peace and comfort are; and you never *can* know till you come here one of these days and spend a week or so with us. Which I hope you will do, and bring Mrs. Conway. We are in the air, overhanging the valley 700 feet, and my study is 100 yards from the house. This is not my vacation, mind you—I take that in winter. I am booming along with my new book—have written ⅓ of it and shall finish it in 6 working weeks.

Tom Sawyer proofs come in slowly; received and read Chapter 8 yesterday.

With warmest regards and best wishes—

Yrs Ever

Mark

Mrs. Clemens says you do not need to be a prophet in order to convince her that she would "Enjoy London" now.

---

[1] Obviously, EB had sent a set of electros—of the illustrations—to Chatto & Windus and had requested payment. Ultimately (after letters to Eustace Conway on 14 August, and to Mrs. Conway on 28 October 1877), MT wrote Chatto on 7 November 1877, "It would not be fair to let you pay the whole cost of a blunder which was not yours but a subordinate's—in which case let us divide the expense, and shake hands across the bloody chasm." But when a similar situation arose with *A Tramp Abroad* (see letter 97 below), friendly arbitration was not in evidence.

81. To Elisha Bliss

Elmira

8 August [1876]

Private

Friend Bliss:

Everything O.K. So that's all right. I will remark, though, in passing, that no proposition has ever been made to Dustin of *any* kind—and none received *from* Dustin—so that report falls to the ground. I have made propositions to no publisher.[1]

Yes, I like the idea of issuing Nov. 1st—or *Dec.* ⟨1st or⟩ 15th,— whichever date seems *best*. What I am after is the *best* date ⟨of the three⟩. Choose it yourself. If you think it best to issue Dec. 15, and begin canvassing 4 or 5 weeks before that date, all right. That would make it essentially a holiday book and give it its very best chance, perhaps.

But if you prefer another date, let it be Nov. 1st, so as to get the month or 5 weeks' canvassing done *before* the election.

I think the advantage lies with Dec. 15—don't you?

But whichever date is chosen, let us make sure to be out promptly on that very day, and with an edition that will amply supply every order, so that there shall be no complaint on *that* head.

I remember, now, you explained the inexpediency of offering prizes, once before. So that may as well be dropped.

I want the "Atlantic" notice of "Sawyer" to be put into the prospectus and in the slips that go to editors, and a line or two of it in your advertisements, for I think it will have a good effect. I wish I had some of the English notices, but I suppose they have been thrown aside and lost at my house in Hartford, as I did not order any newspapers to be forwarded here.

I have just returned Chap. 10, or 11, I forget which—of Sawyer. They are admirably clean, nice proofs. One does not curse and swear over them.

I have received Warner's book, and it is a very handsome piece of typography etc. Haven't read but 1st Chap—only got it last night.[2]

Let me know which of the two dates of publication you decide to use.

The enclosed notice, from the Spectator has just come. I have bracketed good sentences in it, but it is all good, and possibly you can find use for it.

Company here to dinner—so I will quit.

Yrs

Clemens

---

[1] See letter 61, above, to Aldrich, which does propose taking a book to Dustin. EB's letter to which this is a reply is apparently lost, so the specific allegations are unknown.

[2] Warner's *My Winter on the Nile Among the Mummies and Moslems,* which was issued by the American Publishing Company in 1876.

82. To MONCURE D. CONWAY

Hartford

2 November [1876]

My Dear Conway:

Belford Bros., Canadian thieves, are flooding America with a

cheap pirated edition of Tom Sawyer. I have just telegraphed
Chatto to assign Canadian copyright to me, but I suppose it is too
late to do any good. We cannot issue for 6 weeks yet, and by that
time Belford will have sold 100,000 over the frontier and killed my
book dead. This piracy will cost me $10,000, and I will spend as
much more to choke off those pirates, if the thing can be done. Ask
Chatto if he gave Belford Bros permission to publish.[1]

Ever Yours

S. L. C.

[1] Belford Brothers, a Canadian firm, "have been in the habit of publishing
Chatto and Windus works by agreement" (Conway to MT, 9 December 1876),
but in the case of *Tom Sawyer,* "Chatto and Windus have had no
correspondence or negotiations, verbal or of any sort whatsoever, with Belford or
any other publisher" (*ibid.,* 16 November 1876). On 4 November, Conway
wrote mailing his assignment of the *Tom Sawyer* copyright; but in his letter of
10 January 1877, MT said, "I see I am not so well situated here to fight Belford
as you and Chatto are. The English copyright stands in your name—or Chatto's
—so you and C. go to work and prosecute Belford and collect that royalty. I
couldn't do it without having your copyright transferred to me." In any event,
Chatto telegraphed Belford on 15 November 1876, "Tom Sawyer is English
copyright" (Conway to MT, 16 November 1876). Belford replied, " 'We today
recd your telegram in reference to Tom Sawyer. We should be very sorry to
conflict with your interest in any way in Canada. We know Americans are in the
habit of taking out copyright in England, but we doubt if it would hold there: we
are well advised that it gives no right in Canada. We shall be glad, however, to
hear further from you on the subject' "; and Chatto wrote back that " 'hearing
they were issuing an edition of that work they considered it was only right to
inform them that the book was English copyright, and added that all the necessary
steps had been taken in the country for the securing of the same' " (Conway to
MT, 9 December 1876).

83. To MONCURE D. CONWAY

Hartford
13 December 1876

Dear Conway
   It's a mistake, I am not writing any new book.[1] Belford has taken
the profits all out of "Tom Sawyer." We find our copyright law
here to be nearly worthless, and if I can make a living out of plays,

I shall never write another book. For the present I have placed the three books in mind, in the waste basket, but if I should write one of them, Chatto shall have a say in it.

The Canadian "Tom Sawyer" has actually taken the market away from us in every village in the Union. We cannot accomplish anything against the newsdealers because the newsdealer is privileged to sell a pirated book until we give him personal and distinct notice, that that book is copyrighted.[2] The Publishers say that as near as their lawyers can make it out, English copyright is not worth anything in Canada, unless it be recorded in Canada, within sixty days after publication in England. . . .[3]

Saml. L. Clemens

[1] On 28 November, Conway had written, "Chatto writes in some anxiety about your new book on the North Pole. I told him you would naturally let him have it."

[2] In two letters, EB elaborated the American Publishing Company's position. On 11 December 1876, he explained, "The difficulty is that we have *to prove* that the news dealer *knew it* was a *copyrighted* book, to sustain our case. Such has been the construction put upon the law by lawyers. It is hard doing this. Every one will claim they did not know of this fact and were not responsible for selling it." An undated fragment, obviously of the same period, pointed out, "I learn that to hold a copyright in Canada—taken out in England, it is necessary to have it recorded in Canada also within 60 days of its publication in England—or it is lost. I fear your copyright in Canada is worthless."

[3] One "lawyer" involved was Orion Clemens. On 11 December EB wrote MT that "I send Orion some of our notices to serve on anyone he has opportunity to, and want him to watch the sales and go for anyone that sells after such notice." On 1 February 1877, Orion sent EB a statement explaining that he had visited four bookstores in Keokuk and warned them against selling *Tom Sawyer*. He asked a "leading lawyer" what he should charge for this service, and enclosed a bill for $50. EB sent the letter and bill to MT on 5 February "for expression of an opinion as to its justice." EB settled the bill by paying Orion $15 (*MTHL*, p. 255).

84. To Frank Bliss

Heidelberg
13 July [1878]

Dear Frank—

Yours of June 28th. arrived last night, making the trip in the usual time, 14 days. If I were to send you the power of attorney now, you would receive it July 27th.—ten days too late. I am very sorry you didn't start it a couple of weeks earlier. I hope things went satisfactorily and that your father remains in his place. I should have voted for him, of course.[1]

As I wrote you, a week or so ago, I am making fair progress,[2] but of course it isn't *great* progress, because it costs me more days to *get* material than to write it up. I have written 400 pages of MS—that is to say about 45 or 50,000 words, or one-fourth of a book, but it is in disconnected form and cannot be used until joined together by the writing of at least a dozen intermediate chapters. These intermediate chapters cannot be rightly written until we are settled down for the fall and winter in Munich.

I have been gathering a lot of excellent matter here during the past ten days (stuff which has never been in a book) and shall finish gathering it in a week more. Then we shall leave, and be on the wing for 2 months, during which time I shall not be able to write more than 200 pages, perhaps. Can't tell, yet. I shall be mostly on foot, with Twichell, the first 5 or 6 weeks, and shall write up in full every night if not too tired.

If you should need to write me in the meantime, direct to Heidelberg, care Koester & Co., Bankers, and I will ask them to forward it.

Yr truly,

S. L. C.

---

[1] After the publication of *Tom Sawyer,* no significant MT letters to the American Publishing Company are apparently extant until this one. During 1877, MT was involved with the staging of "Ah Sin," a Bermuda trip with Joe Twichell, and some abortive plans with Slote, Woodman and Company. And indeed, this letter is not to Frank Bliss in his capacity as Treasurer of the Company. On 8 March 1878, apparently still irate at EB for the failure of *Tom Sawyer,* MT made his contract with the younger Bliss for "manuscript of original matter in quantity sufficient to make a volume when published of size suitable to sell by agents as a subscription book." Whether the trouble mentioned in the present letter involved MT's complaints about *Tom Sawyer* or not, Frank Bliss was obviously requesting a proxy for MT's shares of American Publishing Company stock to support a vote of confidence in EB by the directors of the Company.

[2] On the manuscript describing his current trip to Europe, *A Tramp Abroad.*

85. To Frank Bliss

Lucerne
20 August 1878

My Dear Frank—

I find it is no sort of use to try to write while one is traveling. I am interrupted constantly—and most of the time I am too tired to write, anyway. Since Twichell has been with me I have invented a new and better plan for the book. Therefore I shall tear up a great deal of my present batch of MS. and start fresh. I shan't be able to go to work in earnest until we settle down in Munich in November. Up to this time all of my prophecies have failed—so I won't venture any more. I will only say that when I *do* get to work, I will mail my chapters to you as fast as I write (and approve) them.

I have instructed Twichell to keep the title and plan of the book a secret. I will disclose them to you by letter, presently, or through Twichell—but I do not want them to get into print *until the book is nearly ready to issue from the press.*—They are in themselves a joke—and a joke which the public are already prepared for is no joke at all. . . .[1]

Ys Truly

S. L. Clemens

---

[1] MT's secret plan was to write a book about a journey announced as a walking tour, but actually making use of every other possible means of conveyance. Howells learned the secret in January 1879 (see *MTHL*, p. 249); the reader was to have learned it in a preface to *A Tramp Abroad*, unused in the book and printed here for the first time:

To the Reader.

Perhaps you were about to say that formerly I went Abroad as an Innocent, but that this time, fortified with experience and guile, I went Abroad as a Tramp. ⟨But that inference would not be quite right, while at the same time it would not be wholly⟩ Let us not argue this question. When I chose my book's title, I only intended it to describe the nature of my journey, which was a *walk,* through foreign lands,—that is, a tramp; but the more I think of how little I cared whither I went, or how long it took me to go, or whether I saw anything or found out anything when I got there, so long as I had a lazy, delightful, irresponsible high-holiday time on the road, the more I perceived that in using the word Tramp I was unconsciously describing the walker as well as the walk. Very well, let it go at that. Tramps are increasing; by and by they may be in the majority; in that day a Tramp will be elected President of the United States: I seem to have a future before me.

I went abroad to visit some countries which I had not seen before. I meant to traverse them on foot. It was a vast undertaking, but I believed that by getting a little lift here and there when I was pretty tired, I could accomplish it. If I succeeded, I should have something to boast of as long as I lived; I should be admired and looked up to as a man who had conceived and carried out one of the most formidable projects of the age.

But I meant to have a good time, just the same, and I had it. I had been at work a long time; I was not going to walk to tire myself, but to rest myself. I was off for a satisfying, comprehensive, and elaborate holiday,—a holiday in the open air, rather than in cities and picture galleries.

I had a couple of light minor purposes, also: to acquire the German language, and to perfect myself in Art.

                                                                 Mark Twain

Paris, July, 1879.

86. To Joe Twichell

                                                               Munich
                                                      23 January [1879]

Dear Joe—

I've got to write to Mr. Bliss and Frank through you, for I don't know their address. I have the idea that Frank said they might leave the publishing company during the summer.

I only want to say to them this: I am doing my very level best, but I don't want to attempt any more prophecies as to date of completion of the book. My prophecies seem to fail, every time. I work *every* day that some member of the family isn't sick. This does not give me a great deal of time, but I make the most of what I *do* get.

Very well, then,—as to items: I have torn up 400 pages of MS, but I've still got about 900 which need no tearing. They suit me very well. So the book is half finished. If anybody will tell me how long it will take me to write the other 900 in a way which shall satisfy me, I shall be under many obligations to him. I know *one* thing,—*I* shall fool away no time—*I* want to get through.

I have found my lost Swiss note-book.[1]

I shall make from 10 to 20 illustrations for my book with my own (almighty rude and crude) pencil, and shall say in the title page that some of the pictures in the book are from original drawings by the author. I have already made two or three which suit me. It gives me the belly-ache to look at them.

When the MS is done I shall ship it right along, without copying, and run the risk.

I can't venture to ship any of it yet, for I may want to alter the first part in several important particulars.

That's all. Now as to *you* Joe, I'm going to write you presently.[2]

We thought our youngest child was dying, three days ago, but she is doing pretty well, now.

Yrs Ever

Mark.

[1] MT had lost a notebook of his and Twichell's walking tour (see *MTB*, pp. 636–637, and *MTL*, p. 349.)
[2] The letter intended for Twichell is in *MTL*, pp. 347–351.

87. To FRANK BLISS

Paris
15 April [1879]

My Dear Frank—

I have been sick—sick—and sick again—with rheumatism and dysentery. I have spent four-fifths of my six weeks' residence in Paris in bed. This is an awful set-back. I hired a den a mile from the hotel and went to work as soon as I reached Paris, but my fire went out and I was laid up the very first day. I only got fairly and squarely to work again a week ago, and had to go back to bed again to-day—more dysentery, or rather, a threat of it which frightened me. I am working, every chance I get, and that's the best I can do. I am hoping to be able to go right along, now,—I believe my diseases are about played out.

I have been able to talk, if I couldn't write. Been interviewed by the "World" representative. Said interview will not be printed immediately, because it has one feature in it which seems important enough to be issued simultaneously in London and New York. So that feature will be sent to some London magazine (in order to get it noticed by all English papers) and when the magazine is ready to go to press, then the "World" will publish at the same time.—The "World" representative—he is an old lawyer—does me the honor to think I may possibly have solved the problem of International Copyright, and I,—who am no lawyer,—am of his opinion. I'm going to lay the matter before some experts, before I take on any airs in the matter. If I *have* solved it, I can fix those Canadian pirates; and if I haven't, we must rig a purchase in some way, to get Canadian copyright.[1]

Perkins says your father didn't promise to get my stock out of the Pub. Co. free of loss. I ain't prepared to say he did—and I wouldn't want him to do a thing he couldn't do, anyway. But I want him to get rid of all of my stock but about 5 or 10 shares at the best figure he can before he leaves the concern.[2] What is that stock worth, now?

I'm thinking over the Riley matter—I think I'll tell Perkins to let the Co pay themselves the $2000 out of my copyright money, and take a written release from the contract to write another book. I thought that old matter had been settled long ago. Your father once offered to pay me 10 per cent. on the volume of sketches and by jingo I wish I had let him, now—the extra royalty would about clear off the Riley debt.[3] Isn't the sale of the Sketches near enough to 50,000 copies for the extra 2½ per cent to be added? *That* would reimburse me.[4]

I never have mentioned your contract and mine to anybody unless it was Twichell, and I don't think I mentioned it to him. It was not a thing I would be likely to speak of.[5]

Ys Truly

S. L. Clemens

[1] New York *World,* reprinted in Hartford *Courant,* 14 May 1879. MT's concern for an international copyright was no doubt stimulated by Frank Bliss's comment of 26 March, "I wish we could manage to get a twist on those Canada

fellows by securing an English copyright, don't suppose we can, but *if* we could it would make a vast difference in the sales." In Notebook 14 (TS p. 15), MT wrote:

> 12th Apl—Paris—While writing an "interview" for Mr. Richard Whiteing, representative of N.Y. World, I was about to say something about International Copyright, when it occurred to me that a trade-mark case decided in my favor by Judge Lawrence in New York (about 1873) *really established international copyright.*

See note 2, letter 56 above, for MT's trademark case. On 29 May, Frank Bliss wrote MT, "I was in hopes you had unearthed some point of law that would lift Am Authors and Publishers out of the Copyright slough, but by your card I see the thing flatted out."

[2] Anxious over the possibility of EB's leaving the American Publishing Company (see the preceding letter), MT wanted to sell his 200 shares of stock; actually he did not dispose of them until May 1881 (see *MTBus,* p. 157). On 29 May 1879, Frank explained that "A.P. Co. stock don't seem to sell very fast . . . guess it can be bought pretty low."

[3] On 13 February, EB had written MT pointing out that the $2,000 advanced Riley for the diamond mine book had never been repaid (see *MT&EB,* p. 130). On 29 May, Frank Bliss wrote, "Now why not just write Perkins and say that you consider 'Tom Sawyer' as filling the bill on that Riley contract." See also MT's letter to Frank dated 10 June, letter 89 below.

[4] See MT's letter to JRO, letter 64 above. Frank Bliss replied on 29 May, " 'Sketches' has reached a sale of something over 30,000 copies I think by this time, though it is nearly a year now since I had charge of the records you know."

[5] MT was responding to Frank's statement on 26 March, "It is beginning to get noised about that I am to publish your book. . . . Should you say anything in your letters to any one here respecting the publication of the book please don't mention that our contract is not of recent date." Frank Bliss's company managed to publish *The Autobiography of Buffalo Bill,* but before *A Tramp Abroad* was ready to issue, the younger Bliss returned to the American Publishing Company.

88. To FRANK BLISS

Paris
10 May 1879

My Dear Frank—

I received a rather impertinent letter from Mr. Drake [1] a week ago, mentioning reports and inquiring somewhat particularly into my affairs,—on behalf of the Company, I suppose,—but I suppose he can wait for an answer as long as I have waited for one to the letter I wrote the Company on the same subject 3 years ago.

I am making good progress, and hope to have the book done before the end of July.

Now as to illustrations. I remember your father telling me the artist's and engraver's work for the Innocents Abroad cost $7,000. Of course we can knock down a deal of that expense, now, by using the new photo-processes. I've got an artist, here, to my mind,— young Walter F. Brown; you have seen pictures of his occasionally in St. Nicholas and Harper's Weekly. He is a pupil of the painter Gerome, here, and has greatly improved, of late.

He is willing to make the pictures for my book about as cheaply as the photo-people here will put them on the plates for. There are two or three of the processes suited to different styles of work, and I shall have occasion to use them all. Brown has been to the process men and got their figures, and the result is this:

If you will send me *Eleven hundred dollars, gold,* to Paris, you shall receive, in return for it,

10 full-page plates	@ $18.	....	$180.00
25 half-page do	@ 9.	....	225.00
75 quarter-page do	@ 4.50	....	337.50
100 sixth-page do	@ 3.	....	300.00
210 drawings	..... Totals	......	1,042.50

I say $1100 instead of $1042 to cover little possible mistakes in over-sizing the plates. I would suggest that another $50 be added to make reasonably sure of covering such mistakes.

Our government will charge 25 per cent duty on the cost of the *plates,* nothing on the artist's work. (I have been consulting the law, at the consulate.) This will add $125 or $150 to the total cost (I don't know what the freight will be on a box of plates,)—and the total cost of the 210 pictures will then be, say, $1325 or $1350, *artist's work included.*

These pictures will cover a space of—

10 full-page	— — —	10	pages.
25 ½- "	— — —	12½	"
75 ¼ "	— — —	19	"
100 ⅙ "	— — —	17	"
		58½	pages.

That is a *general* idea of the size of the pictures. I may use only 6 or 7 full-page pictures, and split up the other 3 or 4 into smaller ones; I may use some ⅓-page ones, and fewer ¼-page. And so on— but the amount of space covered by pictures will remain the same and cost the same.

In addition I propose to give several pages of space to *my own* pictures, but these will only increase the above picture-bill at the rate of $9 a page for processing the same (and duties)—I think I won't charge you anything for artist's work, although I've had a good deal of trouble with these things and thrown a world of mighty poor talent into them.

Brown agrees to submit all pictures to me and re-draw them till I approve of them. He also agrees to superintend the process business and see that the work is properly done.

If all this work is done here, the plates will be finished by the time I finish my last chapter, and the MS and the plates will cross the ocean in the same ship. But if the pictures are made in America that will cause a delay, and the artist will have to over-hurry his work besides.

I enclose proofs of plates made for this book by the processes, so that you can judge of their merit and of Brown's drawing.

We meant the Matterhorn accident for a full-pager, but had to guess at the size. If you agree to these propositions, send me a copy of the Innocents, and also send me two or three Innocent *pages* in a letter, per same mail—I shall be sure to get one of them, then.

If these propositions suit you, send me this cablegram at once, and Brown will go right to work, for there are stacks of MS ready:

"Clemens, care Munroe, Banker—Paris—*Yes.*"

Put no date, and no signature, of course.

If you don't agree, send the same cablegram with *No* in place of yes—because I want this thing off my mind, so it won't be intruding on my work.

If you agree, ship the money along, and I will pay for the artist's work and the plates from time to time as they are approved and delivered into my hands. The best way will be for you to hand the money to Geo. P. Bissell & Co and let them send me an ordinary *letter of credit* for the amount.—I can then keep it separate from my own money.

The proofs I send are in the rough. They have not been cleaned up. They are not on clean white paper, either.

Please reply at your early convenience.

Ys Truly

S. L. Clemens

¹ Sidney Drake, a Director of the American Publishing Company.

89. To FRANK BLISS

Paris
10 June 1879

Dear Frank

All right—have just written Perkins that Tom Sawyer fills the Riley contract, and instructed him to have the Co endorse all my contracts as completed and deduct $2000 from copyrights now due, in satisfaction of the Riley debt.[1] What I wanted the "yes or no" for was on the *artist's* work—of course I did not care where the plates were made. I have not a doubt that you even beat their French work which looks very shabby to me.[2]

Dan Slote [3] has the best process in the world, but I suppose we can't use that, because in his process the pictures are not transferred, but drawn on a hard mud surface. It looks like excellent wood engraving whereas *all* these other processes are miserably weak and shammy. How clean and strong the Innocents pictures are!

Yes, will leave space for some pictures to be drawn at home, as you suggest. I shall have one full page made here by a fine wood-engraver if he will cut it for anything under $100,—otherwise will send it over and let Dan Slote's artist try his hand on it. It is a thing which I *manufactured* by pasting a popular comic picture into the middle of a celebrated Biblical one—shall attribute it to Titian.[4] It needs to be engraved by a master.

Yrs Truly

S. L. Clemens

[1] On 26 June 1879, Charles Perkins, MT's Hartford attorney, replied, "I have had the Am Pub Co. indorse on all the contracts with you that your part thereof has been performed, and July 1st when they render their a/c, I will settle the $2000 matter."

[2] In a letter of 30 May, Frank had objected to the processing of illustrations in Europe: "I think the production of the plate can be done *better* here and at *less* price. It can be done here for about 5 to 6 dollars for a full page."

[3] Dan Slote not only published MT's self-pasting scrapbook and *Punch, Brothers, Punch,* but was also involved in the Kaolatype illustrating process to which MT refers in this letter and in which he invested heavily in 1880.

[4] "Titian's Moses" was printed as the frontispiece to *Tramp Abroad.*

90. To Frank Bliss

Paris

10 June 1879

My dear Frank—

Brown sent you some 35 drawings today—and one or two by "Harris" (my imaginary "agent") and one by myself.

I don't like those stipple processes half as well as I thought I should and am glad the plates are not to be made here. Pen and ink on plain paper looks much cleaner and stronger.[1] I have paid for the 2 or 3 plates made here—$14.60 and shall not have any more made. I shall leave several pages for your artist over there to fill up with after-thoughts as you suggest.

Ys Truly

S. L. Clemens

[1] Frank had objected to the stipple effect of some of the illustrations in his letter of 30 May, fearing the engraving "would be likely to fill up with the ink and make a bad mess of the thing."

91. To Frank Bliss

Paris
13 June 1879

[No salutation]

P.S. Perhaps you'd as well not have any of the pictures processed till you get them all, Frank. Then you could better determine which of them to make large and which to make small. It is only a suggestion—you must do as seems best, you know.

Ys Truly

S. L. Clemens

92. To Frank Bliss

[Paris]
17 June 1879

My Dear Frank—

Please "process" that waiter with the bottle, and a few other of the pictures and send proofs for Brown to judge by. I suppose he wants to know what *sort* of a process it is, so he can draw to its best capacities.[1] He brought some pictures last night which please me exceedingly.

Yrs

S. L. C.

[1] Frank Bliss wrote a long reply on 27 June describing various processes, techniques, and printing devices for insuring maximum effectiveness in illustrating.

93. To Frank Bliss

Elmira
8 September 1879

My dear Frank:

A stranger writes me that the A.P. Co. have had a new book of his under consideration for some time. Now if we publish my new book through the A.P. Co. let us have a written agreement with them that they shall not canvass *any* book *but mine* between this present date and a date *9 months after the actual publication and issue* of my forthcoming book.[1]

They put off the Innocents a whole year in direct violation of contract in order to run in two new books—but no matter about that, my object in having them was to have *an entirely* unencumbered field—and if I return to them, I don't want *any* books (new or old) canvassed but mine until my new book shall have had its full run. Will you fix this?

You will perceive that my book is not finished. I shall finish it here, after the M.S. comes back to me. There is nearly matter enough but I shall probably *strike out* as well as *add*.

Yrs Truly

S. L. C.

This letter is not dictated by malice, but only in the interest of "business."

---

[1] EB completed an addendum on 1 November 1879, agreeing "not to publish any other new book within 9 months from the time of publication" of *A Tramp Abroad*. MT sent the original contract and the transfer agreement to Perkins on 9 November, asking him to look them over and reword them if necessary to make sure the American Publishing Company would be "strictly bound" by the contracts.

94. To FRANK BLISS

Elmira

9 August [i.e., September] 1879 [1]

My Dear Frank

When you return the MS to me by Express don't forget to mark it "Value $500."—or $1000. When shall you be done with it? I ask because I want to know whether to go and visit my Fredonia folks now or wait till I have revised the book. I am not in any hurry for the MS. but I want to know how to date the aforesaid visit. Telegraph or write me.

Yrs Truly

S. L. C.

---

[1] The date of this letter is an obvious error, since the Clemens family did not return from Europe until 3 September.

95. To Moncure D. Conway

Elmira

19 January [1880]

My Dear Conway—

Yours and Harrison's [1] have arrived—the former containing your kind greetings and the latter a draft equivalenting £219.1.6—for both of which pray receive my thanks. I have acknowledged to Mr. Harrison by letter of this date in due business form. Prosperity to Chatto!—since he helps the prosperity of others—mainly the humble and deserving, like you and me.

Dod-rot the new book—as John the Baptist would say—it hangs along drearily. I read proof of the *middle* chapter yesterday—can't tell how long before it will issue from the press. A big edition has already been sold by subscription in the past 2½ months—so I suppose I am twelve or fifteen thousand dollars better off—or maybe more—though I haven't got the money yet. Bliss has been instructed to furnish advance sheets to Chatto as fast as possible, and I don't doubt he does it. . . .

Yrs Ever

Mark.

---

[1] Apparently a bookkeeper or accountant for Chatto & Windus.

96. To Elisha Bliss

[Hartford]
20 March [1880]

Friend Bliss—

I like the book exceedingly well; it (Sketches) [1] is handsomely gotten up, (barring the old type) and I believe it is going to take. Roughing and Gilded Age sold nearly double as many copies, in this length of time, so I imagine the Canadians have been working us heavy harm. I am glad no big newspaper has had a chance to give it a black eye with a left-handed notice—for in your accompanying statement I see distinct evidence that if the Gilded Age had been kept away from the newspapers, it would have given excellent satisfaction and its early sale would not have been "knocked." It now sells nearly up to Roughing It—and there never was any reason why it shouldn't—except the newspapers. You keep my books strictly *out* of the newspapers and we'll find our profit in it.

Check for $977.23 received—all right. The old books sell handsomely, yet, though there is a decrease, I believe, as compared with past years. That was owing to the long absence of a *new* book (and Canada,) I judge. The sale will pick up again, now, I judge, if the new book gives good satisfaction.

This ought to!

Kaolatype consists of 1000 shares at $25 per share—$25,000. I am President, Charley Perkins, Secretary, and Dan Slote Treasurer etc. Dan has an able assistant who was long head of a vast printing bureau in the City government. I own near four-fifths of the stock —paid cash for it and have agreed to lend the Co a liberal and sufficient sum every month for 3 months to get the thing going. (But I did this latter thing after I had myself hit upon a new application of the patent which I think puts non-success about out of the question.) You are a deal safer to come in *now*, I think, than you would have been when I bought. I have put off one man who had a disposition to buy some stock at par, because he is a stranger to this sort of business and could be of no use to us, but if you want some at par for cash down, all right, provided you don't go over 100 shares. However, if you will wait till the middle of summer you will be a great deal *more* safe—for if you pay 100 premium for it then, you will *know* it to be worth the money; and on the other hand it may possibly be worthless, and then you will be wise and stay out.

Ys Truly

S. L. C.

---

¹ The word "Sketches" is written in the top margin of the letter. It apparently refers to the illustrations in *A Tramp Abroad*, about which MT might obviously have been expected to comment.

97. To Moncure D. Conway

Hartford

20 April [1880]

My Dear Conway:

I started to write the enclosed ¹ to Chatto & Windus, but I saw I was too angry, and so it would be better for you to convey to them in inoffensive language that I am not in the publishing business, and that as long as you are in London and Bliss in Hartford I will have nothing whatever to do with electros, dates of issue, or any other matter of the sort. Jesus Christ, how mad I am! This man is *forever* ignoring Bliss and writing *me* about electros and matters strictly within Bliss's province.²

Will I (not Conway, not Bliss, but will I put aside my own matters and) "kindly see that a complete set of the electros of the illustrations are immediately dispatched to us, etc." *Why* should I give such a loose order for 300 plates, and be responsible for it? It is unbusiness-like and absurd. I will do nothing of the sort. I have enclosed Chatto's letter to Bliss and told him to return it to me at once, to enclose to you. I have told him that if he chooses to consider Chatto's order in the light of a business transaction, fire away and fill it—but not on my responsibility. He is merely the salaried servant of a Company, and it isn't likely he will venture.

Well, it gravels me through and through, that Chatto waits from July '79 to April '80—8 or 9 months, without asking a solitary question about the book, and then pitches into *me* about the miscarriage.

Bliss's address: American Publishing Co., 294 Asylum st., Hartford, Conn.

No book of mine has made so much talk here, since Innocents Abroad—and to my infinite surprise and delight, it is strongly *complimentary* talk. Howells's "Atlantic" notice has just arrived, and pleases me exceedingly. I enclose it.

I am very very sorry I never could make Chatto understand that I cannot act as agent between him and Bliss. I tried to so act, once, in the matter of Tom Sawyer electros, and the result was trouble and unpleasantness. That "let me out."—I like Chatto exceedingly, and shall continue to like him, but I won't saddle myself with business matters which are out of my province.

Yrs Ever

Mark

Chatto has not had time, yet, to get the elder Bliss's letter; so he orders (or rather, gets *me* to order) more than 300 electros without any idea of what they will cost. I made Frank Bliss promise to cable to-day as follows:

"Chatto, Publisher, London. Electros making—price $450";—so he would have a chance to cable and stop their manufacture if he wanted to.

Now I am done with this business—if Chatto wants to know how the electros are progressing or anything else about them, he *must* write Bliss, and *not* me.

Yrs

Mark

P.S.—21st: I sent down the letter and Frank Bliss answered in person, in place of his father—his father quite ill and not allowed to talk business. There was nothing for it, then, but for *me* to order Chatto's electros for him and sign a paper making myself and estate responsible for the $450 if Chatto dies or defaults.

This is simply a hell of a way to do business.

P.P.S.—I meant to enclose Chatto's letter, but Frank Bliss wanted to keep it, as being in a kind of vague and spectral way an order for electros.

[1] The fragment to Chatto & Windus (in Berg) follows:
Dear Sirs—
   Mr. Conway is my business agent. Let us suppose that you desire to know several things, to-wit:
   1. How many pages in the book?
   2. Will it issue before Xmas '79?
   3. Will it issue before Apr. '80?
   4. *When* will it issue?
   5. If, between Aug. 1st 1879 and March 1st 1880, we never ask a single question nor order a single electro, shall we be in a position to complain when we hear that the American edition is out without us?
   6. How shall we proceed, and whom shall we address, in order to procure electros?
   If Mr. Conway could not answer these questions on the spot, he would write to *Mr. Bliss* my publisher, and get the information.
   I have nothing to do with publishing my books; and I *won't* have anything to do with it, either here or in England. With Mr. Conway right at your elbow, you keep writing to *me*. When you want electros, you write *me*.—I have no electros, and never have *had* any electros. Why do you not write Bliss, who *has* electros? When things go wrong, you complain to *me*. My dear Sirs, through Mr. Conway I send you advance-sheets (looking to it *myself* and seeing that it is done) for a royalty—it is *all* I have ever agreed to do—it is all that I have ever had the slightest intention of making myself responsible for.
[2] MT was obviously still smarting from the fiasco over electrotypes for *Tom Sawyer*, but neither Chatto nor Conway was willing to admit the American Publishing Company was any purer than they. On 3 May, Chatto wrote, "We are on tenterhooks of anxiety for fear of a threatened unauthorized reprint of your *"Tramp Abroad"* at a shilling, which we shall be powerless to oppose. . . . Mr. Bliss by issuing the American Edition without giving us sufficient notice, has contrived very seriously to emperil your English copyright." The next day Conway replied to the present letter: "I must say that Bliss did not do his duty. I do not refer to the electros but to the fact that the proof of the text of the book was not in Chatto's hands until the work was out in America. There was over 100 pages of the book short here when the book was issued. That was recklessness on Bliss's part to your English advantages and interests which we may (though I hope not) have some difficulty in protecting."

98. To ORION CLEMENS

[Hartford]
24 October 1880

Private.

My Dear Bro:

Bliss is dead.[1] The aspect of the balance-sheet is enlightening. It reveals the fact, through my present contract, (which is for half the profits on the book above actual cost of paper, printing and binding,) that if Perkins had listened to my urgings and sued the company for ½ profits on "Roughing It," at the time you ciphered on cost of Innocents, Bliss would have backed down and would not have allowed the case to go into court. I felt sure of that, at the time, but Perkins was loath to go for a man with no better weapon to use than a "scare"—and Bliss went into the accounts and details and satisfied Perkins and his expert that 7½ per cent *did* represent half profits up to a sale of 50,000, and that after that the publisher had a mere trifling advantage of the author. So we dropped the matter.

I did a lot of ciphering, and struck for 10 per cent on the next book. Bliss stood the raise, but "proved" that paper was so much higher that 10 represented more than half profits.

I never bothered about the next 2 books—I cared nothing about them; being busy cursing from $500 to $1200 a week out of Raymond; but *this* time, the play being long ago dead, I did take an interest. I told the directors I wouldn't publish with them at any figure, because their business was too much spread out; Bliss [2] had resigned; so I gave him the contract, at ½ profits. Then he was ashamed to leave the company to perish; so he asked my permission to transfer the book to them; and I said I was more than willing, since they would be obliged to publish only *my* book during the first 9 months. Well, as a consideration for the book, he required them to allow him one-half of the *company's* entire profits for 3 years!—and they were exceedingly glad to comply. For it saved the company's life and set them high on their pins and free of debt. Frank has taken his father's place, and the business goes on.

Keep these things utterly private—mention them to nobody.³

I have lost considerably by all this nonsense—sixty thousand dollars, I should say—and if Bliss were alive I would stay with the concern and get it all back; for on each new book I would require a portion of that back pay; but as it is (*this in the very strictest confidence*), I shall probably go to a new publisher 6 or 8 months hence, for I am afraid Frank, with his poor health, will lack push and drive.

Out of the suspicions which you bred in me years ago, has grown this result—to-wit, that I shall within the twelve-month get $40,000 out of this "Tramp" instead of $20,000. Twenty thousand dollars, after taxes and other expenses are stripped away, is worth to the investor about $75 a month—so I shall tell Mr. Perkins to make your check that amount per month, hereafter, while our income is able to afford it. This ends the loan business; and hereafter you can reflect that you are living not on borrowed money but on money which you have squarely earned, and which has no taint nor savor of charity about it—and you can also reflect that the money you have been receiving of me all these years, is interest charged against the heavy bill which the next publisher will have to stand who gets a book of mine. . . .

With love from us

Y Affy

Sam.

$25 enclosed.

---

¹ On 13 September, Frank Bliss had written, "Father pulls along pretty slowly. Is very much better than he was a month ago. Still it is slow work building up a new man on a foundation so well worn out as his was; however I hope to see him at this table here at the office again before a great while."

² Frank Bliss, not Elisha.

³ A garbled version of this portion of MT's letter is in *MTL*, pp. 389–390; the rest of the letter is also printed there.

99. To Chatto & Windus

Hartford
1 December 1880

Dear Sirs:

Yours of Dec. [actually November] 15 [1] is just received, with the four notes, and I have to thank you for the pleasant surprise which so handsome a sale of the book furnished me. The largeness of the sale in the United States has surprised me, too, considering the confounded activity of our friends the Canadian pirates, for they managed to get advance-sheets from the several steam-press establishments here, and were on the market almost as soon as we were. I think they hurt us to the extent of 20,000 copies, perhaps, but we have sold 70,000 in spite of them.

I mean to have the "Atlantic" people delay my articles hereafter, so that I can "simultane" with you.

Yours faithfully

S. L. Clemens.

Your $6,000 makes it sure that I shall get $50,000 out of the "Tramp" for the twelve-months' sale, from 1st of last March.[2]

---

[1] Chatto's letter of 15 November sent four notes for a total of £1245.17.6, which MT was acknowledging here.

[2] MT was exaggerating. On 13 September, Frank Bliss had reported American sales as 55,000; he asserted, "The Tramp has been pegging along rather slowly the past few weeks, as the weather has been so hot that canvassers and workers of all kinds have been resting." Conway was so elated at the immediate reception of the book that on 20 December he told MT he was inserting the following paragraph in the *Athenaeum*:

Mark Twain's "A Tramp Abroad" has been a remarkable success in a pecuniary sense. Though by no means cheap, it has reached its eightieth thousand in the United States, while the Canadian appropriators have sold about 20,000 copies of their reprint. The Canadians have not failed on this occasion to add their contribution to the cumulative argument in favour of international copyright. They are said to have managed to get advance sheets from the steam press at Hartford, Twain's own town, and to have been in the market almost as soon as his own publishers.

III

"The Publishing of My Book"s

(1881–1884)

> "There were things about the publishing of *my* books
> which you did not understand. You understand them
> now, but it is I who have paid the costs."
>
> MT to JRO, 21 December 1883, Harvard

By 1881, Mark Twain was virtually a full-time investor and entrepreneur. A scrap of paper in MTP (DV 158) listing his "outgo since Jan. 1, '81" includes $10,000 for "my new book," $3,500 to the Fredonia Watch Company, $3,000 for Kaolatype expenses and $14,500 for the "Engineering Co.," $5,000 for the typesetter, $4,500 for stocks, $10,600 for the Crown Point Iron Co., and $2,000 for legal expenses. The list is undated, but was probably written early in 1882, and represents business payments and investments of over $53,000.

The Kaolatype was the largest drain on his income for several years, and deserves comment here because it brought Charles L. Webster onto the scene as Clemens's business agent. Pamela Moffett, Clemens' sister, announced to her son Samuel on 26 July 1881, "It seems from Charley's letters that your uncle Sam is putting all his business into his hands." Again, on 9 December, she wrote her son, "There is a pile of money in the Kaolatype business for somebody though it is not on a paying basis yet. . . . All it needs now, is to become known. They are getting out a book of specimens of their work: ten thousand copies of the first edition, to be scattered all over the country." Mark Twain, Charles L. Webster, and Charles Perkins were the President, Vice-President and Treasurer, and Secretary of the Kaolatype Company, whose vicissitudes are described in *MTBus,* pp. 150–180, and more succinctly in *MTB,* pp. 726–727. Briefly, the basic process of engraving on a clay surface over a steel or brass plate ultimately was subjected to a vast elaboration—for example, Clemens proposed its adaption by a brass-casting process to stamping book covers and printing wallpaper. By 1883, there was a complex comedy of errors being acted out, including lawsuits, charges of arson, and an attempt at reorganization (*MTBus,* pp. 209–210). In 1886, Clemens wished to sell his share of the Company (*MTBus,* p. 365, and letter 165 below); and in 1887 (Notebook 22, TS p. 32), he wrote, "Next year capture 500 Kaolatype infringers." The only enduring monument to Kaolatype is the binding of the first American edition of *The Prince and the Pauper,* on which Twain persuaded Osgood to use the engraving process.

The large majority of letters included in this section are to Osgood, who finally succeeded in becoming Mark Twain's official publisher with the issue of *The Prince and the Pauper.* Osgood had an enormous handicap in comparison with Elisha Bliss: he knew nothing about the mechanics of subscription publication. It was necessary for him to rely heavily on Twain's advice and commands, and in addition he made the mistake of employing the American Publishing Company's apparatus to distribute his subscription books.

When James R. Osgood & Company finally went bankrupt on 2 May 1885, *Publishers' Weekly* announced that "the firm has published several expensive works by subscription, and one cause of the present embarrassment is that, while these books are ready for delivery, and the firm has contracts to the amount of thousands of dollars with perfectly responsible persons, the latter, on account

of the hard times, are unable to receive the books at present"
(quoted in Carl J. Weber, *The Rise and Fall of James Ripley
Osgood* [Waterville, Maine, 1959], p. 222).

Osgood was inept enough at the mechanics of subscription
publication, but as the following letters suggest, he attempted at
least to accommodate Mark Twain as much as possible. Though he
was more docile than Elisha Bliss had ever been, he still made the
mistake of substituting his own business sense for the humorist's on
one crucial occasion with disastrous results. And in Charles L.
Webster—a relative, a hireling, but experienced enough by 1884 as
Osgood's New York general agent to manage subscription apparatus—Twain found a temporarily satisfactory successor.

Webster was in a peculiar position during 1883 and 1884: as an
employee of both Osgood and Clemens, his loyalties were divided.
And he made costly mistakes which were in part responsible for
Twain's rupture with Osgood. For example, when he prepared to
dump copies of *Life on the Mississippi* into the trade, he advised
"Uncle Sam" to authorize the binding of 14,000 additional copies
(CLW to MT, New York, 25 October 1883). When the author
complained the next year about Osgood's binding 10,000 books
"which he knew there was no sale for" (*MTBus*, p. 245), Webster
denied any responsibility (CLW to MT, New York, 17 January,
1884).

Nevertheless, Webster did defend Osgood (and showed his own
growing awareness of subscription method) when Twain insisted
the American Publishing Company sold more of his old books than
Osgood did new ones (CLW to MT, New York, 9 January 1884):

> There are a variety of reasons why he [Frank Bliss] should make a
> larger sale of the old books for the last three months than Osgood
> has made on the new book.
> 1st People of different tastes and ideas have six different works to
> select from instead of one. They can select a book for an adult or
> for a boy, a book with short sketches, or a continuous story, of western
> travel and adventure, of eastern, or of continental Europe. They can
> select books varying in price from $2.75 to $8.00 as originally pub-
> lished, and thus fit all pockets. Again they can get all these books at
> *half price retail* or $1.38 for Sawyer, and $1.75 *retail* for Innocents.

With all this selection, and at these low prices, it is not strange that the American Pub. Co. sell books, indeed it would be strange if they did not. . . .

Now in the corresponding three months in 1880, viz. from Oct 1st to Jan 1st after the Tramp's issue, there were sold by the American Pub. Co. but 3901 books; the statements show this. Osgood must have sold as many if not more the last three months, because Gill sold 2500 under his contract with me as I understand. I ordered over a thousand and this makes over 3500 from these two sources and I should say that the other nine General Agents certainly ordered more than enough to swell it to a good deal over 4000. So Osgood has done as much probably. No, the mistake was made in the start, not now.

Understand this argument is not to justify Osgood's mistakes in regard to the book, but to show that at this late day one new book should not sell as much as six old ones, at a reduced price, as we have to hold the price of Miss high. . . .

By the time of this elaborate explanation the fledgling Charles L. Webster & Co. was ready to try its own wings.

100. To James R. Osgood

[Hartford?]
Sunday. [1881] [1]

My Dear Osgood—

That concern is not going to bust, I reckon. They have sold *4,000* copies of my *old* books in the 3 months ending Dec. 31.

Have examined their inventories, and find their liabilities $80,-000, and their assets $84,000. No copyrights are mentioned as assets. They've got everything inventoried away up yonder! One of their "assets" (continued from year to year,) is a debt of Bret Harte's! ($2,000.) Others are considerable sums which the impecunious distant relatives of the late publisher owe. The plates of my six books are inventoried in the aggregate at $8,300. They *ought* to have been inventoried as old type metal—and inferior at that. I think they would have come nearer the truth if they had made their assets $50,000.

My books (cloth) are set at a cost of 50¢ for Sawyer, and 65 and 70 for the big books.

Ys Truly

S L C

[1] This letter was undoubtedly written very early in 1881. MT had just received his royalty statement through 31 December, and the thoroughness of the American Publishing Company's inventory suggests that it was undertaken shortly after EB's death as the management passed into new hands.

101. To James R. Osgood

Hartford
12 February 1881

My Dear Osgood:

Mrs. Clemens will decide in a day or two.—Will that do? Meantime, many thanks for the invitation. She can go, if we can persuade the friend who is with us (Mrs. Fairbanks) to stay while we go.[1]

Now as to Gebbie.[2] He failed of his appointment yesterday (as usual). He can make no more appointments with me. If he will treat with me *through you,* (if you are willing,) all right—but there ain't any other way. If you will make a contract with him, for me, for that Cyclopedia, I will give you a commission of 2½ per cent on what I get out of it, if you are willing to take hold of the thing—if the terms are such as I can approve. I should want him to show that I would get $50,000, with a possibility of more, for it is a big, stupid, laborious piece of work. It would be easier and pleasanter to write a book out of my own head. I would employ Howells to help me [3] (but Gebbie would have nothing to do with paying *him*—that is my affair). I should want Howells's name to appear with mine, if Gebbie were willing—it costing G. nothing.

My idea was to charge Gebbie 70 percent of the profits above cost of manufacture of the book—that is to *propose* 70 per cent., and then let him beat me down toward or to 50. Not unreasonable, since he probably expects to sell the book on my name rather more than on the contents.—I should want G. to go and see you *personally*, instead of contracting by U.S. mail.

Are you willing? Shall I refer him to you?

⟨And if you didn't trade, couldn't you get the whole job for Howells?⟩

Ys Truly

S L Clemens

---

¹ The reference is presumably to a trip to Boston which MT ultimately made alone on 23 February (see *MTHL*, p. 360, n. 3).

² George Gebbie, a Philadelphia subscription publisher, had proposed "the publication of a book, similar to Burton's Encyclopaedea of Wit and Humor illustrated with *new* steel and wood Engravings" (Gebbie to MT, 14 July 1880). Gebbie was preparing to sail for Europe; however, before leaving he made contracts for portaits of several humorists (*ibid.*, 17 July 1880). Upon his return, Gebbie announced he would "visit Boston inside of two weeks and will do myself the pleasure of interviewing you" (*ibid.*, 29 October 1880). On 12 January 1881, he announced an impending visit to Hartford and apologized for not having called sooner; and again on 30 January, he advised, "I will be in Hartford on Friday next." See further, *MTHL*, pp. 346–350.

³ Howells had accepted the offer to help on 17 January 1881 (*MTHL*, p. 347.

102. To JAMES R. OSGOOD

[Hartford]

7 March 1881

My Dear Osgood—

First and foremost—*yes*, send me a collection of etiquette books; Mrs. Fairchild's idea is a mighty good one, I think.¹

Now here's my American "rightful Earl of Durham," a sort of second or third cousin of mine.² If you approve my suggestion, send him $10 *on account*, and charge said $10 to me, of course—but after that, you and him for it. If he writes you anything worth printing you'll probably take it and pay something for it—otherwise you'll drop him.—*I* think he'll write you a gassy, extravagant,

idiotic book that will be delicious reading, for I've read some of his
rot; and it is just the sort of windy stuff which a Kentucky tramp
who has been choused out of an English earldom *would* write. By
George I believe this ass will write a serious book which would
make a cast-iron dog laugh. You take him in hand, now; but mind
you make him understand that if he attempts to visit me or write
me, you will cease from business intercourse with him at once.
Dern him, I can't be bothered with him.

If you approve all this, mail to him the enclosed letter.

I expect settlement-cheque from Bliss about Wednesday or
Thursday; and as soon as it comes, I shall forward to you that
Cyclopedia-item for the papers [3]—for I haven't heard anything
from Gebbie yet.

I have written Bliss to give me statements of cost of paper,
printing, binding—and shipping-expenses. The statement which
he *did* give me went but little into particulars—simply: 62,000
sold; $106,000 received; profit, $64,000; Clemens's half $32,000.
Cost of cloth copies, (and packing,) 67 cents each.[4] Bliss says you
can't make 'em for 47 cents—nor 50 cents—nor a penny less than
65.

Ys

S L C

Please send me a lot of *prepaid* envelops with your address
printed on them, and charge to

Yrs

S L Clemens

[1] Mrs. Charles W. Fairchild had suggested a burlesque etiquette book which
MT began but never completed (see *MTB*, pp. 705–706, and *LE*, pp.
191–208).

[2] Jesse Leathers, who proposed writing an autobiography; see *MTHL*, pp.
358–360, 869–871.

[3] An undated fragment (Harvard, TS in MTP) is presumably the item for the
papers to which MT refers:
It is rumored that Messrs. J. R. Osgood & Co contemplate the issue of a

Cyclopedia of Humor, with Mark Twain ⟨or W. D. Howells ⟨and possibly both,⟩⟩ to do the compiling and editing.

My Dear O—Ask Howells if he objects to the above form—if he doesn't, fire away.

Yrs
S L C

[4] The statistics refer to the first year's sale of *A Tramp Abroad.*

103. To James R. Osgood

[Hartford]
26 March [1881]

My Dear Osgood—

Now before you forget it, send me some of those damphool "ready letter-writers." [1] I want some "Forms" for epistles.

Thanks for the figures. They foot up $31,000 for 62,000 books; Bliss's foot up $42,000 for the same number.

I think that if I had had you to hurl items through the press and prepare the market for the "Tramp," the sale would have been double. Bliss never had a bit of sense about working the newspapers.

Ys Truly
S. L. Clemens

[1] JRO replied on 2 April, "The *envelopes* you mention no one here knows anything about."

104. To James R. Osgood

Hartford
30 March 1881

My Dear Osgood—

Yes, must have nice pictures, and a generous sufficiency of them, too.[1] Make the limit the figure you suggest—$2,800.

Please send me the enclosed dam book.² Got the others. Much obliged.

Howells don't seem to have no taste. The Earl's literary excrement charmed me like Fanny Hill. I just wallowed in it. I do not think you ought to publish it yourself, but I *do* think you ought to use your influence with Aldrich.—But you never will. You are as dainty and effeminate as Howells; so I know perfectly well that you will simply urinate on the Earl's MS and send it back to him without other comment. It is what Howells used to do with poems of sentiment when I sent him any.

> Truly Yrs
>
> S L Clemens

I returned Earl's MS to you today.

¹ For either the Cyclopedia of Humor or *The Prince and the Pauper*.
² *A Fair Barbarian* by Mrs. Francis Hodgson Burnett, which JRO published in 1881 and reported sending to MT on 2 April.

105. To James R. Osgood

> Hartford
> 23 May 1881

Dear Sirs—

Enclosed please find $160.76.¹

What is the last item—"London, 6 vols?" I have puzzled my dam head of trying to recoleck it.²

Yes, I prefear to have the "Prince" account kep entirely seperit.

All right Osgood—come along.

> Yr Truly
>
> S. L. Clemens

Please send me No's 68 and 142 of Harper's Franklin Square Library (Green Hand and Sailor's Sweetheart.) ³

Would also like to get hold of "Tom Cringle's Log" and "The Cruise of the Midge," [4] if they are still in print.

S L C

[1] On 8 February 1876, JRO had advised MT that a charge account had been set up for him: "We shall render you a bill once a month but you can pay when you like. I have given such orders, and you may now fling your postals recklessly." The present payment was for such a bill.

[2] As has the present editor, but with no success.

[3] The first volume was anonymous; the second, by W. Clark Russell. Both are merely listed in Notebook 15 (TS p. 25) with no further reference.

[4] Michael Scott wrote both titles, which were originally issued in *Blackwood's* and published in book form in 1836.

106. To James R. Osgood

Hartford
30 May 1881

My Dear Osgood—

I signed the contract and sent it.[1] And again, now, that clause about sharing losses comes troubling me. For although such a thing is exceedingly unlikely, there *might* be a loss instead of a profit— and I would have to pay my proportion of that loss and *$6,200 besides!* (the money which I stand pledged to pay to Howells and Clark whether the book pays or not.) Come, old man, add a codicil specifying that that $6,200 shall stand as a cash payment on my proportion of the loss. No, I won't *require* this—couldn't if I wanted to!—but I submit it for consideration and prayer.

Yr Truly

S L Clemens

[1] For "Mark Twain's Cyclopedia of Humor," dated 20 May 1881, on which MT was to receive 70 percent of profits above costs of manufacture or to pay 70 percent of losses resulting from publication.

107. To Frank Bliss

Hartford

30 May 1881

Dear Frank—

The 1st of July I shall expect to be paid half the profits accruing upon Tramp Abroad up to that time. I don't know whether that is the letter of the contract or not,[1] but it is the spirit of it. It having now been demonstrated that 10 per cent represents less than half the profits, there can be no reasonable use in the company's retaining a part of my money 9 months in order to demonstrate it again. I think you will see this as I do.

Ys Truly

S. L. Clemens

[1] MT *did* know that his request did not correspond to the letter of the contract, for Charles E. Perkins had explained the matter to him on 23 June 1880; the contract provided for quarterly payments of 10 percent royalty but only an annual accounting of half-profits.

108. To Benjamin Ticknor [1]

Branford

1 August [1881]

My Dear Ticknor—

We go hence to *Elmira, N.Y.*, three days from now, and *that will be my address for the following six weeks.*

As to the pictures,[2] they clear surpass my highest expectations. They are as dainty and rich as etchings. I would like to have you print twelve or fifteen full sets of them for me, each picture in the centre of a sheet of fine India paper about double the size of this I am writing on, (I mean the sort of paper they print etchings on—or any other paper that will best bring out their excellencies,) and bind each set simply and neatly in boards. Can this be done at a reasonable expense? I want to give them to a few especial and particular friends.[3]

You tell me to send these back. What do you want 'em back, for? I wish to look at them.

Put titles under the pictures yourself—I'll alter them in proof if any alteration shall seem necessary.

I am going to the annual Educational blow-out at Ashfield, Mass.,[4] some time between Aug. 15 and Sept. 10, and shall hope the date will be after Aug. 21, so that I can "meet up" with ole Brer Osgood, as uncle Remus would say.

Truly Yrs

S. L. Clemens

[1] Both Benjamin H. Ticknor and Thomas B. Ticknor are listed on JRO's letterhead; presumably all letters addressed merely to "Ticknor" are to Benjamin, JRO's partner (see Weber, p. 181).

[2] Illustrations for *The Prince and the Pauper*.

[3] The India-paper collection of illustrations ultimately became an edition of the book itself (see the subsequent letters). They were originally intended for Susy Clemens, Koto House, E. H. House's adopted daughter, and Winifred Howells.

[4] Charles Eliot Norton's annual Ashfield Academy Dinner; see *MTHL*, pp. 364–366.

109. To Benjamin Ticknor

Elmira

14 August [1881]

Dear Ticknor—

I'll suggest *one* point for the circular—to-wit: that you don't forget to glorify the illustrations; and also that you call attention to the historical accuracy of the costumes.

The more I examine the pictures, the more I am enchanted with them. If it is going to be too extravagantly costly to make 20 books of them on India paper—a large item of the expense is the mounting, doubtless—maybe we can print them on a heavy *tinted* paper and survive the outlay. Let us talk of this when I am in Boston August 26ᵗʰ. But I don't know but I shall have to borrow enough money to get *one* set printed on India paper, anyway. Merrill ¹ probably thinks he *originated* his exquisite boys himself, but I was ahead of him there!—in these pictures they look and dress exactly as I used to see them in my mind two years ago. It is a vast pleasure to see them cast in the flesh, so to speak—they were of but perishable dream-stuff, before.

I hain't got no proofs, yet—but there may be some in the post office now.

The Great Seal wasn't to be engraved—ole Brer Osgood forgot that, I reckon. I'm afraid to put it in—we will talk about that, August 26.

Truly Yours

S. L. Clemens

¹ F. T. Merrill, illustrator of *The Prince and the Pauper.*

110. To Benjamin Ticknor

Elmira

9 September 1881

My Dear Ticknor—

I didn't think about there being any hurry; and besides, I wasn't expecting any delay. I got the cover-design last Sunday—mailed it to New York that evening; expected it to be in our artist's hands by 9 A.M. Monday; expected it to be *out* of his hands (in the form of a type-metal facsimile,) some time during Wednesday; I hoped it would reach Chelsea that night, be cast in brass and finished-up on Thursday and be in your hands and ready for the press on Friday.¹

But everything went wrong, of course. The design did not reach our artist until some time on *Tuesday;* the Thanksgiving or Prayer-holiday ² stopped the work on it yesterday, no doubt; and now comes a telegram to say it won't be ready for the brass founder till *Monday.*

So I am instructing my nephew to take the spelter-cast to Boston Monday night, and get it cast in brass, in Chelsea, Tuesday.

I am not foreseeing any difficulty about it;[3] but if our work *should* be inferior and unsatisfactory to you, you can fire away and have the plate *cut,* by the die-sinkers. Webster will bring you the original design.

I shall be sorry if it turn out that I have caused you a week's delay, but hellandamnation I wasn't dreaming of such a thing.

Truly Yours

S. L. Clemens

You haven't told me the extra cost of gilding the whole thing instead of printing a part of it black.

[1] MT was using the cover design of *The Prince and the Pauper* to experiment with a refinement of the Kaolatype process. On 7 September, he had written to CLW, "Trot that design through; and when you have it cast in spelter, ship the cast to Providence and ask them to cast it in brass with their utmost nicety—cast it and re-cast it till they get a perfect plate. Then let them ship it to Osgood to be finished up by a first-class finisher."

[2] A prayer day for the recovery of the wounded President Garfield, who died anyway.

[3] Difficulties did arise, however; on 19 October, MT wrote JRO from Hartford: "I'm very much afraid that those process-pictures are too shallow to stand much of an edition—they'll fill up easily and wear out quickly. I could have done them to perfection in Kaolatype, (if I had known it then), and about as cheaply and quickly, and a dern sight deeper and stronger. That is, I *think* I could have done them to perfection—it won't do to swear to anything, these days" (University of Texas).

111. To James R. Osgood

Hartford
2 October 1881

Dear Osgood—

Have just arrived. Yes, I agree to the soundness of your construction of the Canadian matter.[1] So you can go ahead and set up the types for Canada whenever you please.

I will go to Canada when notified.

Now what steps must I take to make that *bona fide* transfer to Chatto. Only a mere piece of paper, like any other bill of sale, I suppose? Draw me up one, and I will sign it and send it through you to Chatto.

I may run up to Boston Thursday of this or early next week.

Ys Truly

S L Clemens

[1] JRO had written MT a detailed letter on 29 September, outlining his plans for obtaining legal control over Canadian printing of *The Prince and the Pauper* and preventing a repetition of the *Tom Sawyer* piracy. Basically, the publication of an authorized Canadian edition together with an Imperial copyright in the name of Chatto & Windus, JRO thought, would prevent piracy. Samuel Dawson, a bookseller who had helped to draft the Canadian copyright act, provided advice and ultimately issued an "authorized" Canadian edition.

112. To James R. Osgood

Hartford

24 October 1881

My Dear Osgood—

Here is an article which I have been three years building.[1] Scribner's folks have asked for an article, and I was going to send them this; but I reflected, and this is the result: *this* must go into the North American Review, else every ass of a reader will believe I invented these things, instead of experiencing them. That would simply exasperate me. The subject is entirely worthy of the Review; and besides I have treated it with the seriousness which it deserves. Won't you send it to the Review for me? If they don't want it, *then* we'll go to the Century—but not otherwise. I want to "simultane" it with some grave enough London magazine, or with one of Chatto's magazines, and also with the Australian Review— we forgot all about simultaning when we sold to Scribner before [2] —so we unintentionally left Chatto out, that time.

Ned House has got some awfully curious instances, and I want him to write and print them. They mustn't be lost. Will you tell him?

I've got some more myself—going to make another article, by and by.

Ys Truly

S. L. Clemens

¹ "Mental Telegraphy"; the *North American Review* apparently refused the article, prompting MT's sarcasm in letter 115 below.
² Scribner's published *The Century* (*Scribner's Monthly* did not begin until 1887); thus MT speaks of Scribner's and *The Century* synonymously. JRO had sold them MT's "A Curious Experience" for $400 in May 1881 (JRO to MT, Boston, 11 May 1881); the article appeared in the November issue.

113. To JAMES R. OSGOOD

[Hartford]
27 October 1881

Dear Osgood—

In setting up and printing in Canada,¹ we run one risk—that the sheets may be bought or stolen, and a pirated edition brought out ahead of us. How would it do to leave out a signature, (in our Canadian reprint, up yonder,) here and there, until a few days before Canadian publishing-date?

Howells's notice is superb.² And it will pitch the key for the rest of the American criticisms. You are going to send books, now, to —— to —— to whom?—the press in general, or to only certain wise ones. O, no, I remember, now—*can't* let a copy go out, lest it be construed as "publication." (I have got a very good memory, but can seldom find it.)

In a hurry, to catch the morning mail,

Yrs

S L C

¹ The plan to print *The Prince and the Pauper* in Canada was soon replaced by the more practical and less dangerous alternative of shipping sheets of JRO's edition, with some signatures removed, to Montreal.
² Howells' review of *The Prince and the Pauper* appeared in the New York

Tribune on 25 October 1881, p. 6; it was written from his reading of the proof, for the volume was not issued until December.

114. To JAMES R. OSGOOD

Hartford
28 October 1881

Dear Osgood—

How would it do, to set up the first and last signatures in Boston, and do the rest in Canada? You see, what I'm after is a *preventive;* it is preferable to even the best of cures. Those sons of up there will steal anything they can get their hands on—possible suits for damages and felony would be no more restraint upon them, I think, than would the presence of a young lady be upon a stud-horse who had just found a mare unprotected by international copyright. In the one case, theft and piracy is the fateful doom; in the other, copulation and adultery.

What day are *you* going to Canada? That's the day that I'm going. Name it.

Ys Truly

S L Clemens

Say—I'll pay all your expenses, you know.

Especially if there is any little game you play for amusement on such trips.

115. To JAMES R. OSGOOD

[Hartford]
1 November 1881

Dear Osgood—

I forgot. Howells's review ought to be *"nuggeted,"* (I mean, the most telling remarks mustered together,) so as to make 3 or 4 stickfuls of bourgeois, then printed on slips and supplied to every canvasser, so that *he* can supply the same to his village editor along with press copy of book. Maybe you've already done this, but I thought I'd make sure.

I perceive by the letter from His Supremacy, God Almighty, Editor of the North American Review,[1] that he is as nervous and scary as he used to be when he tried to run the affairs of the peculiar people and made a mess of it. I reckon he is a little sore about amateur philosophers since his Mr. Jere Black has got such a ludicrous roasting.[2]

The Century wants an article.[3] Now here is my idea: send it there, but strike out the nom de plume, and sign it S. *Langhorne* (part of my own name)—and I want to simultane with Chatto and with the Australian Review.—Wherever "Hartford" occurs (which is only once, I believe,) change it to "Boston."

They can pay what they please—or nothing.

There is not a statement in the article which is either untrue or in the least degree exaggerated. Yet there isn't one in it which would be believed, with my nom de plume at the bottom.—Will you send it to the Century, or shall I?

Rose [4] is a scoundrel, and *won't* do as he agrees. Mr. Dawson is mistaken. My knowledge of him is not second-hand.

Derned if *I* can think of anything to suggest except taking a set of plates to Canada to print from. If that will answer in place of setting up the book there, I should recommend that.—They wouldn't need to be electrotyped, but only stereotyped. And in any case, if we ain't on hand there a *week* beforehand, the C. edition won't be out on time, I judge.

You might use Dawson's imprint and put the copyright entry and title in the name of some Montreal hotel clerk, if you know one. What's the objection to that? There *ain't* any, is there?

You probably get a damsight of information out of me—and intelligent assistance. Well, I always do my best, anyway.

Ys Truly

S. L. Clemens

¹ Allen Thorndike Rice, who purchased the Journal in 1876 and popularized its contents.

² In the August 1881 issue, Robert Ingersoll had written an article on "The Christian Religion" (pp. 109–128), to which Jeremiah S. Black had written a rebuttal (pp. 128–152). In the November issue (pp. 477–522), Ingersoll "roasted" Black's rebuttal in "The Christian Religion, Part II."

³ The article was "Mental Telegraphy"; see MT's description of his tribulations with his MS in his prefatory note to the printing of it in *£1,000,000 Banknote*, pp. 45–46.

⁴ George M. Rose, president of Rose-Belford Publishing Company, who had pirated most of MT's books; see Gordon Roper, "MT and His Canadian Publishers," *American Book Collector*, X (June 1960), 13–29.

116. To James R. Osgood

Montreal
28 November 1881

Dear Osgood—

Have just returned from visiting Mr. Dawson. He has printed an edition of 275, and they are ready to be put into the paper covers. ⟨—and said covers are ready.⟩ He wanted to know what price to put upon the book, so that he could state it in his announcement. I said I believed our idea was, to put a *prohibitory* price on it, to keep it out of the pirates' hands until we had reaped our market. But he knocked that argument as cold as Gilsey House civility with the simple remark that if the pirates want a copy and can't get it here on the 2d, they can wait a day and get it from Boston.

He seemed to think it would not answer at all to put the price of this little paper-covered volume at a heavier figure than $1. *I said I would write you immediately, and you would telegraph him and set a price.*

⟨Hell, I wish you were here!—for just this moment I've struck an idea. It is this: let Dawson put this book at *15 cents* a copy; not advertise and not issue⟩

But I reckon tain't much of an idea, after all. Hurry up here dern your skin.

Yrs

Mark.

I knew I should have a lot of
dam *business* on my hands, if you
didn't come with me.

117. To James R. Osgood & Co.

[Hartford]
28 December 1881

Dear Sirs—

Sylvester Baxter, of the Herald, sends me this.[1] Now please set
your detective forces to work and find out who that Hartford
correspondent is. I judge he is connected with the Am. Pub. Co. of
this city. If so, I can make it valuable, as I shall begin suit against
that concern pretty soon, now, (keep this to yourselves), for
swindling me. Save this Herald scrap and return it to me. By the
middle of January I shall experience a let-up in this protracted out-
pour of cash, and shall then waltz into that gang with affectionate
enthusiasm. Find me that correspondent.

Please send me one of those China-paper books [2]—or hand it to
Ned House; it is for his daughter.

Ys Truly

S. L. Clemens

Osgood, remind me to speak of a short-hand reporter to travel
with us in the spring.[3] I want a bright, companionable *gentleman.*
Maybe Baxter can name him for us.

---

[1] In a "Literary Chit-Chat" column in the New York *Herald* of 19 December
1881, p. 5, there was a brief description of the plot of *The Prince and the
Pauper*, together with the comment, "Those who saw the book in manuscript
hastened to assure the world that there was no fun in the book, much to Mr.
Clemens' disgust, who wisely thinks that he is nothing if not funny."

[2] See letter 108 above.

[3] Down the Mississippi; see letter 119 below.

118. To James R. Osgood

[Hartford]
29 December 1881

My Dear Osgood—

I enclose a review by Rev. E. P. Parker, D.D.,[1] which is excellent, and is vigorous and outspoken in its commendations.

You must have sufficient material, now, from which to select plums for a new and powerful circular—that is if any more powerful one than the last is needful or possible.

Ys Truly

S L C

[1] Parker wrote an anonymous review which appeared in the Hartford *Courant* on 28 December, and wrote MT the same day identifying himself as its author.

119. To James R. Osgood

[Hartford]
31 December 1881

Dear Osgood—

Never mind. Crane says the coal-firm's young phonographer will suit me, and the firm would like him to have the trip and the holiday as a testimony of their satisfaction with him.[1] He will not be expensive.

Better send the India-paper books here, I guess—I don't see no prospect of getting to Boston pretty soon.

Are you paying general agents 60 per cent? Years ago I remember hearing Bliss say that if he should allow a general agent more than 50 when a book was new, the ⟨b⟩ scoundrel would rush them immediately into the bookstores. Still, I also remember that the books *were* rushed into the bookstores when new, whatever the percentage was.

Have you evidence of the American Pub Co working against us upon which I could found a suit? Am going for them anyway, and might as well have 2 suits as one.

Think of those thieves declaring *another* dividend! This is the second one since the end of last June, when they hadn't ten cents in their treasury.[2] Webster stepped in there yesterday, and found them, as usual, with no work of a fatiguing nature going on. Bliss said I had probably found out by this time the mistake I made in leaving an experienced subscription man to go to a green one. He said Osgood had minutely studied and copied all the methods invented by *them,* and was using the machinery (agencies) created by them. Webster should have remarked that Osgood was not employing *all* of it, but only the inferior and subordinate limbs— but he didn't think of it, I reckon.

My New York lawyer will begin to move in my American Pub. Co. suit early, now. I shall want to show that the Co paid more for paper and binding than they needed to pay; and I shall want you to help me do this, through figures obtained from Fairchild[3] and bookbinders. I judge I can ⟨scare⟩ get my copyrights out of those fellows; and then they may just as well shut up shop.

Ys Truly

S L Clemens

[1] The young phonographer is unidentifiable; Theodore Crane was MT's brother-in-law and an officer in the Langdon Coal Company. Eventually, MT employed Roswell Phelps, a stenographer for the Continental Life Insurance Co. of Hartford. Phelps and MT signed a contract whereby MT paid the secretary $100 a month, all traveling expenses, and a dollar per thousand words of transcription.

[2] Two reports of the Bradstreet Company call MT's statistics into question. On 10 March 1881, Bradstreet's reported a surplus capital of $28,000 for the American Publishing Company; on 29 July they listed a cash value of $20,000 and capital stock value of $50,000 for the Company.

[3] Possibly Charles Fairchild, a friend of Howells' whom MT visited frequently in Boston. His authority to provide evidence for MT cannot be determined.

120. To James R. Osgood

Hartford
4 January 1882

Dear Osgood—

India-paper books received all right.

The McMillan matter [1] belongs to you and Dawson to decide—
it is a matter of pure business. I don't care how many of the
Canadian edition are sold *in the British Possessions*—simply don't
want them to get over the line. Mr. Dawson has put on a high
price so that they *can't* be sent to the U.S., no doubt.

My position is simple: just so [there are no] shipments of the
Canadian books to the U.S., I do not care what arrangement is
made with McMillan and others.

Yes, I remember discussing the discount to General Agents. It's
only just *now,* in view of current events,[2] that I am impressed with
the idea that all that we give them, over 50%, is thrown away; for
the *canvasser* is the lad that does the work, and *he* ain't going to get
any more or less than his regular 40% in *any* case.

No, we can't keep the books out of the stores—and moreover, we
don't want to; we only want to *let on* like everything that we *do*
want to—otherwise the canvassers would sail into us.

(Look here! Why shouldn't we be our *own* general agents in
N.Y., Phila and Boston, another time? We could work the
bookstores and divide the swag.) . . .

Ys Truly

S L Clemens

---

[1] From the context, the matter apparently involved distribution of MT's book
in British possessions other than Canada. Presumably JRO or Dawson had
received a letter of inquiry regarding exports.

[2] In Notebook 16, February to September 1882, TS p. 43, is the statement,
"Osgood said he would divide the $2500 loss by defaulting general agent with
me." The unidentified general agent in all likelihood prompted the current
interest in discounts and the suggestion that JRO serve as his own general agent
two paragraphs later.

121. To JAMES R. OSGOOD

[Hartford]
7 January [1882]

Dear Osgood—

Glad to hear that decision of the Toronto pirates' lawyers.[1]

I am meditating a little assault of a rather venomous nature upon Whitelaw Reid,[2] and maybe you better drop in and consult about the judacity of it if you are going to pass through here within a few days.

Ys Truly

S. L. C.

[1] Although Canadian pirates were a topic of correspondence in late 1881, and Belford and Clarke were to become defendants in a lawsuit in late 1882 and 1883, the "decision" of early 1882 is obscure—especially so since a pirated *Prince and the Pauper* was issued by the Rose-Belford Publishing Company in April 1882.

[2] Charles Dudley Warner had told MT that Reid's New York *Tribune* was attacking MT persistently; so a "venomous" assault, including a malicious biography of Reid, was plotted—only to be canceled when the allegations proved false (see *MTHL*, pp. 386–390).

122. To JAMES R. OSGOOD

Hartford
12 February 1882

My Dear Osgood—

I didn't know of anything to suggest,[1] so I waited for an idea. It hasn't arrived. Too brief a pre-canvass, and the subsequent performances of the Bliss gang of general agents, were the main troubles, I guess.—Then there is another—the modern canvasser (not gen'l agent but canvasser,) doesn't canvass. He sublets to an idiot, on a percentage, and sits at home in aristocratic indolence. That is the case here; it is the case in Elmira, N.Y.; it is doubtless the rule.

After a little, it might be a good thing to cut under the unfaithful gen[1] agents by shoving books into the stores at a little cheaper terms than *they* can afford—doing this either openly or clandestinely as shall seem most judicious.

There is just one thing *sure*—we'll have a very different gen[1] agent system, hereafter, and not any Bliss's in it.

House has been sick abed here about two weeks; and most of the time *mighty* sick. But he is mending somewhat, the last two days.

I've got to go to New York for a day, pretty soon. When are you going? And can't you stop over night here? Then I would go along with you—or go with you anyway, if you couldn't stop.

Clark is progressing with the Library of Humor.[2] Enclosed is that rheumatic preventive from Clara Spaulding.

Yrs

Mark.

---

[1] To explain the failure of *The Prince and the Pauper,* published in early January, as a subscription book. In spite of gloomy results, MT kept up a bright public attitude, as his 11 January letter to H. H. Boyesen (CWB) suggests:

I was mightily delighted with your review of my book, and am very glad that the work impresses you so favorably. I was doubly solicitous—anxious, shall I say?—this time, because the thing was a new departure, both literarily and publicationally, for I went for the bulk of the profits, and so published the volume at my own expense, opening with an edition of 25,000 copies, for the manufacture of which I paid $17,500. Yes, I was solicitous, for a while, but that is all gone by, now. I find myself a fine success, as a publisher; and literarily the new departure is a great deal better received than I had any right to hope for. . . .

[2] Charles H. Clark, an editor of the Hartford *Courant,* was doing the preliminary editing according to an agreement JRO committed to paper on 1 April 1882 (*MTHL,* pp. 398–399).

123. To James R. Osgood

Hartford
4 March 1882

Dear Osgood—

I's gwyne to sen' you de stuff jis' as she stan', now; an' you an' Misto Howls kin weed out enuff o' dem 93,000 words fer to crowd de book down to *one* book; or you kin shove in enuff er dat ole Contrib-Club truck fer to swell her up en bust her in two an' make *two* books outen her.[1]

Dey ain't no use to buil' no index, ner plan out no 'rangement er de stuff ontwel you is decided what you gwyne to do.

I don't want none er dat rot what is in de small onvolups to go in, 'cepp'n jis' what Misto Howls *say* shel go in.[2]

I don' see how I come to git sich a goddam sight er truck on han', nohow.

Yourn truly

S L Clemens

P.S. I wrotened to Cholly Webster 'bout dem goddam plates en copyrights.[3]

---

[1] Though the contract for *The Stolen White Elephant* was not drawn until 10 April, MT sent material with this letter and also had JRO examine the files of the *Atlantic Monthly* for his contributions. JRO replied on 15 March (*MTHL*, p. 398). The "Contributors' Club" was a column Howells established in the *Atlantic* for anonymous paragraphs (see *MTHL*, p. 156).

[2] On 8 April, JRO reported that Howells suggested omitting ten items; see *MTHL*, p. 400.

[3] The reference is obscure. In 1882, CLW was experimenting with the Kaolatype process for the cover of *The Stolen White Elephant*, as he had for *The Prince and the Pauper*. He was also accumulating "evidence" against the American Publishing Company in an attempt to retrieve MT's copyrights by proving that they had fraudulently exaggerated the costs of manufacture for *A Tramp Abroad*.

124. To James R. Osgood

[Hartford]

7 April 1882

My Dear Osgood—

1. I have issued, after a prodigiously long canvass, as follows: Roughing It, 43,000; Gilded Age, 43,000; Tramp Abroad, 48,000.

2. In the first quarter after issuing, we sold, of each, 10,000 to 20,000, say.

3. In the *second* quarter after issuing, sales dropped down to where the "old" books were.

Doesn't this simply mean that the sale marked "2" *consists mainly of a tumbling of the books into the trade, by General Agents and canvassers?*—and that the effect of it is observable in "3?"

Yes, sir, I think a subscription book has just two lives: One drawn from the public *before* issuing; and one from the trade, *after*.[1]

Ys Truly

S L Clemens

I have written the Introduction to the Portuguese Phrase Book.[2]

Did you send some brass stamp patterns *whose cost you already know,* to Webster to duplicate for experiment. Said you would.[3]

P.S.—$1500 or $1600 is steep for an author who is already deep in 2 expensive law suits.[4] Tell you what I will do. You sacrifice yourself for your guild, and I will for mine: You pay ⅓ of this trade-mark exploit and I will pay the other ⅔.—How's that? [5]

Ys

S L Clemens

---

[1] MT's elaboration of these mechanics of publication is the only extant vestige of his plan to remove *The Prince and the Pauper* from the subscription market because of its poor sale. On 31 July, JRO advised, "The responses we receive from the agents seem to indicate a good sale for 'P & P' for the rest of the year. We have therefore concluded it will be wiser to give up the notion of withdrawing it from the subscription sale until next year."

[2] Pedro Carolino's *New Guide of the Conversation in Portuguese . . . ,* was published with MT's introduction by JRO in June 1883.

[3] CLW's attempts to make satisfactory cover patterns and illustrations ended in failure. JRO wrote MT on 5 June: "Anthony is going to make a parcel of the drawings and Kaolatype reproductions which I will send forward to you today by express. He will also write a letter giving the artist view of the objectionable features in the reproductions." On 15 June, MT told CLW, "When I got to Boston the pictures had been sent to Hartford, so I did not see them until I got back. I listened to what they had to say, and examined the pictures when I got home. To my mind yours were better than the Moss, but as the artist did not feel

so, I gave orders to have the rest done by the Moss Company. An additional reason for this was, that they said you charged double what Moss charged." Inexplicably, however, the same letter confided that JRO wanted "to buy a shop-right outright for Boston or take it on a royalty" (Webster, TS in MTP).

[4] MT's lawsuit with Belford and Clarke came before the Circuit Court of the United States, Northern District of Illinois, in November 1882. MT held that the publisher had violated his trademark by publishing a volume, *Sketches by Mark Twain* in 1880. Prior to the suit, during the summer of 1882, JRO had served as MT's advisor in getting the suit ready for court. On 18 July, JRO reported that Thomas William Clarke—the humorist's attorney in the case—estimated costs at $1,100 to $1,500.

[5] On 31 July, JRO wrote, "Suppose I do this. Clarke estimates the cost of counsel to defend the suit at $250 to $300. I'll pay this cost—viz. opposing counsel's fees, whatever they may be—and this will relieve you from any imputation of paying Belford's bills."

125. To JAMES R. OSGOOD

[Hartford]
Friday [1882]

Dear Osgood—

All right, call it Apl. 17—and start from *New York,* at 6 P.M., Pennsylvania road (ain't it?) *Hotel car* all the way to Chicago—[1] dam sight better than a mere dam sleeping car. How does this strike you?

I reckon I can get the Sketches ready in time, though publishing books don't pay for the trouble of writing them—only this one don't *have* to be written.

Yrs

Mark

[1] These are the instructions for the first leg of the long-delayed trip down the Mississippi.

126. To James R. Osgood

Hartford
3 June 1882

My Dear Osgood—

Have written to ask Spofford if my copyright is perfect on my several books.

I find no fault with Mr. Clarke's bill; but if Spofford charges me $11 apiece to tell me whether my copyrights are good or not, I shall be most unspeakably surprised.

I guess I won't try to scare these thieves here till I find how the other copyrights stand. If none of them are sound, I shall have to keep mighty still, of course.

I see no harm in a trade-mark suit in Chicago, to assail the pirates on that one little volume of Sketches; for if I lose it I surrender only that one book to them—and that one I can spare.

If Simon Sterne tells Clark[e] he won the other case on trade-mark pure and simple, why not sail in?

There *must* be copyright articles in that pirated volume of Sketches—for some of them must have appeared in the Atlantic or Galaxy. I could tell if I had the book—and if proving that would answer our needs.

Yr Truly

S L Clemens

I have sent Clark[e] a check in full.
I re-enclose his letter—you may need to keep it.

127. To James R. Osgood

[Hartford]
19 July 1882

Dear Osgood—

Won't you please send to Commodore Rollingpin [1] and get a photograph of Capt. Isaiah Sellers' Monument in Bellefontaine

Cemetery, and let our artist make a ⅔ or a full page picture of it. I stole my nom de plume from him,[2] and shall have considerable to say about him, for out there he was "illustrious."

Ys Truly,

S L Clemens

P.S. And now, of *course*, the very man I want a favor of, would be the man whose house in Magazine street, we drove by without stopping at—Capt. John A. Stevenson. He has the article—my first —which made Capt. Sellers so angry. Said he would give it to me, but at the time I didn't think I needed it.—But I do. Won't you ask Bixby to get it for *you*? Say you want to see it, and will return it if required. And send Stevenson a White Elephant.

Ys,

S L C

[1] John Henton Carter ("Commodore Rollingpin") was a journalist and humorist in St. Louis, and had interviewed MT in May. See *MT&HF*, pp. 286–287.

[2] See *MTB*, pp. 149–150, for the standard history of the pseudonym and Paul Fatout, "MT's Nom de Plume," *American Literature*, XXXIV (March 1962), 1–7, for a variant version. An illustration of a "Cemetery" on p. 430 of the first edition of *Life on the Mississippi* may be the result of the present request.

128. To JAMES R. OSGOOD

[Elmira]

18 September 1882

Dear Osgood—

Welcome home![1] I have been half dead with malaria ever since you left; and these last few days am two-thirds dead. I work all the time, but accomplish very little—sometimes as little as 200 words in 5 hours.[2]

What is worse than all is that I find I still lack about 30,000 words, whereas a few days ago I thought it was only a third of that

—dismal miscalculation! I shall peg along, day by day, but shan't be through when we leave for home 2 weeks hence.[3]

Truly yrs

S. L. C.

Poor Lem Gray [4] died of his injuries—was buried Aug. 23d. The others got well.

---

[1] JRO had left for England on 8 August and returned to the United States on 18 September. While in England he had arranged with Chatto & Windus for the English edition of *Life on the Mississippi* (JRO to MT, London, 2 September 1882).

[2] The composition of *Life on the Mississippi* had been difficult in spite of the River trip. In an undated fragment (TS in MTP), MT asked JRO to "set a cheap expert to work to collect local histories of Mississippi towns and a lot of other books relating to the river for me." On 22 July, W. Rowlands replied for JRO that they were mailing *Emerson's Magazine* with J. A. Dallas's "Up the Mississippi" and "a lot of books relating to travel in the U.S. by English people in the first half of this century; twenty-five volumes in all."

[3] JRO was anxious to begin work on the new volume; on 22 September he wrote:

Now we must go to work at once on the prospectus-books. For this purpose we need the title and a selection of pages including type and cuts. Also your preface, or such introductory or explanatory matter as you choose to prefix. We particularly need the title at once, that we may have the cover-stamp prepared. Anthony tells me that there are about 100 cuts ready, or nearly so, (about one-third of the whole number proposed) and that he will soon be needing more copy to go on with. Let me hear from you as soon as possible on these points, as we can make no progress until they are settled. . . .

[4] The *Gold Dust*, on which MT and JRO had ridden during their River trip, exploded while JRO was in England. Lem Gray was the pilot; see *Life on the Mississippi,* Chapter XXXVII.

129. To James R. Osgood

Hartford

18 October 1882

Dear Osgood—

I am sending Webster to talk with you. I would like him to take pretty full charge of the matter of running the book, if this will disadvantage you in no way.[1]

Please tell him about the man you spoke of. He can use him in Chicago, maybe.[2]

Ys Truly,

S. L. Clemens

[1] Though CLW had been a business manager and office boy for MT in a number of other enterprises, and had touched on matters of book manufacture when he wrestled with the American Publishing Company and experimented with Kaolatype for MT's books, this letter is the first step in CLW's eventual career as MT's publisher. The original plan was for CLW to become general agent for New York for JRO's subscription department; on 27 September, CLW told MT, "I talked the Agency matter over with Osgood; he told me to tell you that he liked the idea very much. . . . He said that I would have to get a better office near the book business." By January 1883, CLW was apparently supervising a number of sales details for the book (see the following letter). On 6 November, JRO wrote MT, "I told Webster last week that as soon as I heard from you indicating that there was not likely to be any delay in the publication of 'Life on the Mississippi' I should write to him and have him come on here. My idea was to arrange all the details of the working of the N.Y. office, and to plan a three weeks' expedition for Webster to the other centres of distribution, as a preliminary step to selecting and starting the general agencies. We are now all ready to do this, and I only await your information that the suggested revisions are not likely to cause delay." On the delay, see *MTHL,* p. 418.

[2] On 2 April 1881, JRO had written MT, "We have already received a letter from Hinckley, the Chicago man, and have replied to him that 'A Handbook of Etiquette' would be a trade-book, that the 'Cyclopaedia of Humor' would not be published for a considerable time . . . and that we shall have another book ready for subscription sale next autumn. Have asked him to state particulars as to territory covered by him, invited proposals and promised not to assign the territory until we have consulted thoroughly with him." Hinckley had been a bookkeeper for the American Publishing Company whom EB sent to Chicago to open a branch office in the 1870's. On 11 October, CLW wrote MT a long letter outlining Hinckley's advice:

> I have seen Hinckley. He has a list of about 500 agents that have sold your books; also another list of about seven thousand persons who have applied for agencies from all over the west. He has also about $600 worth of old books at 55% off. Most of them yours which he wants to get rid of. He says he will let us have all the old ones at 55% off and throw in his lists etc. at $250.00 extra *or:* he will take $500.00 for all his lists of agents and applicants for agencies with good will etc. and all papers relating to agency. . . .
>
> He thought that the business could not be run entirely at the N.Y. end even with his lists because most of his Western agents were poor men and could not pay for large batches of books at once, but had to take a few at a time C.O.D., that if we sent a few at a time C.O.D. from so long a distance as N.Y. the express charges would eat up the profits. He said they should be sent in large batches by freight to Chicago and then small lots C.O.D. to adjacent places would cost comparatively little. He thought we might work it to advantage if we had a small depot here for storage and a trusty man to send out the books

and we could do most of the correspondence and advertising in N.Y. but he thought it better to have a regular agency here though with his thunder he thought we might do a good business. . . .

He did not favor a long canvass of three months as a great many good agents were poor and could not live on nothing during the canvass. He thought a good many good agents would be lost if the canvass was so long, as they must have money to live on before. He said we could probably handle the large cities west from N.Y. but not the country towns where the poorer agents lived, they should get their goods at Chicago. . . .

. . . Now my conclusions are 1st if you run this office it will be necessary to have a depot for storage and distribution run by a good trusty man.

2nd It is important that we get a list of the agents that have been selling your books.

3d We must see by those lists, together with the lists of sales who are the best agents and retain only the good ones trying new men in place of the bad ones.

In that way we can probably run the thing from the other end. . . .

On 24 October, CLW acknowledged a check for $500 from MT to purchase Hinckley's list of agents.

130. To James R. Osgood

[Hartford]
[29 December 1882?] [1]

Dear Osgood—

I shipped all but "8th batch" to you last night.[2] Went to my copyist's house this morning to see what was the delay, and found she is laid up with the persistent enemy of this book, *scarlet fever.*

But they said my MS (8th batch) had been removed from her room and disinfected with carbollic acid as soon as the disease was determined. So I brought it away and expressed it to you. Enclosed find express receipt. Maybe you had better give it another good disinfecting before you meddle with it, or let your children get hold of it.

Will you telephone Fairchild that we are in quarantine, and say I am going to write and thank him for his invitation as soon as I get over the exhaustion of this ten days' revising and correcting?

Truly yrs

S L C

[1] The date is inferred from a statement in MT's letter of 15 January 1883 to George Washington Cable: "2½ weeks ago my secretary went home with scarlet fever" (*TG*, p. 89).

[2] In letters of 29 and 30 September, W. Rowlands acknowledged three shipments of manuscript: pp. 130–160, 161–212, and 213–238.

131. To James R. Osgood & Co.

Hartford
6 January 1883

Dear Sirs—

Yes, make two sets of the plates and dies, and print 50,000 copies of the book. Bliss usually issued with upwards of 40,000 orders, and only 20,000 books to supply them with.

In proof-reading I shall cause you no delay—but I don't answer for Mrs. Clemens, who has not edited the book yet, and will of course not let a line of the proof go from here till she has read it and possibly damned it. But she says she will put aside *everything* else, and give her entire time to the proofs.[1]

No, I don't want to read proof of the old Atlantic matter—but I want it read *almighty carefully* in Boston, and *no* improvements attempted.

We must give Webster all the thunder-and-lightning circulars and advertising enginery that is needful.[2] We must sell 100,000 copies of the book in 12 months, and shan't want him complaining that we are the parties in fault if the sale falls short of it.

When you have decided what to condemn in the last batches, run down here with it——no, I'll run up there; it might get lost in transitu.

Ys Truly

S. L. Clemens

Please send me ½ dozen White Elephants;
Also Japanese Legends:[3]

Also "Short Sayings of Great Men."

S L C

¹ Additional correspondence from MT about the proofreading of *Life on the Mississippi* is published in Caroline Ticknor's *Glimpses of Authors* (Boston, 1922), pp. 136–141.
² Although MT speaks as though CLW were in complete charge of the book, CLW's letter of 14 April 1883 suggests more accurately his relationship to the other ten General Agents in JRO's subscription machinery:
  In regard to the other General Agents, Osgood is running them. Most of my business with them lately has been, *furnishing them* with agents. I have sent them 186 names of agents in their territory and have received but about a dozen in return. However I guess they are doing well as Mr. Osgood says they are ordering books well and appears entirely satisfied.
³ E. H. House's volume.

132. To James R. Osgood

[Hartford]
15 January [1883]

[No salutation]
Old Man, you must glance through all the proof-slips (after Atlantic chapters) for about Baton Rouge and maybe in other places I have added footnotes and other stuff which you have not seen. I put in some Southern assassinations along there.

There will be 20 to 25,000 more words than necessary; so the scissors can be freely used. The whole family sick, here.

Yrs

Mark.

133. To James R. Osgood

[Hartford]
17 April 1883

Dear Osgood—
Nevertheless I am right. The big sale is always before issue—

after issue, the agents immediately load up the bookstores and canvassing ceases.[1]

March—21,585. *That's* all right; but the 17,635 under "Apl & May" *ought* to have been bound and delivered (not only) to the Am Pub Co *along with* the 21,585 in March—no, *before* March. *All* those 39,000 books were ordered *before* March 1—and mighty few were subscribed for *after* Mch 1.[2] You say "IF they had 40,000 orders on day of publication and didn't fill them for 3 months it was bad management." It ain't an IF—it is what happened.

The orders that come in after the ISSUE of a subscription book don't amount to a damn—just write that up amongst your moral maxims; for it is truer than nearly anything in the Bible.

As to the White Elephant, do as you and Charley prefer.

If I *should* go to New York, we'll take the same train and try the Shelburn. But the thing is uncertain and unguessable now, for if Mrs. Clemens continues to gain at *this* rate and no faster she will not be able to spare me from the sick room before Xmas.

Truly Yrs

S L C

[1] MT's oft-repeated maxim became the center of a dispute over *Life on the Mississippi* in which the humorist's logic was proved false. On 9 April 1883, CLW reported his inspection of the binder's statements for MT's American Publishing Company books: the statistics proved that "you are clearly wrong" in the idea that EB issued with an enormous canvass already completed. "I don't think you have cause to be disappointed, I think you will sell as many of the new book as of *any* you ever wrote *not excepting* Innocents, but it can't be done in a minute, but it *will* be done in the same time." In another letter on 14 April, CLW echoed Hinckley's advice: "I know that the great bulk of *my* sales will come after the book is out. Some of my agents can't commence canvassing until after it comes out, they can't live." MT obviously remained unconvinced, as the present letter proves; JRO replied on 18 April, "Perhaps you are correct: but I don't quite believe it. The sequel will show."

[2] Apparently MT refers to the bindery's records for the first three months' sale of *A Tramp Abroad:* MT's point is that there were advance orders for 40,000 copies which were not filled for over three months. This "revelation," together with his certainty that Frank Bliss was cheating him on royalties, led MT to have CLW examine his old contracts. In a letter of 23 April, CLW revealed that a clause in the Riley Diamond Mine book contract stipulated that "matters of difference as to the meaning, or private understanding of contracts heretofore

made between said parties are hereby settled and adjusted"; *A Tramp Abroad* would therefore be the only book over which MT might sue. But in addition, CLW noticed that all the contracts forbade the publication of other volumes by MT during the "preparation and *sale*" of the American Publishing Company volumes. Since the older books were still selling, "if these contracts were construed literally they clearly debar you from writing anything else as long as that Co. sees fit." Judiciously, CLW advised that "the less we bother the Amer. Pub. Co. the better off we are."

134. To JAMES R. OSGOOD

Hartford
21 December [1883]

Dear Osgood—

No, I shall not do or wittingly say anything to interrupt our friendly relations. I am sorry I made that remark, since it hurts you; but it was not new matter—it had been conveyed, before, through Webster.[1] And I said to Webster distinctly, "I will not have ill blood with Osgood, nor any but honest speech, plain but without bitterness—*State my case,*—leave the rest to Osgood and me."

In Boston I could not bring myself to talk. It was a festive occasion,[2] and not a proper time to discuss the failure of a book which could not have failed if you had listened to me.[3]

I am peculiarly situated. The Prince and Pauper and the Mississippi are the only books of mine which have ever failed. The first failure was not unbearable—but this second one is so nearly so that it is not a calming subject for me to talk upon. I am out $50,000 on this last book—that is to say, the sale which should have been 80,000 (seeing that the Canadians were for the first time out of competition,) is only 30,000.—

Now I did not want to say *anything* which could not be said through Webster, because I did not want to run the risk of saying or writing one word which might mar the pleasant relations existing between you and me. I have never for a moment doubted that you did the very best you knew how—it is impossible to doubt that—but there were things about the publishing of *my* books which you did not understand. You understand them now, but it is I who have paid the costs of the apprenticeship.

Damn that remark in that letter the other day, I did not want to make *any* remark. But it was based upon the fact—and it is unquestionably a fact—that the publisher who sells less than 50,000 copies of a book for me has merely injured me, he has not benefitted me. Legally one pays the same rate for an injury as for a benefit, but not morally. In the beginning, you may have contemplated the possibility of a sale which should fall short of 50,000; but I had had no experience of that kind and never once thought of it. I could not have engaged to pay any royalty at all on 30,000, and would not have engaged to pay much on 50,000 if the sale stopped at that.

If it is necessary that we talk together, and if it seems to you best, we will do it; but let us not write about it—for writings do not successfully interpret the feeling of the writer. My remark seemed sharp and unfriendly to you—consequently it lied, as to my feeling. Your reply closes sharp and bitter to me. It may have sounded a false note. If you will stop over here, any night, we will talk; and if bitter things are to be said, I will do my best to see that only you say them, and not I.

Truly Yours

S. L. Clemens

[1] On 8 December JRO had written:

Mr Webster has delivered me your message, which I must confess astonishes me. I cannot believe that on reflection you will confirm the attitude in which he represents you to stand at present.

We are deeply conscious of having done everything which anybody could have done for this book. We have worked harder over it and had more trouble and anxiety in connection with it than any book we ever had to do with. So far from being a source of undue profit to us, we have done the business at an unprecedentedly low commission. If it is a failure it is not due to lack of intelligent, conscientious and energetic effort on our part.

[2] MT was in Boston on 17 December; see *MTHL*, p. 454, and *MTBus*, pp. 229–230.

[3] MT's insistence that advance orders must reach 40,000 before the successful issue of a subscription book continued to be his main source of irritation at JRO, in spite of its patent illogic; indeed, it remained his cardinal publication rule (see

MTBus, pp. 248–249). But there were additional causes for complaint which can be deduced from CLW's letters to MT. CLW reported that the Cincinnati general agent, Forshee & McMackin, had flooded the trade market with books sent through the American Publishing Company (16 August 1883); on 31 August, MT replied, "Telegraph O. to cancel Cincinnati" (Webster, TS in MTP). The next month, CLW reported Douglass Brothers Agency in Philadelphia were also dumping in the trade (6 September 1883). On the other hand, CLW decided in October that books *ought* to be sold to the trade, appointed Watson Gill to sell to bookstores at less than $2 a copy, and advised MT to have JRO bind 14,000 copies of *Life on the Mississippi* in sheets in preparation for the avalanche of sales (25 and 30 October 1883). At about the same time, MT wrote in Notebook 17, May 1883—August 1884 (TS p. 25): "Tell O that dumping the b[ook?] means the end of the cvass.—therefore I wish can* to begin on the new one 1 month later—so let the dump fall Nov. 1."

135. To James R. Osgood

Hartford
17 January 1884

My Dear Osgood—

I have thought, and thought; and as a result, I wish to accept the kind offer which you made yesterday, if you are willing to let me.[1] I hope you can and will stop on your way up. I am not well content with myself over yesterday's talk, yet I do assure that I never *meant* to be unjust toward you in a single word or thought.

Truly Yours

S. L. Clemens

[1] The nature of the offer is obscure, but it probably involves the complete removal of JRO from the subscription selling of MT's books. At first the plan was apparently to assimilate CLW into JRO's company, for JRO wrote, "I understand we are fully agreed as to the policy of giving up the present office and organization in N.Y." for which JRO was paying a portion of the rent (JRO to CLW, 4 February 1884, Webster, TS in MTP). On 2 February, however, JRO wrote MT a letter to which he received only a telegram for reply: "Charley is equipped with full authority and also with amplest possible instructions" (JRO to CLW, 4 February 1884, Webster, TS in MTP). In addition, there was some sort of arrangement about the publication of *Huckleberry Finn*. In his 4 February letter to CLW, JRO announced, "We therefore await the receipt of any proposition you may have to make regarding the new book," and on 21 March, he wrote MT, "In a note just received from Chatto & Windus they write 'Please

give us early information of the progress of Mark Twain's Huckleberry Finn.' Shall I reply to this, and if so, how?" Finally, CLW told MT, "I talked about his [JRO's] *imprint* being in the book over mine and told him that we were likely to publish it ourselves" (New York, 5 February 1884).

136. To James R. Osgood

Hartford
20 March 1884

My Dear Osgood—

I received the $5,000, added a like amount and paid off that old endorsement (total loss, shan't get back a cent of it—and shan't play with endorsements any more for pastime.) [1] I have no further present pressures; so I don't doubt that the acceptances will answer every purpose. [2]

Yes, *do* fix that prize business; [3] and apply crucial tests to any individual who claims to have sold 400 copies. Privately, I don't believe any individual did sell that many, but of course I don't know. As to that 900-claim—well, you can be very sure that *that* requires a rigid scrutiny; and you can be about as sure, too, that it won't survive that scrutiny.

Publicly, I'm confined to the house with rheumatism; but under the holy seal of secrecy I reveal to you that it is *gout*. I suppose this comes of high living when I was a boy—corn-dodgers and catfish.

Ys Truly

S L C

[1] The reference is unidentifiable; it may involve the clearing up of accounts for *Life on the Mississippi*, which was taking place in March 1884 (see *MTBus*, pp. 243–246). On 18 March, JRO had written, "I have been in N.Y. since Saturday, and your letter asking for $5000. was enclosed here to me with other letters by my brother, who tells me he has forwarded check to you. We have rendered a detailed statement of the whole a/c to Webster, and he is coming over to Boston early next week to look into a few items which he does not understand, and we shall then arrive at an exact balance."

[2] In Notebook 17, May 1883 to August 1884, MT wrote (TS p. 26):
About middle October, '83, Osgood owed me $33,250.
Paid me $5,000 by check.

Gave me acceptances at 3 months from Oct 15, for $5,000, $10,000, and $5,000 ($20,000).

Leaving $8,250 unprovided for.

On 22 April, MT asked CLW if the acceptances had arrived (*MTBus,* p. 250); and on 10 June, CLW reported that JRO had "sent me their note for $6,844.65 Four months. The balance they owe is 6749.66 and the extra $134.99 is interest for 4 mos. which they have added making $6,884.65. They said that they needed money and that Bissell would discount it if we needed it."

3 MT had apparently endorsed the idea of prizes for agents selling the most copies of *Life on the Mississippi* (see *MTBus,* p. 207). JRO replied to the present letter on 21 March, "Webster is going over that prize question when he comes."

137. To James R. Osgood

[Hartford]
24 May 1884

My Dear Osgood—

The left-over sketches received.[1]

I have mailed you a 1601; but mind, if it is for a lady you are to assume the authorship of it yourself.

I have invented a new game of billiards, and I want you to stop over with us, next time you are passing Hartford, and try it on. It is meaner than cushion caroms—a good deal meaner.

Truly Yours,

S. L. Clemens

1 MT's last extant business letter to JRO acknowledges receipt, apparently, of those items left out of *The Stolen White Elephant* (see letter 123 above). Nor are there any extant letters from JRO to MT after this date, excepting a receipt for $3,000 "for all our rights in sundry contracts this day assigned" (5 February 1885). Nevertheless, even though business correspondence came to an abrupt halt, the two men remained on friendly personal terms (see *MTHL,* p. 510, and Weber, pp. 226, 244).

IV

"I Am Webster & Co., Myself"

(1884-1887)

"I am Webster & Co., myself, substantially."
Mark Twain to the Editor of the *Herald,* Elmira, 6 July
1885 (MTP)

W HEN Charles L. Webster replaced Osgood as Mark
Twain's publisher (and undertook as well the jobs of handy man,
errand boy, and private investigator), Webster was for some time
too busy chasing wild geese to worry about publishing books. He
was searching for actors to perform in "Colonel Sellers as a
Scientist," making contracts for an abortive comic almanac, worrying about lawsuits, and trying to clear up affairs with James R.
Osgood & Company. Webster and Mark Twain had executed some
kind of informal agreement concerning the publication of *Huckleberry Finn* on 1 May 1884, to which Webster referred in a letter
of 5 April: He "had Whitford draw . . . a contract between us."
And on 8 March and 5 April 1884, he wrote Mark Twain about
bindings and illustrations for the novel.

By mid-1885, Charles Webster was a full-fledged publisher, and
a more formal contract of partnership (labeled "No. 2") was drawn
on 20 March. In it, the humorist agreed to advance "all capital
necessary to conduct and carry on the said business." Webster

169

received a salary of $2,500 annually, plus one-third of all net profits to the amount of $20,000 and one tenth of the profits after that. (He was prevented, however, from removing more than a fraction of the $20,000 from the Company.) Mark Twain received a 70 percent royalty on new books and 60 percent on old ones bought from Osgood. He received an 8 percent interest on the capital he advanced; and he received two-thirds of net profits until Webster had earned $20,000, and nine-tenths after that. Finally, both partners had to agree on book contracts.

The mechanics of printing and selling volumes appealed to Mark Twain less than the glamorous adventure of "capturing" them. When Kate Field wrote him about possible interest in a book exposing Mormonism, Mark Twain's answer was almost plaintive:

> I should be very far from unwilling to publish such a book in case my business decks were clear. They are not clear now, however, and it is hard to tell when they will be. They are piled up with contracts which two or three years—and possibly four—will be required to fulfil. I have even had to rule myself out, and am now an author without a publisher. My book is finished and ready, and I have spent nearly ten thousand dollars in its preparation; but it is pigeon-holed indefinitely, to make room for other people's more important books. (In this line of business we generally publish only one—and never more than two—books in a year.) I think I could write a very good moral fable about an author who turned publisher in order to get a better show, and got shut up entirely. (Lilian Whiting, *Kate Field* [Boston, 1899], pp. 446–449.)

Nevertheless, he continued to insist "we must have that book" on literally dozens of occasions.

Because of the Grant *Memoirs* and *Huckleberry Finn* (and not because of any of the other books Mark Twain felt he "must have") the Company prospered. It prospered to such an extent, in fact, that Webster somehow persuaded Mark Twain to revise the one-sided copartnership No. 2. On 21 January 1886, an amendment ("No. 3"?) gave Webster the right to withdraw more of his share of the profits (except on the Grant volume), raised his salary to $3,000, and lowered the interest rate on Mark Twain's capital from 8 to 6 percent.

As affairs became more and more complex, and Charles L. Webster's duties took him to Rome to interview the Pope, Webster's assistant began to assume more duties—among them, that of Mark Twain's correspondent. Fred J. Hall began as a stenographer for the Company—it was he who transcribed some of General Grant's dictations for the second volume of the *Memoirs*. On 28 April 1886, another "Articles of Copartnership" ("No. 4") was signed: "In consideration of the premises and of the sum of one dollar ($1), by each party paid to the other," Hall was made a copartner. He was to receive $1,500 annual salary and one-twentieth of all the firm's net profits except those from Grant's volumes, after which Twain and Webster would divide the remainder on the formula of the earlier contracts. Hall agreed that in the absence of Webster, he was "to have the entire active management and control of said business."

During late 1886 and 1887, Mark Twain's letters were more and more often addressed to Hall, in part because the author was already dissatisfied with Webster's decisions and attitudes (letters 176 and 182 below) and in part because Webster's health was declining. In 1887, Twain made a codicil limiting his financial responsibility to the Company (letter 187 below), and showed considerable coolness in having to share with Webster the losses arising from an embezzlement of funds by a bookkeeper named Frank Scott (*MTBus*, pp. 389–390).

By the end of 1887, the vast and elaborate subscription house which Webster had organized was completely in the hands of Mark Twain and Fred Hall.

138. To Charles L. Webster

[Hartford]
29 February 1884

Dear Charley—

Let us canvass Huck Finn and Tom Sawyer both at once, selling both books for $4.50 where a man orders both, and arranging with the Pub Co that I shall have half the profit on all Sawyers so sold, and also upon all that *they* sell while our canvass lasts.

Also, canvass Finn, Sawyer and Prince all at once—a reduced price where a man orders the three.[1]

It's a good idea—*don't forget to arrange for it.*

Yrs

S L C

P.S. I have put in my whole time, yesterday and today (and shall for several more days,) writing original matter for Prang's calendar.[2] Besides other stuff, I have written special squibs for 10 of the months and all the national holidays. My time is worth from $100 to $500 a day, according to what I am doing.

Now then, it would be unfortunate to do all this work and then have eventual trouble and misunderstanding. So you'd better look very carefully into that contract. If Prang is going to have but one price for the calendar, and that price a dollar, it is all right—10 cents to me is correct. But don't you think there ought to be a clause saying that *if* he should conclude to charge any higher price for any or all of them, my royalty in that case shall be 10 *per cent?*

It isn't the amount of extra money involved that is bothering me particularly—it is the dread of a loose, unclear contract. Carefully look into the thing and get it just right.

S L C

¹ CLW replied on 1 March, "Your idea about the three books is certainly good," but ultimately the American Publishing Company declined to cooperate (see letter 144 below).

² As CLW had explained in his letter of 6 February, "I have made an agreement with Prang & Co. whereby they pay for the manufacture of the almanac, and give you 10% on the retail price of each copy sold; they to compile it from your old books and you to edit the same if you wish." The notion of calendar epigrams died (to be revived in "Pudd'nhead Wilson's Calendar") when Prang wrote CLW on 4 March 1884, "We are afraid that Mr. Clemens's writings are not adapted for this purpose, and that we shall have to give up the idea, unless indeed the Author would make up the deficiency which can hardly be hoped for."

139. To Charles L. Webster

[Hartford]
14 April 1884

Dear Charley—

Keep it diligently in mind that we don't issue till we have made a *big sale*.¹ Bliss never issued with less than 43,000 orders on hand, except in one instance—and it usually took him 5 or 6 months' canvassing to get them.

Get at your canvassing early, and drive it with all your might, with the intent and purpose of issuing on the 10th (or 15th) of next December (the best time in the year to tumble a big pile into the trade)—but if we haven't 40,000 orders then, we simply postpone publication till we've *got* them. It is a plain, simple policy, and would have saved both of my last books if it had been followed. There is not going to be any reason whatever, why this book should not succeed—and it shall and *must*.

If we make any change, it must be simply a change from 40,000 to 50,000 before issuing. The Tramp issued with 48,000.

Be particular and don't get any of that *old* matter into your canvassing book—(the *raft* episode.)

Yrs

S L C

Susie has invented a musical game [2] which we may perhaps publish, anonymously.

I think we'll publish "1002," [3] anonymously, in a 15 or 20 cent form, right after Huck.

S L C

[1] *Huckleberry Finn.*

[2] No further indications of this invention of MT's daughter are extant.

[3] See *MTW*, pp. 59–60, for a discussion of "1002," a final Arabian Nights' tale.

140. To CHARLES L. WEBSTER

[Hartford]
7 May 1884

Dear Charley—

I returned the book-back.[1] All right and good, and will answer; although the boy's mouth is a trifle more Irishy than necessary.[2]

Did you say paper had been offered you at 7¢ which you could hardly tell from 8¢ paper—or to that effect? [3] If so, why not take it?

I've got some business to talk with you—notion to print a very small book for railway circulation.[4]

You might come here a day before you are due at Crown Point,[5] and go from here there *via* Springfield and Albany, perhaps.

Ys

S L C

[1] The cover design for *Huckleberry Finn,* which CLW had sent on 5 May.

[2] After choosing E. W. Kemble to illustrate the novel for $1200 instead of a cheaper artist named Hooper (CLW to MT, 3, 5 April 1884), the publisher had to soothe the humorist's dissatisfaction and persuade the artist to rework many illustrations: on 23 May he sent MT seventeen drawings "which are much better than the last. . . . Kemble has fixed the last lot so that they are all right." On 29 May, he promised, "In regard to Kemble's pictures, I think they will come out all right. . . . However, I shall not relax my efforts to get better work out of Kemble." See also, *MTBus,* pp. 255–256, 260.

[3] CLW replied on 12 May, "I can get the same [paper] as was put into the

Miss. which cost 8¼ cents, for 7¾¢, and a fair quality for 7½ cents, but I am going to try the mills and can possibly get a better grade."

[4] Probably "1002," mentioned in the previous letter. Throughout the first half of 1884, CLW reported to MT his unsuccessful negotiations with the American News Company (31 May) and the Union News Company (4 June), both of whom declined to discuss the possibility of a twenty-five cent railroad book without seeing a sample of the book. CLW proposed a book consisting of 25,000 words: "By setting it in Pica and printing it on cheap but *thick* paper we can get in 150 pages with say ten illustrations, and then make the book as *thick* as one of Funk & Wagnalls 25¢ books that contain 225 pages and no pictures." Finally, on 6 June, MT wrote, "The cheap book is given up—but keep your figures, we might need them another time" (*MTBus,* p. 258).

[5] MT owned stock in the Crown Point Iron Company, which he was apparently trying to sell, and CLW went to a reorganization meeting as MT's proxy on 14 May 1884. On 22 May, he reported, "The Crown Pt. trip did no good. They turned out Gen. Hammond as Pres. and elected the old directors, and also elected the same supt. The stock would not sell at any price. They said it might come up a little in time, but everyone on both sides had all they wanted."

141. To Charles L. Webster

Hartford
23 May 1884

Dear Charley—

Accept Raymond's offer.[1]

The paper bargain is splendid—and also the bargains for binding.[2]

I am mortal glad to hear you have got everything squared up with Osgood.[3]

Order 30,000 copies of Huck Finn to be printed and bound.[4] The same to be paid for in cash on delivery.

Of course get into the contract as good terms as you can for subsequent editions to consist of 2,000 or 3,000 or 5,000 each.

Begin your canvass early, and *drive* it; for if, by the 5th of December, we have 40,000 orders, we will publish on the 15th, and "dump" books the same day and catch the holiday trade. Otherwise we will continue the canvass till we strike the full figure of 40,000 orders.

Now let's never allow ourselves to *think* of issuing with any *less* than 40,000 while there's the ghost of a show to get them.

Did you get from Osgood the sketches that were crowded out of the White Elephant?[5]

Yrs

S L C

---

[1] John T. Raymond had offered to play "Colonel Sellers as a Scientist" in one-night stands from which the total receipts would be "three or four hundred dollars—and to pay a royalty of one hundred dollars would leave me on the wrong side of the ledger" (*MTBus*, pp. 253–254). He had made an alternative offer, the details of which are unknown (*ibid.*). On 1 September, CLW relayed to MT some of Raymond's misgivings: "He don't like the English Earldom idea, nor . . . the idea of materialization of dead bodies. . . . He would like to have some of Sellers schemes,—say the fire extinguisher—succeed, and have Sellers become suddenly very rich." Raymond decided the play would not be successful and withdrew his offer.

[2] On 22 May, CLW reported that by having "two mills bidding against each other *strong*," he had procured paper for 6 87/100 cents: "I have agreed to take 900 reams which will cost $4,018.95, and this amt will make 30,000 books and 1,000 prospectuses." The contracts for bindings were better than JRO's: "The binding of P. & P. and the new book is the same, but while their binding costs: sheep, 55 cents, mine cost 35 cents, or *20 cents* per book *less*. Their Half Mor. cost 70 cents, mine 60 cents. Their cloth 22 cents. I have not let that contract yet, but have one bid of 20 cents. These prices of theirs are without wrapping &c, while wrapping *is included* in my prices, which makes another difference in my favor." On 29 May, he reported accepting a 17½ cent bid for cloth bindings.

[3] MT apparently refers only to CLW's statement in his letter of 22 May, "In regard to Osgoods, . . . we agreed on a basis of settlement and they have promised to send me a statement of balance this week." Affairs were, in fact, far from settled.

[4] CLW had written on 22 May, "How many cloth books shall I contract to bind at 20¢ or less? How many books shall I print in sheets?"

[5] See letter 137 above. On 2 July, MT claimed JRO had not returned illustrations for "1002" or all of the "left-over" material from *The Stolen White Elephant* (*MTBus*, pp. 263–264).

---

142. To Charles L. Webster

[Hartford]

18 July 1884

Dear Charley—

When you strike something which you want to *recommend* that we tackle, go ahead and recommend it and give your reasons. But a mere blind conundrum, without either recommendations or reasons, is a sort of thing which I don't want the bother of trying to answer.

Now in the matter of that campaign book,—which is *business*, pure and simple, and clear out of my line—you just work out the answer yourself, and then tell me what it is, if favorable.[1] I am not finding fault, I am merely establishing a judicious and useful rule, for the future.

Ys Truly

S. L. C.

[1] This letter was prompted by CLW's letter of 10 July:
Hubbard Bros. have a campaign book, "Blaine and Logan," a book of about 400 pages, and perhaps 50 cuts, very well gotten up. It to retail @ $2.00, and they sell it for 62½% off for *cash*.
    There is one objection; they grant free territory to everyone, so that it is impossible to tell what ground has been worked. Do you think it worth our while to take hold of it, or do you think it would clash with our book this fall?
On 15 July, CLW told MT, "I have given up the Blaine book, as it will . . . interfere somewhat with the canvass of the new book."

143. To Charles L. Webster & Co.

[Elmira?]

[August 1884?] [1]

[No Salutation]
    C L Webster & Co
_____
    Publishers of Mark Twain's later works, viz:
The Adventures of Huckleberry Finn———
The Prince and the Pauper———
Life on the Mississippi———
The White Elephant & Other Sketches

By an arrangement with the American Publishing Co. of Hartford, we are enabled to furnish Mark Twain's earlier works upon the same terms granted to the customer by that house. These books are—

The Innocents Abroad
Roughing It
Sketches, Old & New
Adventures of Tom Sawyer
The Gilded Age
·A Tramp Abroad

Orders taken for all or any of the ten books.

Don't you need some such circular, Charley?
We want to *canvass* those old books (all the 10) and keep them driving.

N. B. We want the Century's warbook—keep on the best of terms with those folks.[2]

SLC

---

[1] This letter was obviously written before the one immediately following, which drops the plan to canvass the American Publishing Company imprints along with *Huckleberry Finn.*

[2] *The Century* was running a series, "Battles and Leaders of the Civil War," to which Grant contributed three articles. MT persisted in being interested in publishing *The Century's* collection (see letter 148 below), and it may well have been the first spark of inspiration for the Grant volume. The collection was published in book form by *The Century* in four volumes, edited by Robert U. Johnson and Clarence C. Buel, in 1887–1888.

144. To CHARLES L. WEBSTER

Elmira
1 September 1884

Dear Charley:
That question appears to answer itself: if the Am. Pub. Co. will not give you terms on Tom Sawyer which will afford you a profit, does not that end the project?[1]

When you send me pirate ads ² which are calculated to enrage me, I wish you would also send me a form for a letter to the Am. Pub. Co to fit the case. You lay me liable to make trouble under a sudden and frantic impulse when there is no occasion for it. Besides, the episode unfits me for work for a week afterward. I have lost $3,000 worth of time over this pirate business, and I do not see where any good has been done, unless the erection of a quarrel with the Pub. Co can come under that head.

If you would *help* me get along with the Pub Co. we could doubtless manage them to our advantage; but I have no diplomacy in my own nature, and you don't suggest any to me. Try to remember that I fly off the handle altogether too easily, and that you want to think twice before you send me irritating news.

As to the prizes,³ you can think that out and decide upon it much better than I can. It is not my function to help arrive at conclusions in business matters. The thing should not be submitted to me except in a completed and determined form—then my function comes in: and it is merely and solely to *approve* or *disapprove*.

This is the first summer which I have lost. I haven't a paragraph to show for my 3-months' working-season. But there was no help for it—been in the doctor's hands the greater part of the time.

I have foolishly gone so far with the Am Pub Co that I must now go on, if Whitford thinks it a winning case—which he won't.⁴

We shall reach our hotel the evening of Sept. 16. And thenceforward we can *meet* when there is business to be discussed —it is the only good way.

Ys truly

S L C

Do not imagine from anything in this, that I misappreciate you. No, I am at loggerheads with *myself*.

---

¹ Frank Bliss proposed terms so difficult that it was impossible to bring the plan mentioned in letter 138 to fruition. CLW explained that "It seems impossible to make any arrangement whereby the other Gen. Agts. can sell 'Huck Finn' and

'Tom Sawyer' together, at a reduced price, as in order to do so they must have 'Tom Sawyer' billed to them at 60% off at the very *least*. The American Pub. Co. won't bill them to *me* for a cent less than that, so that taking freights, etc out, I would lose money to bill them to Gen. Agts at 60%" (30 August 1884).

² On 23 August, CLW had written, "The enclosed advertisement appeared in *today's* Frank Leslie's Illustrated Newspaper. Something must be done about it soon." On the envelope, MT wrote "Alabama Pirates." The Frank Coker News Company of Talladega had first published an advertisement for MT's books in the New York *World* in June (*MTBus*, pp. 261–262); it continued to appear until February 1885 (*ibid.*, pp. 264, 286, 304) in spite of MT's threats to sue Bliss for not protecting his copyrights (*ibid.*, p. 262).

³ In his letter of 30 August, CLW included a schedule of "prizes," whereby any agent selling 50 copies or more received five free copies for every fifty sold. CLW asked, "If you think the above too high a premium let me know. . . . Possibly we might strike out the prize for 50 copies, and make the first one for 100."

⁴ On 3 September, CLW advised MT, "It is undoubtedly your business to protect those [books] you have the copyrights for. Alexander & Green will look into the matter and sue the pirates if there is any remedy. Your case against the Pub. Co. is, as yet, weak."

145. To Charles L. Webster

Janesville
19 January 1885

Dear Charley—

No, it is *business*—and so I don't want anything to do with it.¹ You are there to take care of my business, not make business for *me* to take care of. Your security is perfect, but I want no business that I must look personally after. That is my objection—I have no other.

I don't wish to buy Osgood out,² but you might, if you want to. It might possibly be a better thing than buying the 3-story house,³ good as that doubtless is.

When we get Osgood's Jan. statement—if you ever get it out of him—it will probably show that the books (in *his* hands) are worth, for the 3 years yet to run, from $40 to $60 apiece. You might offer him a lump sum of $150 for his ownership in the 3. For his ownership in the Library of Humor you could venture to offer but little, for he produces and runs the book, and gets but 30 per cent of the profit—and there'll be a *hell* of a profit, of course, in *his* hands.

I am very tired, from much RR travel today.

When are Osgood and Am Pub Co and Slote going to show their Jan. statements? [4]

Yrs

S L C

You say not a word about that Bromfield and Rice business.[5]

---

[1] This outburst was prompted by CLW's outlining a business proposition for the patent bed clamp (see *MTBus*, pp. 279–280, 284, 291) in a letter of 10 January 1885: The "bed clamp man" would receive a salary of $1,000 annually; costs were then to be repaid; MT's advance repaid; and net profits divided half-and-half.

[2] On 17 January, CLW forwarded JRO's letter of 16 January, offering to sell rights in all MT's books, not only the *Library of Humor* for which CLW had been negotiating. On 5 February, CLW purchased JRO's rights for $3,000.

[3] CLW purchased a "three story brown stone house on 126th St just off of 6th Avenue, one of the best locations in the upper city" and asked to borrow $4,500 from MT to help finance it (17 January). The following letter includes MT's counter-propositions.

[4] On 19 January, CLW replied that JRO's "sales were so small that he did not think it worth while to make out a statement." Slote had just sent a check for $240.24, and Bliss had just sent his statement and a check for $1,138.54.

[5] During CLW's absence from the office, a clerk named Bromfield had given Thorndike Rice Chapter XXI of *Huckleberry Finn* for consideration for publication in the *North American Review*. CLW sent Rice a bill for $200, and the price was apparently too high. In addition, CLW offered the opinion that "too much [of *Huckleberry Finn*] is being printed and am not in favor of giving it out in this way" (9 January). See also *MTBus*, pp. 290–292.

146. To CHARLES L. WEBSTER

Minneapolis
25 January 1885

Dear Charley—

Even $2 is much too low for the bed-clamp.—If I go into it eventually, it must be at $2.25 each for small size, and $3 for the large.[1] There is no money in the thing at any cheaper rate.[2] You didn't give me the main item: What do the annual *receipts* at present reach?

I want nothing to do with business myself, and so I do not wish to lend money which *I* must keep track of; but I'd just as soon write J Langdon & Co to lend you $4,500 on those securities as not. They will do it. Shall I write them? Or, shall I *buy* $4,500-worth of the house at the price you paid, and thus own that proportion of the property myself? If that suits you, draw that amount from C L Webster & Co and make out and send to Livy the necessary papers —for I should want my share of the house to be in her name.

If you should come across another dog-cheap house, I will buy *with* you—but I don't wish to buy alone.[3]

Make Osgood furnish us his Jan *statement*. On that and other data you will know how to offer him *little* enough for the Library and my other books. We can strike up a trade with him yet, I guess.

Osgood has only 12,000 Mississippi's left? Then 6,000 have been sold since our last settlement I judge.

If we *can* only get a twist on the Am Pub Co![4]

As to *terms*,[5] you and I will go and call on Bliss when I return, and see if he will lie to *me* as he has done to you.

I ought to have staid at home and written another book. It pays better than the platform.[6]

Yrs

S L C

[1] On 19 January, CLW explained that "the bed clamp man" "thinks it would not do to ask over $1.75 for the crib size, or $2.00 for the bed size."

[2] CLW was of the sounder opinion that there was no money in the bed clamp at any price: "You haven't asked my opinion, but I will say; I have no doubt that it will prove a failure. It is so entirely foreign to our business that I think it unwise to go into it" (19 January).

[3] On 21 January, CLW reported "a splendid chance to buy another house the other day," and MT apparently could not resist the speculation. But in his letter of 30 January, CLW advised he had "obtained the money [the $4,500] elsewhere" and did not wish to share the investment in his home with MT. "However," he added, "if I see another chance to buy a cheap house as an *investment,* I will let you know."

[4] In the 21 January letter, CLW mused, "If I could only get your old books from the American—and thus you get all the profits. . . . Your books are a mine to the American their only source of life, and they make vastly more than you. On Innocents Abroad you make 17½ cents for every copy sold and they make 72½ cents. . . . They played a sharp game on you in the start and must have made several fortunes and are still reaping golden results, and if there is any way to get hold of them I believe in doing it."

[5] In the same letter, CLW accused Bliss of falsely representing his situation in the arrangement proposed in letter 143 above. By CLW's figuring, the American Publishing Company was offering him only a 60 percent discount on the prices of MT's books, but giving more than that to his own general agents.

[6] MT was in the midst of his 1884–1885 lecture tour with George Washington Cable.

147. To Charles L. Webster

Columbus
10 February 1885

Dear Charley—

Glad to be rid of Osgood.[1]

I am not able to see that anything can save Huck Finn from being another defeat, unless you are expecting to do it by tumbling books into the trade, and I suppose you are not calculating upon any sale there worth speaking of, since you are not binding much of an edition of the book.[2]

As to notices, I suggest this plan: Send immediately, copies (bound and unbound) to the Evening Post, Sun, World, and the Nation; the Hartford Courant, Post and Times; and the principal Boston dailies; Baltimore American. (*Never* send any to N.Y. Graphic.)

Keep a sharp lookout, and if the general tone of the resulting notices is *favorable,* then send out your 300 press copies over the land, for that may *possibly* float a further canvass and at least create a bookstore demand. No use to wait for the magazines [3]—how in *hell* we overlooked that unspeakably important detail, utterly beats my time. We have not even arranged to get English notices from Chatto and shove *them* into the papers ahead of our publication.

Yrs truly

S L C

[1] After pointing out "it would be folly for me to buy the book [the *Library of Humor*] of Osgood as you suggest, for, on reading the contract I see that Osgood is to furnish the capital for its manufacture and sale" (23 January), CLW reported the purchase of all MT's rights in his letter of 7 February: "I think this is a splendid bargain for you as you can now control your own books."

² On 23 January, CLW had requested $5,000 to pay for binding 20,000 cloth, 2,500 sheep, and 500 half-morocco copies of *Huckleberry Finn* and 500 prospectuses. On 4 February, CLW answered the present letter: "I am not going to fall into Osgood's mistake and have 15000 copies on hand unsold. I have my paper ready and 30,000 printed and can bind 5000 copies in a *week* if I wish."

³ On 7 February, CLW pointed out that Richard Watson Gilder could not review *Huckleberry Finn* in the March *Century* and "says it will be a hard squeeze to get it in April no. and would not promise me." For CLW's reply about other press notices, see *MTBus,* p. 303 and *MT&HF,* p. 368.

148. To Charles L. Webster

Hartford
16 March 1885

Dear Charley—

Your news is splendid. Huck certainly *is* a success,¹ and from the standpoint of my own requirement. This result sets my fears about at rest as regards the General's book.² It *insures* a sudden sale of 250,000 copies of the first volume.

Pity but that first volume were *completed.*³ As I understand it, it lacks 2 or 3 chapters. Well, if the lack is at the *end* of the volume, we will end the volume *without* them; if they are to be supplied by another hand, they may begin the 2d vol., not mar the 1st, which must be *all* General Grant, if possible.

Keep on good terms with the Century people.⁴ We will presently prove to them that they can't *afford* to publish their war book themselves—we must have it.

Livy told me the other day that she wished to warn you against overwork. Your letter shows that you need such a warning. So I warn you myself to look out for that—overwork killed Mr. Langdon, and it can kill you. . . .

Yrs

S L C

P.S. Your scheme for filling special orders at our office for the General's book, and thus getting the commissions extra is good.⁵ Don't forget to reserve that right.

¹ On 14 March, CLW had written, "I have *sold* 39,000 books," and detailed the fact that none of MT's earlier books had reached that sale in so short a time.

² On 28 November 1884, CLW first wrote MT about General Grant's *Personal Memoirs,* then running serially in *The Century:* "Col Fred Grant writes that he will see you on the subject of his father['s] new book at any time." On 6 December, CLW told MT he had offered General Grant $50,000 "and have not heard from him since." On 3 February 1885, CLW made an alternative offer of 70 percent of the net profits (CLW to U. S. Grant, 3 February 1885, TS in MTP). MT thought "it would be a grand thing if we could get the General's book on those terms" (*MTBus,* p. 299) though much later, in 1887, when the Grant family accused CLW of falsifying accounts, MT remembered vindictively that he had suggested a flat fee of $500,000 for Mrs. Grant (Notebook 22, September 1887 to September 1888, TS p. 10). The General's family apparently approved CLW's offer, too, for on 25 February CLW persuaded MT to amend their copartnership again because "we have now entered upon the publication of a book that will call for an additional expenditure of time and money, and its success will be largely due to my personal efforts."

³ Grant's perilous health endangered the completion of the book and prompted rumors in newspapers that it was being ghostwritten by General Adam Badeau (see *MTBus,* pp. 319–320). On 22 April, CLW voiced the belief that "Genl. Grant will yet write that second volume." And he provided MT with frequent progress reports on the accumulation of manuscript: "I have obtained the first 313 pages of manuscript which brings us up to Shiloh" (22 April); "We have Appomatox *complete*" (2 May); "We got about 20 pages today" (14 May); and, finally, "I have all of the first volume in type and . . . the second volume. . . is now finished" (22 July).

⁴ *The Century* was miffed because it assumed the right to book publication of the Grant material in the *Battles and Leaders* volume after its appearance in the magazine. On 22 April, however, CLW reported, "All matters with the Century Co. are satisfactory and pleasant. . . . All future articles in the Century will have this footnote 'Personal Memoirs of U. S. Grant,' and Copyright 1885, by U. S. Grant." In return CLW had offered "not to publish first vol before Dec. 1st next, and second vol before Mch. 1st next giving them three months notice" (CLW to MT, 15 April).

⁵ On 5 March, CLW had written about his scheme to "Reserve the right to fill all subscriptions made by letter or otherwise to the N.Y. office, at the *full* retail price."

149. To Charles L. Webster

Hartford
4 April 1885

Dear Charley—

Now the dam typesetter is in lucrative shape at last—provided Pa[i]ge signs the papers to-day, as he promises.¹ It is in perfect working order (the machine is,) and stands ready and willing to submit itself to any test an expert chooses to apply. A new and valuable addition has been made to it, too—viz: a *type-tester,* which permits no type to enter the machine (while distributing) without its *strength* being tested by the application to it of six times as much impact as it will afterwards get in the machine. If it breaks, the tester throws it out. Formerly there was danger of a type breaking in the machine and causing damage, delay and expense.

The new terms: Pa[i]ge sells the whole thing *outright* (including future improvements), to Wm. Hamersley,[2] for $350,000 cash and a royalty of $500 on each machine manufactured (or sold, whichever it is,) Pa[i]ge reserving foreign countries. Formerly Pa[i]ge was to sell us only the right to make 1000 machines —now the number is unlimited. Formerly it was estimated that each machine would cost $1600; now only $1000. Formerly it was proposed to sell them at $5000 each; that is still the idea; and Hamersley says the head man of the Herald will stock his office with them at that price—said he would do it.

Pa[i]ge engages to furnish working models for 8 different sizes; also—for wages hereafter to be determined, he will personally superintend the construction of the first 400, if the new Co shall desire it.

It is estimated that 400 will cost $400,000, the plant $800,000, Pa[i]ge's $350,000, his royalties $200,000. Total, $1,750,000, and the plant will *remain*—$800,000.

Hamersley's proposal to me, is, that I sell the thing out to a Co who will give *him* $250,000 and *me* $250,000 of the new stock (or a sum in cash, or a bully royalty, whichever the Co shall prefer;) that the Co also pay to Pa[i]ge $350,000 cash, of course. Thinks said Co should have a capital of $2,000,000 and give him and me a fourth between us in paid-up stock; or have a capital of $1,500,000 and give us some cash or a royalty.

Hamersley is going West for 3 weeks, but will send you a copy of the Pa[i]ge contract when completed, and will try to see you for an hour, about next Friday, on his way West.

I'd rather have $250,000 in non-assessable stock than $100,000 *cash.*

Then you can sail in again, with the experts and capitalists, and start a new trade with them; and this time the thing will doubtless be a success, and with a better margin for profit than before.

Bank book received—they didn't notice how I spell my name. How many books sold? [3]

Yrs.

S L C

[1] MT had been investing in the Paige typesetter since 1881. On 9 December 1881, Pamela Moffett told her son Sam that the Kaolatype "is very small indeed, compared to another enterprise Sam has set Charley to work on. This is some new invention. They want to start with a capital of five hundred thousand dollars, a stock company. Charley took a lot of prominent men to Hartford the other day to examine the machines." In late 1881 and in 1883, CLW did serve as a general supervisor of MT's interests in the typesetter (*MTBus*, pp. 171–173, 211–213); and on 31 December 1884, he had reported to MT a proposal from W. A. Paton, an investor in the typesetter, to reorganize the company with $1,000,000 of stock and to pay Paige $10,000 a year for ten years. The present letter is the first one extant in which MT intruded typesetter affairs upon CLW *after* the publishing company was fully launched and a full-time concern. See *MTBus*, pp. 330–331, for another 1885 letter.

[2] William Hamersley was the Hartford City Attorney and a principal stockholder in the Paige typesetter.

[3] On 24 March, CLW had reported a total sale for *Huckleberry Finn* of 43,500. Sales must have dropped sharply, however, for in a later letter (31 July 1885), CLW explained that "when an agent sees any great quantity of books in the stores it discourages him and he quits at once, they acted that way with Huck."

150. To Charles L. Webster

[Hartford]
4 April 1885

Dear Charley—

The Advertiser and the Republican still go for me daily.[1] All right, we may as well get the benefit of such advertising as can be drawn from it.

So, if the idea seems good to you, add this new page—this "Prefatory Remark," and insert it right after the copyright page in all future editions.[2] I would ⟨bind up a hundred of them or more and send to the princi⟩ bind up a few copies immediately and send to all the New York and Boston papers, and to a scattering few western ones—and don't *mark* them; but when you are ready to ship them get W. McKay [Mackay] Laffan (go to see him at Harper & Bros.) to drop the Prefatory Remark into the Sun, with a mere quiet editorial comment to the effect that we are inserting this in deference to a generally expressed curiosity on the part of the public to know whether Huck is a real or imaginary character.

You might print a proof of the P. R. and hand it to Laffan for publication *immediately* (before Gen Grant dies and absorbs all newspaper interest,) without waiting to bind up and send off the books.

Ys

S L C

Prefatory Remark

Huckleberry Finn is not an imaginary person. He still lives; or rather, *they* still live; for Huckleberry Finn is two persons in one—namely, the author's two uncles, the present editors of the Boston *Advertiser* and the Springfield *Republican*. In character, language, clothing, education, instinct, and origin, he is the painstakingly and truthfully drawn photograph and counterpart of these two gentlemen as they were in the time of their boyhood, forty years ago. The work has been most carefully and conscientiously done, and is exactly true to the originals, in even the minutest particulars, with but one exception, and that a trifling one: this boy's language has been toned down and softened, here and there, in deference to the taste of a more modern and fastidious day.

---

[1] See *MTHL,* p. 535, for a summary of the criticism of the Boston *Advertiser* and the Springfield *Republican.*

[2] The idea did not seem "good" to Mrs. Clemens, and these orders were revoked (*MTBus,* p. 309).

151. To Charles L. Webster

[Hartford]
8 April [1885]

Dear Charley—

I hope it is your idea that C L Webster & Co shall be a general agency and have New York and a fair area of territory around it, and receive the usual general agent's commission.[1] Such a commission on fifty or 100,000 volumes would make a handsome addition to the firm's assets.

Yrs

S L C

[1] The present plan is apparently an extension of the mail-order proposal outlined in letter 148 above. CLW did indeed reserve a metropolitan New York general agency (Watson Gill worked the Western counties) which he expanded further in late 1887 with W. E. Dibble as supervisor (see letter 197 below).

152. To Charles L. Webster

[Hartford]
17 June 1885

Dear Charley—

I enclose a note from my friend Charley Clark of the Courant, and one from his friend and Gerhardt's (Fewsmith.) If F. is *the very best man* in Newark for a canvassership, the New Jersey General Agent will want him and take him—otherwise he will be sagacious and allow him to get left.[1] We are not hunting for *possible* capacity, we are hunting for *known* capacity.

S L C

[1] CLW had announced to MT that he would appoint agents "at once" as soon as he finished work on the Grant prospectus (22 April 1885), but whether Fewsmith was appointed is unknown.

153. To Charles L. Webster

Elmira
28 July 1885

Dear Charley—

Part of my business can be done—after a fashion—by letter: the rest must wait. I wanted to consult as to the advisability of issuing *both* volumes Dec 1. Don't throw this suggestion overboard without giving it serious thought.[1]

If we publish but one vol Dec 1, the bookstores will have signs and advertisements out within a week, promising it at half price, and also promising to furnish the second at the same easy terms if people will wait. That will stop the canvass, kill it dead as a coffin-nail. And it will do more than that. People who have subscribed and paid for the first volume will get out of taking the second on one pretext or another—hoping and expecting to get it cheaper from the bookstores—and so we shall have a great edition of the second volume left on our hands.

If we publish only the one volume, *general* agents will be afraid to load up the bookstores with it, lest we come down on them; but if we issue both vols Dec. 1, the general agents will themselves privately load up every bookstore in the land—the very thing we *want* them to do—and then tell us to lump it if we don't like it.

This scheme will kill the canvass, from Dec 1 to March 1 or April 1—and after that, canvassing will revive again. If we publish both vols Dec 1, and the general agents know it beforehand and agree to it and approve it, they will privately make arrangements to pile 50,000 sets into the bookstores. I think this is sure.

If we publish both vols Dec 1, we need not care what the critics say about the book—but if we publish only one, we run some risk.

Now my instructions to you are,—unless after careful weighing, you disapprove my idea—to send a circular to the general agents, proposing to publish both vols Dec 1—"to satisfy a strong public desire"—and as we suppose *they* would also prefer this, we give them the opportunity to approve it, if they can do so by unanimous vote. In which case you will send them a later circular appointing

Dec 1 for the issue of both vols, so that they can so inform their canvassers.

What I suggest now, is, that you draw up the circular—it will not take 5 minutes—and give it to Mr. Hall, to hold till he hears from you. Give it solid thought on shipboard;[2] then if you find you approve, cable Hall to "issue circular"; if you find you don't approve, you needn't cable anything.

Yrs truly

S L C

---

[1] CLW apparently gave the matter no more than several minutes of thought before he threw it overboard. His reply of 31 July pointed out comprehensively that printers and binders could not undertake the chore, that simultaneous publication would violate the agreement with *The Century,* and that close supervision of General Agents would prevent dumping. CLW also had "many other good reasons that would take too much time to explain here."

[2] CLW made a trip to England and the Continent to secure contracts for publication of the Grant volumes.

154. To Charles L. Webster

[Hartford]
30 October 1885

Dear Charley:

I wouldn't have made Col. Fred so good an offer as that.[1] Half profits up to 60,000, and 60 per cent of the profits on all sold *after* that would have been a plenty good enough offer.[2] Suppose his book should sell 51,000 and stop there? We couldn't afford to give him 60% on that. Your offer would be right and fair on a stipulated sale of 75,000, but on a sale of 50,000 it trims our actual profit down to $15,000 or less. If he finally refuses your offer you can comfort yourself with the reflection that you were as liberal as the prospect for his book would really permit.

No, we can't take Badeau's book in any event[3]—for two very good reasons: 1. If it be cleanly, decent, and respectful, it will have but a poor sale. 2. If it be malicious, and try to undermine the General's character and reputation, it may be expected to have a great sale, but we can't touch it.

I think you are right about that correspondence; [4] it will be more likely to help our book than hurt it. . . .

Ys truly

S L C

[1] Colonel Fred Grant was an extremely difficult burden to MT and CLW: he gave an interview at the time of his father's death which announced he was not at all certain Grant's *Memoirs* would make two volumes (FJH to MT, 10 August [1885]); he gave *The Century* permission to use a deathbed photograph of his father which CLW had intended to publish exclusively—"What right he has is not clear, but it does seem that he is a particularly unfortunate business man" (CLW to MT, 1 August 1885). He was intractable in the death-mask fiasco (*MTBus*, pp. 343–346; CLW to MT, [16 December 1885]: "I can't do a thing with Col. Grant"). He altered the proof of the second volume of the *Memoirs*— "I found it so changed and patched that it made me nervous. . . . it seems to me that General Grant's words should be changed as little as possible" (CLW to MT, 25 December 1885). The present reference, however, was to a biography Colonel Grant was proposing: "He contemplated writing the life of his father, taking it up where the Autobiography left off, and carrying it down to the time of his death" (FJH to MT, 29 September [1885]).

[2] On 29 October, CLW told MT, "I have offered Col Grant ½ profits on his book up to 50,000 and if it sold more than 50,000 to give him 60% of the profits. . . . he was not pleased with the offer said he had had a better offer from other publishers than we gave on the Genl's book."

[3] In the same letter CLW suggested, "It might be a bright move to gobble up Badeau's book in case Col Grant goes to other publishers." Badeau's *Military History of Ulysses S. Grant* was reissued by D. Appleton in 1885; his *Grant in Peace,* which MT and CLW discuss in subsequent letters as if they intend to publish it, was issued by S. S. Scranton & Co., of Hartford, in 1887.

[4] The present reference is presumably to one of Badeau's volumes, for CLW's 29 October letter said, "If the Badeau letters come out at the right time it will boom our book. We can take a back seat and see the fun go on and seem to have nothing to do with it." A volume of Grant letters was soon to become a topic of discussion, too (in letter 156 below).

155. To CHARLES L. WEBSTER

Hartford
11 November 1885

Dear Charley:

R. M. Daggett, late U.S. Minister to the Sandwich Islands (an old friend of mine,) has submitted to me a book which I shall be very glad to have, under certain conditions. It would make a book the size of one of Gen. Grant's volumes. It was constructed by Daggett and the king of the Sandwich Islands, working together, and consists of the (historical) Traditions and legends of the natives, reaching back connectedly 1500 years, and of course is very curious—and *new*. It is fresh ground—untouched, unworn, and full of romantic interest. I have read three of the legends, and they impress me favorably.

I told Daggett that what was required for success was a *good* book; and that the other nine-tenths of the requisite of success was that there should be a big name back of the good book. So I said that if he could get the King to let his name appear as part author, we *wanted the book*. (In fact I wanted it anyhow, but I didn't say so.) I said we preferred to keep up our standard, and be known in the world as a house that publishes only for Kings and full Generals.

It is the King who tells the ancient native legends (or Sagas) to Daggett, and Daggett writes them down—and connects them, very plausibly into an historical chain, with names and dates and details.

Daggett is to be at San Diego, California, until the middle of December, and I said we would confer together and tell him what we require. This is what I suggest:

1. That without the King's expressed collaboration, we will pay what I was paid on the Innocents Abroad—15 per cent of the profit above cost of manufacture.

2. With mention of the King as collaborator in the introduction, we will pay 40 per cent of the profits.

3. With *both names in the title page* as authors, we will pay 60 per cent of the profits.[1]

Keep this thing quiet. We will talk when I come down. And keep this letter handy for reference.

Daggett thinks he can get the King to consent to nearly any reasonable thing. With a sufficient concession from him, I would rather have this book than *any* that is offering now. It can be fascinatingly illustrated.

Daggett stayed with me 2 days—left yesterday.

My friend Redpath came yesterday on the part of Rice,[2] and talked 3 hours. Several "toppy" telegrams arrived from Rice in the meantime, one of them ordering Redpath "not to concede too much." When Redpath left, he telegraphed the printers to stop the press on the Lincoln book and prospectuses till further orders, and telegraphed Rice that Webster & Co would not yield a jot or tittle on the Diary,—not a line of it would be permitted to appear.

I forbade the publication of Col. Grant's chapter in the Lincoln book, but with this reservation: that if in the judgment of Alexander & Green the publication of that chapter would be no harm to our book, I would withdraw the prohibition. (I don't mind that chapter—I only mind the opportunity it gives Rice to *advertise* the book, and the Canvasser to swear it is written mainly by General Grant's hand.)

When you go to Canada about the 28th of November to copyright the General's book,[2] I may possibly like to go along if not needed on American soil by any etiquette of law. That is, if you are going to Ottawa.

I am all right again, and can come down when needed, but do not care to go, otherwise.

Ys truly

S L C

P.S. I think Rice thinks he can make Col. Grant uncomfortable because he accepted that check. One of his telegrams (I tell you privately—as I was meaning to do in the case of the other telegram) says that the mere returning of the check isn't going to satisfy him, since he has announced the Diary.

---

[1] CLW believed that "there would be no novelty to the book unless the King's name appeared as author 'assisted, (if you like) by Mr. R. M. Daggett,' such a book would have a market value, and would undoubtedly have a large sale" (13 November 1885).

[2] After the argument with Thorndike Rice over excerpts from *Huckleberry Finn* (see letter 145 above), Rice hired Bromfield as his office manager. Rice then decided to issue a volume of *Anecdotes of President Lincoln* by subscription, using Bromfield's knowledge: "Now he undoubtedly comes to Colonel Grant with this argument: My Mr. Bromfield was with Mr. Webster a

year and a half; he is thoroughly well acquainted with his methods; he knows all his General Agents; therefore, we can take your book and work it just as successfully as can Mr. Webster" (CLW to MT, 6 November 1885). The book may have been Colonel Grant's proposed biography of his father; but of more immediate concern were some autobiographical dictations by General Grant, which Colonel Grant had removed from the *Memoirs*—some of the material "about Butler being bottled up on the Peninsula. . . . was thrown away as of no use" (CLW to MT, 13 November). Fred Grant had sold the material to Rice for inclusion in the *North American Review* (see *MTBus,* p. 340) in violation of the contract restricting for three years the publication of any "other book, article or writing" (CLW to MT, 6 November). CLW was adamant about refusing to allow publication of this "Diary": "Rice stole Huck Finn. He stole Bromfield (for which thank God) he has approached Mr. Hall and tried to bag him, next they tackled the most efficient office boy who resisted their charms, now they try to steal some of the memoirs . . . and they also steal the design to our cover. Rice will be after our agents next and then take our children" (13 November). Grant appealed to CLW, however (*MTBus,* p. 343), and Rice's volume appeared with General Grant's material.

[3] CLW made a contract with Sampson Low, Marston & Co. in August 1885; "this royalty covers Great Britain and the colonies with the exception of Canada which belongs to us" (CLW to MT, London, 22 August 1885).

156. To Charles L. Webster

[Hartford]
20 December 1885

Dear Charley—

It is important, now, that you secure the letters [1] and get the contract signed pretty soon, so that we can publish it next December and so get it out a year in advance of the Pope's book. The reason is, that I've got another hundred-thousand-dollar book on a string, and it is one which the owners would like to have come out ahead of any other book of ours, and we must have a good excuse for putting it off, if possible. It is a book which we *must* have; and although all the publishers are hot after it we can get it. It is offered to me by an old friend of mine, and also by the person in chief authority, who is an enemy of mine of long standing.[2]

Don't you really think you had better get the letters *before* you pay any money? I'm a little afraid of a demand for a higher rate than we are now paying. And there'll be an offer to take in a partner,[3] too, as a consideration, I'm afraid.

Do you want to come down and ask for the letters? Or do you want me to come and consult about a plan of procedure.

Be sure to go to Mr. Dana and secure the Pope's book.[4]

Yrs

S L C

[1] Mrs. Grant's edition of President Grant's letters to her (see *MTBus*, p. 346).

[2] The "old friend" is unidentifiable, but the "enemy of mine of long standing" was William C. Prime, whose books MT had ridiculed in *Innocents Abroad*. The book was *McClellan's Own Story*. Prime served as intermediary for the volume, made business arrangements (Prime to MT, 31 December 1885, and 29 January 1886), and apparently read the proof (*MTBus*, p. 355). Prime told MT (24 January 1886), "I am not going to negociate with the numerous publishers who have written to me. Harpers want to do the book—on the subscription plan."

[3] Jesse Grant, another of the General's sons, apparently was trying some gentle blackmail—offering the Grant letters in return for an interest in CLW & Co. CLW refused to consider the matter (see letter 157 below).

[4] How Charles A. Dana controlled the rights to the *Life of Pope Leo XIII* is obscure. But MT repeated the command on several occasions (*MTBus*, pp. 348, 349). The contract with Bernard O'Reilly for the biography was signed in early May 1886 (*LLMT*, p. 247).

157. To CHARLES L. WEBSTER

Hartford

19 March 1886

Dear Charley—

It isn't good policy for anybody connected with our publishing firm to be under a fire of newspaper criticism this year. Our interests and those of our clients are too large to be jeoparded for the few dollars that might be squeezed out of a play (a play which isn't worth a damn and is going to fail.) Burbank is a personal friend and a first rate fellow, but I won't allow that play to be played this year or next, upon *any* terms.[1]

Did you complete the contract with Prime and pay over the $10,000?[2]

I suppose you can easily get the McClellan book ready for the September canvass; but unless His Holiness's book is in your hands by July 1, you can't start *it* at the same time, can you? Wouldn't it answer if you issued McClellan's book Dec 1, and began the canvass for the Pope's on *that* date? I suppose they won't be the same canvassers.[3]

Yrs

S L C

P.S. Jesse Grant is to call on me at the Normandie at 9 or 10 A.M., Wednesday, March 24. It will be necessary that I see you first, and take your opinion on the propositions.[4] So if you can look in a little before 9, he can wait till I have talked with you.

---

[1] A. P. Burbank had written MT on 17 February about reviving "Colonel Sellers as a Scientist" (*MTHL*, p. 555). The "fire of newspaper criticism" would apparently have involved complex litigation over the right to produce the play (see *ibid.*, pp. 554–563).

[2] CLW replied on 20 March, "I have signed the contract with Mrs McClellan and Dr Prime and have the manuscript in the safe. I have paid $5000.00 of the $10,000 which they are to have." Earlier, CLW had reported, "I have had a talk with Mr. Prime this morning and I told him we were strong in the opinion that one volume was the proper form for the book. He acquiesced if we could get 700 pp in one volume. I told him we could at $3.75, the same price as Blaine's, so that is decided" (12 February 1886). James G. Blaine's *Twenty Years of Congress: From Lincoln to Garfield,* published by subscription by the Henry Bill Publishing Company, was coincidentally to become important to MT later the same year (see letter 160 below).

[3] The 20 March reply noted, "I can easily get the book ready to canvass by September. . . . I also expect to run the Pope's book at the same time if I get manuscript in time. They will be worked by an entirely different class of agents and will not conflict with each other."

[4] CLW had suggested on 10 February, "The most dangerous thing in this world excepting selecting a partner for life is the selection of a *business* partner. However, I think I could get along if you made any arrangement as I should expect to have my own way as per our contract and I would not relinquish that right." Again, on 20 March, CLW announced, "I would go very *slow* about taking in new partners. I don't want to part with any of my interest but if you wish to sell any of yours I have no objection to the Grant boys, but they should have *nothing* to say about the conduct of the business." The Grants did not become partners, but a statement of the sales of the *Memoirs* to 1 April 1887 allows a puzzling additional 12 percent royalty on sales "from the General Agency," above the 70 percent of the contract. Perhaps the Grant family received the additional royalty because of some arrangement regarding the New York general agency CLW was establishing.

158. To Charles L. Webster

Hartford
6 June 1886

Dear Charley—

Hadn't you better offer Gen. Badeau 10 per cent royalty for his "Grant in Peace?" [1]

It promises to be an interesting book—gossipy and entertaining to all kinds of readers—and as it is a Grant book, it ought to be kept in the family, I judge.

10 per cent is one-third of the profits. I suggest that figure because the book is worth more than that other General's [2] (to whom you pay 25¢ per vol—which is one-quarter of the profits) and worth less than Gen. McClellan's, on which we pay one-half profits. . . .

Yrs

S L C

[1] See letter 154 above. On 6 September, FJH wrote, "I have seen Colonel Grant. He says they have no objection whatever to our publishing the book by Gen'l Badeau." Further, FJH had "written General Badeau: we would be pleased to examine the manuscript, and we think that we can make arrangements to publish."
[2] Perhaps General Winfield Scott Hancock; see letter 163 below.

159. To Fred J. Hall

Elmira
12 July 1886

Dear Mr. Hall—[1]

That sounds like a good book, and we ought to have it; but we could not do it justice in the handling if we tried to publish it next winter, because our hands will be more than full with the Pope's and General McClellan's books.

Our copartnership contract would not allow me to take the book without Webster's assent; and he would not like to make a decision from the other side of the ocean. In fact he could not, for he is going to be prodigiously driven, making the European contracts for the Life of His Holiness.

I hope the matter can stand over without prejudice to Dr. Fulton's book ² till Mr. Webster's return.

Truly Yours

S. L. Clemens

You will need to communicate with Dr. Fulton or Mr. Dana; so I have written the foregoing in such a way that you can enclose it to either of them if you choose, along with what you will say yourself.

When are you going to send Mrs. Grant another check? The supply of money on hand must be getting perilously large by this time.³

I can take care of twenty or thirty thousand dollars myself whenever you think it will relieve your bank burdens.⁴

Please give me a list of the gift-copies (the people's names) I ordered of Gen. Grant's book, and the styles of binding stipulated. Several of the second volume have not reached the parties yet, I think.

I ordered my coachman, Patrick McAleer, to draw on you to pay for a pair of horses, but I doubt if he gets them.

Ys Truly

S. L. Clemens

¹ CLW had left for Rome on 23 June, and FJH was in charge of the office during his absence.
² No other correspondence mentions this volume. However, it may refer to John Fulton's *The Beautiful Land. Palestine, As It Was and As It Now Is: Historical, Geographical, and Pictorial, Along the Lines of Our Savior's Journeys*, published in 1891 by the Standard Columbian Company of Chicago.
³ Mrs. Grant's famous first check had been paid on the anniversary of the signing of the contract, 27 February (CLW to Cyrus W. Field, 27 February 1886, TS in MTP). MT's concern over large supplies of money is explained by CLW's letter of 26 February: "I dislike to carry so large a bank account, so I have decided to give Mrs. Grant a check. . . . I do not for a moment think there is any danger with either of our banks here still such a thing is possible and as we

are liable to Mrs. Grant for amts *collected,* the safest way is to pay now." Still, FJH advised MT on 15 July that CLW "left special instructions to have that matter stand until he returned. Mrs. Grant understands and has consented to wait until he comes back."

⁴ In his 15 July letter, FJH advised that MT's share of the Grant profits was $63,142.87 and offered a check in whatever amount MT named.

160. To Fred J. Hall

Elmira
14 July 1886

Dear Mr. Hall—

Mr. Howells has enclosed me this.¹ Under this decision no doubt it is possible to go for that pious son of a dog, John Wannamaker of Philadelphia. Refer it to Alexander & Green; and if they approve, let the attack begin.²

Ys Truly

S L. Clemens

¹ FJH's reply refers to "your letter of the 14th . . . inclosing a page from the Publishers' Weekly" (16 July). The reference was to an article "Protecting Subscription Books," *Publishers' Weekly,* XXX (10 July 1886), 37–38, announcing the decision of Judge Hammond that a trade bookseller's purchase of Blaine's *Twenty Years of Congress* constituted a "copyright piracy" against Blaine and the Henry Bill Publishing Company.

² FJH's two letters of 16 and 23 July outlined the advice of Alexander & Green: "The first step of our lawyers . . . will be to get an injunction against Wannamaker to restrain him from selling the books, pending the decision of the Court" (23 July). MT attended the hearing, but the court refused to grant the preliminary injunction ("Subscription Book Decisions," *Publishers' Weekly,* XXX [14 August 1886], pp. 204–205).

161. To Fred J. Hall

Elmira
16 July 1886

Dear Mr. Hall:

No, I don't think I shall need any money of any consequence before fall, or perhaps the end of the year. But a bank might break on us, and so it might be wise to put into government bonds or a safety deposit vault all the money not needed to run the business; this in order that none of us may get crippled, and that the necessary capital may be on hand when wanted for the Pope's book and Mrs. Grant's second payment. We were nervous before about keeping a great stock of money on hand, and it was a wise nervousness, I think.[1] I am all the more nervous because I believe the copartnership contract requires me to furnish all the capital; and so I could get worse hurt by an accident than my brother partners.

I miss from my list *Mrs. A. W. Fairbanks, Cleveland, Ohio,* (cloth.)

Unless *Mrs. J. Langdon and Mrs. T. W. Crane, Elmira,* (both *tree calf,*) are subscribers, they also belong in my list. They have not received the second volume yet. Can you tell by your records whether they are subscribers or not?

Keep an eye on the Sun, and if Father O'Reilly [2] doesn't tell of Charley's private interview with the Pope (which I hope he will, for it will be good matter to put into your circulars,) we must get the fact of his private audience mentioned in the newspapers ourselves.[3] It is a valuable card. It may come to us through Roman newspapers, for it could hardly pass unnoticed.

Yours Truly

S. L. Clemens

---

[1] On 20 July, FJH replied that he agreed "it would be a good idea" to transfer money to a safety deposit vault. He also said the firm had $248,000 in the U.S. National and Mount Morris banks, and $186,000 in accounts receivable. On 19 July, however, Daniel Whitford, attorney for Alexander & Green, advised FJH, "I do not think it would be good policy to withdraw any considerable amount of currency from the Banks and place it in Safe Deposit Vaults" (MTP).

[2] Bernard O'Reilly was the author of the Pope's biography. MT's expectation that O'Reilly's description would appear in the *Sun* suggests an arrangement as correspondent which would explain Dana's intervention in the contract for the Pope's biography (letter 156 above).

[3] "Both the Sun and the Tribune mention the fact that Mr. Webster had a private audience with the Pope, but they do not give any particulars," FJH replied (20 July). "Would it not be well," he proposed, "to let the matter rest until we are ready to bring out the prospectus of the Pope, and then get it noticed in the papers, giving full particulars."

162. To Fred J. Hall

Elmira
21 July 1886

Dear Mr. Hall—

I find that Mrs. J. Langdon's tree calf was a presentation copy; so I judge that Mrs. T. W. Crane's was, also.

There are still two cloth presentation copies to be sent, but I can't recal the names. Look on the presentation list. You must have such a list. It is not likely that the 1st vol would be sent out and no provision made for the 2d.

You are right. The visit to the Pope should be held back till the canvass opens.

Macy has Grant books for sale cheap. We must assault him, next.

Ys Truly

S L Clemens

163. To Fred J. Hall

Elmira
17 August 1886

Dear Mr. Hall:

It is good news. I have written the General [1]—straight off.

I told him General Grant's business representative reported to him that our firm was the best equipped in New York for the service required; and that the person employed from Rome to make similar inquiry "returned the same verdict to the Roman Cardinals." I closed with: "Mr. Webster will return from Rome early in October. May I send him to you when he arrives?"

Truly yours

S L Clemens

P.S. Is Mrs. General Hancock preparing a book for us? Has a

contract been made with her? I have forgotten what was finally done in the matter.[2]

[1] Presumably General Philip Sheridan, whose *Personal Memoirs* would be published by CLW in 1888. On 2 October 1886, FJH wrote MT that he was assured by friends of General Sheridan that "he intended to place the book in our hands." CLW told MT on 8 November, "The contract with Genl Sheridan is signed. . . . The contract is on the half profit basis."

[2] Some attempt may have been made to secure a Hancock book when the General died in February 1886 (see *MTBus,* p. 355). At any rate, FJH replied on 18 August, "We have no agreement with Mrs. Hancock, as the affair was not in definite enough shape to make one." Mrs. Hancock's *Reminiscences of Winfield Scott Hancock* did appear under CLW's imprint.

164. To Fred J. Hall

Elmira
19 August 1886

Dear Mr. Hall:

1. I want to get the name and address of every *daily* newspaper in the U.S. and Canada that contains fully 2 *pages of new matter daily.*[1]

I don't care for those that contain less than that;—that is to say, less than 35,000 ems.

2. Where practicable, I would also like to know *about* how many 1000 ems of new matter each of said papers prints daily.

These data could be listed in this way:

Tombstone Gazette, 2 pages new matter daily—16,000 ems to the page.

T. *Journal,* 2½ p. new matter, 18,000 ems to the page.

T. *News,* 5 p. n. m. 40,000 ems to the page.

I wish you would go in person and put this job into the hands of some advertising agency—Rockwell's [Rowell's][2] or some other. I want it done *well*—not in a slipshod way. I want the report to be entirely trustworthy.

I would rather the measurements of matter were made in New York than ascertained by sending circulars of inquiry to the newspapers. Let them get a copy of the paper itself, and *do their own measuring.*

Make a bargain with them for this work; and when it is finished, pay the bill and charge to me.

And greatly oblige

Ys Truly

S L Clemens

You had better carry this letter with you, and read the several requirements to them, and see that they set them down clearly and correctly and *intelligibly*.

I don't wish to be known in this, or have anything said about it. You are a member of CLW & Co, and that is sufficient. What you want with these data is none of their affair.

One more thing. Which doubtless they can also get for me:

1. I want a list of the several printers' unions (*compositors' unions*) in the U.S.; and where they are located, and how many members each contains. This will no doubt be easily procurable from headquarters—office of the *National* Typographical Union.

I want to know where each of these Unions *is*—and what its strength is.

---

[1] Letters 166, 168, and 169 below explain this scheme. FJH's replies of 26 August and 6 September (MTP) outlined delays and problems in the project.

[2] "Rowell," FJH replied, "refuses to undertake it at any price." P. B. Bromfield did the work for $325 (Notebook 21, TS p. 20).

165. To FRED J. HALL

Elmira
25 August 1886

Dear Mr. Hall:

Won't you please take Mr. King [1] up, and sell the unsold United States rights in the Kaolatype patent to him on the terms proposed by him? You are hereby given full power of attorney to act for me in the matter and sign all necessary papers for me. And I hereby revoke all existing powers of attorney concerning my Kaolatype interests.

As to whether he is "good" or not, it isn't of any consequence to me. And greatly oblige

Ys truly

S L Clemens

[1] Perhaps a Horace King, whose name and the address "Thompsonville" appear in Notebook 21, TS p. 28. Apparently FJH did not complete the sale— see *MTBus,* p. 365.

166. To Fred J. Hall

Elmira

28 August 1886

Dear Mr. Hall:

I am very much obliged to you. Now I will try to make the job less hard for the gentleman. Instead of requiring the actual facts, we will take the newspaper foreman's word.

You've got a newspaper Directory in your office. Let him get the names from that, and send a note addressed to the *foreman* not the proprietor, of each, asking how many ems of new matter, ads included, his paper averages daily; and say the information will not be used publicly. (Enclose a stamped and printed return-envelop.) Also printed blank to be filled—about like this:

Office of the ———

———, Sept ——— 1886.

Our daily average, of new matter, including ads., etc., is about ——— ems.

Foreman.

Perhaps one of the advertising agencies will let its name be used in these circulars as the collector of the statistics, although they refuse to do the *work*. Without some such backing we should get no statistics that were serious or trustworthy. Let us do it in this way or not attempt it at all. The plan which I proposed before is too cumbersome. I imagined that Rowell would have the country dailies on file in his establishment, and that there wouldn't be more than 600 or maybe 700 of them, and so it couldn't be much of a job to measure them.

We don't need the statistics of New York, Boston, Phila, Chicago, Cincinnati, Chicago, St Louis, New Orleans and San Francisco. It's the country dailies that are important for my purpose.

Please take a glance (by office boy) at your Newspaper Directory and tell me the *aggregate* number of dailies in the U.S., *big cities* and all.

Ys Truly

S L C

167. To FRED J. HALL

[Elmira]
4 September [1886]

Dear Mr. Hall:

I think we ought to have that book [1]—not for a lump sum, but for 20 cents on each and every copy, of whatever binding. The large sale would be in N.Y. city, in our own general agency.

Would we be liable in libel suits? [2] I suppose so. Therefore Mr. Whitford had better read it and mark the worst of the libelous passages for expunging. Then you might propose the above terms, and if they prove unsatisfactory, ask the owner to wait till Mr. Webster's return. I'd rather he would do that, anyway.

Ys Truly

S L Clemens

¹ FJH had written on 3 September, "We have just been offered a book which is likely to attract attention. It is written by Ex-Superintendent [George W.] Walling of the New York Police and Detective Force. . . . In this book, he gives the inside of a great many celebrated cases; for instance: The complete history of Stewart's body. . . . the Nathan Murder case."

² FJH's 3 September letter went on, "It was to have been published by a firm in the City here . . . but one of the members . . . brought it here, and said that some of the statements made were so strong, that they were afraid that it would raise a storm." Walling's *Recollections of a New York Chief of Police* appeared in 1887, over the imprint of the Caxton Book Concern, Limited.

168. To FRED J. HALL

[Elmira]
11 September 1886

Dear Mr. Hall:

Answer him thus:

Dear Sir:

We only asked the question because Mr. Clemens (of this firm) instructed us to ask it, and to apply personally at headquarters; observing that it could probably be answered without difficulty, as the information was doubtless contained in a printed pamphlet. If he had purposed making an improper use of it he would hardly have sought it in so unclandestine a fashion; and we will risk the postulate that if he had supposed he was invading a privacy, he would have forborne from seeking it at all. He is interested in a printing invention, and wanted to get an idea of how large or how small the market for such things might be, and so has been collecting every sort of information that bears upon that industry, immediate or remote.

When will Webster arrive? ¹

Yrs

S L C

¹ On 20 September, CLW wrote from London, "We sail . . . next week Wednesday [29 September], the first date that I could get a steamer everything on all lines being taken."

169. To Fred J. Hall

Hartford
30 September [1886]

Dear Mr. Hall:

Please send me $6,000 and charge to my account.

You say Mr. Bromfield has sent out 1289 circulars and received 418 satisfactory answers. It is a much better result than could have been prophecied. When I came to reflect upon that form of application for the information, I was afraid nobody would furnish it. A simpler and much surer plan would have been to send stamp for sample copy of every daily paper, and then personally measure the contents. We should have got *facts,* then; now we get romance. Still, it'll answer.

Let Mr. Bromfield take his time, and wait till he can give me the information *all in one. dab.* There is no hurry.

Ys Truly

S L Clemens

170. To Charles L. Webster

Hartford
17 November 1886

Dear Charley—

I should say, make perfectly conscienceless terms with him— terms which will absorb all the profits—and take his book.[1] He choused me out of a good deal of money, 13 years ago as coolly as ever any other crime was committed in this world.

A few copies will sell in every large town—and the canvasser will always know just who are the stock-meddlers, and therefore just who to tackle.

Yrs

S L C

P.S. Here's a letter from Gilder. I should think a book on England from Smalley would sell.[2] It would be exceedingly interesting—that I *know*. We couldn't pay more than ¼ profits, or 7½ or 8 per cent royalty.

It may be that we have already enough books.[3] But anyway, I wish you would do Smalley and Reid the courtesy to call on Smalley at once and talk about the book—for it or against it as shall seem best—and explain to him that I would be there with you but that I am tied up at home with an equinoctial precession of guests, complicated with engagements, but can come presently if desirable.

S L C

[1] Henry Clews, a prominent banker; on 15 November, CLW had written, "Henry Clews wants us to publish a book written by him entitled 'Twenty Eight Years in Wall St.,' being personal recollections of eminent capitalists." How Clews "choused" MT in 1873 is not known. His book was published by the Irving Publishing Co. in 1887.

[2] Richard Watson Gilder apparently suggested George W. Smalley, a correspondent for the New York *Tribune* (hence the mention of Whitelaw Reid in the next paragraph), as author of a possible subscription book. Smalley's *London Letters and Some Others,* consisting of articles originally written for the *Tribune,* was published by Harper & Brothers in 1891. See further MT's telegram to CLW of this same date (*MTBus,* p. 368).

[3] The notoriety of the success with Grant's *Memoirs* was causing an avalanche of offers by prospective authors. In late 1885, General W. T. Sherman mailed MT a manuscript called "Notes of Travel" (of a tour of Europe in 1871–1872) which MT rejected (Sherman to MT, 15, 25 September and 9, 16 October 1885). In a letter dated "September ? 1886," James Redpath offered MT Donn Piatt's book for publication. On 13 September, FJH wrote that Mr. Stevens, "The Philadelphia gentleman, who lost both his wife and daughter on the yacht disaster" had "written a book of personal reminiscences" he offered the Company, but FJH "took the liberty of very courteously refusing."

171. To Charles L. Webster

[Hartford]
6 December 1886

Dear Charley:

Don't you think it would be better to take a page or a ½-page of the Century—the quarter-page crowds your matter so.[1]

I have read "Grant in Peace"[2] up to the present time, and there hasn't been a dull chapter thus far. It is mighty well written, too.

I will tackle Stanley.[3]

Please send a cloth "Mississippi" to Miss Mary E. Mathews, and charge to me. (Postmark enclosed—seems to be New Windsor, MARYLAND.)

Yrs

S L C.

[1] MT refers to the advertising space which CLW was taking regularly in *The Century*. CLW replied on 7 December, "I *had* already taken a page in the Century which will be occupied next month." In late 1887, MT apparently blamed CLW for this extravagance (Notebook 22, TS p. 17).

[2] See letter 158 above. CLW & Co. lost the Badeau volume, presumably because there could be no guarantee of immediate publication. As late as 26 January 1887, CLW told MT, "Gen'l Badeau has . . . accepted terms 10% of retail price." On 6 November 1888, CLW wrote MT from Fredonia,

Don't let the Badeau case worry you at all. . . . Badeau has absolutely *no case*. He withdrew his manuscript (in *answer to a letter from us offering to let him do so*) before the time set for its delivery to us. After he had possession of his manuscript he wrote me that he should feel at liberty to make arrangements elsewhere. . . . Thus by his own act he removed from us the possibility of carrying out the contract were we disposed to do so by withdrawing the manuscript and by previous publication.

A clipping from the New York *Sun*, 7 March 1889 (Grant Scrapbook, II, 136, MTP) clarifies the matter: "Gen. Adam Badeau has begun suit against Charles L. Webster & Co. to recover $22,500 damages for their failure to publish his work, 'Grant in Peace,' which he declares the firm agreed to put before the public, printed and bound, as a companion volume to the Grant 'Memoirs.'" Publication was interrupted, the clipping continues, when CLW required that an additional clause, allowing Mrs. Grant the opportunity to "alter the matter in such a way that it will be unobjectionable to her," be added to the contract. Badeau "positively refused, however, to emasculate his work at the dictation of any human being. There was more correspondence. . . . Finally Gen. Badeau . . . got the manuscript eventually and had the book published by a Hartford firm."

[3] CLW had written MT on 30 November, "A book from Stanley would be a good hit. Can't you use your influence with him for one?" See further the subsequent letter, below.

172. CHARLES L. WEBSTER

Hartford
14 December 1886

Dear Charley:

When a stranger offers me a book which we don't want, I decline it promptly, without adding it to your burdens of that sort; but this Lieutenant Owen [1] is not quite a stranger, so I have told him I would refer his matter to you, who will write him and deliver a verdict. Of course you could decline because we don't re-issue other people's failures; but I reckon the plea of our already overcrowded decks may answer better. [2]

I have suggested, in a long letter mailed yesterday, an Autobiography to Stanley, [3] and shown him how he can write it in the cars (he is a stenographer) in 105 days, one hour's work a day. I said that he could have our crowned-head rates—half the profits; and that I didn't see why he shouldn't clear $50,000 out of it, though that was a guess and would prove wrong in one direction or the other.

I see by this morning's paper that he is likely to sail for Europe and Congo tomorrow. All right; he has of course received my letter this morning, and will have time to chew on it at sea. As a result, he will quite certainly give us either these coming adventures at Stanley Falls *or* an Autobiography. (if he survives those Arabs.) But I'd rather have the Autobiography.

Ys truly

S L Clemens

---

[1] William Miller Owen had published *In Camp and Battle with the Washington Artillery of New Orleans. A Narrative of Events During the Late Civil War from Bull Run to Appomattox* . . . with Ticknor & Co. in 1885. CLW apparently did not reply to Owen's letter—or not promptly enough, at any rate—for MT wrote in Notebook 21 (TS p. 34): "Why didn't you answer W. Miller Owen? Too many of these complaints."

[2] On 7 December, CLW announced that General Logan had offered a volume. On 28 December, he asked MT if they might approach Mrs. Custer for her book;

and in the same letter CLW proposed buying Logan's book from his widow (he had died on 26 December) at a higher royalty than he had offered the General (see also *MTBus,* pp. 371–372). A letter of 24 December gives a good idea of just how overcrowded the decks were:

> Everything is working well. McClellan is selling well, Mrs Hancock has accepted our offer, Genl. Sheridan is at work, and the Pope's book looks as good if not better than ever. As soon as the agents slack up on McClellan I shall put them on that and Crawford [General Samuel W. Crawford's *Genesis of the Civil War*] then Mrs Hancock then Sheridan or perhaps Logan if he accepts as I think he will.

³ CLW had written Stanley, too, and had suggested to MT the possibility of a *"novel* on African adventure for boys that would sell like smoke" (4 December 1886). On 7 December, though, Stanley wrote CLW, "I see no prospect just now of being able to write a book." The possibility was revived, however, in 1889 after CLW had retired from the firm (*MTBus,* pp. 392–393).

173. To CHARLES L. WEBSTER

Hartford
4 January 1887

Dear Charley—

Yes, ½ profits is the right offer to make—his wide reputation entitles him to that—and if anybody wants to offer him more, we withdraw from the competition.¹ The book will sell first-rate—tip-top—but ½-profits from us is as good as 75 per cent from any other house.

(Pond's "colossal" check was $10,000, I guess.² I am betting $25 to $5 that it wasn't $25,000. If Pond wants to earn an honest penny, just beguile him into taking me up. Pond never deals in small adjectives—"colossal" is a tame word for him.) If we can't clear $40,000 for Beecher, at ½-profits, it'll be the author's fault, not the publisher's; that is, it will mean that he isn't as good a card as we think he is.

Truly yours

S L Clemens

¹ On 3 January, CLW had written that Henry Ward Beecher had decided to write his autobiography and "seemed to think that . . . other things being equal, he would rather have us publish it than any one else." CLW liked the idea

because he wanted to "switch off of War books if we can." Additional lettters from CLW (18, 20, and 26 January and 14 February) add further details: Beecher was to turn over the plates of his *Life of Christ* and both it and the autobiography were to be issued (in spite of *MTBus*, p. 375). Beecher showed CLW a synopsis of the autobiography—"a story of his 'inner life'. . . . Detail and minutia of his life at every stage, as a child, youth, young man, just entering the service of 'Christ' (?) and minister" (CLW to MT, 14 February).

² Major James Pond had worked as intermediary with CLW and told him that "some parties" had "placed a check of not very small dimensions upon his [Beecher's] desk" to persuade him to write the autobiography. "What the check was I do not know, but when Pond spoke about it, he pointed to the ceiling, said it was way up" (3 January). Pond attempted to obtain a $5,000 advance for Beecher and $4,000 for himself (18 January). CLW offered Pond a $1,000 bonus and an additional $500 upon delivery of the manuscript of the autobiography; Pond "went off saying he could and would not do it unless he got something out of Beecher" (20 January), but accepted this deal (26 January).

174. To CHARLES L. WEBSTER

Hartford
13 January 1887

Dear Charley:

Upon further reflection, I see a probable three quarters of a million dollars' profit in L's proposed book.¹ There's a dead-certain half-million, I judge.

Now as to the proper division of the swag. Suppose you offer L *one-quarter* of said swag, we to take the ¾. If that doesn't seem satisfactory, maybe the offer of a *third* will.

IF Mr. W. will put up *all* of the necessary money (receiving it back out of the first returns,) that book is a greenback-mine.

I got delayed and didn't get down to L's after my talk with you; so you better arrange a meeting per telephone, and go down and talk with him. This isn't a "big" thing—it calls for Pond's word: "colossal."

Yrs

S L C

¹ According to *MTBus*, p. 374, William M. Laffan of the New York *Sun* was business agent for a catalog of the art collection of William Thompson Walters, which was not finally published until 1897. In Notebook 21, TS p. 34, MT

calculated terms for an offer for the book whereby Laffan's and Walters' profits increased according to the number of books sold (only 1,000 copies would be published); they would receive a total of $97,500 on the 1,000 volumes. See further letter 198 below.

175. To CHARLES L. WEBSTER

Hartford
1 March 1887

Dear Charley:

I think well of the Stedman book,[1] but I can't somehow bring myself to think *very* well of it. My notions are too long to write; but you look in here, on your rounds, and we will swap ideas.

There are two books which ought to be written, and which would sell steadily, like cyclopedias.[2] We can get them done. We will talk about that, too.

The Pope's canvassing-book would sell a Choctaw Bible, it is so handsome. Brer Simeoni got in with his left, just in time; and got in in admirable good form, too.[3] That book is going to *go,* sure.

Truly Yours

S L Clemens

[1] On 25 February, CLW wrote that "Mr. Stedman has been to me and explained the character and scope of the work." Edmund C. Stedman and Ellen M. Hutchinson were at work, of course, on their *Library of American Literature* in ten volumes, which would remain an albatross to the Company until the bankruptcy. The plates of five of the volumes were already made by W. E. Dibble of Cincinnati (who will appear later, to assist in the final demolition of CLW's and MT's partnership). CLW felt Dibble would be willing to sell plates and rights for less than his $10,000 investment; Stedman and Hutchinson would complete the remaining five volumes for $500 a volume and an 8 percent royalty. CLW proposed offering Dibble $8,000 and meeting the other terms (26 March). (See further, *MTBus,* p. 379.)

[2] Unidentifiable. One may have been a volume which MT tried to persuade Samuel E. Moffett to write in 1885: "I have a subject which I am not competent to handle, but you are: to wit, *Picturesque Incidents in History and Tradition;* a 500 or 600-page octavo, to be written by you and published (with illustrations) by Chas. L. Webster & Co., by subscription." MT believed that "such a book, ingeniously contrived, captivatingly written, will sell handsomely, largely, and will *keep on* selling, permanently" (Elmira, 21 July 1885).

³ CLW had written on 26 February that a "splendid letter" from Cardinal Simeoni, Prefect of the Propaganda, had arrived in time to be included in the prospectus of the Pope's biography.

176. To CHARLES L. WEBSTER

Hartford
10 April 1887

[No salutation]

All right now you are talking a language which I understand make yourself easy I will come down in a day or two as soon as I have finished blocking out a novel begun last night ¹

S L Clemens

¹ The background of this telegram is extremely complex. In mid-March it was discovered that Frank M. Scott, a bookkeeper, had embezzled $25,000 from the firm over a period of more than a year. MT was indignant because "⁹⁄₁₀ of the steal *before* Feb. 27, '86, was mine, no doubt" (Notebook 21, TS p. 41). In addition, Scott had first become suspect in August or September 1886, but on the advice of Whitford was not questioned (*ibid.*), "They [Alexander & Green] advise you to keep a thief's hand in my pocket" (*ibid.*, p. 43). MT demanded a complete reorganization of the Company (*ibid.*, pp. 45–46), and in an undated fragment CLW forwarded a proposition: The Grant volume would be figured in with the other volumes of the Company rather than separately; MT would receive straight half-profits on his books; he would leave $50,000 capital in the Company, and receive complete statements each three months. In response, MT drafted an

Answer to the proposition.
A tri-monthly complete statement, with check, *imperative.*
A desk in the office for my agent, and free access to the books, balance-sheets, and every detail of the business.
Capital furnished from time to time as it is needed. The amount needed must be proven in a plain, clear, business-like way, to me or to my agent. No interest charged.
⟨On books of mine when published by the concern, I to receive, as *author* ½ profits.⟩
Strike *new* books of mine out of the contract.
I want $6,000 for the needless and perilous retention there of $100,000 for a year.
Where is the agreement of 50¢ each on "Mississippi?" Is it in writing?
When I put up $50,000, it will be in a new concern entitled S L Clemens & Co.—that or "The Mark Twain Pub. Co."
Then I might not *need* to furnish capital.
On 8 April, CLW replied to the answer: "I cannot deal with my partner in

business through the intervention of an agent. . . . no business can succeed where partners deal with each other at arms length." Further, "I must say frankly that I do not think you are doing your duty by me in neglecting to come to the office and talk matters over with me and be intelligently informed in relation to the business." The present telegram, then, was MT's reply to this strong appeal; and matters were apparently smoothed over by a new contract (*MTBus*, pp. 378–379, 382–383); but MT chose to communicate "per F. G. Whitmore" ([6] April 1887 and *MTBus*, pp. 380–381) and see letter 188 below, to Orion.

177. To Charles L. Webster

[Hartford]
25 April 1887

Dear Charley:

Thank goodness the Mississippi is out of the way at last.[1] I was very tired looking at the pile.

If you've got Prince and Pauper in sheets, I wish you would bind 2 in *tree calf* and mark one in gilt letters H. B. Stowe, and the other M. Warner,[2] and send both to me.

The other day Mrs. Stowe said "I am reading your Prince and Pauper for the *fourth* time, and I *know* it's the best book for young people that was ever written!"

Yrs

S L C

P.S. Six years well earned![3]

[1] CLW had written on 23 April, "I have sold the whole batch of the Mississippi's over 9,000, for more than cost, a splendid sale and mighty glad to get rid of them as I needed the room." The reference is to the remaindered stock purchased from JRO and sold to Watson Gill.

[2] Margaret, who had performed in Susy's production of *The Prince and the Pauper*.

[3] CLW's 23 April letter had begun, "Scott was sentenced by Judge Gildersleeve to six years at hard labor in Sing Sing States Prison yesterday."

178. To Charles L. Webster

[Hartford]
28 May 1887

Dear Charley:

You can mail the enclosed; and if you make Alden [1] an offer, I think *one-third* of the profits is plenty to offer for it. The *name* of publishing the book is something to us, but the sale won't go above 30,000. The offer would have to be for a book containing *175,000* words—for "89 chapters" is too indefinite.

Garabaldi is stale enough already; so we shouldn't want to contract for his book for 1892, but for next year—before he gets *too* stale.

You may know what to offer for translating, but I have had no experience in that line.[2]

Truly yours

S L C

P.S. Joe Jefferson's MS is delightful reading,[3] and I see that it has this additional great advantage: it is quite largely a book of *foreign travel,* and the illustrations can be made to show up that feature prominently, and the advertisements can further whoop it up.

His address is Hohokus, Bergen Co. N.J. You could write and suggest an appointment; and after you shall have concluded a bargain with him, get him to make some of the illustrations himself.

I think forty per cent of the profits is a fair offer to make him— the book to contain about 175,000 words, estimating 5 letters to a word.

I shall bring his MS to New York presently, or if he needs it I will bring it down on any day required. Such things should not be expressed—unless he has kept the original.

Yrs

S L C

¹ W. L. Alden, of the American Consulate General in Rome, wrote MT on 12 May, offering an autobiography of Garibaldi "of 89 chapters, and 693 pages of MS." CLW replied on 1 June that it would be impossible to secure a copyright: "I think we had better let foreign publications alone until we get international copyright."

² Alden had proposed translating the volume himself and asked MT to advise "what you would pay me."

³ Joe Jefferson had first written MT on 8 May 1887: "I have just written an Autobiography, and am flattered by offers . . . but as one is only endowed with a single life, it behoves him to be careful who takes it. . . . Would you care to look at it?"

179. To Charles L. Webster

Hartford
16 June 1887

Dear Charley:

We reach New York en route for Elmira, about the 21st.

I think your arrangement in the Stoddart matter is quite fortunate.¹

I have written Alden.²

Don't lose sight of the enclosed book.³ If we are in condition to take hold of it when finished, a year hence, it may be a first rate thing.

Ys Truly

S L C.

I shall keep "The Man Wonderful" and read it.⁴

¹ J. M. Stoddart was one of three General Agents for the Grant *Memoirs* who defaulted on payments. CLW obtained a judgment against Stoddart for $13,200, and wrote MT on 14 June that he had accepted an offer to settle for $6,500 cash and notes for $4,700. The two other agents, Hubbard Bros. and R. T. Root were also defending suits at this time, Hubbard for $32,000 and Root for $36,000 (CLW to MT, 14 June, 1887).

² MT had written Alden on 28 May, suggesting his uncertainty over the book: "It might be a great strike, and also it might fail of that" (CWB). On 14 June, CLW asked MT, "I have very little time, as I start for the West to-night;

therefore, if you can, I would like to have you write to Alden in regard to the book." MT jotted "Write Alden" on the envelope, and presumably rejected the Garibaldi volume in a second letter.

³ The reference is uncertain. In addition to volumes already mentioned, MT and the Company had corresponded about offers from "Sir Roger" Tichborne for his autobiography and Paul Boyton "of amphibious fame, who proposes to write a book of his adventures" (CLW to MT, 26 March [1887]; *MTBus*, pp. 380–381), and about a "work on Mexico, written by a lady who has spent a great many years there and lived among the people" (FJH to MT, 4 April 1887), which MT advised publishing "if you can obtain the book . . . for a very low royalty; 2½ to 3 percent" (F. G. Whitmore to FJH, n.d.). Or it may more probably be the Delmonico's cookbook, to be mentioned further in subsequent letters.

⁴ Chilion B. and Mary A. Allen had published *The Man Wonderful in the House Beautiful. An Allegory Teaching the Principles of Physiology and Hygiene, and the Effects of Stimulants and Narcotics* in 1883; the volume was reissued in 1891, over the unlikely imprint of The Man Wonderful Co. MT may have referred to it as "the enclosed book" in the paragraph above, and contemplated publishing it.

180. To Fred J. Hall

[Elmira]
12 July 1887

Dear Mr. Hall—

If your prospectus for Kalakaua's book is ready it might be well to rush into the canvass now while this flurry is up.¹ But it is not a long-lived flurry ²—a steamer or two will see the end of it.

Truly Yours

S L Clemens

¹ On 13 July, FJH replied that "there are a great many drawings and wood-cuts under way, so that if you decide to rush the book [of Hawaiian legends], it can be done without much trouble." He also reported that "the Crawford book is all printed, and will be out probably in a week; and I am just returning to the printer the last galley proofs of the Hancock book."

² In 1887, David Kalakaua's monarchy was threatened by a revolutionary movement which resulted in a new constitution limiting his powers.

181. To FRED J. HALL

Elmira
15 July 1887

Dear Mr. Hall:

No, if the prospectus were actually ready to issue it might be worth while to take advantage of the King's little flurry, but there isn't enough permanency to the flurry to do us any real good, and might disarrange Mr. Webster's plans, anyway.

It appears by your letter of day before yesterday that you have received Am. Pub. Co. check for $163.20 and Slote's check for $477.24. So my one blank book outsells my 6 printed ones!

You may send those two amounts to me—they made confusion last year by getting mixed into our firm-accounts.[1]

Now I have this idea—which I would like you to submit to Mr. Whitford:

If you will send to Mr. F. G. Whitmore, Hartford, and get my Am. Pub. statements running back several years (or possibly you may have them yourselves), and compare them with this new and amazing $163-statement, it must appear that those people can't work my books to advantage, and so they (perhaps) might be compelled to annul the contracts.

2. If they reply that my reputation is dead and that that is the trouble, you can disprove that by showing your *own* statements of sales of my books. (By the way, how much of this $163-worth were sold by *you* in the last 3 months? There is fraud or a mystery here.)

By their showing, their present profit on my books is only about 12 or $1300 a year, and mine about a third of that. Now then, suppose I offer them three-years' purchase for my contracts—say $4,000—they to destroy the plates, for I should want new ones, unless they were willing to sell me the plates at twice the price of old type-metal. And if they refuse my offer, bring suit for annulment of my contracts.

I would like to know what Mr. Whitford thinks of my project.

Ys Truly
S. L. Clemens

[1] A. H. Wright had written MT on 13 July that the two checks had been "placed to your Cr.[edit] on our books." MT, still suspicious and distrustful of the state of the business, wanted the amounts sent directly to him, and FJH complied on 18 July.

182. To CHARLES L. WEBSTER

Elmira
3 August 1887

Dear Charley:

I have to confess that to me our outlook is disturbing. I suppose the Pope's book and the McClellan book together will not more than pay the expenses of the last year and a half—you will correct me if I am wrong. Meantime we have suffered three serious diminutions of "futures," so to speak—in fact they amount to disasters: I refer to the loss of the Grant Letters,[1] worth to us $60,000 profit perhaps—one can only guess, of course; heavy diminution of value of *de luxe* Grant Memoirs, by reason of the loss to us of its chiefest feature of value (the insertion of samples of the General's manuscript,) and finally the reduction of the Beecher autobiography to a biography,[2] which is about the equivalent I suppose of reducing a dollar to a fourth of that sum: a serious matter still, even if the Beechers should consent to come down to a 10 per cent royalty, which they ought to do. By these misfortunes not less than a future $100,000 has escaped our hands. The only extremely promising book left is the Lieutenant General's, and it is not immediately usable to fill up the tank. We are still paying in money to J Langdon & Co on the great coal mine purchase of three years ago, and must continue to do so, or at any rate lie out of dividends, until 13 months hence; and if we should require money for this to a considerable amount, the outlook promises that we cannot with certainty look to you for it:

Therefore, I beg you to put the Library of Humor [3] in the works without waiting for pictures, and push it through, publishing the 15th of December. If somebody's book must be turned over to the spring, let it be a stranger's. If the canvassing book can with *certainty* be gotten ready and distributed by the 12th or 15th of September, let me know, for I want relief of mind; the fun, which was abounding in the Yankee at Arthur's Court up to three days ago, has slumped into funereal seriousness, and this will not do—it will not answer at all. The very title of the book requires fun, and it must be furnished. But it can't be done, I see, while this cloud hangs over the workshop.

I work seven hours a day, and am in such a taut-strung and excitable condition that everything that *can* worry me, does it; and I get up and spend from 1 o'clock till 3 A.M. pretty regularly every night, thinking—not pleasantly.

Charley, I want a *perfect* copy of Fred Grant's letter,[4] for my Autobiography. I was supposing I had about finished the detailed private history of the Grant Memoirs, but doubtless more than one offensive chapter must be added yet, if Fred Grant lives.[5]

Truly Yrs

S L Clemens

[1] The Grant family—specifically Colonel Fred—had become suspicious of the bookkeeping on the Grant *Memoirs*, questioning whether large legal expenses might validly be a part of "publication costs." CLW insisted to MT that they were (21 and 23 April 1887), and MT agreed (*MTBus*, p. 380). Apparently MT decided that the Grants would retaliate by withdrawing their plan for the letters and their willingness to dispose of the manuscript in a *de luxe* edition of the *Memoirs*.

[2] On 30 March, after Beecher's death on 8 March, CLW wrote MT: "I want your approval by telegraph to the publication of a 'Biography of Henry Ward Beecher, written by his son Wm C. Beecher and his son in law Rev Saml Scoville assisted by Mrs Henry Ward Beecher and largely compiled from his notes and papers.'" In the margin MT noted, "Telegraphed: 'I approve the book and the terms. Close the contract.' (April 1/87.) S L Clemens."

[3] On 17 February 1887, after a query from MT (*MTBus*, p. 376), CLW had replied, "It would never do to publish that [*Library of Humor*] out of our house; as you are a partner it would look as though we had had a row or as though you doubted the ability of your own house. . . . The book cannot get too old, it will always sell, and as soon as we get some of the important pressing things off our hands we will publish it."

[4] On 22 July, Fred Grant had written CLW a letter (TS in MTP) claiming that an audit of the Grant accounts by his accountant persuaded him that the firm owed his mother approximately $104,000 more than she had been paid. On

the envelope of his copy of the letter, MT wrote, "Fred Grant's queer letter." Later, on 10 August, FJH told MT, "I saw him [Grant] a few days ago . . . and from his words and manner I judged that he had no idea we would allow his claims."

[5] All of the extant autobiographical dictations concerning the Grant *Memoirs* are dated 1885, so the offensive chapters may not have been added.

183. To Fred J. Hall and Charles L. Webster

Elmira
15 August 1887

Dear Mr. Hall; and of course C.L.W:

Thank you very much for the report.[1] That is what I should like to have now and then. It makes everything clear, and one can see where he stands.

We are learning new points on one thing, every day: and that is, that it takes a great book to stand big royalties. A book must sell 30,000 copies at $3 to $3.50 cloth, to stand ½ profits; it must sell 20,000 to stand ⅓ profits (10 per cent royalty); 15,000 to stand 7½ per cent; and a 10,000-copy book is not worth much at *any* terms —for us.

I would offer Joe Jefferson only 8 per cent.[2] And if the thing were to do over again we would try Sunset Cox at that figure.[3] I am afraid his sale won't go above 12,000 copies. I guess Joe Jefferson at 15,000 to 20,000. The highest royalty I ever got (while *I* was green), was 10 per. cent.

Now as to the Library of Humor. It will sell 30,000 copies without illustrations, and 50,000 *with* them; so Webster is right about the propriety of illustrating, I believe.[4] I suggest that you get *Kemble* as artist; and that you get him right away, if he is getable; and that he make 200 pictures—a few of them full-page, the rest ¼, ⅓, ½-page, and so on, to go in with the text.

And so you will need to instruct Mr. Clark to make the book— what? ⟨170,000 words?⟩ You can figure it out. ⟨It is about that.⟩ Pictures occupy say 70 pages of space; index, title, etc, and tops and bottoms of chapters, 15 or 20 more: then you'll want about

500 pages of solid *words*. Are there 400 words on a page? if so, you'll want 200,000 words;—more likely 250,000, maybe.

I don't want to get caught out and "left." After all my recent eloquence, you say if I "wish it" you will have "under way" the Library of Humor. I don't recal, now, what it was I wrote, but dear me I meant to be *urgent!* And my idea (whether I got it on paper or not), was, to get an absolute date set for the canvass to begin, and another for the publication. And that is what I am up to, *now,* you see. Can you name the 15th of January with *certainty,* for the canvassing-books to be ready and the canvass to begin? And the 1st of April as the day of publication? Now whack me out an answer to these conundrums, Charley; and if yes, you can stir up Mr. Clark as soon as you please, and shove the book into the works.

This present book (I mean the "Yankee at King Arthur's Court,") will be finished by the end of the year; I allow myself time enough, because when we leave for Hartford I shall have but 500 pages of MS finished—just ⅓ of the book—and in H. I shall not have the uninterrupted rush that I secure to myself here. But it may never go to press; for it is a 100,000-copy book, if Huck Finn was a 50,000-copy book, and I shall wait until I see at least an 80,000-copy sale ahead before I publish. (You see, I went back and read my 350 pages of MS through, yesterday, and found out that I am making an uncommonly bully book—and am swelled up accordingly.)

Yrs

S L Clemens

[1] In response to MT's depression in the previous letter, FJH mailed a report on the state of the business on 10 August (CLW had been in bed with neuralgia since his return from the West in July, and apparently returned to the office only intermittently from this time on). The outlook was good; there were no outstanding debts except MT's undrawn profits. Both the Pope's book and McClellan's were selling well "considering the time of the year." Neither FJH nor CLW was interested in the Grant letters—"great as Grant was, the people . . . have had enough of it." Both men expected the Beecher biography and the *Life of Christ* to sell satisfactorily.

[2] Jefferson wrote CLW on 20 October, after having been offered this contract, "I presumed from the long silence that followed my correspondence with Mr. Clemens . . . that you had given up the idea of publishing my book. Being under this impression, I began negociations with another firm" (TS in MTP).

[3] On 7 July, FJH had written that S. S. Cox had offered the Company his *Diversions of a Diplomat in Turkey*. On the envelope MT wrote, "Yes, we want Cox's book" and authorized a 7 or 8 percent royalty (*MTBus*, p. 384).

[4] The 10 August report to MT had conveyed CLW's opinion that "the large public who read your books have become accustomed to seeing them characteristically illustrated. A book with 'Mark Twain's' name attached to it, without illustrations, would be a disappointment and materially injure its sale."

184. To CHARLES L. WEBSTER

Elmira
16 August 1887

Dear Charley:

Oh, no, I would give her our cordial permission.[1] And I would make it the rule of the house to give *any* respectable author permission to use extracts amounting in bulk to even a whole *tenth* of any book of ours—he to name page and matter as this lady has done. I quite understand that $\frac{1}{10}$ of the Memoirs would be all of 100 pages. *And a very generous advertisement for us, gratis*—well worth having. It isn't a newspaper's *review* of a book that makes the book sell; it is the *extracts* copied from the book that does it. To be consistent damned donkeys, Houghton Mifflin[2] ought to forbid the use of extracts in reviews of their books. But I suppose a fool never is consistent.

Ys Truly

SLC

Why, the Hancock book does indeed promise well.[3]

[1] On 13 August, A. H. Wright wrote for CLW, forwarding a letter requesting permission to reprint material from the Grant *Memoirs*. On 17 August, FJH advised, "We have written the lady . . . that she might use the selections indicated in her letter."

---

² MT's dazzling generosity concerning permissions is partly explained by his growing concern over permission for the *Library of Humor*—especially from Houghton Mifflin. See the following letter.

³ On 13 August, Wright had reported on the initial sales of the Hancock book: "The first agent we sent out took 27 orders the first week. The second agent took 14 in two days."

185. To Charles L. Webster & Co.

[Elmira]
23 August 1887

Hartford
June 10, 1887

Dear Sirs:

⟨This is as far as I got, in a blast at Houghton, Syphillis & Co,¹ designed for publication. But it would not do to print what I was going to say.⟩ ⟨You see by the date that I meant to manufacture a "Correspondence."⟩

That's all right. Get H.M. & Co's terms for the use of the matter we want. If one may judge by what the Atlantic pays those authors for the stuff when it is *original,* and what they dribble out to them in royalties in a year, when it has gone into book form, the sum won't be very heavy. I should say that ⅔ of a cent a word would be plenty high enough for that second-hand matter; for they pay those very authors an average of less than 2 cents a word for their original matter. Their highest-paid prose man ⟨except myself,⟩ was Dr. Holmes, and he got $18 per Atlantic page—which is 2 cents ⟨and an invisible fraction⟩ per word.

Let me hear what they want to charge. If they crowd me too hard, I will use the matter without their consent, and let them sue for "exemplary" damages. But I should want this purpose kept private until our book was out.

Yrs

SLC.

Come to think, are there any Selections in the Library from *Howells's* books?[2]

If not, I must have Mr. Clark make some at once.

SLC

---

[1] FJH's letters of 17 and 22 August report difficulties in obtaining permission rights, because Houghton Mifflin "are very offish."

[2] On 3 January 1886, MT had written "Dear Charles" Clark, "You perceive that nothing—in Howells's opinion—is necessary but a selection from his own humor; then the book will be finished" (TS in MTP). On 18 July 1887, FJH had pointed out to MT, "I do not find any selections from Mr. Howell's works." On 13 August, MT wrote Clark again (TS in MTP), suggesting the difficulty of securing permissions and proposing to "rake together an *uncopyrighted* page or two from Warner and Howells."

186. To FRED J. HALL

[Hartford?]
2 September 1887

Fred Hall

Consider the propriety of telegraphing those people[1] that all the manuscript must be in our hands by the 20th of this month or there can be no question that the book will be a failure.

Ys Truly

S L C.

P.S. I was going [to] telegraph this to you, but don't like that vehicle. If those people cannot be frightened into completing the Beecher book in three weeks, I think the book will not only fail but will so clog our hands as to heavily damage one or two *other* books.

---

[1] The Beecher family.

187. To Charles L. Webster or Fred J. Hall

[Elmira]
5 September 1887

Dear Charley—or Mr Hall—or both: [1]

You need to be careful about the cook-book,[2] in the matter of date. There will be no date open for it for about two years; and they will have to be told this, of course. Gen. Sheridan occupies all the fall of next year, by himself.[3] The only other choice date for a canvass to begin is Jan 1, '89, which will have to be left open and free for a possible 100-ton book;[4] "Yanks and Johnnies"[5] will follow it, and it might be that the cook book would be pushed still forward indefinitely. I really doubt the wisdom of taking that or any other book for a year to come, except a 100-ton one. Indeed I very *strongly* doubt it.

Truly Yrs

SLC

[1] The present letter is in response to a visit to Elmira by FJH on 30 August to discuss business prospects, and to a "scheme for publishing" mailed to MT on 2 September. The "scheme" proposed the following publication schedule:

Hancock's *Reminiscences*, 20 September 1887
S. S. Cox's book, 15 November 1887
Beecher biography, 1 December 1887
Mrs. Custer's *Tenting on the Plains*, 15 December 1887
Library of Humor, 28 February 1888
"Sandwich Islands," 15 April 1888
Life of Christ, 30 May 1888
Sheridan's *Personal Memoirs*, 1 December 1888.

"Sandwich Islands" was Daggett's and Kalakaua's volume, not the Bill Ragsdale novel MT had worked on in 1884 (see *MTHL*, p. 462). MT's displeasure with the schedule was reflected in a notebook entry (Notebook 22, TS p. 9): "We are forced to suddenly change from 2 in a year and a half to an attempt to *do 7 in 9 months!*"

[2] FJH had presumably brought the offer of a cookbook from Alessandro Filippini, chef at Delmonico's. MT was unimpressed and in the "scheme for issues" suggested "Royalty 5%—if we decide to take it."

[3] The letter of 2 September had pointed out that "As this book is one that will attract a great deal of attention, and draw the agents, it is advisable not to issue any other book during the time of the active canvass and sale of this, for except the [other] book was of a peculiar character it would merely mean to sacrifice it, as no agent could be gotten to take hold of it."

[4] Presumably *A Connecticut Yankee in King Arthur's Court.*

[5] William H. Van Nortwick's *Yanks and Johnnies; or, Laugh and Grow Fat,* a humorous volume the firm published in 1888.

188. To ORION CLEMENS

Private

My Dear Bro:

These are secrets—not to be spoken of, and not to be referred to in letters to me or to others. The firm of C. L. Webster & Co. have paid out in cash in the 6 months ending Sept. 1, $105,000 cash, about a third of it unnecessarily; but still we cleared $23,000 in spite of it.[1] After this, things are going to be done on a business-like basis, and the half-year ending Apl. 1, will make a better showing. I woke up 6 weeks ago, to find that there was no more system in the office than there is in a nursery without a nurse. But I have spent a good deal of time there since, and reduced everything to exact order and system—insomuch that even Webster can run it now—and in most particulars he is a mere jackass. I could never interfere before; the former contract was so ingeniously contrived that for two years I have had no more say in the concern than the errand-boy; and to ask a question was to invoke contemptuous silence, and to make a suggestion was to have it coolly ignored. During two years I couldn't get the shadow of a statement as to the condition of the business. If Webster wanted the contract changed (for his advantage,) he *demanded* the change—never asked for it; and I had to comply; but he made one grab too many, last April, and turned the tables on himself. He knew I had been spending $5,000 a month here for a year on a project of mine, and that this was to continue for another year; so he got frightened and demanded and *required* that I put up a permanent cash capital of $75,000 for the publishing-house to save it from destruction in case I ruined myself. (Formerly I had to furnish *limitless* capital and be responsible for everything.) It was offering me my emancipation-papers, and I did not lose any time in signing the document.[2]

Up to that time he had been all insolence; but he is the gentlest spirit in this region since—perfectly tame and civil. And stands criticism like a pupil; stands being reminded of the numerous ways in which he has betrayed the fact that he is not the miracle of a publisher he supposed he was, but a blundering, ignorant apprentice. He had the hardihood to turn Donelly's Shakspeare book [3] away without asking me anything about it; so used to violating the old contract that he forgot he was no longer master, and fell into the old habit. Of course he didn't know he was throwing away $50,000; he was merely ignorant; had probably never heard of Bacon and didn't know there was a controversy. This won't happen again.

My Library of Humor is going into the works, now, and I have appointed the day, and cleared the field for it.[4] For two years he would not touch it. He made the mistake of his life last April.

Your Bro

Sam.

P.S. The play? [5] I took it off the stage to remodel it. Shall put it on a year hence if I get time to fix it.

[1] In spite of a surface harmony, this letter to Orion and MT's notebook entries for the same period show that distrust had in fact already destroyed the partnership. Notebook 22 contains entries like these: "Sept. 1, '87. Two (books) in a year and a half. Loss upon the one, $32,000; profit on the other, $15,000. Expenses, $30,000. Net loss, $17,000 [$47,000?]" (TS p. 9); "You had 35,000 in bank about June 1st . . . and only $13,000 a month later" (TS p. 18). On TS pp. 9–13 is a diatribe of such vitriolic character (presumably written very early in September and based upon his reactions to both the Scott defalcation and the Grants' alienation) that any notion of continuing the partnership would have been obviously impossible.

[2] The contract of 1 April 1887 (in CWB) limited MT's capital investment to seventy-five thousand dollars, increased CLW's salary to $3,800 annually and provided a salary of $2,000 for FJH. FJH received one-twentieth of the net profits, and MT and CLW then divided the remainder, two-thirds and one-third.

[3] On 9 July, MT had decided he did not want Ignatius Donnelly's *The Great Cryptogram* (*MTBus*, p. 384); on 10 August, however, FJH did report that "Donnelly offered us his Shakespeare book, but Mr. Webster thought it best to decline it, especially as the author wanted all the profits."

[4] A number of FJH letters in late 1887 discuss the progress of the *Library of Humor*: after talking about illustrations with other artists (3 and 21 September 1887), he contracted with E. W. Kemble for $2,000 (19 September); Houghton Mifflin finally gave permission (22 and 28 September); and the manuscript arrived from Clark and was being prepared (22 September, 3 October).

[5] "Colonel Sellers as a Scientist."

189. To Fred J. Hall

Elmira
8 September 1887

Dear Mr. Hall:

I think it is the very book [1] we want—though you see you have left me in the dark again as to an essential feature: *how many words does it contain?* Make him an offer of 5 per cent. If he agrees, close the contract. If he doesn't, keep at him, and yield a little till you get him.

We will bind the *book* itself and deliver it immediately into the hands of the subscriber, without any canvassing-book. [2] Begin the canvass and delivery June 1st—at people's houses; afterward at all the watering places and summer resorts, east and west. *They* concentrate the very people we want.

We will make *two* cloth editions—one large-type octavo (to be offered to a person first—at $3.50; and if that is too high for him, offer him the other)—a small-type 12mo. at $2.50. The big one to contain good portraits of the Delmonicos and the author, with signatures.

But of course we can't make the big one unless there are 200,000 words and upwards. We want a $5-binding, too.

Be ready with your facts Wednesday morning, when I look in.

Ys Truly

S. L. Clemens

[1] On 7 September, FJH had written a long glowing letter describing Filippini's cookbook, and pointing out that the Delmonico family "are willing to do anything in their power to forward the sale." The description succeeded in changing MT's opinion of the volume.

[2] FJH had suggested in his 7 September letter that the volume could be prepared for publication as a "slow and steady-selling book," without any need of intensive canvass. It appeared in 1888 with the title, *The Table: How to Buy Food, How to Cook It, and How to Serve It.*

190. To CHARLES L. WEBSTER & Co.

Hartford
18 September 1887

Dear C. L. W. & Co:

Here is a systematic and orderly scheme which I have worked at a good deal, the last two days, and have finally got it to suit me. It cannot easily be improved, if at all. It has some large advantages:

1. This system of royalties can be proposed without a blush, to the biggest author, and also to the littlest one. (Try it on the cook book.)

2. By it we *cannot* lose on any book which is important enough for us to be willing to publish it.

3. It gouges no author, and it permits no author to gouge us.

The system will vary but in one case. When we *know* an author will sell more than say 60,000, we may possibly have to promise an addition of 1 per cent to the 12 after a sale of that number.

I have put in those trade and subscription statistics, purposely that they may be *used* in talking with authors, in order that they may see the fairness of sinking the plates and paying only 5 and 6 per cent royalties on the first 20,000 copies sold. The statistics are not guesses, they are *facts* within my personal knowledge (provided the Sherman one is right—I got it from General Grant). If you will familiarize yourselves with these facts and arguments, and use them, you will be able to capture *any* author's book, it makes no difference who he is.

Please keep the scheme private, and study it. But let no clerk see it. Don't type-writer it. We don't want to give away a good idea to other publishers.

S L C

Just and Equable Scheme of Royalties.

An itemized and accurate account shall be kept, showing just what the "plant" or plates of a book cost us.

When receipts have *repaid* us that, the payment of royalties *shall then begin,* but not sooner. We will "sink the plates" always.

ROYALTIES.
(estimated on a $3.50 book,
and paid on cloth basis, only.)

	Author gets
On the first 10,000 copies, 5%———	$1750
" second " " 6%———	2100
" third " " 10%———	3500
Total	$7,350

On all above 30,000 copies, the author to receive a royalty of *12 per cent.*

On first 10,000, we deduct $5,000 office expenses and $1750 for author, leaving $3,250 profit. On second 10,000 we clear about $5,000; on third, about $6,500; on the rest, $5,800, or nearly 60% of the profit.

"TRADE" METHODS.

The average book-seller hardly ever orders more than 3 copies of a new book. (Do not take our word, but go and ask.) These go over the counter the first day, and he orders no more. He tells the customer he is "out," and proposes to take the customer's order. The customer doesn't care enough about it, and no sale is made.

RESULT, AND ARGUMENT.

Bret Harte's greatest sale was on his first book, "The Luck of Roaring Camp," when he was at the zenith of his popularity. This sale was 26,000 copies in 2 years. The price was $1.25 a copy, the royalty was 10%, or 12½ cents on each book. Result to Harte in 2 years, about $3,000!

We can sell 3 copies of *any* book where the trade can sell 1. Moreover, we always charge about a third more for a book than the trade can venture to ask for it. In this case we would have sold

75,000 and charged $2 a copy. And we should have handed Harte $15,000 instead of $3,000.

Aldrich's greatest sale was "The Story of a Bad Boy"—13,000 in 10 years! price, $1.50; royalty 10 per cent. Result, about $2,000. We should have charged $2 and sold 40,000. Result to Aldrich, $6,800, instead of $2,000.

Howells's greatest sale was "A Foregone Conclusion"—started at $2 and presently reduced to $1.50. Sale, 14,000 copies. Royalty, 10 per cent. That was when he was at the top of his fame. We should have sold about 50,000, and paid him $7,200, instead of the sum which he did get, which was short of $3,000.

General Sherman's book—$7 a set—sold 25,000 sets, and he got $25,000, or 50 cents a volume. Assisted by such a name as the General's, we should have quadrupled that sale easily, and paid him $80,000 in royalties, instead of $25,000.

The "Innocents Abroad," sold by subscription 160,000 copies at $3.50. Royalty all through, 5 per cent. Result to the author, about $30,000. By our graduated system of royalties, he would have received $62,000.

Very few authors can sell an edition of 3,000 in the trade aside from those above enumerated. Those who can do it can be counted on the fingers of the two hands.

The author of The Innocents Abroad tried 2 books in the trade. One of them sold 6,000 copies, the other sold 10,000. Total, 16,000. He has tried 10 books by subscription. Total sales, 618,000 copies.

P.S. I am going to Boston Tuesday to discuss with Houghton. Clark goes with me.

Next, I shall get the Am. Pub. Co's consent.

I will have Clark send you all of the stuff as soon as I have arranged with Houghton. Then you want to get the artists at work instantly.

When I first projected the Library of Humor, I placed the sale at my usual figure for a $3.50 book—60,000 copies in 6 months. I have raised on that, now—to 80,000. That is my bottom estimate.

Clark says it is a magnificent book, and nobody can glance into it without buying it, even if he has to sell his shirt. Therefore, the canvass must be extended. It must last from Jan 1 to *March* 15, even if we have to crowd the next book into pretty narrow quarters to do it.

Please note that change:

Canvass begins Jan 1, and ends March 15.

When I come down, presently, we will think the thing all over and definitely arrange dates for the succeeding books as well as we possibly can for their advantage.

The matter shall be in the artists' hands 4 or 5 days hence, and we want them to make written agreements with us and get right to work.

There is $40,000 for the firm in this book, and we want to have the plates ready early,—and give ourselves plenty of elbow room to work in.

Yrs

S L C

191. To Charles L. Webster & Co.

Hartford

14 October 1887

Dear CLW & Co—

You may write Uncle Remus; and if he doesn't consent I will then take him by the hair myself.

You may also write Stockton and if he says no, I will take *him* by the hair.[1]

If you've got that detailed statement ready, you may mail me a copy; for I had my palate cut out several days ago, and it promises to never get well again and I'm forbidden to travel while it remains in this infamous condition.

I've thought of a new and better way to offer copyright terms to authors—and so we will postpone offers till I see you and tell you about it.

Ys Truly

S L Clemens

---

[1] For permissions. FJH wrote MT on 13 October that Appleton and Scribner had agreed to the use of Harris's and Stockton's material if the authors agreed. FJH reported on 28 October that Appleton and Belford and Clarke had granted permissions and that all copyright holders were cooperating.

192. To CHARLES L. WEBSTER & CO.

Hartford

17 October 1887

Dear CLW & Co:

I should say that we do not want the book of Gems at any price.[1]

What arrangement have you arrived at with Laffan, on the Baltimore book?[2]

He is going away.

Ys Truly

S L C

---

[1] On 28 September, FJH reported that a Mr. G. F. Kunz, "the gem-expert at Tiffany's," had written a book on gems, very expensive "to get up." Other rejected offerings of the Fall were:

A biography of Dio Lewis by Mrs. Lewis (FJH to MT, 26 September).

A revised edition of the Bible (*ibid.*)

William D. O'Brien's *Encyclopedia of Ireland* (*ibid.*)

Dr. Chalfant's *Life among the Convicts* (29 September).

A history of the G. A. R. proposed by General Fairchild (*ibid.*)

A cookbook by Flora Haines Longhead (3 October).

Dr. J. H. Douglas, *The Last Days of General Grant* (5 December).

Mr. Thompson, *Anarchy* (on the Haymarket riots) (27 December).

An autobiography of Lillie Langtry (29 December).

[2] The Walker art book. MT had written earlier on 5 September (*MTBus*, pp. 385–386), reporting that Laffan was talking of going to Europe. No replies are extant.

193. To CHARLES L. WEBSTER & Co.

Hartford
19 October 1887

Dear C.L.W. & Co:

Your letter received concerning statement.[1] You may send me $10,000; also the firm's note or receipt for $12,073.47 to complete the $75,000 capital required by the contract. I shall look for the statement in a few days.[2]

Ys truly

S L Clemens

[1] MT had received a complete itemized statement of the Company's affairs through 1 October 1887, the margins of which he filled with peevish queries:
Rent in 4 places?
Where is the Phila. judgment and compromise-money?
Reported before?
When is this to issue?
How much of this is profit to us?
In summary, the Company took in $124,262.50 from April to October, and paid out $105,328.10, leaving a balance of $18,934.40. In the present letter, MT requests the majority of this cash on hand plus a note which accounts for more than the remainder.

[2] Instead, he received a frantic letter (21 October, TS in MTP) from CLW: "You have made a great mistake some way and I fail to see where you got the figures to make it." CLW explained, "The paper which you took a few days ago showed only 'Receipts' and 'Disbursements' but *not* Assets and Liabilities to Author etc. . . . On sales for the last six months there is nothing to divide but on sales *prior* to April 1st collected *since* to be divided according to the old contract there is as stated before $12191.40." MT's share of the profits was $9,086.85, but CLW was "so low in cash that I do not dare" to pay the full amount. Instead, he promised to forward $5,000 the following week.

194. To CHARLES L. WEBSTER & Co.

Hartford
27 October 1887

Dear C L W & Co—

The $5,000 has been endorsed on the last receipt.[1]

Young Burton will get his father's MSS together and hand them to me.[2] Rev. Parker or Twichell will read the proofs here.

Which shall you prefer to do?—have the plates made here, or in N.Y?[3] They can't *bind* a book here, at all. Composition 25 cts.

There will be between 600 and 700 pages octavo, at 380 words to the page.

We will sell it at $4. *cloth,* and $3 or $3.50 to the clergy.

We will have no general agency, but use a canvasser only.[4] I am on the track of the one we want: a young insurance-policy canvasser, who hunts the State on his bicycle, is a member of Burton's church, and so is his father; the latter is a pillar—even a pier—of that church.

This is a case where a steel portrait is a quite valuable addition to a book. You know the man for the work—; so let him take the enclosed and put his masterwork on it.[5]

Ys truly

S L Clemens

P.S. The enclosed printed slip is for the ENGRAVER. By studying it carefully he will learn to know his man before he begins his work. Please *impress that upon him.* I want him to make as noble a portrait as his subject was.

[1] See n. 2 to the preceding letter.

[2] MT and CLW had disagreed on the wisdom of publishing the late Rev. Nathaniel Burton's *Yale Lectures on Preaching* (*MTBus,* p. 387).

[3] Although CLW did sell the volume, it was manufactured almost entirely in Hartford. FJH shipped paper to the Star Company (FJH to MT, 6, 15, and 17 December 1887). It was apparently sold from Hartford as well (see letter 196 below).

[4] Yet in Notebook 22, TS p. 39, after an entry dated 18 November, MT wrote, "Canvass Dr Burton *now.*" Later (TS p. 42), he wrote, "Do not begin on the Burton book till the MS is *all* ready, and the words carefully counted."

[5] In Notebook 22, TS p. 34, MT wrote: "Nov. 1. Will take 3 or 4 weeks to make Dr B's steel—$300"; and on 6 December, FJH asked how many copies of the engraving were required.

195. To CHARLES L. WEBSTER & Co.

[Hartford]
13 November 1887

Dear CLW & Co—

I believe it would be a good idea to keep "Memorandum Book for Constant Reference" and in it have headings, thus:

> Library of Literature
> Library of Humor
> Cox's Book
> Custer's Book
> The Cook Book
> etc., etc.,

and in it enter notes for guidance, which might slip the memory and get lost.

Then, under The Cook-Book heading, enter this as a reminder:

Better take out Canadian copyright, or the pirates will kill us with a cheap edition. And while in Canada it might do no harm to take out English copyright also, and send Chatto a set of stereotypes—not electros.[1]

Ys

SLC

---

[1] Letters of this period (Chatto & Windus to CLW, 3 October; CLW to Chatto & Windus, 19 October, 3 December) discuss simultaneous publication of the *Library of Humor,* but not the cookbook. Many pages in Notebook 22 discuss the method of English prepublication (TS pp. 48–53).

196. To CHARLES L. WEBSTER & Co.

[Hartford]
24 December 1887

Dear C L W & Co—

That is a good woodcut.[1]

I am glad the prospectus is coming out on time.[2] I think your arrangement of it is thoughtful and well devised.[3]

That paper came, and the printing of the Burton book has begun. Also the canvassing—with good promise.

Truly Yours

S L Clemens

[1] MT refers to a woodcut of himself for the Stedman *Library of Humor*. He had disapproved an earlier engraving (*MTBus*, pp. 388–389) and on 27 December, CLW wrote, "I am very glad that you like the wood cut. I was not at all pleased with the old one, and therefore had the new one made."

[2] The "scheme" of 2 September had called for the agent's dummy of the *Library of Humor* to appear on 1 January 1888, and MT was becoming more and more disturbed at the possibility of the book's delay. On 24 December, FJH wrote that although work was progressing on the *Library of Humor*, "We thought it was best to get the Custer book out and printed, but we have not started to sell it yet, for the simple reason that the Cox book is going very well and our Agents have just started on it." MT wrote on the envelope, "Hold back the Custer book," and repeated the order in a letter of 29 December (TS in MTP). He also exploded in his Notebook (22, TS p. 47):

Pub. next to nothing during 2 years and then pile everything in together and make one bk kill another.

Lib Humor ought to have issued and sold 100,000, fall of '86, stead of being balled-up with Custer and Cox in the winter of 87–8. . . .

What did you print the Custer book for?

Did you bind it?

[3] In a letter of 23 December, FJH explained the selection of material for the prospectus, with some interesting implications about the subscription-book formula:

We thought if it was composed principally of extracts from well known pieces by prominent authors, many would say in looking at it, that it was merely a collection of old matter . . . and for that reason most of the extracts given in the prospectus are from the less prominent writers, and extracts which comparatively few people have read. Then, to meet the objection that might arise from people who would wish all the standard humorous pieces, we have put in a number of full page illustrations as *inserts*. . . . Besides we have prepared an index of authors . . . and our agent can turn to that and show at once that all the prominent pieces are in the prospectus, besides a vast deal of matter that is comparatively new.

197. To CHARLES L. WEBSTER

Hartford
28 December 1887

Dear Charley:

I am quite willing, since it commends itself to you as a good move.[1] If you wish to relinquish and sacrifice toward this new salary the extra $800 a year added to your own salary to make up your private loss by Scott's defalcation,[2] good—otherwise never mind it. I gave my word at the time, and will not retreat from it, of course; though reflection, later, convinced me that I already had a heavy enough load left on me by Scott.

I suppose the larger the local General Agency can now be made, the better it will be for us all, so long as it isn't made too large for Dibble to handle effectively.

I shall be down Saturday noon to attend another troublesome dinner and will drop in at the office.

Truly yours

S L Clemens

[1] On 27 December, CLW wrote, testily, "Although under our partnership agreement I have the sole right of employing whomever I please and of discharging whomever I please, still in a matter of as much importance as the present I feel it my duty to consult you." CLW believed that "our subscription department is the weakest part of our business," and that W. E. Dibble of Cincinnati should be brought in to manage the New York General Agency of the Company. "I find that I can get Mr. Dibble by giving him a salary of two thousand dollars ($2,000.00) a year and one-fourth of the net profits of the local agency. . . . I have talked it over with Mr. Dibble and with Mr. Hall, and we have come to the conclusion that it would be very desirable for us to have him on those terms." FJH was soon to lose his interest in Mr. Dibble (see letter 202 below).

[2] In April 1887, CLW had somehow lost $4,000 of his own money on Scott's embezzlement, in addition to the firm's loss; he had persuaded MT to increase his salary to $3,800 in order to make up this loss over a five-year span. In reply to MT's suggestion that he give up the additional $800, CLW wrote a letter (29 December); on the envelope MT later jotted, "Webster ill and about ready to resign." CLW protested:

I do not see the justice in me relinquishing $800 of my salary and paying it to Dibble toward his when I get but a third of the profits. My salary has always been small I think I can say without fear of contradiction. . . . You talk as though you were paying me the salary, this is not so. I earn it myself. . . .

My health is poor and if it is thought that I do not earn my salary I am willing to make some arrangement to retire from the firm but as long as I am a member I do not feel like relinquishing any of my share in the firm.

Dibble was hired, though the terms of his contract are obscure. CLW wrote several letters to MT about company business early in 1888 ([17], 20 January, and 9 February), but to all intents the Dibble affair was his last significant involvement with the firm. On TS p. 58 in Notebook 22, MT wrote the epitaph to the partnership:

Feb. 16, 1888. On the 13th we at last got Webster to retire from business, from all authority, and from the city, till April 1, 1889, and try to get back his health. How long he has been a lunatic I do not know; but several facts suggest that it began in the summer or very early in the fall of '85,—while the 1ˢᵗ vol of the Grant Memoirs was in preparation and the vast canvass.

V

"Never ... Any Trouble"

(1888–1891)

"I cordially approve, detail by detail, of what you have done, and of what you have planned to do. You and I will never have any trouble."

Mark Twain to Fred J. Hall, Hartford, 11 January 1889

T HE YEAR 1888 was almost as trying for Mark Twain's publishing house as 1894 would be; affairs veered close to bankruptcy (according to the monthly statements prepared by A. H. Wright, the cash on hand for many months of the year was less than $2,000). Wright and Fred Hall made pleasant predictions that business would improve, and finally by the end of the year, sales of the Sheridan *Personal Memoirs* did brighten the accounts. And Mark Twain found the perfect scapegoat for the almost insolvent situation in nephew Charles L. Webster.

Before he retired in February, Webster had capped his dealings with the Grant family by writing a pathetic remonstrance in reply to their threats to sue for additional royalties they believed the Company owed them. By pointing out the vast profits the Grants had received from his own superhuman efforts, Webster apparently quieted Colonel Fred Grant. But he also exposed his growing defensiveness and hostility. Apparently some arrangement with the force of a contract ("No. 6"?) eased him into an almost involuntary retirement. When he began planning in November to reassume the direction of the Company the following April, Mark Twain and Fred Hall proposed buying him out of the organization. After lengthy negotiation (see letter 201 below), Hall purchased Webster's share of the Company for $12,000 and the task of rebuilding the organization began.

There is the question of whether Webster or Twain or Hall was responsible for the perilous condition of the Company. Webster made too many contracts for books (both Mrs. Custer and Daggett were to complain), and too many advance royalty payments for undelivered manuscripts (the Beecher family's $5,000 advance was also to cause trouble in 1888). The practice of dumping books into the trade finally backfired, for Hall wrote Twain, "several good men . . . refused to take our books on any terms, because the booksellers got hold of them, and we also know four or five *good* canvassers on the 'Huckleberry Finn' whom, so far, we have been unable to secure, because they say the trade get the book as soon as they do" (2 May 1888). Civil War books under contract had to be published even though Fred Hall became convinced that *"war literature of any kind and no matter by whom written is played out"* (FJH to MT, St. Louis, 15 October 1888). The fact remains, however, that Twain and Webster had been partners and that Webster's decisions were always subject to veto. In other matters— finances, bookkeeping, and the reliability of employees—Webster did appear to have been slipshod. Nevertheless, Webster himself saw the dramatic decline in the Company's worth after he left as proof of the urgent necessity of his own return; Twain and Hall saw in it proof of the long-lasting effects of Webster's incompetence.

Once Webster was completely out of the organization, the process of retrenchment began. Hall's notion of establishing a back list of books led to the building up of a "trade book" department (by the time of the completion of *Pudd'nhead Wilson*, Charles L. Webster & Co. was to have no subscription apparatus with which to sell it). The overproduction of books led to the establishing of $30,000 credit with the Mount Morris Bank (FJH to MT, 14 August 1888) who were used time and again (and would remain one of the largest and most intransigent creditors at the bankruptcy proceedings). With the help of *A Connecticut Yankee,* the firm stayed afloat in 1888, 1889, and 1890, "clearing $50,000 a year for three consecutive years, and piling every cent of it into one book— *Library of American Literature*" (*MTL,* p. 546). In spite of that substantial profit, a need for economy combined with Mrs. Clemens's poor health would lead to the closing of the Hartford house in 1891 and the taking up of more or less permanent if itinerant residence in Europe.

Until 1891, then, Charles L. Webster & Co. functioned as a partnership, with Mark Twain and Fred Hall working fairly harmoniously for a longer period of time than anyone would have thought possible. After 1891, Fred Hall was left substantially on his own.

198. To Fred J. Hall

Hartford
7 May 1888

Dear Mr. Hall:

The proposed book was to be infinitely grander and finer than any ever issued in any country in the world.[1] There were to be 600 copies for Europe and 600 for America, all marked and numbered —and the plates then broken up. Price, $1,000 apiece. All the canvassing to be done by a single individual; his commission $100 a copy; his total profit something over $100,000; ours $700,000, or $800,000 after paying back the original cost, of $200,000 or $250,000. I said there was reputation in it for us—and cash. We should have realized that fact, but Captain Boyton's ten-cent adventures were in the way,[2] and we couldn't get up an interest in anything above that juvenile level.

Laffan was to go to Europe and get the artists, *and* the man to write the letter-press (the mighty Wolf of Paris),[3] and superintend clear till the plates were made and the books printed and placed in our hands—a matter of 2 or 3 years.

But since then I have found a job for Laffan which will pay him $210,000 in ten or twelve months,[4] and of course he wouldn't leave that till it is finished, to tackle the art book. In fact I could not *let* him. So we will leave the art book unmentioned for a year, and then maybe take another shy at it.

I like the Gen. Howard book idea pretty well.[5] Now please write to me as if *I* were Gen. Howard. Make me a formal proposition; tell me in detail your requirements, and state what terms you will grant me if those requirements can be met. Then I will make corrections if any are needed and we'll mail it to the General.[6]

Ys Truly

S L C

[1] The Walker art collection catalog. On 5 May, FJH wrote asking, *"Is it too late now to do anything with this book?* As the cost of getting it up would be borne by someone else . . . it seems rather a rare opportunity."

[2] Boyton's book, published in 1892 under another imprint as *The Story of Paul Boyton . . . A Book for Boys, Old and Young,* continued to irk MT, because CLW had apparently thought highly of it. Notebook 22, TS p. 37 records this tirade against CLW:
What about Laffan's book? Inquired since? Only once? Been a Boyton book for babies how many times would you go?
Or to Jo Jefferson?
Or Donnelly.
Loss, $100,000 on 3.

[3] Albert Wolff, French dramatist, journalist, and author of children's books, had written the text for *Cent chefs-d'oeuvre des Collections Parisiennes* in 1884.

[4] On 12 March, Laffan and MT signed an agreement whereby they traded $\frac{1}{200}$th interests in the Paige typesetter and "a certain invention for quadruplexing cablegrams." Laffan was apparently set to work raising money for the enterprises (see Notebook 24, TS pp. 24–25).

[5] FJH's 5 May letter had enclosed "a letter and also two chapters from a manuscript by Maj. Gen. O. O. Howard"—possibly Howard's *My Life and Experiences,* issued by subscription from A. D. Worthington of Hartford [*ca.* 1907].

[6] On 12 May, FJH wrote, "I have made the corrections in the letter to General Howard, and it will go forward to-day."

199. To Charles L. Webster & Co.

Elmira
15 July 1888

Dear C L W & Co:

Why are these bills sent to Chatto? Chatto has bought no plates of you; Dawson has bought no plates of you; yet you send bills for plates to both of these people.[1] Please apologize to Mr. Chatto by the first mail; you cannot be too prompt in repairing this injury.

We've got to ask Mr. Dawson to see us through with the Sheridan book; and we've got to ask Chatto to see *him* through. And then are we to ask them to pay some more of our bills for us?

Please refer to this matter the next time I am down, and I will explain my idea of this Canadian business.

To lose Canadian copyright on a book like Sheridan's could cost us $30,000 and more, and—however, we will talk, when I come.

I was glad to get Mr. Wright's letter. You are certainly getting pretty low, but when your nose goes under you can borrow of the bank, as you suggest.[2]

We can't allow Scribners to have Winchester,[3] of course. When they have selected what they want, please count the words and see that neither of the 2 articles overruns 000 [4] words; or at least that the 2 together do not overrun 000. That is all I care for. I do not wish to inspect or examine what they select. The copying must be done *in our office* of course. Cannot let the original go out of our sight.

Now as to Gen. Miles. I should say "We are full." [5] If we can't sell the Custer book we can't sell any smaller reputation's book. But if you differ from me I will yield; only stipulating that you write to Miles the same letter you wrote to Gen. Howard.

In keeping your eye on the sharp look-out for everything affecting the Sheridan book, you are doing just right.[6] We must build as big an edition as is called for, cost what it may.

Truly Yours

S. L. Clemens

Their persistence about Winchester is not pleasant; it is about as cheeky as it would be if we were girls and had promised them something,—supposing they meant kisses—and they come and try to collect our maidenheads.

[1] Chatto & Windus and Dawson were publishing English and Canadian editions of the *Library of Humor,* and FJH had obviously billed them erroneously for plates. MT's orders about Chatto & Windus (FJH to MT, 6 March, 2 May) and Dawson (FJH to MT, 19, 21 April) were followed; and on 17 July FJH wrote, "apologies have been sent to both Dawson and Chatto and no such mistake will occur again."

[2] Wright had mailed a statement on 9 July showing a cash balance of $2,829.77. On 11 July FJH had written that "we will have to raise money" to pay for manufacturing the Sheridan volumes "by giving notes to the Mt. Morris Bank." On 14 July, Wright sent another statement showing that cash reserves had dropped to $1,422.14. On the envelope, MT wrote:
    Observe this: 2½ years ago, when we hadn't the slightest use for money, Webster insisted on keeping $100,000 in bank right along, to "keep us strong." And then he went to work and wasted it, squandered it in every idiotic way he could think of. Behold the result. We need $30,000 to build General Sheridan's 100,000-copy edition, and we've got $1500!

[3] On 18 February, FJH wrote MT that General Sheridan was being bothered by Charles Scribner regarding an earlier agreement to allow parts of his book to appear in *The Century;* on the envelope MT wrote, "Sheridan. No—*one* long article—say 10 pages—worth $3,000." A lengthy debate took place (FJH to MT, 19 April, 22 June, 3 July), and finally a member of *The Century's* staff read the manuscript in the CLW & Co. offices. He selected two passages for anthologizing, "Sheridan's observations on the Franco-Prussian war and the ride to Winchester. We told him that there would be no objection to the former, but the ride to Winchester must not be published in magazine form" (11 July). Finally, on 3 August, FJH reported a settlement: Scribners "will content themselves with one article, this one article covering General Sheridan's experiences from Gravelotte to Sedan." Later in the year there was further discussion about whether material from the Sheridan *Memoirs* could be allowed in the *Century's Battles and Leaders.* . . . FJH notified MT on 5 September that Robert Underwood Johnson had produced a letter from MT to Richard Watson Gilder agreeing to excerpts; FJH agreed to the inclusion of material in a supplemental volume scheduled to issue in 1889, but not in the volume to appear in December 1888 (5 September). MT wrote, lamely, on the envelope: "I *did* agree, as far as *one* end of a firm could, but I *didn't* promise to get the other end's consent, or even ask for it."

[4] MT apparently had not decided exactly how many words would satisfy the agreement by the time he wrote this letter, and mailed it with only the string of zeroes present.

[5] FJH's 11 July letter announced two possible books, a book on the West by General Miles "of Indian-war fame," and an Edison autobiography (to be revived later). Nelson A. Miles's *Personal Recollections and Observations . . . ,* also to be discussed further, was published in 1896 by the Werner Company.

[6] On 14 June, FJH explained rather heartlessly that the best plan for the Sheridan *Memoirs* was to have it ready to issue "and await the result of

Sheridan's illness"; if he recovered, a long canvass could be worked, and if he died, the Company "would be in a position to drive things lively." In reply to the present letter, FJH reported that he had "suggested to Colonel Sheridan [the general's brother] that when the reporters interview him he try to bring in something about the book." When Sheridan died on 5 August, however, FJH decided not to issue the volume immediately: "Undoubtedly there will be some movement started to raise a fund for the benefit of the General's family. Now if Col. Sheridan . . . will say that they do not care for any such subscription, but that if the public will buy his book, a great portion of the profits going to the General's family, it will be the best method of subscribing towards the family's support."

200. To Fred J. Hall

Hartford
12 November 1888

Dear Mr. Hall:

Mr. Wright has been here and I said he could freely unbosom himself, provided I might repeat everything he should say.[1] When he was through I said I saw only one thing which needed explanation on your part.

If you need him and want him in your subscription department, take him—he will give you no further trouble.[2] If you do not want him do not take him. If he is valuable—make use of him; but if he isn't—Don't.

It is not proper for me to influence you, and I won't. Personally I have only this to say against him—he has been very indiscreet.

When a switchman has wrecked a train, they then consider him a warned and valuable man, and they keep him. Mr. Wright can never do you any harm again, and possibly he can be valuable to you.

If he is personally disagreeable to you, that is another matter. I told him a man can't have a subordinate around him who is personally disagreeable and unconquerably so. He thought he could make himself agreeable to you. I told him I could not make a request of you in his favor—I could only undertake to acquiesce in what you should decide; he must plead his cause himself I could not do it for him or interfere in the matter.

I was not harsh with him. At least only at first; after that it was a business-like and rational conversation. I will detail it to you when I go down next week.

Truly yours

S L Clemens

¹ A. H. Wright, who had been keeping the books of CLW & Co. since Frank Scott's embezzlement, wrote MT on 5 November: "There are a number of points which it would be well for us to talk about at your earliest convenience, *which are of great importance to you* and should be investigated *at once.*" Wright claimed specifically that he was "not allowed to keep the books in a proper manner nor as they are kept in any well managed house."

² FJH had written on 10 November, "I discharged Mr. Wright this morning." On 16 November he reported that "Mr. Wright is now canvassing for us. . . . I think he is better in this capacity than any other."

201. To Fred J. Hall

Hartford

12 November 1888

Dear Mr. Hall:

I approve, all through. Doubtless Mr. Wright concluded it would not be good politics to come and see me. If so, his conclusion was sound. I am glad he is disposed of. Now, let an expert examine his books.[1]

Let your press-copies of Sheridan reach their many destinations ten days before publication, with urgent attention called to the fact that no notice should appear before publication-day, lest the foreign copyrights be crippled.[2]

Yrs

S L C.

I don't hear from Whitford. I have a letter from W (dated election-day) proposing to resume command next April.[3]

¹ "The expert finds that the books have been honestly kept, . . . but very badly" (FJH to MT, 16 November 1888). Wright had written on 10 November, "I am very sorry indeed Mr. Clemens that you should think it necessary to resort to this means of disposing of me, as I have been of great service to you in the past. . . ." An undated fragment in MT's hand refers to Wright: "I am not conspiring with you to injure Mr. Hall. I *did* want to afford you an opportunity —since you seemed very much to desire it—to give me private information of a contraband nature about the business—but I did not consider myself to be conspiring." Finally, on 21 November, FJH told MT that Wright "comes to the office, to hand in his orders, . . . and seems to think that he still has some authority here. . . . he seems to have developed a settled spirit of revenge. . . . he is unprincipled and at times has a very ugly disposition and would stoop to anything. . . . I judge from the way he has been talking that it would be safer to have nothing whatever to do with him."

² On 19 November, FJH replied: "We sent the books to the New York papers, under a special form of receipt, that they were not to publish until the 26th. We find this morning that the 'Times' have broken their agreement, and come out this morning with a review of the book."

³ After apparently warning FJH earlier, CLW wrote MT a long letter from Fredonia on 6 November: "I feel that by April 1st I shall be able to resume business with my old time activity." CLW proposed putting the business on what he called a "peace footing," and publishing new books only when an impressive one was offered. Included, too, was a suggestion of FJH's incompetence: "Now from vague reports that I get it seems that the splendid Sheridan book is not going satisfactorily. I know it *should* sell and will with proper management but I shall say no more. I wish to complain of no one." The possibility of CLW's return sent MT, FJH, and Whitford scurrying about with counterproposals, defenses, and offers. FJH wrote a lengthy explanation of the business during his months in control, comparing sales with corresponding months of the previous year to show the improvement (5 November). FJH opened negotiations with Annie Moffett Webster (CLW's wife and MT's niece) to buy out CLW's share of the partnership (FJH to MT, 7 December). CLW thought the offer (apparently slightly under $10,000) "a pittance" and proposed his alternative: "If the other members of the firm will *secure* me against liability *past present* and *future* and give me $15,000 . . . I will sell all my interest in the firm property and give the use of the firm's name for five years" (CLW to Mrs. Webster, Fredonia, 10 December 1888, TS in MTP). MT meantime contemplated three possibilities: (1) selling the *Library of American Literature* immediately for $45,000; (2) selling CLW the entire business except for a share of the profits on the Sheridan volumes; or (3) collecting his own $75,000 investment and his share of the Sheridan profits and then "let the old regime return Apl. 1 and go unassisted to destruction" (Notebook 23, TS pp. 29–30). On 17 December, FJH recommended to MT that CLW's counteroffer be accepted; but two days later, he reported that Whitford and Mrs. Webster had agreed that CLW could not be secured against past liabilities. The parties compromised on a $12,000 price and all papers were signed in late December (FJH to MT, 24, 27 December; Contract No. 7, 22 December. Webster, TS in MTP).

202. To Fred J. Hall

Hartford
11 January 1889

Dear Mr. Hall:

The substitution of brains for guesswork was accomplished when you took Webster's place last February, and I see by your letter that the use of brains in place of guesswork is to remain the policy of your administration.[1] I cordially approve, detail by detail, of what you have done, and of what you have planned to do. You and I will never have any trouble.

The new contract suits me, thoroughly. If you should ever find that it is unfair to you in any way, do not hesitate to speak up and say so, so that the wrong may be righted. We are not sailing a pirate ship any longer; we have discarded the pirate ways and the inalterable pirate laws, along with the pirate himself.

I never read the contract until yesterday afternoon; I knew it would contain what had been agreed upon, and have in it no clandestinely-inserted pitfalls and ambuscades; and so, as I have been busy for a week preparing a reading for Baltimore,[2] I took all the time to it I wanted.

I have talked with Mrs. Custer, and she feels much more contented, now.[3] I said, wait until we get out of this rush, and then we will push her book and do our very best with it.

Truly yours,

S L Clemens

---

[1] Among the innovations: Dibble was demoted to a canvasser because of his inefficiency (FJH to MT, 19 May 1888) and replaced by Horace Granfield at a smaller salary (*ibid.*, 8 January 1889); after long negotiations, the Beecher family repaid their $5,000 advance and took back the manuscript of the *Life of Christ* (31 July, 17, 21 September, 13 December 1888; 15 January 1889). A "corps of lady canvassers" was contemplated for selling the cookbook (5 November 1888), and the Grant family compromised the old differences (4 January 1889); and FJH managed to unload the stock of a number of old volumes to Watson Gill (16 January 1889). Bromfield and Co. bought the old stock of the Beecher biography for $4,000 (31 January).

[2] With Richard Malcolm Johnston (see *MTB*, pp. 877–878).

[3] Mrs. Custer had complained about the neglect of *Tenting on the Plains* in

December 1888, attempting to purchase the rights and to place the available copies of her book in the hands of another publisher. FJH disapproved, because "it will be noised around that we made a failure of the book" (FJH to MT, 7 December 1888). MT apparently mollified Mrs. Custer and sales did indeed improve in the spring of 1889 (FJH to MT, 16 January, 18 February).

203. To Fred J. Hall

[Elmira]
2 July 1889

[No salutation]

The first article in the St. Nicholas for January last, shows that R. B. *Birch is an artist* who is capable of illustrating my book admirably [1]—I judge he wouldn't need any help from Merrill or anybody else. Suppose you make a note of his name.

Yrs
S L C

July 3, 2:30 p.m. Mr. Crane is still alive, but that is all.[2]

[1] *A Connecticut Yankee in King Arthur's Court.* FJH had reported that two copies were typed up (16 April), and had been read by both himself (8 May) and E. C. Stedman (14, 17 May, 5 July). The search for an illustrator had begun several months earlier: apparently MT had asked FJH to query A. V. S. Anthony, JRO's business manager for *The Prince and the Pauper,* in order to locate F. T. Merrill, the illustrator. Anthony had replied (20 March), enclosing Merrill's address and offering his own services. R. B. Birch illustrated Tudor Jenks's poem "The Pygmy Fleet," the lead item in the January *St. Nicholas.*

[2] Theodore Crane died on 3 July after suffering a paralytic stroke in the fall of 1888; see *MTMF,* pp. 262–264.

204. To Fred J. Hall

Elmira
24 July 1889

Dear Mr. Hall,—

Upon reflection—thus: tell Beard [1] to obey his *own* inspiration, and when he sees a picture in his mind put *that* picture on paper, be it humorous or be it serious. I want his genius to be wholly unhampered, I shan't have fears as to the result. They will be better pictures than if I mixed in and tried to give him points on his own trade.

Send this note and he'll understand.

Ys

S. L. C.

---

[1] Dan Beard, whose illustrations for a story called "Wu Chih Tien, the Celestial Empress" in the March *Cosmopolitan* had attracted MT's attention (Notebook 23, TS p. 49), had made up a sample illustration which FJH forwarded to MT (5 July). On 19 July, he reported Beard's terms for illustrating:

> He wants $3,000 for illustrating your book. . . . in all, some two hundred and fifty or sixty illustrations. This is for very careful work, and undoubtedly he will make the drawings at this price very fine. He can make a cheaper grade of drawings for less money, but we told him we would submit these figures to you. We paid Mr. Kemble $2,000 for making two hundred and four drawings, these of course were off-hand sketches.

MT apparently wrote a letter agreeing to these terms and including some directions for Beard's work which the present letter cancels; although the letter by MT is no longer extant, the following comments were written by Franklin Whitmore, obviously at MT's dictation, on the back of the envelope containing FJH's 19 July letter.

> I prefer this time to contract for the very best an artist can do. This time I want pictures, not black-board outlines and charcoal sketches. If Kemble illustrations for my last book were handed me today, I could understand how tiresome to me that sameness would get to be, when distributed through a whole book, and I would put them promptly in the fire.

On 23 July, FJH had written, "I note what you say about his [Beard's] seeing Mr. Stedman also about the quality of the pictures, that is, to have more or less humor in some of them, but not too much. Will try to give Mr. Beard the correct idea as to just what you wish." The next day, FJH wrote again concerning Beard's illustrations: "It took Kemble, if I remember rightly, about two months to make two hundred drawings for your 'Library of Humor' . . . but the drawings that Mr. Beard is to make are to be elaborate and full of detail work. Although he and his brother are going to devote all their time to them, even at that rate they say it would be impossible to have the thing completed before the first of November." FJH proposed making a cover stamp first, having a dummy prepared as early as possible, and printing and proofreading as the illustrations were completed. "By the time the last illustrations are ready covers for the first Edition of the book will be made, three-quarters of the book will be illustrated and printed, the only thing will be to make plates for the last few chapters and print them. In this way we can get the First Edition on the market by the middle or the latter part of November."

205. To Fred J. Hall

Elmira
20 August 1889

Dear Mr. Hall:

You are perfectly right. The proof-reader must follow my punctuation *absolutely*.[1] I will not allow even the slightest departure from it.

Instruct Chatto to issue in London *December 6*.[2]

Issue in Canada Dec. 8.[3]

In U.S. Dec. 10.

Ys

S L C

[1] The schedule for publication FJH outlined in his 24 July letter required very rapid proofreading in Elmira. MT suggested literal copysetting and FJH replied on 29 July, "Now in regard to reading proof of the book, I will see that it is compared with the greatest of care and made to conform exactly with the manuscript." (FJH had carefully collated the two typed copies to insure that Stedman's corrections were preserved in both [17, 19 July].) By 19 August, though, a proofreader had violated the instructions: "With reference to reading proof of your book, the punctuation as it is in the Manuscript is different entirely from the punctuation as our proof reader conceives it ought to be. *I told him plainly, that he must have no opinion whatever regarding the punctuation, that he was simply to make himself into a machine and follow the copy. Is this all right?"*

[2] FJH had envisioned difficulties with prepublication in England if his publishing schedule were followed, for sheets of the complete American edition would not be ready until immediately prior to the American issue. In addition Chatto & Windus wished some corrections (see *MTL,* pp. 524–525). Ultimately, Chatto "received all the proofs" (Andrew Chatto to MT, 22 November), deposited a copy of the English edition in the British Museum, and sold a copy to secure copyright "although the bulk of the copies of our edition will not be ready for delivery to the general public before the 13th of this month" (Chatto to MT, 6 December). Also, Chatto pointed out that "not a word of yours has been cut out or altered, except as regards keeping the title to your original wording 'A Yankee at the Court of King Arthur' " (30 December).

[3] Canadian copyright was endangered by Chatto's desire to change the text of the English edition; the Canadian text had to be identical with the English one, but previous practice had been for CLW & Co. to supply their sheets to Dawson (FJH to MT, 5 August 1889). But Samuel E. Dawson, through whom MT planned to publish in Canada, had unfortunately left the book publishing business (Dawson to CLW & Co., 9 August 1889, TS in MTP), so the arrangements described in the next letter had to be made.

206. To Fred J. Hall

[Elmira]
5 September 1889

Dear Mr. Hall:

I made the confusion myself, then.[1] Well, I might have expected it. I apologize.

Yes, send to Howells just what you send to me—revises that have been well weeded of errors.[2]

Send what you think best to Chatto. I should think that after my corrections have been made, the matter is ready for him, whether it go in slips or in sheets.

Why should he need a set of our sheets for copyright purposes. Won't his own printed and bound book answer? Oh, I see: You mean we can get ours to him earlier than he can get his own ready, and then clap on a title-page and a binding, and publish the book before waiting to get his own edition ready. All right.

We are much obliged to Mr. Dawson, and will do anything he wants us to do.[3]

I like the Canadian contract.[4]

Please tell this Jeweler's Weekly for me—well, anything you please: for instance, I am too much pressed.[5] You can say the same to all other applicants, without sending me their letters.

August panned out very nicely. I endorsed the note and mailed it to-day.[6]

Ys

S L C

---

[1] Work was progressing at a rapid pace on *A Connecticut Yankee*. FJH wrote on 21 August, "We mail you today the first batch of page proofs." The next day he sent a cover design, noting that "Beard has taken the liberty of leaving out the word 'Connecticut' in the title. He says that it is not unusual to shorten the title on the cover when it is long and that too much lettering would not look well." On 3 September, FJH explained the "confusion" referred to in the present letter: "The misunderstanding occurred by your saying in one of your letters, the first on the subject, that you wanted corrected *proofs* sent Mr. Howells. Then in a later letter you told us not to forget to send *sheets* to Mr. Howells. Using the word proof at first and later sheets, confused Mr. [E. H.] Rosenquest."

[2] On Howells's proofreading, see *MTHL*, pp. 608–614.

[3] Dawson had assisted FJH to arrange a contract with the Rose Publishing Co. of Toronto, whom Dawson himself had suggested. MT had proposed paying Dawson for this work (FJH to MT, 19 August), but Dawson would agree to accept only a set of the *Library of American Literature* (FJH to MT, 3 September).

[4] FJH enclosed a copy of the contract with his 3 September letter. It stipulated that Rose (who had flooded the American market with cheap copies of *Tom Sawyer*) would not sell *A Connecticut Yankee* in the United States or sell his edition for less than $1.50.

[5] FJH had forwarded a letter—presumably a request for a contribution—on 4 September with the question, "Do you wish me to decline in your name such requests unless they come from some first class and well known source, or shall I refer them to you?"

[6] August ended with $859.18 cash balance, and a $4,000 note due at the Mount Morris Bank on 11 September.

207. To Fred J. Hall

Hartford

24 November 1889

Dear Mr. Hall:

I send you a little book by George Standring.[1] My idea is, you as a publisher copyright the first title-page (the one for the cover);

Get it out in paper covers;

In clear, good-sized type, leaded;

On very cheap paper;

Sell it through the *trade*, only;

Make the price 15, 20, or 25¢ as they may prefer;

Pile on the printers, (night and day if necessary), and have it out and *placed on the book-sellers' counters the day we publish the Yank;* [2]

Send a copy *with the Yank* to every paper we send the Yank to, Dec. 10 or 12—if we conclude to send the Yank to the press.[3]

Get the World's permission to use slip No 1.[4] If you can't, leave it out.

Ys

SLC

¹ George Standring's *People's History of the English Aristocracy*. Earlier, FJH had written MT cryptically, "We note what you say about the 'Royal Grants' " (30 July).

² The mechanics of preparing *A Connecticut Yankee* for the press had continued all fall. On 30 July, FJH agreed, "We shall be careful not to get any religious matter in the Prospectus." He also suggested the possibility of trade publication as an alternative to the subscription method, but MT vetoed the plan (FJH to MT, 30 July, 5 August 1889). FJH reported the agents' opinions "that the church could not possibly hurt it; that it was the Catholic church that would principally attack, and that they were not book buyers anyway" (8 October). Prospectuses were ready on 10 or 11 October and FJH planned to "commence the canvass at once" (FJH to MT, 10 October). MT approved the idea of making a signature of Beard's illustrations for the agents' use (*ibid.*, 16 October), and on 29 October, FJH reported that *"The Yankee is all in type."* Complete sheets of the book were printed by 15 November (FJH to MT, 11 November).

³ On 25 November, FJH replied, "I think it would be a good idea to give the book out pretty freely to the press." Later, he explained that papers taking review copies of the book were required to agree not to publish reviews before 8 December, since that might constitute American "publication" and damage English copyright.

⁴ Apparently the New York *World* had printed part of the material MT wished to include in the pamphlet.

The affairs of Charles L. Webster & Co. were considerably more complex in 1889 and the first half of 1890 than the few extant Mark Twain letters would suggest. In addition to *A Connecticut Yankee*, the firm published Alfred R. Conkling's *The Life and Letters of Roscoe Conkling* in 1889 and contemplated the publication of an eleventh volume in the *Library of American Literature*. It tried desperately to secure the half-promised volume from Stanley (Hall even made a trip to England in the matter), and declined Bernard O'Reilly's insistent offers to revise and update his biography of the Pope. The two partners began their consideration of E. B. Sanford's religious encyclopedia, and Hall argued Mark Twain out of issuing a fifty-cent *Prince and the Pauper*.

In January 1890, Hall conferred with Sampson Low, Marston about Stanley's book only to discover that James R. Osgood, now Harper's London agent, was "pressing him hard" (CLW & Co. to MT, 16 January 1889). After losing the contract and returning to this country, Hall became involved with experimental advertising and sales schemes: a circus-poster advertising *A Connecticut Yankee*, a ten-cent pamphlet half full of advertising, a plan to employ college students as canvassers in the summer. Books—including an exposé of the Masons, a volume by Carnegie, a travel book by De Witt Talmage—were simmering; but the firm's financial affairs continued to be unimpressive. "There was a gross profit made out of the business last year [1889] of fifty thousand dollars. . . . Of this . . . eight thousand four hundred went to you ($8,400.00), twelve thousand two hundred and fifty to Mr. Webster ($12,250.00) and twenty two thousand two hundred and thirty four was put into the Library of Literature in excess of receipts from the same" (FJH to MT, 16 April 1890). The working capital of the Company was increased (see letter 208 below) but Mark Twain apparently complained about his share of royalties, for Hall wrote on 27 June, "I appreciate the injustice of taking money due you as an author and putting it into the manufacture of other people's books. . . . The mere fact that you are a member of the firm is no reason why you should wait for your royalties any more than Mr. Stedman, Mrs. Sheridan, or anyone else." Still, Mark Twain did wait; extant correspondence shows that rather than draining CLW & Co. of money to finance the Paige typesetter, Mark Twain could not collect even the amounts due him from the sale of his books, much less dividends or any return of his capital.

208. To Fred J. Hall

Hartford
19 April 1890

Private.

Dear Mr. Hall:

Mr. Whitmore has $10,000 or $12,000, and it is about all he has in the world. He would like to lend it to us at usurious interest—8 or 10 per cent. Or, still better, he would like to buy a small interest in the firm with it and come in under you to work 6 days in the week on a salary, making himself as useful as he can.[1] I told him to lay the matter before you.

You might do this, if you like. Take the money on interest for a year, and hire him in the way you hire your other help—that is, as I understand it, make his commissions pay his salary. Then, at the end of the year, if you like each other, discuss the sale of an interest or drop the subject.

But even if he were a partner, it ought to be expressed in the contract that he must be always subject to your *orders*. He suits me very well, for my uses, and he would still come up here and do up my work every Sunday, and retain his present salary ($500 a year.) Of course you might find him useless to you; so it would never do to sell to him without a full year to study him in. He is perfectly honest, and can be entirely trusted; but on the other hand there is nothing of the negociator in him; he couldn't make a contract with an author or a binder or a printer; he often has good judgment, but seldom any courage.

After I hear from you—well, I wait till I do.

Truly Yours

S L C

P.S.
Private.

Mrs. Clemens is dead opposed to it. She says take the money and pay as much interest for it as you want to, but keep entirely clear of the man. She says he would not be agreeable to you,[2] and would be a constant fret and discomfort to you. Well, I believe she is right.

He wanted his proposition laid before you, and of course he had a right to that consideration. But you needn't hesitate to make any reply to it you want to—by letter to him or by conversation; or by message through me to him, just as you prefer.

Ys

S L C

---

[1] Franklin Whitmore had worked for CLW & Co. in 1888 as a General Agent for the *Library of Humor* (FJH to MT, 4, 9 June 1888). His $10,000 occurred to MT as a possible answer to FJH's plaintive request for more money to run the organization (16 June). Although the idea was supplanted by a $25,000 loan from the Mount Morris Bank (FJH to MT, 5, 14 May 1890) and a $10,000 loan from Mrs. Clemens (letter 212 below), it was to recur to tantalize the partners later in the year when MT sought investors for a stock company to finance the *Library of American Literature* (letter 211 below).

[2] When Whitmore had worked as General Agent for Hartford County in 1888, FJH had voiced some reservations: "We gave Mr. Whitmore permission to work Hartford County on this book, but he has done absolutely nothing with it, so we have written him, asking him to relinquish the 'Library of Literature,' as we would not like to have any trouble with the General Agent who wants Connecticut" (FJH to MT, 11 July 1888).

209. To FRED J. HALL

Hartford

30 June 1890

Dear Mr. Hall:

The letter accounts for Arthur Steadman: idiotcy runs in the family.[1]

It requires no notice of any kind. Treat it with contemptuous silence—that and all similar letters from that pair of quite too wonderful people.[2]

If he should ask (with his mouth) to know what has become of this one, I have put it in the waste basket.

Ys Truly

S L C

[1] Arthur Stedman, the son of Edmund C. Stedman, apparently was an employee in the CLW & Co. office. Later he was to become the general editor of the "Fiction, Fact, and Fancy Series" and editor of Walt Whitman's *Autobiography* for the Company.

[2] E. C. Stedman had seen a circular for CLW & Co.'s "Great War Library," a uniformly-bound collection of the Grant, Sheridan, McClellan, Hancock, Crawford, and Custer volumes, together with General W. T. Sherman's *Memoirs* —published earlier by Appleton and issued by FJH in 1890 from old sheets with a new title page (FJH to MT, 17 April 1890). The complete set was advertised for $30, and Stedman wrote FJH a letter of protest (27 June 1890), claiming that "it is adverse to our common interests, and to the spirit of our contract, to call this new series a 'Library,' and to make it so nearly uniform with our 'Library of American Literature.' " FJH enclosed the letter with his own of 28 June: "Mr. Stedman evidently thinks that because he used the word 'library' on the 'Library of American Literature' that that word was thereafter to be stricken from the English language. He also seems to think that because we publish a book of his compilation that it gives him the right to interfere in our business generally, which, in my opinion, is a piece of unmitigated impudence."

210. To Fred J. Hall

[Hartford]
15 October 1890

Dear Mr. Hall:

Just as you vote yourself on Mr. Stoddard's book,[1] consider me as voting.

I don't think much of the Edison book suggested;[2] still, as a trade book it might pay for the plates, and even a little profit, maybe.[3] (I am supposing of course that *he* doesn't write it. He couldn't. Never has a minute. Still, if you will remind me next time I am down, I will send Geo. Lathrop to ask him if he will dictate a book for us into the phonograph. I should think he could do that.)

Also, remind me and I will talk with Booth if you like:[4] though I smoked with him till midnight in his rooms four or five nights ago and Aldrich and I tried to persuade him—etc.

Ys

S L Clemens

[1] William O. Stoddard's *Inside the White House in War Times* was published by CLW & Co. in late 1890, the first trade book issued by the firm. FJH reported on 17 November that Stoddard's book "is a small affair all around." He also advised that the only other new book—E. B. Sanford's *Concise Cyclopedia of Religious Knowledge,* which the firm had been contemplating for over a year (FJH to MT, 19 June, 5 July 1889, 15 February 1890)—was ready: "The canvass of it of course will be slow and altogether different from the canvass on your books."

[2] An Edison book had been first proposed in 1888 (FJH to MT, 11 July). FJH renewed the discussion with his letter of 7 October suggesting a "book from Edison, written in a way that will make it of general interest, on electricity—say, a book bearing some such title as this—'Electricity; its uses and possibilities.'" Other volumes which MT did not think much of in 1890 were a travel volume by De Witt Talmage (FJH to MT, 15 February), a volume on *The Social Arts* by Ward McAllister (18 April), and a volume titled *Justice and Jurisprudence* (30 June). Discussed this year and published later were Annie Jenness Miller's *Physical Beauty. How to Obtain and How to Preserve It* (15 October) and Mary Young Ridenbaugh's *Biography of Ephraim McDowell, M.D.* (14 May).

[3] In late 1890, the firm tended toward trade publication. *A Connecticut Yankee* had not sold well—23,000 copies in seven months (FJH to MT, 16 July 1890), which FJH pointed out "is not satisfactory" (8 August). And other subscription volumes were equally uninspiring. On 29 November, FJH contrib-

uted his analysis of the company's situation: "The truth of the matter is just this: That we are developing a new line in our business and developing it rapidly—it is the trade line. Outside of 'L.A.L.' three-quarters of the business we have done in the past six months has been in the trade line. It is a permanent line and the only way we can dispose of old books, and it is a line through which we can increase our business indefinitely." Again, on 13 December, arguing for an arrangement to publish Chatto & Windus books in the United States, FJH suggested, "Outside of 'L.A.L.,' I think the future of our business will depend quite largely upon the trade." The present letter suggests that MT, too, was examining titles for possible trade publication.

[4] In a letter no longer extant, FJH had apparently suggested a volume by Edwin Booth.

211. To Fred J. Hall

[Hartford]
23 October 1890

Dear Mr. Hall:

Come up next Tuesday, and let me know your train. I shall be away until Monday night.

When you come, tackle Whitmore and beguile him with an offer of 8 or 10 per cent for the use of $10,000 for a year.[1] But make short work of him. If he hesitates, drop him.

Ys Truly

S L C

[1] The enormous expense of the *Library of American Literature* and the installment method of sale had led FJH to consider establishing a stock company to finance the venture (FJH to MT, 8, 13, 26 August 1890), and he remembered MT's letter of 19 April (letter 208 above). On 14 August, he mentioned, "It has occurred to me that possibly Mr. Whitmore's money, of which you spoke some time ago, may still be uninvested and he might like to put it, or part of it, into L.A.L. stock."

212. To Fred J. Hall

Hartford
11 November 1890

Dear Mr. Hall:

Mrs. Clemens lends the $10,000 at 6 per cent.[1] Please send her the firm's note, and make it a year.

Ys

S L Clemens

(Her mother lends it to her.)

---

[1] Negotiations with Whitmore had apparently broken down, and Mrs. Clemens was called in as a substitute.

213. To Fred J. Hall

[Hartford]
30 November 1890

Dear Mr. Hall:

I couldn't reach you with a telegram Saturday afternoon or today because I do not know your residence-address or Whitford's—please furnish me with both.[1]

I couldn't talk business with Gill,[2] because there wasn't any witness to testify on our side; but I talked social stuff for 3 hours, had him to dinner, etc., and he went away saying you and he could no doubt straighten everything up without my help (which I hoped might be, for I am nursing a sick child[3] and Mrs. Clemens is in Elmira where her mother has just died,)—my hands are pretty full.

I liked Gill for one thing—he didn't enlarge on the business when he found how I was situated. He had said he only wanted existing contracts lived up to. To which I answered, in effect, that contracts are always able to take care of themselves when they are clearly and not confusingly worded; and that we always live up to our contracts.

I know you will do the right and fair thing; and I shall endorse your action and back it up.

Truly Yours

S L Clemens

---

¹ FJH complied on 2 December.

² Watson Gill, who had purchased 5,000 copies of various CLW & Co. imprints (see letter 202 above), was complaining about the Company's entry into the trade book field. At first, FJH proposed to violate CLW's old agreements (29 November 1890), but after seeing the conciliatory tone of the present letter, he "patched up a truce" (2 December), which disintegrated at year's end when Gill demanded damages and a new contract making him CLW & Co.'s sole trade outlet (19, 26 December). FJH concluded "to cut loose from him after our present contracts expire, as we can do the business he does for us at more profit to ourselves" (27 December).

³ Probably Jean Clemens's first epileptic seizure; see *MTHL*, pp. 633–634.

214. To FRED J. HALL

Hartford

27 December 1890

Dear Mr. Hall:

I don't believe Whitford.¹ Webster was too big a coward to bring a suit when advised against it. The real mistake was in trusting law business to an ignorant, blethering gas-pipe like Whitford. I am not saying this in hatred, for I do not dislike Whitford. He is simply a damned fool—in Court—and will infallibly lose every suit you put into his hands.² If you are going to have any lawsuits with Gill, I beg that you will either compromise or have some other law conduct the thing.

I am mighty sorry for you, but this result was to be expected.³ If I were you I would ask Whitford to present a modified bill—or better still, present it to the parties he won the case for.

Merry Xmas to you!—and I wish to God I could have one myself before I die.

Ys Ever

S L C

¹ On 26 December, FJH had written:

I suppose you have heard that the Little matter is decided against us and that we shall have to pay, in a short time, $3,000.00, besides lawyers' fees. . . . I think we would have won the suit had Mr. Webster's testimony been a little different; but he took the matter into his own hands when on the witness stand and talked more than was required. At the beginning of the suit Little offered to compromise for $800.00, and Mr. Whitford advised Mr. Webster to accept the compromise, but Mr. Webster thought it best not to, and we must now pay $3,000.00 and several years accumulation of lawyers' fees.

When J. J. Little & Co. had printed half the Grant *Memoirs,* CLW contracted with other printers to supply the unexpected demand. In 1885, Little sued for breach of contract and won a judgment in the amount of $1,950 (miscellaneous clippings, Grant Scrapbook II, 122, MTP). On appeal, the suit was won again, and on 5 January 1891, FJH told MT, "We have paid the Little judgment of some $2900.00, but have not received the bill for lawyers' fees yet." In Notebook 25, TS p. 18, MT wrote in December, "If W. disapproved of the Little suit, why did he consent to appeal it? To get a compromise?"

² Whitford had been losing MT's court battles with E. H. House over the dramatic rights to *The Prince and the Pauper* during 1890 (see Paul Fatout, "Mark Twain, Litigant," *American Literature,* XXXI [March 1959], 30–45), and the present outburst is undoubtedly the result of accumulated displeasure.

³ MT was filling his notebook with entries suggesting growing dissatisfaction with the organization of the Company: "Reduce your and O.'s salary. . . . Also your legal costs. Who made the execrable estimates on the Yank. Show them to me. . . . The business cannot afford your salary (which is ⅖ more than Slee's) nor Whit's" (Notebook 25, TS pp. 17–18).

215. To FRED J. HALL

[Hartford]
3 February 1891

Dear Mr. Hall:

It's an excellent idea.¹ You will find Major J. B. Pond at the Everett House, and he will give you a list of Stanley's dates and engagements. If Stanley is too far away, you can write him. Use the enclosed letter in person or by mail, just as you prefer.

Truly Ys

S L C

[1] On 2 February, FJH, announcing publication of Herbert Ward's *My Life with Stanley's Rear Guard,* suggested that Stanley "might want to make a final reply in small, cheap, book form. How would it do for you to suggest the idea to him and to let us publish the book, getting it out in, say, 50 cent and $1.00 form?" Stanley wrote that his contracts forbade such a book and suggested William Bonny as a substitute (FJH to MT, 9 February 1891). Stanley's "Rear Guard" had been left behind while the "Advance Guard" pushed forward in its search for Emin Pasha without, its members apparently felt, adequate instructions or sufficient communication from Stanley.

216. To Fred J. Hall

[Hartford]
13 February 1891

Dear Mr. Hall—

What does the $7000 stock of Religious Cyclopedia represent?—sheets, or bound copies?—and how many? [1] Can we afford to tie up so much money in an untried book when we are paying 8 per cent interest? [2] I should think plates and 3,000 sheets would be a sufficient venture on almost any untried book; then bind as ordered. We run the risk of this one's keeping us paying interest on unavailable stock as in the case of the Genesis and some of Webster's other ventures.

Big editions are no doubt an economy after a book has proved itself, but not before, I should think. I would not tie up much in an Indian book if I were you. [3] I would rather tie it up in a Religious Cyclopedia—much rather.

My apprehension comes from old and sore experience. We printed and *bound* 50,000 Mississippi's, and the orders stopped at 32,000. Webster gave the rest away—as he strenuously wanted to do with the 40,000 extra Grant sheets that he printed. [4]

Truly Yours
S L Clemens

[1] FJH had forwarded a Profit and Loss Account and Balance Sheet for 1890 with his letter of 10 February, which listed a $7,000 debit on the Sanford *Cyclopedia.* On 16 February, he explained that the volume had been expensive to produce and that many copies had been sent to religious newspapers for review; 4,000 sets of sheets had been printed and 1,000 copies bound.

² On the Mount Morris Bank notes, which now totaled $23,666.68 (FJH to MT, 5 January 1891).

³ Howells had sent a prospective volume for MT's consideration: Captain John G. Bourke's "Crook the Pacificator" (FJH to MT, 14 February), later published by Scribner as *On the Border with Crook* (see *MTHL*, pp. 634–635).

⁴ To Watson Gill; see letters 202 and 213 above.

217. To Fred J. Hall

[Hartford]
13 February 1891

Dear Mr. Hall:

Yes, wait till you hear from Miles.¹ Meantime, if you like, dictate a new letter to Miles (such a one as you would approve,) and send it to me and I will put it in my handwriting and mail it to him.

Yes, I wrote Howells.²

Ys

S L C

¹ FJH pointed out (12 February) that a book from Miles had been under discussion earlier and that "it would be wiser, don't you think, to wait until we hear definitely from General Miles before committing ourselves any way to Captain Bourke?" In addition, Bourke wrote advising that he had promised Charles Scribner "the first look at the manuscript" (FJH to MT, 14 February).

² *MTHL*, pp. 634–635.

218. To Fred J. Hall

[Hartford]
15 February 1891

Dear Mr. Hall:

This is from our good friend Grace King. Read and return it to me. I think there is only one thing you can say: that if the man's friends will secure 1000 subscribers at $3 per vol (single *cloth* vol); or 500 at $6; or 300 at $10 we will undertake it; and that this will manufacture the books and leave $1500 to divide between the widow and us; that they must expect no considerable sale else-where. Well, say *something* which I can send to Miss Grace. I'm not particular what.[1]

Truly Yrs

S L C

[1] The volume Miss King attempted to place with CLW & Co. was probably *A History of Louisiana,* written by her and John R. Ficklen. Later, she wrote MT, "In order to get any returns for my School Hist. of Louisiana—I had to publish it myself—that is with my collaborator" (New Orleans, 8 December 1893).

219. To FRED J. HALL

Hartford
27 February 1891

Dear Mr. Hall:

Within please find the note.[1]

I'm feeling better about the Sherman book now. It had a doubtful look before, with us, apparently, to do the staking.[2]

What is the very *quickest* you can issue it? Its market is best for the next 30 days, I think; then nearly as good for 30 more; then comes the fading quickly out.

I have written 10,000 words on a book whose canvass is to begin *September 1,* and issue Dec. 10 with 75,000 orders—and not a single one short of that.[3]

Ys Truly

S L C

[1] One of the Mount Morris Bank notes—renewed for the third time (FJH to MT, 26 February).

[2] General Sherman had died on 14 February, and his family "want us to get out a $1.50 edition of the book; to re-set it; and they are going to have James G. Blaine bring the book down to date—that is, write an appendix taking Sherman's life up where he left off in his Memoirs and bringing it down to the funeral at

St. Louis" (FJH to MT, 25 February). FJH suggested that the Sherman family should supply the funds for the undertaking, and advised MT he had received their check for $3,500 to cover the costs (26 February).

³ *The American Claimant.* FJH replied on 28 February: "I am glad you are writing a new book and I have a plan to propose regarding its sale whereby we think we will have the seventy-five thousand orders by the time we issue it, and what's more there will be some money in it—the profits will not be all swallowed up in getting the book out and on the market, as it was to a great extent on the 'Yankee.' " The plan was apparently to issue a cheap edition in conjunction with other MT volumes; see letter 222 below.

220. To Fred J. Hall

Hartford
10 March 1891

Dear Mr. Hall—

The dummy is very nice.[1] No doubt *cork* is the preferable thing if not too expensive.—

We will talk the whole thing over when you come up. We are both too busy now.

I am mighty sorry for those vexations [2]—and sorry, too, that you've no amelioration of them to depend upon but Mr. Blaine's written promise, which isn't worth a damn. Except that you can attach it in facsimile to your book if the Shermans will permit,— and they ought not to object.[3]

Y

S L C

[1] Of the history game, in which MT's interest had been revived earlier when he told FJH, "Come quickly, and discuss my historical game. It is the important feature now" (Hartford, 17 February 1891, Berg). FJH found a man to prepare a dummy board (FJH to MT, 25 February), and promised to have it ready by early March (28 February, 4 March). On 9 March, he queried MT concerning patents and copyrights for "Mark Twain's Fact and Date Game."

[2] Blaine had procrastinated on the preparation of the appendix to the Sherman volume, and FJH was especially perturbed because he had announced Blaine's contribution in his advertising (FJH to MT, 9 March).

[3] On 12 March, FJH replied that "The Shermans say that if Blaine should disappoint us we have full permission to publish his letter."

221. To Fred J. Hall

Hartford
29 March 1891

Dear Mr. Hall:

How many subscriptions to LAL does a first-class canvasser capture in a month? I've got an advertising-scheme.[1]

Ys

S L C

I have suggested to Father Sherman that his and his brother's generous letter to our firm be held in reserve until somebody complains of Blaine's absence from the book, then publish it immediately.[2] I have also suggested that the words *"at least in your first issues"* be left out. We don't need Blaine in *any* issue I guess.

---

[1] What specific scheme MT refers to here is uncertain, but on 30 March, FJH replied that "we would consider an average of (1) order a day good work, making him earn over 12.00 a day." The constant drain of the *LAL* persuaded FJH to borrow $15,000 from personal friends, the Barrow family, if MT would furnish another $20,000 and "we would be put firmly on the high road to prosperity" (17 March). On 20 March, the figure had risen to $100,000. MT wondered (Notebook 25, TS p. 29), "Shall we, or can we, *sell* a ⅓ interest in the business for $100,000?" Also, "Get the $15,000 and let the rest wait till we get the LAL higher. We can't show a steady and large monthly increase on LAL. . . . Sell a ⅛ to Stanley for $100,000. Or preferably ⅙. Or to Chatto" (*ibid.*, p. 31).

[2] With MT's letter is one from the Sherman brothers urging CLW & Co. to issue the volume as soon as possible without waiting for Blaine's material. Blaine's material arrived at the CLW & Co. office on 30 March and FJH thought it "really fine" (FJH to MT, 30 March).

222. To Fred J. Hall

Hartford
9 April 1891

Dear Mr. Hall:

If I tried either (Mrs. Carlyle),[1] I think it would be a few sheets, not plates. In my opinion it isn't worth bothering with in any form.

Please ransack your safe for my old contracts with American Publishing Co. and if you can't find them require them of Webster, who has without doubt carted them off in obedience to his native disposition to smouch all unwatched property. I think the contracts may enable me to forbid those people to issue cheap editions without my privity and consent. If I ever give consent I ought to require better than the present terms. We will issue cheap editions [2]—especially if they do not approve. They seem to think we have asked their advice—and by letter.[3] Damn their advice, we have no use for it. And as for their approval, I wish to avoid acquiring that, by all legitimate means.

                                                                    Ys

                                                              S L C

[1] FJH's plan to print some Chatto & Windus titles had resulted in Ward's book, offers of Sebastian Kneiff's *My Water Cure* (Percy Spaulding to FJH, London, 26 February), and plates of George R. Sims's *Tinkletop's Crime* (FJH to MT, 11, 13 April 1891). On 7 April, FJH reported to MT that Chatto & Windus were offering either sheets or plates of Mrs. Alexander Ireland's *Life of Mrs. Carlyle.*

[2] The temptation to issue cheap editions of MT's books had been tantalizing both author and publisher for a year: on 22 May 1890, FJH had argued against MT's proposed cheap edition of *The Prince and the Pauper*, which would ruin the market for his expensive subscription editions; but on 18 July 1890, FJH decided to try to arrange with the Book Trust Company for the publication of MT's books "in fifty cent form." On the back of the letter MT wrote, "A good idea. Tell him to exploit it." Again on 11 March 1891, FJH suggested "a cheap edition of your books, say, 'Huck. Finn' to start with. . . . One bookseller this morning . . . said he would take 500 right off. . . . Mr. Granfield thinks that there would be no trouble whatever in securing advance orders of from twenty-five to thirty thousand copies of the cheap edition." The next day, he added further, "a big jobber . . . says he can sell thousands of a 1.00 edition of Huck Finn. He would probably be willing to order in five thousand lots." Smitten with the idea, MT figured profits on such a scheme (Notebook 25, TS pp. 28–29):
    Your best chance is to prospect the Game, and if it promises well, out with it. *$10,000.*
    Next the cheap Huck—rush it out. *$10,000.* . . .
    Why not follow Huck, 2 months later with $1 Yankee? *$10,000.*
    And both a few months later
    With White Elephant (using the *present* plates) at 50¢ in paper. *$5000.* . . .
    And follow the above, a few months later with *$1 P. & P. $10,000.*
[3] On 3 April, Frank Bliss wrote MT regarding a $1.00 *Huckleberry Finn,*

"After considerable thought we cannot help regarding such a move as a mistake and one which may interfere largely with the sales of the books which we publish. . . . if 'Huck. Finn' is in the market at $1.00 it will be liable to cause book buyers to compare that with our higher priced books and very likely refuse ours." FJH was almost gleeful at Bliss's letter: "It is first rate and the strongest argument possible in favor of the cheap edition. I am glad that they feel as they do. The truth is that they haven't the capital or energy to get out a cheap edition of their books. . . . I think it will force them into making some arrangement with us whereby we can get out a uniform edition of your books" (8 April).

223. To FRED J. HALL

Hartford
4 May 1891

Dear Mr. Hall:

I don't think very much of Mr. Bok's offer.[1] He has engaged a short story of Mr. Howells at $5,000, and Howells has sold the use of a long story to the N.Y. Sun for $10,000.

Won't you appoint a meeting with Col. Cockerill managing editor of the World,[2] and see if you can sell him the use of this 70 or 75,000-word story for $10,000? If not, ask for his best terms. And if you fail with him, I will tackle Wm. M. Laffan. The World has engaged some stories of Bret Harte and others.

I am thinking of naming this story "The American Claimant."

Yrs

S L C

You can mail the enclosed to Cockerill and ask for an appointment.

[1] Edward Bok had visited FJH on 25 April, hoping to obtain *The American Claimant*. But as FJH pointed out to MT, "he would . . . want to know something of the character of the book before he could make any offer" (25 April). On the envelope of the letter, MT wrote a note to "Brer" Whitmore, "Let us telegraph I will see him." Bok visited with MT on 1 May (Bok to MT, Boston, 29 April 1891), and then discussed financial matters with FJH on 2

May: FJH reported, "The very best that I could get out of him was four thousand dollars, he to have the story illustrated by Kemble or Frost and to sell us electrotypes at one-third the original cost."

² FJH replied on 11 May that he had tried to see John A. Cockerill twice but without success; see letter 225 below.

224. To Fred J. Hall

[Hartford]
13 May 1891

Dear Mr. Hall:

All right, accept Mr. Curtis's offer of $6,000.¹ I'd rather have that than $8,000 from those other papers. You want to have in writing the date that *we* can issue the book; and how long we may canvass *before* issuing and before *they* have finished the serial publication (6 weeks?)—so that we *can* publish by subscription in case we should *wish* to; though we don't insist upon canvassing before they finish if they object to it. But we *do* want a date for our issue fixed, so that we can be sure to secure our English copyright by *pre*-publication a few days over there.

Ask if they pre-publish in England. If they don't, we must be very careful. In fact the surest way will be to have Chatto sell the temporary use to some periodical over there, they to begin the serial publication a day or two *ahead* of Curtis every number.

The check you sent me was not signed, but I have signed the firm's name "per S L Clemens." ²

Truly Yours

S L Clemens

¹ Bok's offer of $4,000 was raised to $6,000 by Bok's employer, Cyrus Curtis, owner of the *Ladies' Home Journal*.

² For a settlement on the copies of *Life on the Mississippi* remaindered to Watson Gill (FJH to MT, 11 May).

225. To FRED J. HALL

Hartford
13 May 1891

Dear Mr. Hall:

Don't begin to send that monthly check of $70 to John O'Neil till *July 1*, instead of June 1.[1]

Col. Cockerill's retirement from the World explains why he couldn't see you.[2]

Don't let Curtis *syndicate* the story.

I have the impression that the Sun and the World do not syndicate theirs. Think I got it from Howells.

Ys

S L C

[1] The Clemens family gardener, who came to work in October 1885 (Notebook 20, TS p. 25) and was being retained as a caretaker during the family's trip abroad.
[2] Cockerill resigned from the *World* in May 1891 to become editor of the New York *Commercial Advertiser*.

226. To FRED J. HALL

Hartford
20 May 1891

Dear Mr. Hall:

Please see Laffan, who will probably send you to (McCluny,[1] this is not quite the name, I think) the manager of the newspaper syndicate, and see if he wants to syndicate the story in England, and what he will pay, and whether the requirement to limit it there to a *monthly* serial would embarrass him.

That stipulation in the contract bothers me and makes me reluctant to sign.[2] I told Bok I should want unembarrassed control of the English end, but this detail may embarrass it, I'm afraid.

Curtis seems to think the *American* copyright could be damaged by previous *weekly* serializing in England. If that is his only objection it is hardly valid. Previous publication in England is at present necessary to secure English copyright, but no amount of previous English publication can hurt American copyright. Otherwise *I* should be the first one to holler.

Laffan sent Mc up here a day or two ago to offer me $300 per Century page for a few European letters for the syndicate papers.[3] This is three times as much as Curtis is offering for this story.

Mc wanted to call on you (he is acquainted with you), and get the Sellers story for his European syndicate, and I told him to go and do it and arrange terms with you.[4] This is better than bothering Chatto—and fully as profitable.

After you've seen him you will know whether the "monthly" requirement is going to bother us or not.

In case I've got to come down after you've talked with Mc or Laffan, telegraph me. I am ever so much obliged to you for the trouble and travel you have put in for me on this matter.

Truly Yours

S L Clemens

P.S. All the *rest* of the contract pleases me entirely.

S L C

[1] Samuel S. McClure, who had established the McClure Syndicate in 1884.

[2] A contract with Bok had been drawn up by FJH, "of course, to be entirely subject to your approval" (22 May). MT objected to a clause which specified that any English periodical publication must be in a monthly rather than a weekly magazine: "Bok's principal objection to having the articles come out in Weeklies is that the Weeklies would, perhaps, be sent over here, or extracts and comments on the story would reach America ahead of what was coming out in his paper" (FJH to MT, 21 May).

[3] On 28 May, FJH reported that McClure had agreed to purchase some European travel letters: "For all letters containing not less than 3500 words he is to pay you $1,000.00 per letter. If they contain more than 3500 words so much the better. If the letters contain less than 3500 words he is to pay you at the rate of $300 per thousand words."

[4] On 21 May, McClure offered $12,000 for *The American Claimant* (FJH to MT, 22 May); Bok's contract was returned to him (*ibid.*, 28 May), and FJH

proposed a peace mission to Philadelphia because Bok "may feel rather sore about it" (1 June). On 29 May, FJH outlined the McClure contract: McClure received world serial rights, copyrighted in the name of Samuel L. Clemens, and paid $10,000 on receipt of the contract and an additional $2,000 when the story was half published. He would begin publication in January 1892 "because the newspapers will pay very much more for material then than they will in summer." Actually, McClure paid $2,500 in June 1891 and proposed paying an additional $2,500 on publication of the first installment, another $2,500 on the appearance of the second installment, and $4,500 when the story was half published (FJH to Franklin Whitmore, 11 June 1891).

227. To Fred J. Hall

[Paris]
17 June 1891

My Dear Mr. Hall—

A cablegram informs me that my type-setter sale has fallen through.[1] Therefore you will now have to modify your instalment system to meet the emergency of a constipated purse; for if you should need to borrow any more money I would not know how or where to raise it.

If you made the first instalment $5, and the others $4 per month would that relieve you sufficiently?[2]

It is merely a suggestion—maybe good, maybe bad.

We leave Paris tomorrow, but my *permanent address* is

Ys truly

S. L. Clemens, Care Drexel,

Harjes & Co, Paris

Write me weekly.

[1] Notebook 25 is peppered with reminders about MT's plans to reorganize the typesetter organization; perhaps the most satisfactory summary is in *MTB*, pp. 909–911. The present collapse was of efforts to sell his interest in the typesetter for $250,000 to Marshall H. Mallory of the religious periodical *The Churchman*. Although Mallory agreed to "go on and work at it [reorganization] with all my heart," he also found it impossible to make any progress or to pay an initial $5,000 (Mallory to H. C. Robinson, New York, 15 June 1891, MTP).

² The foolhardy arrangement for selling the *LAL:* a subscriber agreed to purchase eleven volumes, paying $3 a month when the volumes were delivered. But as soon as the agent returned to the office, he received a commission of just over $12 for the entire set. Therefore, the more new subscribers for the edition, the larger CLW & Co.'s deficit. What MT proposes in the present letter is that the subscriber pay $5 on receiving Volume I, and then $4 for the next seven months. MT summarized the paradoxical situation in which greater prosperity meant larger debts (Notebook 25, TS p. 32):

What we want to know *exactly,* is this:—and is this so?

  1. Up to 200 subs. a month, we can take care of ourselves.
  2. On every 50 added, per month, we need to borrow what?—the canvasser's $12.24? Say $600 per 50?
  3. Or *half* the gross money coming in—which is $35 per set. Borrow $17.50 per set?

228. To FRED J. HALL

Aix-les-Bains
10 July 1891

(Address, Brown Shipley & Co
        London)

Shall be present at eight or ten Wagner operas at Baireuth—shall be there from July 31 to Aug. 12.

Dear Mr. Hall:

Please see Johnson or Gilder, and tell them of my present arrangement with McClure, and ask them what they will pay.¹ I could write 6 instalments for them and the 6 for McClure, and so fill up the twelvemonth—and if they don't offer $1000 per instalment and won't pay that, we can't trade.

But *first* see McClure, because if he wants to make a bid he must have the first say.

It *is* my intention to write a book, and take a year or two to collect the material and do the writing.

I haven't sent McClure anything yet, my right arm being still disabled with rheumatism; but it is improving, these last few days, and I hope to begin pretty soon. When I do begin, it is my purpose to send him the letters right along, so that he can print the 6 in 6 successive months.

(Please make and keep a copy of this letter—I must economise my labor and my cramps.)

I am not worrying about Bok,[2] half as much as I would if it were somebody else. He has got a good deal more than a thousand dollars' worth of literature out of me at various times (suspected and unsuspected interviews) and got it for nothing. And I mustn't bother about him now, when every pen-stroke gives me the lockjaw.

By your letter and reports it seems to me that you are doing well and moving along safely and prosperously. The instructions to Mr. Williams are wise,[3] and I am anxious to know the effect upon the canvassers and subscriptions—let me know early. I hope you can carry through the New England deal.

Did you rent your upper stories—or are they going to be more profitable to use? [4]

Shall leave these baths the end of this month, for Germany.

Shall be in France again, all September and October—the family will; I may take a courier and a kodak and go traveling.

November and the winter—Berlin, the family. I may be there, but also I may travel. There are a few summer-places, and also a few winter ones that I want to write about.

With our best regards—

Ys

S L Clemens

P.S. Whatever the Century offers, remember it is *net*. McClure's offer will be discounted 20 per cent by his *commission*. An apparent $1,000 from him w^d be only $800 in reality.

Let us go cautiously and not take up with any offer too hastily. I'd as soon publish an instalment every two or three or four weeks for the next two years as not if I get enough for it.

One a month for $1000 *net* [is] what I would prefer, I think.

Ys

S L C

[1] The six articles on European travel (to which MT is to allude in a number of subsequent letters) were to be expanded by additional articles—here offered to *The Century*—into a book; both the *Century* articles and the expanded book were canceled a month later (see letter 231 below).

[2] Who apparently did complain of his treatment in the arrangements for *The American Claimant*.

[3] No letters from FJH to MT are extant for the period between the latter's departure for Europe (6 June) and 16 December 1891, so that the instructions to Mr. T. Williams and the details of the "New England deal" cannot be reconstructed (but see letter 237 below).

[4] CLW & Co. had moved from 3 East 14th Street to 67 Fifth Avenue in May, and FJH proposed leasing the entire building and then renting out the lofts and upper floors (11 March). FJH leased the loft for $500 and hoped to rent two additional lofts to "Bauman the furniture man" for $2,200 (18 March).

229. To Fred J. Hall

Aix-les-Bains
26 July 1891

Dear Mr. Hall—

Yes, the statement was what I wanted. It made all the details clear. I sent it to Whitmore to be safety-deposited.[1] If it is not too much trouble, make duplicates of that and the monthly statement of book sales, and send them to me and to Whitmore too, telling him he can retain his. Then I will keep mine.

The business does indeed look very very handsome and most promising. It has just about doubled during the year.

Tell McClure I have written and asked Chatto to send you his relinquishment of authority over the German-language rights so that you can accept McClure's proposition for me.[2]

I have begun to try to write a little, but shall probably have to stop again, my hand is so bad. We all send you warm regards.

S L C.

[1] The statement was forwarded with MT's letter of 18 July asking, "You have received statement of old royalties due me from the N.Y. firm. What is the gross amount?—and does it take the form of a loan, with interest payable half-yearly henceforth?" FJH wrote Whitmore on 11 June, "Will forward you in a few days a note bearing interest for royalty due Mr. Clemens that has been absorbed into the capital stock of the Company." It was extremely difficult for Whitmore to

obtain money from FJH during MT's absence; on 2 October, FJH pleaded manufacturing expenses as his reason for delaying payment of $500 to Whitmore.

[2] By contract with MT (rather than by law or copyright agreement) Chatto & Windus presumably held the Continental rights to his books; the McClure proposition is unknown.

230. To Fred J. Hall

Bayreuth
7 August 1891

Dear Mr. Hall:

If I remember rightly, you wrote me that McClure would begin the publication of my story in January (making the second payment at that time,) and finish it in March—or perhaps you said in 16 weeks. If he publishes in a London *monthly* magazine will not that lengthen out the time beyond the 16 weeks and force me to wait a long time for the money and run you into a remote day for publication in book form?

If *not*, I have no objection to the magazine.[1]

I shall send my letters through *you* to McClure.

P.S. By your later letter I see that the publication of the story begins in January (and is all paid for in that month) and that it will be finished in about 10 weeks from first Sunday in January. This being the case, I care not what magazine McClure chooses in England provided it does not change the above agreement.

Yes, I knew you had rented your upper part, but you also had some idea of renting some more—I don't remember what.

Am glad you are extinguishing the Mt. Morris connection and debt—it was what the recent money was sent for.[2]

Truly Yours

S L C

P.S. Suppose you choose as your cable cipher this: Websterco, New York and arrange with the cable offices of both lines and notify me thus by cable to Brownshiply: *"Websterco."* (No signature—I shall understand.)

FJH presumably had reported McClure's contract with the London monthly *The Idler* for serial publication of *The American Claimant*.
FJH forwarded canceled notes (presumably Mount Morris Bank ones) to Whitmore on 5 June ($5,000) and 27 July ("the last one of the last three $5,000.00 checks that we have taken up at the bank.")

231. To FRED J. HALL

Marienbad
24 August 1891

Dear Mr. Hall:

I am mailing to you to-day in separate envelops, 3 letters for McClure.[1] He may publish them in any order he prefers.

Bank the money yourself in New York, (*not* in the Mt. Morris) and if possible get some trifle of interest for the use of it if you can. I shall not want it for some months. In Hartford the bank allows me 2 per cent a year and I draw when I please. Bank it in my name. I enclose some signatures for the bank.

Whitford's letter gives me no information. I don't know whether *I* am to attack or whether it is the business of the House party.[2] If Whitford presents a bill for services for me tell him you have no authority and let him wait till I come home.

The 6 McClure letters are the only ones I am going to send from Europe. I declined the Century offer by cable. To write a big book of travel would be less trouble than to write 6 detached chapters. Each of these letters requires the same variety of treatment and subject that one puts into a book; but in the book *each* chapter doesn't have to be rounded and complete in itself.

I have a fourth letter finished, but it takes longer to trim and fix and *edit* a letter than it does to write it. When the 6 are finished, suppose you make plates of them for a 25 cent book of 35,000 or 40,000 words and have it ready to throw on the market when the last of the 6 is published—you and Chatto both.

Don't you believe it will be well to try the experiment?

I shall write rafts of travel over here, but for a *book*, not serial publication.

Thank you for the statements and letters. They make everything clear.

You still owe the Mt. Morris $16,000. You will soon be clear of that, won't you?

Good-bye—my arm has given out again. I get your letters, none of them miscarry, but I have to use all my strength on the McClure work. With all our kindest regards.

Ys

S L Clemens

[1] The first three McClure letters were "Aix: the Paradise of the Rheumatics," "At the Shrine of St. Wagner," and "Playing Courier."

[2] On 7 August, Whitford wrote FJH that on MT's instructions he had done nothing about trying to get the House case on the court docket to remove the preliminary injunction against MT: "As the case now stands it will not in all probability be moved or stirred up until we move it." In late January 1894, MT wrote in his notebook (Notebook 27, TS pp. 49–50), "House's suit dismissed the other day 'for want of prosecution' with costs in my favor, $24."

232. To FRED J. HALL

[Geneva]
15 September 1891

Dear Mr. Hall:

We arrived here last night and found your welcome letter of a fortnight before. If you wrote Mrs. Clemens the next day as you were intending, it has not come. Other letters which should be here are not here. For the first time our mails have failed and gone utterly to the devil.

The state of the business rejoices me, and I hope you will lose your bet and charge two-thirds of the cost to me.

In Marienbad I saw a great deal of our great American savant Dr. Charles Waldstein. He is at the head of the American school in

Greece, archaeologists, who found what seems to be Aristotle's grave last year; he is also connected with Cambridge University, England, and is there most of his time. He has known personally every European famous in science and art and literature for the last 20 years, and writes sometimes for Harper, Century and the English Quarterlies. He is full of valuable meat, and I want to know if McClure would like to have him in the syndicate. Will you find out and let me know?

I have finished the 4th McClure letter in the rough [1] and written half of the 5th.[2] If I finish that one and write the 6th before my arm retires permanently from business I shall hold myself lucky. It threatens to quit work for good, and I am unspeakably glad I haven't any large literary contract hanging over me.

If the firm's note for $12,000-odd back-royalties does not contemplate half-yearly interest, let it be altered to that. Whitmore is not able to tell me—because he would have to go all the way down to the Safety Deposit to find out.

Ys sincerely

S L C

[1] "Marienbad, A Health Factory."
[2] Either "A German Chicago" or "Switzerland: The Cradle of Liberty."

233. To Fred J. Hall

Berlin
16 October 1891

Dear Mr. Hall—

This is the first time I have taken hold of a pen lately, but I will write a line or two, against the doctor's prohibition—just to say I am glad you are doing so well; and sorry, desperately sorry, that we have to retire even temporarily from the instalment plan—a thing we would not do if I could raise the money to prevent it.

I am glad you are going to move up stairs, that rent-bill is so formidable.

I'm trying to think of a subject proper for a boy's story for McClure, but nothing seems to occur to me. Presently I will take another think.

I hope McClure wrote the Antiquary. Ask him to drop him a line explaining that he can't use him. A dozen people have tried to get me to tackle McClure for them, but I have saved him from all but two—Dr. Wakefield [1] and Dr. Waldstein.

We were unspeakably glad to get your cablegram last night, "Sherman O.K." I had lain awake some nights over that thing with distress of mind. [2]

But look here, I could have sent that cablegram cheaper! Thus:

"Clemens, 7 Körnerstr Berlin. Sherman matter settled."

Seven words—no signature.

O.K. is 2 words. A ten-letter word—like my street—counts for 2 words. My initials are 2 words. Your signature is 1 word. So I guess you paid for 5 words too many.

The reason my initials are not necessary is because I am the only Clemens in this house or in this street, and possibly in this town.

Whenever my letters appear in print, *cut out* 2 copies of each and mail to me in an envelop, and keep one or two copies yourself. Won't you?

I must stop—my arm is howling.

Ys ever

S L C

---

[1] Unidentifiable.

[2] MT became disturbed about the $3,500 advanced by the Sherman family to pay for reprinting the *Memoirs* in a cheap edition. In Notebook 26, TS p. 1, MT wrote:

To Mr. Hall, Oct 4, Lausanne:

Please tell me the terms of our contract with the Shermans, and exactly what we have made or lost. Was the $3,500 a loan, and has it been repaid?

Whatever FJH's answer, letter 235 below shows that MT was satisfied with it.

234. To Fred J. Hall

Berlin
20 October 1891

Dear Mr. Hall:

I want to ask 2 or 3?s

1. What is your plan of publishing my story "The Am. Claimant?"

2. Are you getting the plates ready now?—for there is no time to lose. The book should issue a little before the last instalment appears in the newspapers.

3. Will Chatto have advance sheets as early as he needs them?

Please give me all the details of your plan as soon as possible.

Tell me size, price and book and every particular.

Ys

S L C

The 6 Newspaper Letters.

My idea about these is, that you issue them in paper at 50¢ the moment the 6th one appears in the papers.

2. And that you use cheap paper and unusually large type—say as big as that in Gen. Grant's book, and put across the top of the cover a line in strong type—

Printed in Big Type for
Railroad Use—

or something equivalent to that.

Please ask Chatto to market this and the other book for me with either the new house [1] or Tauchnitz.

---

[1] Charles Wolcott Balestier, who had written Howells asking if MT might be interested in publishing on the Continent through a new firm he was heading (see *MTHL*, pp. 640–641).

235. To Fred J. Hall

[Berlin]
27 October 1891

Dear Mr. Hall:

Mighty glad to get the explanation of the Sherman matter. It is perfectly satisfactory.

I have worked myself to death the last 3 days and nights translating (and making a neat copy of the translation) the most celebrated child's book in Europe, and to-day I mail it to you.[1] It should be in your hands Nov. 7, I judge. I want it on the American market Dec. 10 to catch the holidays.

Can't you *process* each rude picture several times, then trim away from each *all but the portion to be printed with a particular color?*

If a colored picture can't be processed, then *trace* each picture with black ink and make the necessary number of reproductions from *that*. A couple of days ought to suffice to make the cuts and have them ready to print from.

Perhaps you can process the *German letter-press,* too.

I want my translation to be printed on the blank page facing the corresponding picture and the corresponding *German verses.*

Fac-simile the German text and pictures, but set the English verses in very large and clear type—as large as possible—great primer type, I should say—for this is a book for little children 3 to 7 years old.

You can process the *cover* by pasting white paper over the *letter-press* part of it and then sketching in black ink on the white paper the words of the new title which I have stuck onto the outside of the book.

I think I would print the cover a bright lively color, instead of black.

And I think I would use a *paper* cover mainly—with a stiff cover and possibly a *linen* book at higher prices if you or the U.S. Book Co think [it] worth while.

Knock the pot out of the picture where the doctor sits by the bed,

⟨It is too frank.⟩ if you prefer, though I don't see any real harm about it.

Sell McClure the right to use my preface and a piece or two [of] my poetry, with the corresponding German rhymes, in his "Youthful Department." I suggest "The Sad Tale of the Match-Box." He could have the pictures for that made small and yet effective. You needn't be hard on him as to terms—particularly if he can print before Dec. 10 and thus make an advertisement for us. Tell him I would be very glad to accede to his handsome request for a youthful article, but it will be months before I can stop to think about it.

Perhaps it wouldn't be a bad idea to send a paper-covered copy to the principal dealers from whom you might expect orders, as an advertisement to put in their windows—however, you have your own methods, don't mind *me*.

But—take out copyright at once, and also have your circulars ready in as few hours as possible—and don't fail to be ready to deliver *before Dec. 10*—and as long before as possible.

Be sure and know what the *cost* is going to be before you advertise the price—then put on a price which will insure a profit.

If your house is too much driven to take hold and force this thing along, give it to some other publisher on a basis of ½ profits to me ⟨above cost of manufacture.⟩

I shall send a MS of the thing to Chatto. Doubtless he can order *sheets* from Frankfort-A-Main, with my translation printed in them.

⟨You could try ordering sheets if you choose by cable, but you'd have to add my rhymes.⟩

I'll see if the same can be done for you—so you'd have nothing to do but add the *cover*.

If you haven't heard from me by cable by the time you receive this, go ahead and make the book yourself—silence will mean I couldn't manage the thing.

Yrs sincerely

S L Clemens

P.S. I send you 2 copies of "Struw[w]elpeter"—I don't know why. I had a reason but have forgotten it.

---

[1] *Der Struwwelpeter*, published in MT's translation, *Slovenly Peter*, but not until 1935.

236. To Fred J. Hall

Frankfurt
28 October [1891]

Dear Mr. Hall:

Can't buy Struwwelpeter plates or sheets either.

The plates exist in New York, but you probably can't find them. The publication was attempted there, years ago and was abandoned.

Everywhere but in Germany the little book is printed in one color—black. Suppose you do *the same,* and put on a paper cover printed in *two* colors. And do no advertising other than circulars—eh? The plates—*processed,* German text and all—will cost but little, and so there can [be] but small loss if no gain.

But don't publish at all if your judgment disapproves. The thing is not worth taking any trouble about.

You might send a few copies—if you publish—to Chatto, in order to get English copyright, but tell him to look in at the British Museum first, and make sure that the German text and pictures have not been copyrighted there.[1]

If you do *not* publish, sell nothing to McClure, unless you can sell him the temporary use of the whole translation to use serially for a considerable sum—several hundred dollars.

Then at your leisure you could get the book ready in two or three colors for publication *next* fall.

Ys sincerely

S L C

---

[1] MT's concern about the copyrighting of the German text may possibly explain the sudden and complete disappearance of the proposed volume from further consideration, since a German language edition of *Der Struwwelpeter* had been published in St. Louis by C. Witter in 1862.

237. To Fred J. Hall

Berlin
7 November 1891

Dear Mr. Hall:

I made a mistake—I need *two* "Meisterschaffts" (Jan. '88.) Please cut out and send me another one.

You make a most excellent showing for a three-years' up-building of a business which was in ruins. I am anxious to know the result of Mr. Williams's trip.[1] Much depends on it.

N.B. It isn't my *story* that I want cut out and sent to me, but 2 copies of each *newspaper letter*.

Suppose you should make a little 16mo pamphlet of 100 pages long primer, the title page *part of the* sheet—*no cover*—the thing merely stitched together; stereotype and print 3,000. The whole thing would not cost more than $120, I should think. The pamphlet (after sinking the plates) should not cost more than a cent and a half apiece. License a newsboy and let him sell it at 10 cents and keep 4 cents himself. Every time he sells one he makes as much as he would by selling 4 or 5 daily papers, and has no dead stock left on his hands, for his pamphlet is still salable next day. I wish you would make such a pamphlet out of The Jumping Frog sketch and enough matter taken from White Elephant to fill up the pamphlet—print 3,000 and try it on. I believe that by the time you had 50 or 100 such pamphlets made up out of my stuff and uncopyrighted stuff of other people's, you would be able to pay all the firm's annual expenses with the pamphlets and have a profit left. *"The Jumping Frog"—by Mark Twain.*

A strong bold title-page like that ought to sell *just as easily as a newspaper*. I am satisfied that somebody will very soon introduce the 10-cent pamphlet. It is the coming form. Whoever gets in first may master the market. It costs but $120 to try it.

Are there objections to it which have not occurred to me? Would it raise enemies in the trade? Tell me what you think of it.

(*Mem.* The Jumping Frog was first published in the N.Y. Saturday Press, and is not copyright.)

How soon must I send another newspaper letter? I have 2 nearly finished, but don't know when I *can* finish them.

Writing just this note to you will give me lockjaw for two or three days.

Goodbye and good luck.

S L C

---

¹ Mr. T. Williams was contemplating taking over the sales of *LAL*. He considered this set "the work of his life and he wants to make an agreement that will extend over the next eight or ten years. . . . he thinks there is a fortune for himself and for us in the 'Library,' and . . . he will make the sale of 'L.A.L.' the work of his life" (FJH to MT, 16 December 1891). The deal was completed and by 1 January 1893, CLW & Co. was able to add to its list of debts "Mr. Williams' share of profits in 'L.A.L.'; it will at present approximate ten thousand dollars" ("Estimated Selling Value of Stock on Hand—Jany 1st—1893 Belonging to C. L. W. & Co.").

238. To FRED J. HALL

Berlin
8 November 1891

Dear Mr. Hall:

All I ever had in my mind was to make some money for Mrs. Burton because I loved her husband so. I myself am perfectly willing to grant this request of hers or any other, but I mustn't ask you to do it unless you feel entirely willing. Please write her— accepting her proposition, or declining it, or modifying it in any way you like, and I shall be satisfied.¹

And please either enclose this to her or in your own letter explain to her that I am so crippled that the physician forbids me to touch pen or pencil. To write half a page gives me hours of pain.

Ys ever

S L C.

P.S. Nov. 9. No, I don't mean a 10-cent pamphlet of 100 pages *16mo;* I mean *24mo.* That is, say, 4 pages of the pamphlet to *one* page of the Century magazine. Say 200 words to the page,—600 ems—100 pages would be 60,000 ems.

The Century is long primer. Cut a page of it into 4 parts and you will have the sort of page I mean.

In the 10-cent pamphlet (100 of them) there's $100,000 a year profit, or—nothing at all. The experiment is doubtless worth trying.

Very cheap paper is what you want.

S L C

[1] Mrs. Burton may have asked to purchase the remaining *Yale Lectures,* none of which are listed in the ". . . Stock on Hand—Jany 1st—1893 . . ." report.

239. To FRED J. HALL

Berlin
19 November 1891

Dear Mr. Hall—

If you think you might get into a disagreeable dispute with the American Pub. Co. by using the Jumping Frog, use something else. But when I come home I'll use the Jumping Frog and take care of the dispute, for it is quite necessary that I have a controversy with those people some day.

Yrs

S L C

My idea is, that if the 10-cent pamphlet succeeds, to issue those 6 newspaper letters (35 to 40,000 words) as a 15-cent book on thin, cheap paper, and sell it by peddlers in the several cities—organizing a corps of 100 peddlers or more and having a salaried and commissioned agent in each city to run the business.

It may be that the 10 and 15-cent pamphlets are not as lucrative as L.A.L., but I have the conviction that they will turn out to be so.

240. To Fred J. Hall

[Berlin]
22 November 1891

Dear Mr. Hall—

I am returning these proofs in 2 envelops [1]—one envelop won't hold them both.

I have carefully corrected them. You can send one to Chatto if you choose.

Send me 3 copies of the letter concerning Baireuth and the opera. I promised to send one to Labouchère.[2]

Ys

S L C.

---

[1] Presumably the articles on Aix and "Playing Courier" since MT requests three copies of proof of "At the Shrine of St. Wagner" in the last paragraph.

[2] Henry Labouchère, editor of the English magazine *Truth*.

241. To Fred J. Hall

Berlin
27 November 1891

Dear Mr. Hall:

That kind of a statement is valuable. It came this morning. This is the first time since the business began that I have had a report that furnished the kind of information I wanted, and was really enlightening and satisfactory. Keep it up. Don't let it fall into desuetude.

Everything looks so fine and handsome with the business, now, that I feel a great let-up from depression.[1] The rewards of your long and patient industry are on their way, and their arrival safe in port presently seems assured. By George I shall be glad when the ship comes in!

My arm is so much better that I was able to make a speech last night to 250 Americans. But when they threw my portrait on a screen it was a sorrowful reminder, for it was from a negative of 15 years ago and hadn't a grey hair in it. And now that my arm is better, I have stolen a couple of days and finished-up a couple of McClure letters that have been lying a long time.

I shall mail one of them ("Marienbad") to you next Tuesday—registered. Look out for it.

I shall register and mail the other one (concerning the "Jung-frau") next Friday. Look out for it also, and drop me a line to let me know they have arrived.

I shall write the 6th and last letter by and by when I have studied Berlin sufficiently.

Yours in a most cheerful frame of mind, and with my and all the family's Thanksgiving greetings and best wishes,

S L Clemens

---

[1] MT's optimism was infectious—FJH wrote in reply, "The ship is certainly nearing port now." But he cautiously added, "Of course you must not take the profits of that one month as being the average for every month during the year; there will be a steady falling off now until the Spring trade" (16 December).

242. To Fred J. Hall

[Berlin]
1 December 1891

Dear Mr. Hall:

The enclosed is from Mr. Charles Warner's brother George.[1] It has long been and still is, my darling desire to see the Yankee issued in paper covers, without pictures, (cheap paper) at 25¢ a copy—size, 16mo or 12mo or along there somewhere.

I suppose it would cost 3 cents or possibly 4, on cheap paper, after the plates were sunk.[2] You could sell by peddlers, and to the trade (at 33 to 35 off?) and to labor organizations at 20¢ apiece when 10 or more are ordered at one time.

Through George Warner you can get at Hotchkiss, and through him at all the labor organizations in America.

(Privately, there's a chapter or two in the book which will make it a good Democratic campaign document next year.) It could be sold in batches to Democratic Clubs. It is a book that is working its way along in Germany, and I hear its praises in surprising places— from thinkers born to title and nobility.

You should print upon the cheap book the fact that it can be had, bound and illustrated, of C L W & Co. at such-and-such a price.

Nationalist Clubs were formed and they bought 300,000 "Looking Backward"—but here are your Labor Clubs already formed, and numbering a million men, and they have no Gospels thus far except very serious ones and sometimes dreary.

We don't want a 50¢ book, but a 25¢ or a 15¢. My books have all got to be brought down to 25¢ as soon as we can stand it. Write me.

Ys

S L C

[1] George Warner's letter (New York, 17 November 1891, Berg) reports that he had met a labor organizer named Hotchkiss who said, "The Labor folks have got onto it [*A Connecticut Yankee*] and they want a cheap edition. Can't Clemens be induced to print one they could afford to buy."

[2] FJH was perplexed (16 December):

In some way your calculations must have been wrong, when you speak of the book only costing three or four cents. We have gone over it most carefully and with fine type, cheap paper, cheap printing, we do not see how it would be possible (not figuring the cost of the plates) to produce the book under nine or nine-and-a-half cents. . . . I think, however, that a fifty cent and a dollar edition would take.

243. To Fred J. Hall

[Berlin]
22 December 1891

Dear Mr. Hall:

I corrected both Bayreuth letters, and have mailed one to Chatto. I enclose the other to you.

The $1 edition of Huck (only 7000 sold) discomforts me. Evidently there is no sale for that kind of an edition.

I now pin the last rag of my faith on 25 cent editions. Let us see what Huck can do at that.

I think you do not need to begin to select for a "series" this early.[1] My idea was a *10*-cent series; that series having been discarded, there is already a 25-cent series without any selecting. It consists of—"The Yankee at Arthur's Court"—all by itself.

The "series" to *stop with that, if it fails.* If it succeeds, then add—

> "Huck Finn,"
> "Recent Glimpses of Europe," [2]
> "Prince and Pauper"
> "White Elephant," etc. etc.

Of course we've *got* to issue the "Glimpses" at 20 or 25¢—that goes without saying. But the "Yankee" is the real test.

Pages 1 and 2 of your letter approved. (It is dated Dec. 11/91.)

P.S. Dec. 23. Mrs. Clemens urged that I wait over night and then write something pleasant anent the LAL increase of royalty.[3]

But I find it impossible. By your magnificent management and by my sacrifices of money together with grinding and painful economies on the part of my family his book has been saved from a *second* defeat.[4] Has he ever come forward and said, "You are in deep waters—let me help what I can—stop my royalties and take them as a loan for a while?"

If he had played any generosities on us he would have had *me,* for that is my weak side; I should have been obliged to meet him half way. But no, he has contributed nothing but criticism and dissatisfaction so far as I know.

We have *not* sold copies enough to pay the book's half of 5 or 6 years' office expenses. It is still in debt to us for plant and all other expenses. Will those royalties ever be enlarged while the book owes us a single nickel? No. Will they then? Only on one condition— that business *custom and tradition* shall require it. If ever I mix sentiment with business again, I mean to see to it that I don't

contribute all the sentiment and the other man all the selfish-
ness.

Consider! For lack of capital the book's safety is still in doubt,
and at such a time he wants to lay an additional feather on its back!
The man has no bowels; his inside is upholstered with gas pipe.[5]

As to Stedman. I *wrote* 5 books—didn't merely edit them. They
were published by subscription at an average of $3.40 per vol.
(Am. Pub. Co.) Cost of *plant* for the whole, $8,000. Aggregate of
volumes sold, 600,000. Average royalty paid me, 22 *cents* on each
vol.

My first 3 books have sold an aggregate of over 450,000 vols.
On two of them I get a royalty of 5 per cent, and on the other,
7½.

For 15 years I have been trying to get these royalties raised a
little—without success. When I succeed I shall be ready to
entertain a proposition from Stedman.

We took his book after it had failed in another man's hands. We
assumed enormous risks, and (Webster's mind being deranged—it
had previously been non-existent) agreed to pay an extravagant
royalty.

Don't allow Stedman to pester you. Tell him you are willing but
I am *not.* And if you wish, you can add that I see no prospect in the
immediate future that is likely to change my mind. (Privately,
between you and me, I *never* expect to change it. The man has
acted the part of a cold-blooded shark.)

⟨Tell Bok I have caught him in several lies and in one attempt to
swindle, and that I will attend to his case all in good time.⟩

No, I can't afford to help raise Bok into notice.

Among the MSS I left with you are a few that have a *recent* look
and are written on rather stiff pale green paper. If you will have
those type-writered, and keep the originals and send me the copies
(*one* per mail, not two,) I'll see if I can use them.

But tell Howells and other inquirers that my hopes of writing
anything are very slender—I seem to be disabled for life.

Drop McClure a line and tell him the same. I can't dare to make
an engagement now for even a single letter.

I am glad Howells is on a magazine, but sorry he gave up the

Study.⁶ I shall have to go on a magazine myself if this LAL continues to hold my nose down to the grindstone much longer.

I'm going to hold my breath, now, for 30 days—then the annual statement will arrive and I shall know how we feel! Merry Xmas to you from us all.

Sincerely,

S L C.

P.P.S. (Just finished the accompanying "P.S." and finished raging at the eternal German tax-gatherer,⁷ and so all the jubilant things which I was going to say about the past year's business got knocked out of me. After writing this present letter I was feeling blue about Huck Finn, but I sat down and overhauled your reports from now back to last April and compared them with the splendid Oct.-Nov. business, and went to bed feeling refreshed and fine, for certainly it has been a handsome year. Now rush me along the Annual Report and let's see how we feel!

S L C

---

¹ FJH had advised concerning "our 25 cent pamphlet scheme," "we intend to start on [it] just as soon as the holiday trade is over." Ultimately the "Fiction, Fact, and Fancy Series," under the general editorship of Arthur Stedman, would evolve from the present plan—with titles available in both paper and cloth at prices from fifty cents to $1.50.

² MT's proposed title for the collected McClure travel letters.

³ E. C. Stedman had apparently demanded an increase in royalty on the *LAL*. He made the unfortunate mistake of comparing his profits on eleven volumes with MT's—see further paragraphs below.

⁴ The "first" defeat was the inability of W. E. Dibble Publishing Co. to finance the publication of the series.

⁵ MT was so charmed with the felicitousness of his own phrase that he preserved it in his notebook (Notebook 26, TS p. 17).

⁶ Howells accepted the editorship of *Cosmopolitan* in December 1891 (and resigned in June 1892); his last "Editor's Study" appeared in *Harper's Monthly* for March 1892.

⁷ In the first few paragraphs of "A German Chicago."

VI

"I Feel Panicky"

(1892–1894)

"I feel panicky."
Mark Twain to Fred J. Hall, 8 July 1893, *MTL*, p. 588

WHILE MARK TWAIN was in Europe as an absentee land-
lord, Charles L. Webster & Co. continued its collision course
toward bankruptcy. Expenses increased staggeringly, and to offset
them, Hall continued to consider old sheets and stocks of books as
an asset of the firm rather than a liability. Every sale of the *Library
of American Literature* added to the debt, and of more direct
concern to Mark Twain, it was impossible for the firm to pay his
royalties or even his and his wife's interest on their investments. An
annual audit of the Company's finances by the firm of Barrow,
Wade, Guthrie & Co. for 1891 provides startling evidence of the
firm's unproductiveness. At the beginning of 1891, Twain's capital
investment was $74,087.35. During the year, all royalty payments
($9,071.17), interest ($377.05), and his share of the profits
($11,162.19) were turned back into the Company; his share of
operating expenses was deducted ($15,355.97); and the year ended
with the debt to him increased to $79,341.79. Notes to the Mount

Morris Bank were constantly renewed and increased; and although Mark Twain claimed later in life that he "endorsed them without examining them" and later "found that additions had been made" (*MTE*, p. 192), the facts are that Hall made elaborate explanations every time he tried to justify an additional loan.

The point might well be made that Mark Twain's expatriation to Europe was disastrous for the Company, because it was he, not Hall, who knew the subtleties and intricacies of subscription publication from over twenty years of personal experience. On the other hand, Hall's belief that the era of the subscription book (but not the subscription set) was over was shared by Frank Bliss— whose credentials to speak with authority were as impressive as Mark Twain's.

At any rate, the subscription department of Charles L. Webster & Co. faltered while the trade department exploded. The "catalogs" in the final pages of the Webster editions of *The American Claimant, Merry Tales, The £1,000,000 Bank-Note,* and *Tom Sawyer Abroad* represent an impressive investment in a group of the most soporific sounding titles imaginable. *The Publishers' Trade List Annual for 1893* lists seventy-seven volumes for Charles L. Webster & Co.—excluding the eleven volumes of the *Library of American Literature,* and there is no evidence that Mark Twain helped choose (or veto) more than a handful of the new books.

Hall realized the snowball effect, and told Mark Twain on 9 April 1892, "that after next year, instead of making it our policy, as we have heretofore, to push forward and enlarge the firm in all directions, it would be wiser to commence at that time to concentrate; to bend our efforts . . . in keeping what we have, doing it with less expense, and making it more profitable."

Mark Twain, as the following letters show, was intent on his own manuscripts and literary projects, and (as these letters do not show) on the perfection of the typesetter. While he continued to endorse notes, count manuscript words, plan a magazine, and search frantically for investors during the Panic of 1893, the snowball increased in size and speed as it headed toward the precipice.

244. To Fred J. Hall

Ilsenburg
6 January 1892

Dear Mr. Hall:

I enclose check for $1000, which you can endorse over to Mr. Halsey, 15 Wall street,[1] to be invested in Mrs. Olivia L. Clemens's name.

Mrs. Clemens and I are staying here for a few days in the Hartz Mountains. We return Jan. 12 to Berlin.

Address me hereafter

Hotel Royal, Berlin.

I lecture in Berlin Jan. 13 [2]—may possibly return here, but my address will remain as above.

Happy New Year!
S L C.

[1] Noah Wetmore Halsey, of N. W. Harris & Co., who began investing MT's money from serialization—see the following letter.
[2] See *MTB,* p. 935.

245. To Fred J. Hall

Berlin
21 January 1892

My dear Mr. Hall:

Your letter written on Jan. 7th has just reached us. We have not yet rec'd the one written the day before on the magazine matter but it will doubtless come before many days.

Like all your letters it was a great comfort to me. Ever since your letter to me came I have been intending to write you. I have been so thoroughly chagrined at my very unbusinesslike and exacting proposition that you give me six per cent on money that is to be constantly drawn from. Mr. Clemens laughed at me *afterward,* but at the time we let that letter go and was feeling so depressed money wise that he allowed me to send it and put in no protest. Now will you pay me the usual interest on money so deposited? I believe that is three or four per cent.[1]

I am anxious that Mr. C. should take that sixteen thousand that he will have from his story and letters and invest it elsewhere because it surely is very bad to have all ones eggs in one basket so I think it will be well for him now to make small investments when he can outside of Webster & Co. Therefore he intends to invest $16,000. Through Mr. Halsey.[2]

Mr. Clemens has been ill in bed with a very bad cough now for a week, he is better and is going to sit up for a little while today. I write therefore for him. He wishes me to say that you are entirely right regarding the cheap books that not only is it bad to give up the 25 cent editions of his books, but it is not wise at present to publish the letters that after a time he will add something to these and make a dollar book. He desires also that Chatto & Windus do not now publish the letters.[3]

We are delighted that you are thinking of taking a little trip to this side next summer, Mr. Clemens says that you must come to us whereever we are, and that the office must pay two-thirds of your expenses. It is probable that we shall be in Switzerland in July and you need to see Switzerland.

I am ordered to go to some baths the middle of May but I think I shall be through with that course before July.

While I am at the baths we shall locate the family at some quiet inexpensive place.

Trusting you will pardon the many erasures in this work as Mr. C. talks to me while I write. believe me

very sincerely yours
Olivia L. Clemens.

---

[1] Before leaving for Europe MT had written (Notebook 25, TS p. 38), "Want CH W & Co to presently begin to pay 6% half-yearly on $74,000, *and* copyrights and money lent." Mrs. Clemens was obviously expecting to withdraw money from the principal, however, and agreed to the lower interest rate.

² On 5 February, FJH reported that he had deposited Mrs. Clemens' money with Halsey, but had placed a $1,281 royalty check with a McClure payment in the Mount Morris Bank, making a total personal account of $6,781.99 in MT's name.

³ See letter 247, n. 1, for MT's own directions to Chatto & Windus.

246. To Fred J. Hall

[Berlin]
25 January 1892

(Answers to letters of Jan. 7.)

Dear Mr. Hall:

Mrs. Clemens was not able to say it all, day before yesterday—so I will continue. I must be brief, for I am still in bed and hardly able to write. I have been in bed 12 days—touch of congestion of the lungs, and I was careless, supposing I merely had an ordinary cough.

1. The "enclosure" from McClure wasn't enclosed. Doubtless it was about Poultney Bigelow and the Kaiser, etc, enclosed in your note of 12th just received.¹

2. The December showing is great; and the contrast between LAL receipts for last 9 months and corresponding 9 in '90 is startlingly satisfactory.²

3. The letter of credit is here by this time.

4. Yes, you can use my Century war article; also

"Luck" (Harper's Monthly few months ago);

The Mental Telegraphy article (same magazine—December;) also

A Letter to Queen Victoria (same magazine 3 or 4 years ago (Drawer.)

"Meisterschafft;"

Article about an old medical Dictionary (Harper—about 2 yrs ago.)

There may be others but I don't recal them.³

However, I am not able to go on writing. I will cable my approval of every proposition in your letters of Jan. 7.

I am more than satisfied with the Huck Finn result—17,000 copies of an old book is *good*.

You are right—we will not bring the Yankee and the P and P and Huck below $1 for a good while to come—if ever.

As to "Recent European Glimpses"—*suppress it*, till I get time to add a lot of chapters to it.[4] Next summer I mean to do that.

I shall not feel blue again. I am permanently the other way, now.

As to my MSS there—you have ciphered it out right. (See next to last page of your second Jan. 7 letter.)

Good-bye and great luck!

S L C

P.S. You will issue the "Claimant" as a $1 book, won't you?

P.S. Jan. 27. I will enclose a dated check for $2,000 (turn it over to Halsey for investment,) and some undated ones for $1000 each. As fast as money falls in from McClure turn it over to Halsey by means of the undated checks, and have him invest it in Mrs. Clemens's name. Whenever our firm makes a copyright or interest payment to me, turn that over to Halsey in the same way to be invested for Mrs. Clemens and report to me.

Now I am going to ask a favor of you. As fast as Halsey delivers the securities to you I want you to put them in a box in a Safety Deposit Vault, and keep the key yourself; and keep a list of them for reference. I want no mention of them to go to Hartford.[5]

I have been nearly 2 weeks in bed, now, and am tired of it.

S L C

[1] Neither Hall's letters of 7 January nor the note of 12 January are extant. Poultney Bigelow's *The German Emperor and His Neighbors*, published by CLW & Co. in 1892, was presumably offered to the firm by the McClure Syndicate.

[2] A later letter (5 February) suggests FJH's analysis of the Company's financial situation: at the end of 1890, cash profit was $7,029, and at the end of 1891, $16,743. "In addition to this we have increased our good stock about $40,000.00 and our new plates and copyrights about over $7,000."

[3] Some of the material in this list appeared in *Merry Tales*, while the rest was

not collected until *The £1,000,000 Bank-Note.* "The Private History of a Campaign That Failed," "Luck," and "Meisterschaft" were in the earlier volume; "Mental Telegraphy," "A Petition to the Queen of England," and "A Majestic Literary Fossil" were in the later.

[4] Two of the articles, "The German Chicago" and "Playing Courier," appeared in *The £1,000,000 Bank-Note.* The others were not collected until the posthumous appearances of *What Is Man? and Other Essays* and *Europe and Elsewhere.*

[5] MT became embittered with Whitmore in later years because of his failure to make prompt reports (see *MTHL*, p. 710), but the reason for the present secrecy is obscure. Possibly additional money was being sought from MT by the Paige investors.

247. To Fred J. Hall

[Berlin]
2 February 1892

Dear Mr. Hall:

You are going to issue the "American Claimant" as a $1 book the moment it is finished as a syndicate-serial, aren't you? At any rate you are going to issue it as a *book.*

Well, what I want to say, is, have some competent and conscientious person *prepare the copy for the printer,* and read the proofs afterward, for I can't do that or any other work for a good while to come.

Please tell Chatto about this,[1] and make the proper arrangements with him as to date of issue in England and America.

Twenty-second anniversary of my wedding day; been in bed 3 weeks, now, with a mixture of influenza and congestion of the lungs,—mainly the latter, only a touch of the former.

Ys

S L C

[1] MT had written Chatto and Windus himself on 27 January: "Make no preparations to issue in book form the six newspaper letters which I have been writing from Europe. It is my purpose to add to them, next summer or fall, and then make of the whole a *book,* not a pamphlet. Of the five already published I like only three—and not *all* of the three. It is a poor average" (British Museum). Obviously, *The American Claimant* was to serve as a substitute.

248. To FRED J. HALL

[Berlin]
5 February 1892

Address till further instructions. c/o Drexel Harjes & Co. Paris.

Dear Mr. Hall:

The game-board [1] is neat and pretty, but it has a fatal defect. Instead of being filled up flush and level, the printed sheet of figures is stretched across a *hollow,* as from side to side of a slate; as a result, any pressure crushes the sheet in, and splits it in various directions. Also, the backing is not sufficient to hold up the pins; also the pins must be shoved in by force, whereas they ought to enter without force. It will not be well to send any of these boards out—they will come back to you, sure.

I am expecting to be allowed to sit up a little while to-day. We shall see, when the doctor comes.

I am ordered to a warm climate as soon as I can travel. Hence my address is changed back to the Paris bankers as above.

Yrs sincerely

S L C

[1] For "Mark Twain's Fact and Date Game" see letter 220 above.

249. To FRED J. HALL

Berlin
12 February [1892]

Dear Mr. Hall,—

Daly wants to get the stage rights of the "American Claimant." [1] The foundation from which I wrote the story is a play of the same name [2] which has been in A. P. Burbank's hands 5 or 6 years. That play cost me some money (helping Burbank stage it) but has never brought me any. I have written Burbank (Lotos Club) and asked him to give me back his rights in the old play so that I can treat with Daly and utilize this chance to even myself up. Burbank is a lovely fellow, and if he objects I can't urge him. But you run in at the Lotos and see him; and if he relinquishes his claim, then I would like you to conduct the business with Daly; or have Whitford or some other lawyer do it under your supervision if you prefer.

This morning I seem to have rheumatism in my right foot.

I am ordered south by the doctor and shall expect to be well enough to start by the end of this month.

[Unsigned]

[1] Letters to Augustin Daly (12 February and 17 May 1892) preceded the contract (9 August 1892) which gave MT 5 percent of the gross receipts.
[2] Actually "Colonel Sellers as a Scientist."

250. To FRED J. HALL

Mentone
8 March 1892

Dear Mr. Hall:

The fatalest objection of all is that the trade see no promise in the Game.[1] Therefore, my advice is that you put it aside until some indefinite time in the far future—it isn't worth trouble, now, when you can employ your time more profitably on other things. Besides, I am sorry I put my *name* to the Game; I wish I hadn't.

I cabled "Fall" yesterday. I quite agree with your purposes concerning the "Claimant" book.[2]

I have your January statement, which is good for January, and I am glad the future looks well to you and that you are done with Dibble.[3]

Yours sincerely

S L C

Mrs. C. and I remain here 2 or 3 weeks.

---

¹ On 6 May 1891, FJH had reported to MT that toy sellers were willing to take a few of the games on consignment but refused to purchase any outright.

² FJH's letter is not extant, but the cable obviously agrees upon the time to issue *The American Claimant,* which appeared as a $1.50 trade book.

³ W. E. Dibble apparently continued to hold copyrights on the first five volumes of the *Library of American Literature.* To buy Dibble's copyright, FJH agreed to supply him with sets of the series equivalent to $6,000 manufacturing costs—which Dibble then sold, retaining all the profits. As FJH pointed out in his letter of 24 March, "While the bargain is a most valuable one for us, there is a feature of it that I am afraid will make itself felt somewhat in our finances": the Company had to undertake immediate manufacture of 3,000 sets of *LAL* (33,000 volumes), and it no longer received its share of Dibble's profits—$500 to $1,800 a month. Consequently another Mount Morris Bank loan of $15,000 was necessary. FJH mailed five $3,000 notes with the comment, "I do not know that we will need to use these, but I simply do not want to get caught in a hole" (9 April 1892). A year later, MT wrote (Notebook 27, TS p. 14): "Mch. 12/92, is charmed with his Dibble trade—and inside of a fortnight it forces him to *double* that bank burden."

251. To Fred J. Hall

Rome
4 April 1892

Dear Mr. Hall:

Howells and I paid a theatre a lump sum (H. $300; I. $1,700 I think) to cancel a contract and *not* play the piece. We paid nothing to Burbank; he behaved very handsomely in the matter.

Next, I gave him the privilege of reading from the play in public, without his paying me anything.

Next, (by and by,) he wanted to try the piece again, (it was now in his possession and mine), and I gave him $1,200 to try it with. It was a failure. I am out of pocket $2,900 on the piece, I think.

Next, Burbank wanted me to put up money to have the last act re-written and the piece put in shape by a dramatist—4 or 5 years ago. I declined. (Before this, Howells went in with us again and submitted the piece to Herne the actor. Nothing came of it.)

If you talk with Howells or drop him a line, you will find he will resign any rights he may still have.

I will spend no more money in staging the piece or in buying Burbank's or anybody else's interests.

If Burbank wants to stage the piece at his own expense and share the profits (half and half) with me, I am perfectly willing, provided he will get right at it and *do* it, before the public interest dies out. If he can't do this, I think he ought to resign his rights to me. I consider that his rights fairly and properly *ought* to be relinquished, for I did all that could be expected of me when I put up that last $1,200.

If he won't do this, will he relinquish to me for 10 per cent of what I may get out of the piece? If he says *no,* drop the matter out of your mind and I will do the same.

If he says *yes,* then please talk with Mr. Alfred Arnold of 679 Madison avenue, who proposed (March 9) to dramatise the story for Crane the comedian,[1] I to have half of the revenue from the play; no contract for its production to be made without my sanction of terms, etc; I to approve the play or it not to be produced.

Tell him if *Crane* approves the dramatization, that is all I require. It need not be submitted to me. As to terms, he and you can always decide upon those without referring to me. I shall approve what you do.

I wrote Arnold [2] I would treat with him if nothing came of an already existing offer. He answered a few days ago showing that his offer to me still awaited my consent.

Ys

S L Clemens

[1] William H. Crane, whose most notable success was as Senator Hannibal Rivers in Lloyd and Rosenfeld's comedy, "The Senator."

[2] In Notebook 26, TS p. 37, MT wrote: "Rome, Apl. 20. Webster Co. Close with Arnold if you like. Clemens."

252. To Fred J. Hall

Rome
24 April 1892

Dear Mr. Hall:

I enclose the 5 notes for $3,000 each.

I am glad to see that the business has gone to rushing again.[1]

And I am also glad that by the corrected list sent me McClure has so nearly squared up.[2]

We like your project outlined to us for making the business yield dividends and pay debts after this year.[3] It will be a great relief and comfort—to you and to us. I hope you will be able to see your way clear to accomplishing it.

I do not expect to be able to write any literature this year. The moment I take up a pen my rheumatism returns.

Sincerely Yours

S L Clemens

[1] FJH had written on 9 April, "we are doing a splendid business now. The dull streak that we have had for the past month or six weeks seems to be over with." The first volumes of the cheap series (seventy-five cents in cloth, twenty-five cents in paper) were ready: *Merry Tales, The German Emperor* . . . , Whitman's *Selected Poems,* Irving Bacheller's *The Master of Silence,* and Elizabeth Cavazza's *Don Finimondone: Calabrian Sketches.* FJH was also preparing a campaign book for the 1892 elections, "and already have nearly all the matter in type that we can put in before the nominations are made."

[2] FJH had written on 24 March that McClure was $5,500 behind in payments for royalties; on 9 April, however, he confessed to a "decided blunder in making out the statement," since only $2,000 was still due and expected the following week.

[3] FJH's project, explained at length in the 9 April letter, was to concentrate and cut down expenses, pay dividends, and cancel debts, since "it is not to be expected that you and Mrs. Clemens will want to continue to keep the amount of money invested in the firm which you now have, for an indefinite time." Several months later MT wrote in his notebook (Notebook 26, TS p. 58), "After July 1 '92, my royalties are to be sent to me by check, a few hundred dollars per month."

253. To Fred J. Hall

Venice
22 May 1892

Dear Mr. Hall:

Yours of May 9 is here and sounds very good.

I want Mr. Halsey to use his own best judgment in making investments. That is why I don't write and meddle in the matter. Mrs. Crane thinks, with me, that he will do as well without my help as he could with it—and a little better, in fact.

I shall run over home about middle of June and start back to Europe toward end of July.[1] Maybe you can come with me.

I enclose an enclosure. Next time they write me I'll refer them to you, and you can tell them anything you want to—except to promise literature that isn't already written.

Ys sincerely
S L C.

[1] MT was in the United States from 22 June to 5 July.

254. To Fred J. Hall

Bad-Nauheim
22 July 1892

Dear Mr. Hall:

Yours of July 5 has arrived. I am very glad you have added a time-limit, etc., to the Daly contract; it is important.[1]

Give Burbank 10 per cent until $2,500 is reached, then shut him off.

I mail to-day the "Ship" article—8,000 words.[2] It is good and readable. Harpers will pay $80 or $100 per magazine page—say $800 to $950 for the article—if they like it. But maybe McClure will pay $1000. Please try him.

Ys Truly
S L Clemens

Let McClure have a couple of weeks to find out what he can
pay, if he wants it; and you can let him state his price before you
hint at ours. I believe I would rather sell to him than to a magazine
at the same price *net*. I would rather sell to him at $800 *net*, than to
a magazine at the same rate—but all the same I think I ought to
have $1000.

Ys
S L C.

Leave out the Noah's Ark if they want to.[3]

---

[1] On 3 August, FJH explained that the time limit for production had to be
extended from one year to two because Daly "had his next year's work entirely
planned."

[2] "About All Kinds of Ships," unpublished until it appeared in *The
£1,000,000 Bank-Note.*

[3] A burlesque interview of Noah by a German ship inspector, included in the
published sketch.

255. To FRED J. HALL

Bad-Nauheim
24 July [1892]

My Dear Mr. Hall.

I have not sent that "Ship" article yet—been revising it; but I
will mail it within the next six days—and will register it. Please
look out for it about August 12th to 15th.

Part of this delay was because I have written three-fourths of
another article and thought I might finish and send *it*, too; but I
see that it is going to string itself out to two articles, so I will not
wait.[1]

I wish I had seen McClure; I would have said "Give me a
definite figure per thousand words, or I must go to the magazines,
where I can get a definite figure." I wish you would say that to him.

Instead of drawing out that $4,000 (or whatever it is,)[2] in a
lump from your business, no doubt it will be more convenient

for you to send me a letter of credit on Brown, Shipley & Co for the amount. Let the letter begin to run *Sept. 1.* That will be early enough.

You can mail letters to us here (Kaiserhof Hotel) *till Aug. 20.* After that, to Drexel Harjes & Co., Paris, as before.

Ys

S L C

27 July

P.S. I will mail that "Ship" article within the next three days. Inform me when you receive it.

Please send Mrs. Clemens the name and numbers of the investment you told me Mr. Halsey had lately added.

I have just finished a letter about Bad-Nauheim with about six or seven thousand words in it—the amount I used to put in the syndicate letters last winter.

Ys Truly

S L C

---

[1] Unidentifiable—possibly "Down the Rhone" or the letter on Bad-Nauheim referred to in the postscript.

[2] Royalty due on the dollar edition of *Huckleberry Finn.* In Notebook 26, TS p. 56, MT wrote, 'What went with the $4000 that was to come due last May— on cheap Huck Finn, etc.? Been credited to personal account?"

256. To FRED J. HALL

[Bad-Nauheim]
10 August 1892

Dear Mr. Hall,—

I have dropped that novel I wrote you about, because I saw a more effective way of using the main episode—to wit: by telling it through the lips of Huck Finn. So I have started Huck Finn and Tom Sawyer (still 15 years old) and their friend the freed slave Jim around the world in a stray *balloon*,[1] with Huck as narrator, and somewhere after the end of that great voyage he will work in the said episode and then nobody will suspect that a whole book has been written and the globe circumnavigated merely to get that episode in an effective (and at the same time apparently unintentional) way. I have written 12,000 words of this narrative, and find that the humor flows as easily as the adventures and surprises—so I shall go along and make a book of from 50,000 to 100,000 words.

It is a story for boys, of course, and I think will interest any boy between 8 years and 80.

When I was in New York the other day Mrs. Dodge, editor of St. Nicholas, wrote and offered me $5,000 for (serial right) a story for boys 50,000 words long. I wrote back and declined, for I had other matter in my mind, then.

I conceive that the right way to write a story for boys is to write so that it will not only interest boys but will also strongly interest any man *who has ever been a boy*. That immensely *enlarges the audience*.

Now this story doesn't need to be restricted to a child's magazine —it is proper enough for any magazine, I should think, or for a syndicate. I don't swear it, but I think so.

Proposed title of the story, "New Adventures of Huckleberry Finn." [2]

(The foregoing can be shown to editors and McClure.)

Now then, Mrs. Dodge's rate, of $100 per 1000 words, doesn't seem large enough by 50 per cent.

Moreover, this story looks to me as if 50,000 words doesn't afford it space enough.

Won't you talk with Alden of Harpers; and the editor of Harper's Youth's Companion; and McClure; and write Howells? If they don't raise on Mrs. Dodge's offer, please accept her offer for me. Then I will carry the tale to 50,000 words for her and close it in such a way that I can take it up again as a Second Part and finish it. I propose to call it "New Adventures of Huckleberry Finn."

We mustn't simultane in Europe again in a way that will

prevent our issuing the book the *moment* it finishes as a serial in America. Will you take all this trouble for me?

Ys

S L C

P.S.: I have found *this* out, to wit: That Harper's Magazine paid Charley Warner $100 per 1000 words for those Californian articles —$11,000 for 120,000 words. If my market value is below Charley Warner's, it is a case of Since When? I should multiply it by two or three if required to testify.

"Huckleberry Finn and Tom Sawyer Abroad," or

"Huckleberry Finn Abroad"—

I don't quite know which name to give my new book, for Huck writes it and Tom is along. But anyway, one half of the book is done; I have written 26,000 words of it—and can add a million if required, by adding "Africa," "England," "Germany," etc to the title page of each successive volume of the series.

It is easy work, and I enjoy it. There is plenty opportunity for variety and fun. The family are *strenuous* that this first volume shall appear serially in St. Nicholas. Well, I would prefer that, too, but it seems to me that their offer of $5,000 for 50,000 words is just a considerable trifle moderate. Even Warner gets that.

S L C.

[1] In Notebook 26a, TS p. 18, MT wrote, "Began 'Huck Finn in Africa' August 5, 1892."

[2] The postscript, not included in the previously published letter (which ends at this point—*MTL*, p. 566), appears to belong logically to the present set of instructions and description.

257. To Fred J. Hall

Bad-Nauheim
23 August 1892

Dear Mr. Hall:

I will itemise two or three things of importance before they slip

out of my mind, to keep from jumbling them in my letter and
failing to catch your attention to them:

⟨1. Mrs. Clemens has only an incomplete list of the Halsey
investments. Won't you please complete it for her?⟩ Yours of Aug.
12 just rec'd.[2]

⟨I am going to ask Mr. Halsey to watch those purchases for me
and sell them whenever it shall seem best. General Langdon [1]
could authorize you to turn them over to Halsey from time to time
for this purpose. He holds a full power of attorney from Mrs.
Clemens.⟩

2. You asked me what you should do with the $500 left over in
bank from the McClure payments from my personal draft for
$1000. Send it to me in the form of a draft on London.

3. As to the $3,700 royalty. I proposed that you send it to me in
the form of a letter of credit in order *to save the necessity of putting
up the whole sum.* You put up *nothing.* When I draw against the
letter for a few hundred dollars the bank notifies you and you pay
only that minor sum at that time.

That is the way to do it. You may have to give bond, if the firm's
credit isn't demonstrably perfect, but you won't have to deposit any
money.

The reason we have not drawn largely or frequently against our
existing letter of credit was, that we judged the money was in your
business and useful to you; so we have been drawing any stray
sums from Langdon & Co that fell in there to Mrs. Clemens's
credit. ⟨Surely you didn't *deposit* Mrs. C's $10,000 in order to get a
letter of credit. And you won't have to do it in the case of the
$3,700, I should think. What we are after is to draw on you as
lightly as possible—but that ain't going to be any relief to you if
you have to deposit the face value of the letter in the *beginning.*⟩
Still, if it is more convenient for you to send me $500 a month till
the $3,700 is paid, that will answer every purpose.

⟨I wonder if that bloody "Ship" letter has reached you. I mailed
it. I also sent you the registration ticket—but doubtless I ought to
have kept that myself.⟩ Yours of Aug. 12 just rec'd.[2]

I have signed the Daly contracts and will register and mail them to you. You have made a contract which needs no emendations at my hands.

If this blazing weather continues, we shall not go to Florence 2 weeks hence. But it is impossible—it *can't* continue. Mrs. Clemens is hoping that by spring we shall be used to housekeeping in Florence, and that you can then run over and take a month's rest with us and have a refreshing time, and I am hoping the same.

Sincerely Yours

S. L. Clemens

P.S. Aug 23. (Confidential.)

My friend Capt. Frank Mason, U.S. Consul General at Frankfurt a/M. found in Venice, last spring, the *only authentic portrait of Columbus in existence,* and quietly bought it, but by a cable-mistake it was as quietly sold for a song to a rich Chicago gentleman, and poor Mason gets not a penny for a picture which will soon be worth some hundreds of thousands of dollars—I mean, when the well-kept secret bursts out, through the "Century" Oct. 1.

By private letter we know that our Government has recognized the picture as *its* only legitimate portrait of Columbus, and is putting it on a greenback, a postage-stamp, a half-dollar, etc., and will have it on *all government* matters for the Exposition.

Well, Mason owns copyright on all engraved reproductions. He wants a publisher, and hopes to sell 500,000 photogravure fac-similes. His particular friend is high up in the Government part of the Exposition. Name is Curtis—is Secy of the American Republic Department at Washington. Van Dyke of Columbia College does the article for the Century. There is a coolness between Van Dyke and Curtis. However, *one* of them is just on his way from America to talk engraving with Mason. If no contract is made, we will send the thing to you; if you don't want it, tell them who to go to and how to proceed.

Yrs

S L C

[1] Charles J. Langdon, Olivia Clemens's brother; his rank was apparently flexible, for FJH wrote him as "General" Langdon in 1890 (8 November) but demoted him to "Colonel" Langdon in 1893 (11 July).

[2] MT's cancellations and insertions followed the composition of the letter.

258. To Fred J. Hall

Bad-Nauheim
4 August [i.e., September] 1892

Dear Mr. Hall:

Land, you hadn't any flesh to spare! We are all sorry you lost any and we hope you will get it back as soon as possible.

Thanks for the check—it arrived all right.

All right, I'll strike the Harpers for a price. Their page contains 850 words. They paid Warner $100.00 a page for his California articles. I want to write for them at

$200.00 per 1,000 words.

That is, not that they take what I write whether it suits or not, but pay that for what they *do* take. This is about syndicate rates, but I would much rather be with the Harpers than anywhere else if it can be managed. If I aint worth, (commercially, not literarily,) double what Warner is, I want to be finding it out, right away.

What I have to offer Harpers now, (for their *Young People's Magazine*—not the Bazaar or the Weekly or the Monthly—don't forget that) is—

Tom Sawyer Abroad
———
Part I—In the Great Sahara
———
By Huck Finn
Edited by Mark Twain

This part I contains about 40,000 words, and is finished.

If the first numbers should prove popular, I could go on and furnish additional parts without delay, if desired.

I will send this MS to you as soon as the quarantine is raised, so that it can be examined.[1]

My family (tough people to please), like it first-rate, but they say it is for boys and girls. They won't allow it to go into a grown-folks' magazine. Don't forget *that* detail.

By and by I shall have to offer (for grown-folks' magazine,) a novel. Title—

Those Extraordinary Twins

It is the howling farce I told you I had begun a while back. I laid it aside to ferment while I wrote "Tom Sawyer Abroad," but I took it up again on a little different plan lately, and it is swimming along satisfactorily now. I have written about 20,000 words on it, but I can't form any idea of how big a book it is going to make yet. If I keep up my like it will be a book that will *sell* mighty well, I am sure of that. I think all sorts of folks will read it. It is clear out of the common order—it is a fresh idea—I don't think it resembles anything in literature. *I* believe there's a "boom" in it.

Pages 2 and 3 of this letter are in shape so the Harpers can read them if they want to.

If they stand my terms, cable me (through Drexel Harjes & Co., Paris). Put it—"They accept. Hall." If no, put it—"They decline. Hall." If they offer a modified rate, cable it—"They offer——— dollars. Hall." Fill in the blank with the sum which they offer per 1,000 words.

If we can't trade with them, please see Mr. Clark or Mrs. Mary Mapes Dodge and offer this first part of Tom Sawyer Abroad for $5,000. They offered me that for a story of 50,000 words, but I guess 40,000 is enough for the money. Tell them I wasn't able to *promise* a humorous yarn, but I meant to try my hand, upon their suggestion, and see what would come of it.

If you think it safe to send the Sawyer MS while the quarantine is on, cable me—"Send Sawyer."

Our house and servants are all ready for us in Florence, but here we are—*stuck*. Afraid to leave here in these cholera times. We hope the danger will be past in a fortnight, and let us go, but we can't tell.

Yours sincerely,

S. L. Clemens

If the Harpers won't trade, maybe Howells might want the "Twins" at $150 or $200 per 1,000 words—he is used to getting such rates himself.

I'm giving you heaps of trouble, and I wish I could help it, but there aint any way.

P.S. Sept. 5.

The Consul General tells me that the mails will not be delayed or MS injured by the New York quarantine; therefore I shall revise "Tom Sawyer Abroad" at once and mail it to you in a few days.

When you get it please cable me via Drexel Harjes & Co Paris— *"Sawyer received"* (No signature).

As I understand it, Warner gets $10,000 a year (Howells's former salary) for the "Study." The Aug. No. contains 5 pages, the Sept. No. 4½. It is more than $200 a page. Great Caesar's ghost!

If they won't pay me $200 a page would you mind asking them what the difference consists of between the commercial (not literary) value of Warner's stuff and mine?

S L C

---

[1] The cholera epidemic, which MT first heard about on 18 August, was turned into literary material, "The Cholera Epidemic in Hamburg," published in *Europe and Elsewhere.* That date also allows for accurate dating of the present letter, which MT appears inadvertently to have dated "August."

259. To FRED J. HALL

[Lucerne]
18 September 1892

Dear Mr. Hall:

I left a sample of "Tom Sawyer Abroad" in Frankfort to be mailed to you—16,000 words.[1] The rest of Part I (25,000 words) will be mailed to you from Frankfort by and by when it has been copied.

We are on our way to Florence—get there some time or other I hope.

Ys

S L C

---

¹ In Notebook 26a, TS p. 23, MT wrote, "Frankfurt a/M. Sept. 13/92. Shall mail to-morrow 27 typewritten pages of 'Tom Sawyer Abroad'—16,000 words. (113 pages; MS; The whole 280 MS pages make about 40,000 words.)"

260. To FRED J. HALL

[Florence]
5 September [i.e., October] 1892

Dear Mr. Hall:

The August statement has arrived, and is very fine in various ways.¹ The cheap P and P and Huck Finn and Claimant make a good showing.

Watch the American Publishing Co., Hartford, and if they venture to issue any cheap editions of my books, we will stop them. I will drop Whitmore a line and tell him to keep a lookout too.

What ought I to do with the "duplicate" checks?—destroy them, or return them to you? I re-enclose to you the one I cashed last week. Also one which I found in my pocket the other day, and which I think I cashed in Frankfort about the first week of this month. I *did* cash a check then, and got 2 Marks less than this one calls for—and no doubt it was this one and they charged me that trifle for commission and 10 blank checks—for in Florence the checks cost about that rate.

Some day I hope to get to work on the Extraordinary Twins again, but I can't guess how much of a book it will make.

How many cheap Huck Finn's have been sold, up to the present time? I want to see if I can make a rational guess at what I ought to be worth in a magazine.

We are getting slowly settled here—*very* slowly.² I think it will be as expensive as living in hotels—besides the extra cost of getting *started*.

Sincerely Yrs

S L C

[1] In Notebook 26a, TS p. 30, MT wrote, "Copyright royalties for August '92, about $2,000 according to CLW & Co.'s statement. Co. profit, $6,000."

[2] The Clemens family did not arrive in Florence until late September; thus the present letter, like the 5 September one above, appears to have been inaccurately dated.

261. To Fred J. Hall

[Florence]
13 October 1892

Dear Mr. Hall:

I am sending to Harper's an article (8,000 words or 9,000) entitled "A Curious Book." If they do not accept it, Mr. Alden will let you know, and you can send and take it away.

Suppose you wait ten days, and if you don't hear from him, write and ask if he accepts it. If he says yes, and tells you what month it is to appear, suppose you have *it* and the Book itself complete, and the Meisterschafft and some other stuff which I am sending you, in type and printed and ready to issue, at that date, and have advance sheets in Chatto's hands early enough for him to be able to issue simultaneously.

The enclosed (enclosed with the literature itself in a big blue envelop,) is Table of Contents of the proposed book—a book suitable for railroad and summer reading and such-like.

I'll explain the Table of Contents: [1]

    1. Preface—(if I conclude to write one.)

    2. "A Curious Book" is the article I am sending to Harper.

    3. "The Enemy Conquered" is the curious book unabridged—as you will see.

4. The Californian's Tale. ⎫
5. Meisterschaft ⎬ herewith enclosed

6. About Ships—that's the Ship article you've already got. I don't care to publish it in any magazine or newspaper.

7. Playing Courier—(enclosed)

8. German Chicago—   "

9. £1,000,000 Bank Note. Well, I will send *this* to Harper, too. If they don't want it, we'll put it in the book *without* previous publication.

I am suggesting to Harpers that they pay what *they* think is a fair price—then I shall know what to do next time.

I am going to begin another long story, now. But now and then I shall work on that farcical novel until I get it done.

If a little more matter is needed you can send me the syndicate letter which I wrote about the Beyreuth Musical festival, and I will correct it and return it to you. I have lost my copy.

Ys sincerely

S L Clemens

P.S. On second thoughts I concluded to send only the "Curious Book" to Harpers. I've sent the "£1,000,000 Bank Note" to the Century.

Ys sincerely

S L C

¹ For *The £1,000,000 Bank-Note and Other Stories.*

262. To Fred J. Hall

[Florence]
31 October 1892

Dear Mr. Hall:

Yours of the 19th rec'd containing 102.15.11.

Your news *isn't* entirely cheerful, but we will look for better next time.

If you have my 6 contracts with the American Publishing Co., please send them to Mr. Whitmore.[1] If you haven't them, and if Whitford hasn't them, then they are in Fredonia, among the stuff which Webster carted off.

The rest of Sawyer Abroad went to you some time ago. If Mrs. Dodge wants it, let her have it. It falls nearly 10,000 words short of what she wanted for $5,000; but if she isn't willing to pay $5,000, let her pay $4,000.

It is finished, and doesn't need another finish; but I have left it so that I can take it up again if required and carry it on. I tried to leave the improprieties all out; if I didn't, Mrs. Dodge can scissor them out.

Thank you for the news about the Chicago matter—I have kept it still.[2] Get me some more when you can.

Yr

S. L. C.

I enclose the notes, signed.

---

[1] On 31 October, MT also wrote Whitmore:

I will ask Mr. Hall to hunt up my American Pub. Co. contracts and send them to you. I have the impression that one or two of them name the price at which the books were to be sold. If so, I don't care how many cheap editions they issue if they want to pay royalties on three or four times what they get for the books.

If they want to make a *uniform* 10 per cent royalty on *all* the books,—on the old high-priced *and* the cheap editions, all right. I am willing; but otherwise I want them to stop with Tom Sawyer until they can make a counter proposition which shall be satisfactory. Now that they have gone so far with Tom Sawyer as to print 20,000, I don't care to interfere with that, as I am sure that that is a 10 per cent contract.

I once offered to let the elder Bliss issue cheap editions at 10 per cent., but he dissuaded me, saying they would damage the sale of the others; but his son goes ahead without asking any questions.

[2] Undoubtedly in reference to the construction of a Paige typesetter at the T. K. Webster Company in Chicago; but a letter from FJH making specific mention of a "Chicago matter" is not extant.

263. To FRANK BLISS

Florence
31 October 1892

My Dear Frank:

I hear you are issueing a $1 edition of Tom Sawyer.[1] I believe I
have a 10 per cent royalty on that book. *If so, go ahead;* but I
cannot consent to let your firm reduce the retail price of any other
of my books without first making special contracts with me.—The
royalties on several of them were unfair and always have been, the
contracts were gotten out of me by unjust means, and my damage
has already been sufficient.

Truly Yours
S. L. Clemens

[1] In spite of his reservations (see letter 222 above), Bliss issued the dollar *Tom
Sawyer* and, slightly later, a dollar *Sketches New and Old.* MT's antagonism was
aimed more at Bliss's refusal to allow CLW & Co. liberal enough discounts on his
own books; the old wound of 1884 reopened. MT wrote Whitmore on 2
November (Hartford Memorial):

> I wish I could get my American Pub. Co. contracts annulled. Doesn't the
> deliberate violation of the most important feature of a contract annul the whole
> contract? Those people agreed to use their best endeavors to push the sale and
> circulation of my books. The common way, and the best way, is to secure the
> interest of the middle-man by allowing him a big margin of profit. Now
> Webster & Co. are middle men: the A. P. Co. allow them discounts which
> enable them to clear—what? 50 cents to a dollar on each book sold?—No: not
> *ten cents* on *any* book of mine.

Whitmore presumably reported an interview with Bliss, for MT wrote again on 2
December, "Frank Bliss has not written me, but it's all right. I don't think he has
ever told me any untruths, and if he says he is not going to issue cheap editions
of any others of my books, I am satisfied."

264. To FRED J. HALL

[Florence]
24 November 1892

Keep this where you can refer to it.

Dear Mr. Hall:

Yours of Nov. 11 rec'd.

Make it $1.50 book or a $1 book as shall seem to you best.

Put no expense on it.

The article "A Curious Old Book" is the *important* feature, not the "£1,000,000 Note."

The "Curious Old Book" is the most delicious thing that has been offered to a magazine in 30 years, yet Alden declines it because *I* didn't write it![1] God Almighty, but this is "editing" with a gaudy intelligence! I don't believe Gilder is such a fool as that. Try him. If he can get it into the February Century, that would enable you to issue the book by March 1st. You could have your edition ready to issue before the magazine issued. Gilder may make the price as high as he likes, but make it *himself*. The price is not very important on a miscellaneous article, but if I publish "Those Extraordinary Twins" serially the price must be high. It is going to be a full-sized novel, and longer than the American Claimant. I have now written 43,000 words on it, and I think there will be as much more.

Yes, if St. Nick pays for Tom Sawyer when they accept it I'm willing that they defer publication till next Fall; because meantime I could write Part II of it, and then, whether they wanted Part II or not, we could add it to the book when we issue.

Happy Thanksgiving to you!

Ys Sincerely

S L C.

In this same mail I will tell Gilder you are going to offer him the "Curious Old Book."

P.S. I published in Harper's Monthly some years ago, a real good

Letter to Queen Victoria. The idiots put it in the Drawer, *of* course —it's all the sense they've got.

It was in a Xmas No and can be easily found. *That* ought to go into the new book, too.

[1] "A Cure for the Blues" contained MT's long introduction together with the text of Samuel Watson Royston's short novel, *The Enemy Conquered; or, Love Triumphant,* which obviously caused Henry M. Alden, editor of *Harper's Monthly,* to reject it.

265. To Fred J. Hall

[Florence]
7 December 1892

Dear Mr. Hall:

If the $500 draft left your office Nov. 15, it is now 12 days overdue. If this monthly duty is in the hands of the man who went on turning my royalties in to the Company's capital a year or so after being told to send them promptly to me whenever they fell due, he has probably been forgetting again. Within a month this half-year's royalties will fall due, and he will need punching up again, lest he do some more forgetting. I want him to forward $500 a month regularly right along on royalty account until the sum due last July is exhausted, then continuing the same figure monthly on the sum which will fall due Jan. 1.

I wish you would look and see if he is paying Mrs. Clemens's and my *interest* regularly, too. His two samples of forgetfulness suggest that his failing may be constitutional instead of accidental; but that is no matter, if he is punched up now and then.

Somebody (Willard Fiske, I suppose)—has sent me a file of the N.Y. Eve. Post—my favorite paper—from Nov. 1 to 17th, and the election details and comments are nuts to me—also the delicious pre-election "prophecies" of the chiefs of the late Republican party.

Ys Sincerely
S L C

266. To Fred J. Hall

[Florence]
12 December 1892

Dear Mr. Hall—

November check received.

I have lent The Californian's Story to Arthur Stedman for his Author Club Book; so your suggestion that my new spring-book bear that name arrives too late, as he probably would not want us to use that story in a book of ours until the Author book had had its run.[1] That is for him to decide—and I don't want him hampered at all in his decision. I, for my part, prefer the "£1,000,000 Banknote and Other Stories" by Mark Twain as a title; but above my judgment I prefer yours. I mean this——it is not taffy.

I told Arthur to *leave out* the former squib or paragraph and use only the Californian's Story. Tell him this is because I am going to use that in the book I am now writing.[2]

I finished "Those Extraordinary Twins" night before last—makes 60 or 80,000 words—haven't counted.[3]

The last third of it suits me to a dot. I begin, to-day, to entirely re-cast and re-write the first two-thirds—new plan, with two minor characters made very prominent, one major character dropped out, and the Twins subordinated to a minor but not insignificant place.

The minor character will now become the chiefest, and I will name the story after him—*"Pudd'nhead Wilson."*

Merry Xmas to you, and great prosperity and felicity!

Ys sincerely

S L Clemens

---

[1] *The First Book of the Authors Club, Liber Scriptorum* published "The Californian's Tale" in 1893.

[2] A letter to Stedman (Florence, 8 December, Berg) offers the story as a substitute, but does not identify the "squib."

[3] In Notebook 26a, TS p. 51, MT noted: "Dec. 20/92. Finished 'Pudd'nhead Wilson' last Wednesday, 14th. Began it 11th or 12th of last month, after the

King girls left. Wrote more than 60,000 words between Nov. 12 and Dec. 14. One day, wrote 6,000 words in 13 hours. Another day wrote 5,000 in 11."

267. To FRED J. HALL

[Florence]
26 December 1892

Dear Mr Hall:

Carey [1] is right—Royston's name should be changed to some other—also the name of his village—say G. Ragsdale McClintock, of Sunflower Hill, S.C.—or something like that.

Suppose that you get acquainted with *Carnegie* and ask him to lend us money enough at 6 or 8 per cent to run the *L.A.L.* up to 1,000 sets per month—not a lump sum, but only enough per month to cover the necessities of the month.[2] Show him that the possibilities are 2,500 sets a month, and that the history of the book shows that the collections are as sure as they are slow, and not attended by loss. If he won't, then ask him to put his financial head on the problem and tell us how and where to raise the money.

If we could get somebody to back us till we got the book up to 1,000 sets a month, we could then persuade that person or some other to help us up to 1,500 more a month.

Yes, get the *"Mental Telegraphy"* into the book, even if you have to leave something out to make room.

Yes, I got the St. Nick proposition to "split payment," and wrote "all right" to you and to Mrs Dodge.

Merry New-Years!

Yrs

S L C

[1] William Carey, an editor of *The Century* (which also refused "A Cure for the Blues"), pointed out apparently that it would be wiser to substitute a

fictitious name for Royston's; "McClintock" appears in MT's published version.

² Subsequent letters reiterate the appeal to see Carnegie; the next extant letter from FJH (10 March, 1893) explains his reluctance: "We cannot approach Carnegie until we get the experts' statement and the books are closed up for the year." In addition, though, FJH did not approve the idea: "I learn from a man who knows Mr. Carnegie that with all his ability he is a good deal of a busy-body and thinks that in business, as well as in literary affairs, nobody's judgment is as good as his" (FJH to MT, 14 March).

268. To Fred J. Hall

[Florence]
28 December 1892

Dear Mr. Hall:

I am proposing to sell to a friend ¹ enough of your interest and mine in the *L.A.L.* to make a one-fourth interest in the whole, for $200,000. He will decline, as he knows nothing about the book business.

But Carnegie might possibly buy it at that price. You might ask him.

If I were at home or could *get* home, I would suggest that we sell a quarter interest for $250,000 and *stock* the Co.—that is go around among my friends and get them to take from $1,000 to $10,000 of the stock until I made up the quarter million, you and I to own the other ¾ of the property. Couldn't it be done? Ask Carnegie what he thinks of it and what the nominal capital of such a Co. ought to be.

Happy New Years!

Ys

S L C.

I am perfectly sure the mails go astray. Here it is the 28th, and the check which you mailed the 15th—or was it later?—has not arrived yet.²

¹ Possibly Matthias Arnot; see letter 273 below.
² As MT explained to Whitmore (2 December 1892), "I think Mr. Hall does

pretty well. My royalties due there last July were for a couple of years, I think— and the amount was about $4,000. That is being paid me since, by check, $500 a month. My royalties for the past 6 months must be as much as $4,000. That is $8,000 in three years if my memory is right." Actually, a Summary of Royalties on sales from 1 July 1892 to 1 January 1893 showed total royalties of $5,375.57.

269. To Fred J. Hall

Florence
1 January 1893

Dear Mr. Hall,—

Yours of Dec. 19 is to hand, and Mrs. Clemens is deeply distressed, for she thinks I have been blaming you or finding fault with you about something. But most surely that cannot be. I tell her that although I am prone to write hasty and regrettable things to other people, I am not a bit likely to write such things to you. I can't believe I have done anything so ungrateful. If I have, pile coals of fire on my head, for I deserve it!

I wonder if my letter of credit isn't an encumbrance? Do you have to deposit the whole amount it calls for? If that is so, it *is* an encumbrance, and we must withdraw it and take the money out of soak. I have never made drafts upon it except when compelled, because I thought you deposited nothing against it, and only had to put up money that I drew upon it; that therefore the less I drew the easier it would be for you.

I am dreadfully sorry I didn't know it would be a help to you to let my monthly check pass over a couple of months. I could have stood that by drawing what is left of Mrs. Clemens's letter of credit, and we would have done it cheerfully.

I will write Whitmore to send you the "Century" check for $1,000, and you can collect Mrs. Dodge's $2,000 (Whitmore has power of attorney which I think will enable him to endorse it over to you in my name.) If you need that $3,000 put it in the business and use it, and send Whitmore the Company's note for a year. If you don't need it, turn it over to Mr. Halsey and let him invest it for me.

I've a mighty poor financial head, and I may be all wrong—but tell me if I am wrong in supposing that in lending my own firm money at 6 per cent I pay 4 of it myself and so really get only 2 per cent? Now don't laugh if that is stupid.

Of course my friend declined to buy a quarter interest in the L.A.L. for $200,000. I judged he would. I hoped he would offer $100,000, but he didn't. If the cholera breaks out in America a few months hence, we can't borrow or sell; but if it doesn't we must try hard to raise $100,000. I wish we could do it *before* there is a cholera scare.

I have been in bed two or three days with a cold, but I got up an hour ago, and I believe I am all right again.

How I wish I had appreciated the need of $100,000 when I was in New York last summer! I would have tried my best to raise it. It would make us able to stand 1,000 sets of L.A.L. per month, but not any more, I guess.

You have done magnificently with the business, and we *must* raise the money somehow, to enable you to reap the reward of all that labor.

Sincerely Yours

S. L. Clemens.

270. To Fred J. Hall

Florence
24 January 1893

Dear Mr. Hall:

I sent the notes yesterday.[1]

A friend of ours who is intimate with Alden says he was aggravated because he did not get the £1000000 Story; so I stopped my work a day or two ago to see if I *could* write something that would meet his views. However I'll not send the article now yet awhile.

Would it answer for me to publish The Extraordinary Twins through the American Publishing Co.? Mrs. Clemens fears ⟨it would create a damaging⟩ it would damage CL & W to have me publish a new book through another house. Tell me your views— freely.

If the A. P. Co. still have their subscription machinery I should like to try, for there is no money for a book of mine (or anybody else's for that matter) in the "trade." [2]

It may be that I have spoiled my subscription chances by issuing cheap books, but if that is not the case, I would like to pocket $30,000 again on a book as I used to do. And I don't a bit like "serial" publishing.

If you think favorably of my idea, I will come over in March or April and examine into the thing with a view to issuing the book next December.

I like the idea of a cheaply-gotten-up book (£1,000,000). It should be that, no matter what you sell it at.

I am notified that the letter of credit is at the bank—for £985. Then it must be a *new* letter instead of a renewal, for there was £1120 still due on the old letter. Has a mistake been made?

Ys ever

S L C

[1] MT endorsed renewal notes of Mount Morris Bank loans; later he made the mistake of endorsing a renewal for the $15,000 personal loan FJH had made from the George Barrow family in mid-1891 (see letter 221 above), and thus made it a Company liability.

[2] FJH replied (10 March): "There is a good and profitable sale in the trade for any of your books that strike the public fancy. There is no sale at present by subscription for any book that you could write." As for the American Publishing Company, "all the books they sell now are sold through the trade and it is the trade sales of your books that keep them alive, and their subscription sales amount to nothing at all." FJH admitted, nevertheless, that "The 'Claimant' has not sold at all well, and it would make the booksellers a little chary of any new book you might write." The Summary of Royalties for the last half of 1892 showed over $1,000 for *The Prince and the Pauper,* almost $1,500 for *Huckleberry Finn,* but just under $700 for *The American Claimant.* FJH was committed to trade publication by this time, but he also was undoubtedly aware that the subscription book depended on an isolated rural buyer who could not easily patronize a bookstore. By the early 1890's the situation that fostered the

growth of the subscription book salesman had disappeared, and only sets with prestige value were marketable by this method of sales.

271. To Fred J. Hall

Florence
28 January 1893

Dear Mr. Hall:

I want to throw out a suggestion and see what you think of it. We have a good start, and solid ground under us; we have a valuable reputation; our business-organization is practical, sound and well devised; our publications are of a respect-worthy character and of a money-breeding species. Now then I think that the association with us of some one of great name and with capital would give our business a prodigious impetus—that phrase is not too strong.

As I look at it, it is not money merely that is needed; if that were all, the firm has friends enough who would take an interest in a paying venture; we need some one who has made his life a success not only from a business standpoint, but, with that achievement back of him, has been great enough to make his power felt as a thinker and a literary man. It is a pretty usual thing for publishers to have this sort of partners. Now you see what a power Carnegie is, and how far his voice reaches in the several lives I speak of. Do you know him? You do by correspondence or purely business talks about his books—but personally, I mean—so that it would not be an intrusion for you to speak with him about this desire of mine, for I would like you to put it before him, and if you fail to interest him in it, you will probably get at least some valuable suggestions from him.

I'll enclose a note of introduction—you needn't use it if you don't need it.

Yrs

S L C

272. To Fred J. Hall

[Florence]
28 January 1893

Dear Mr. Hall—

Here it [1] is.

Perhaps you would better send him the note of introduction and ask for an appointment—but use your own method; any you prefer.

I have written 1800 MS pages since the 5th of last August, and 1500 of them are still here in my possession (one completed book [2] and one half-completed [3] make 1350 of the 1500.)

What *would* you do with this enclosed operatic man?

Do take him off my hands.[4]

There seems to be no sense in giving opera-privileges for nothing to a stranger—*he* can go and sell them, perhaps. And the worst of it is that the minute you give such a thing away, somebody comes and wants to *buy* it of you—then you curse. Suppose you tell this man he can have a year's permission for a tenth of his royalty—I mean, he to snake off his opera inside the 12 months and his privilege lapses, unless he can show cause and get a renewal of it.

Said privilege to be a privilege *only*—I to do no work and have nothing to do with it in any way.

This man wants my help. It's out of the question—I am too busy.

Ys sincerely

S L Clemens

P.S. Be perfectly free and frank as to my proposal about American Pub. Co.

And there is no great hurry, for it cannot be entertained at all while we are trying to raise more money; and not afterwards unless agreeable to all concerned.

---

[1] Presumably a letter of introduction to Carnegie, although MT refers to it

again in letter 274 below. Another letter, dated 8 July 1893, asks Carnegie to "let him [FJH] submit a project of mine to you and see what you think of it" (TS fragment in MTP).

² *Pudd'nhead Wilson,* the manuscript of which FJH acknowledged on 10 March.

³ *Personal Recollections of Joan of Arc;* see the following letter.

⁴ From the context, it is apparent that someone wanted MT's assistance in adapting one of his books.

273. To FRED J. HALL

[Florence]
3 February 1893

Dear Mr. Hall—

Won't you carry this down to Bowman (of D. Slote & Co.) and ask him about it?

Dan Slote was always robbing me in one way or another until he died; but I have never had any complaint to make of the present firm.

Ys

S L C.

It is D. Slote & Co. 119 William St. And please keep a copy of the letter to D. S. & Co.

I am writing a companion to the Prince and Pauper which is half done and will make 200,000 words; and I have had the idea that if it were gotten up in handsome style, with many illustrations and put at a high enough price maybe the L.A.L. canvassers would take it and run it with that book. Would they? It could be priced anywhere from $4 up to $10, according to how it was gotten up, I suppose.

I don't want it to go into a magazine.

S L C

I am having several short things type-writered. I will send them to you presently. I like the Century and Harper's, but I don't know that I have any business to object to the Cosmopolitan if they pay as good rates. I suppose a man ought to stick to one magazine, but that may be only a superstitition. What do you think? [1]

S L C

P.S. Yes, I think I have already acknowledged the Dec. $1000 and the Jan. $500—and if another $500 was mailed 3 days ago there's no hiatus.

I think I also reminded you that the new letter of credit does not cover the unexpended balance of the old one but falls considerably short of it.

Do your best with Carnegie, and don't wait to consider any of my intermediate suggestions or talks about our raising half of the $200,000 ourselves. I mean, wait for nothing. To make my suggestion available I should have to go over and see Arnot, and I don't want to until I know I can mention Carnegie's name to him as going in with us.

My book is type-written and ready for print—"Puddn'head Wilson—a Tale." (Or, "Those Extraordinary Twins," if preferable.)

It makes 82,500 words—12,000 more than Huck Finn. But I don't know what to do with it. Mrs. Clemens thinks it wouldn't do to go to the Am. Pub. Co. or anywhere outside of our own house; we have no subscription machinery, and a book in the trade is a book thrown away, as far as money-profit goes. I am in a quandary. Give me a lift out of it.

I will mail the book to you and get you to examine it and see if it is good or if it is bad. I think it is good, and I thought the Claimant bad, when I saw it in print; but as for any real judgment, I think I am destitute of it.

Feb. 3—P.S. Dear Mr. Hall:

No, you err, I think, in the matter of the $1000 check. It *was* two payments in one, as you say, but that was because the November payment was overlooked and not sent, if my memory is right. It didn't relieve January from taxation.

I've got the letter of credit—no, it is here in the bank—shall go and get it as soon as I get time. I judge it falls short of the right amount—can tell when I see it.

Arnot, the rich banker, owes me $45,000 on machine-royalties, but I shan't ask him for it until I *know* that the royalties are clearly worth the money. By the conversation which you had with Mr. K., that friend of yours, and from other information, I judge that the royalties are now worth twice that money. Get Mr. K. to find out all about the Paige machine affairs and keep you intimately posted in them. The first machine ought to be finished in May. When it is finished I can apply to Mr. Arnot; and between him and Carnegie perhaps we can get the money we need. If I get $45,000 from Arnot and turn in $20,000 besides, could you and the rest of you in the office put up $35,000 to buy stock with, in the new Co? Then get the other $100,000 from Carnegie or somebody, and the scheme is complete.

Ys

S L C

Get posted and *keep* posted about the machine.

George H. Warner, (brother to Chas. Dudley W.) of 30 State Street New York, has friends in Chicago who might be able to get information, but I would rather he should not know it is I that seek it. You ought to know Geo. Warner, he is a lovely man.

P.S. I think I won't prepay postage any more. Prepaid letters don't sometimes get out of Italy, they say.

---

[1] Olivia Clemens objected to the *Cosmopolitan* (see *MTHL*, pp. 652). FJH agreed (10 March) to the wisdom of "sticking to one magazine so long as they treat you right."

274. To Fred J. Hall

[Florence]
5 February 1893

Dear Mr. Hall:

Check for £102.8.4 received. Thanks; for I don't want to draw on our letter of credit except when obliged.

I shall cable you tomorrow to leave out Ambulinia, Preface and all. If the man who wrote the Preface wrote the story too, then it's a sell, and we can't risk printing it.[1] But who, then, wrote the "Oration" delivered in that Southern village?—for *it* is as idiotic as Ambulinia.[2]

I don't quite understand how we can borrow people's bonds and other securities if we can't borrow their money, which is the same thing. I don't understand the idea, but will examine further and try to.

I signed the notes and mailed them a week or so ago.

I wrote and sent you the Carnegie letter yesterday.

We can't publish Ambulinia, for Johnson might "peach."[3] It will make a big hole in the book, of course.

Yrs.

S L C.

[1] William Carey's concern about "A Cure for the Blues" apparently prompted some misgivings on MT's part that it might be a hoax. The "Preface" to which he refers is a eulogy to Woman.

[2] According to the title page of *The Enemy Conquered*, Royston was the author of "An Address Delivered at Cumming, Georgia, February 1844, on the Rise and Progress of Society and the Formation of Government." Ambulinia is the heroine of *The Enemy Conquered*.

[3] Robert Underwood Johnson presumably believed *The Enemy Conquered* was a hoax; but according to FJH's 10 March letter, "He says he will, of course, not say anything."

275. To Fred J. Hall

[Florence]
25 February 1893

Dear Mr. Hall:

Land, I seem to understand it, now!—the letter-of-credit puzzle
—but I couldn't make out what the trouble was, before.

I have sent "Pudd'nhead Wilson" to you.

I expect to be along soon, myself. If you get *no* cablegram after
March 22, it will mean that I have sailed from Genoa to New York
per steamer Kaiser Wilhelm II on that date.

But you can ship the usual check just the same—Mrs. Clemens
will need it and can cash it.

Say nothing to anyone about my coming. I don't wish to get into
the papers.

I wanted to start earlier but can't manage it.

Yrs

S L C.

276. To Fred J. Hall

[Florence]
8 March 1893

Dear Mr. Hall:

Very good, we will see if we can arrange an "emergency
account" when I arrive.[1]

Make a memorandum of that and of *everything* we need to talk
about and have it ready—then we shan't overlook anything.

Also, be prepared to take a room at the "Glenham" so that we
can talk together two or three evenings undisturbed.

The royalty account shows up well indeed. I must renew the
copyrights on my old books as they expire, and add them to our list.
However, that is a long look ahead—4 or 5 years. The first one—a
little vol. of Sketches, expires 2 years from now.

Could the Oct. or Nov check have failed to reach me? I have no way of knowing. If both of those reached me, then you are right and the $1000-check did include an extra payment.[2]

I shall hope your friend will have good and exact news about the machine when I arrive, so that I can go to Mr. Arnot with a clear case for his eye.

Ys ever

S L C

[1] On 10 March, FJH reported, "I wrote you some time ago about getting an 'emergency account.' This will certainly be necessary before long as it is very embarrassing to run on as small a margin as we are now." On 14 March, he proposed further that the fund should contain $30,000 "in the bank entirely separate from our regular accounts. . . . Whenever we ran a little ahead we could put money back into this fund and use it as a sinking fund to pay off our indebtedness to you and to the Mount Morris Bank."

[2] Discussion and confusion in previous letters about the monthly $500 checks and the letter of credit was apparently settled when FJH sent MT "a detailed statement of just what has been sent you, which no doubt you have received, showing that since we began remitting you we have sent you $500. every month except during January when we sent you $1,000. I also sent you memorandum showing the exact drafts you made against your Letter of Credit and giving you the exact balance, which showed that the amount of the renewal was correct" (10 March).

277. To Frank Bliss

[Florence]
8 March 1893

Dear Frank:

I have yours of Feb. 21st in which you propose to issue a cheaper edition of "Sketches New and Old" and pay me a 10 per cent royalty on it, I to release you from the requirements of the 50,000-clause appended to the original contract. I have acceded by cable, according to your desire—thus:

"Bliss, Hartford, Conn—I agree—Clemens." [1]

Frank, why don't you bill books to my firm on better terms? You discriminate against me on my own books. Don't you sell to all trade houses? And do you make them buy at these prohibitory prices?

Ys Sincerely

S. L. Clemens

¹ Bliss's argument was that a cheap edition was necessary before copyright ran out; see *MT & EB*, pp. 98–99.

278. To Fred J. Hall

[Florence]

13 March 1893

Dear Mr. Hall—

I am busy getting ready to sail the 22ᵈ in the Kaiser Wilhelm II.

I send herewith 2 magazine articles.

The Story contains 3,800 to 4,000 words.¹

The "Diary" contains 3,800 words.²

Each would make about 4 pages of the Century.

The Diary is a gem, if I *do* say it myself that shouldn't.

If the Cosmopolitan wishes to pay $600 for either of them or $1,200 for both, gather-in the check, and I will use the money in America instead of breaking into *your* treasury.

If they don't wish to trade for either, send the articles to the Century, without naming a price, and if their check isn't large enough I will call and abuse them when I come.

I signed and mailed the notes yesterday.

Ys

S L C

¹ Possibly "Is He Living, or Is He Dead?"
² "Adam's Diary."

279. To Fred J. Hall

[Florence]
2 June [1893]

[No salutation]

The $500 monthly draft which should have left New York May 15 has not arrived, and you do not mention it in your letter of the 19th. The $950 came, all right. Perhaps I will cable about the draft if any of the family go to town to-day. The money cannot now reach us in Florence where it is much needed, but we can dip into Mrs. Clemens's letter of credit. We are at a heavy expense, now, in breaking up housekeeping and raking-in old bills.

If the monthly draft can be appointed for a certain day and be always sent on that day without fail, I shall prefer that. We are skimming along like paupers, and a day can embarrass us.

I am terribly tired of business. I am by nature and disposition unfitted for it and I want to get out of it. I am standing on the Mount Morris volcano with help from the machine a long long ways off—and doubtless a long way further off than the Connecticut Co [1] imagine.

Now here is my idea for getting out.

The firm owes Mrs. Clemens and me—I do not know quite how much, but it is about $170,000 or $175,000, I suppose. (I make this guess from the documents here, whose technicalities confuse me horribly.)

The firm owe other sums, but there is stock and cash assets to cover the entire indebtedness and $116,679.20 over. Is that it? In addition we have the L.A.L. plates and copyright, worth more than $130,000—is that correct?

That is to say, we have property worth about $250,000 above indebtedness, I suppose—or, by one of your estimates, $300,000?

The greater part of the firm's debt to me is in notes paying 6 per cent. The rest (the old $70,000 or whatever it is), pays no interest.

Now then, will Harper, or Appleton, or Putnam give me $200,000 for those debts *and* my two-thirds interest in the firm?

(The firm of course taking the Mount Morris and all such obligations off my hands and leaving me clear of all responsibility.)

I don't want much money. I only want first-class notes—$200,-000-worth of them at 6 per cent, payable *monthly*—yearly notes, renewable annually for 3 years, with $5,000 of the principal payable at the beginning and middle of each year. After that, the notes renewable annually and (perhaps) a larger part of the principal payable semi-annually.

Please advise with me and suggest alterations and emendations of the above scheme, for I need that sort of help, being ignorant of business and not able to learn a single detail of it.

Such a deal would make it easy for a big firm to pour in a big cash capital and jump L.A.L. up to an enormous prosperity. Then your one-third would be a fortune—and I hope to see that day!

I enclose an authority to use with Whitmore in case you have sold any royalties. But if you can make this deal don't sell any. Wait a little and see if you can't make the deal. Do make the deal if you possibly can. And if my presence shall be necessary in order to complete it I will come over, though I hope it can be done without that.

Get me out of business![2] And I will be Yours forever gratefully,

S L Clemens

My idea is, that I am offering my ⅔ of LAL and the business for thirty or forty thousand dollars. Is that it?

P.S. The new firm could retain my books and reduce them to a 10 per cent royalty.

S L C

[1] An organization established to finance the production of the Paige typesetter.
[2] FJH was predictably unenthusiastic: "Your plan of retiring from business is feasible but it would be impossible to put it into execution now nor could you get the amount from it that you figure on. You have overstated the balance due you"

(16 June). According to FJH's figures, the firm owed Mrs. Clemens just over $54,000 and MT $12,568 on royalties. MT's "working capital" in the firm was $75,000, a total indebtedness of $142,321.15. But FJH decided that he would leave the firm, too, if MT did. And the panic would make it impossible to "sell your interest for anything like the amount of money you have invested in it nor could you find a purchaser at that price or any other price just at present." The next day, FJH wrote again, explaining that the $75,000 working capital was different from the $66,000 loans:

> When the firm first started you put in some $50,000.00. Shortly after we got the Grant book this $50,000.00 was paid back to you and you were practically just where you started, neither gaining nor losing. You drew out some of your Grant profits, but not all—I remember one check for $40,000.00 and another for $15,000.00. Besides this we have paid Mr. Orion Clemens various amounts for a number of years and for the past year have been paying you certain sums per month. All these amounts are clean gain to you. In addition, however, to the amounts you have drawn out, you have left in some $75,000.00. If to-day you were to get the amount of money loaned by Mrs. Clemens and yourself on notes out of the firm and nothing more, you would still be a great many thousand dollars ahead through your connection with the firm.

If FJH was coyly exploring the possibility of buying out MT on the condition of cancellation of the $75,000 debt, MT showed no interest in such an idea.

280. To Fred J. Hall

[Florence]
3 June 1893

[No salutation]

Whatever money comes from Mr. Arnot, *bank* it in my name (if it comes into your hands) for the present. Deposit it in the Mount Morris until we see whether you can sell my interest in the business as proposed in my long letter mailed today.

If you happen to have sold any royalties, bank that money also in the same place pending the same result.

For if you can sell me out I shan't want to pay any of the Mount Morris Debt, of course.[1]

Yrs Sincerely

S. L. C.

[1] On 16 June, FJH replied that "The Mount Morris Bank has made a demand through Mr. Whitford [the bank's attorney as well as CLW & Co.'s] for $10,000.00. He is very staunch to us and will protect us."

281. To Fred J. Hall

[Munich]
26 June 1893

Dear Mr. Hall:

We have reached here at last, after a much-broken journey—this was rendered necessary by the state of Mrs. Clemens's health. We came here to consult a specialist. We expect him to call to-day. He will probably send us out of Munich to some mountain town.

Yours of the 2d and 9th have arrived, bringing promising news as to the sale of royalties,[1] which was very pleasant, and less cheery news as to the distressing time you are having financially. We were very very sorry you were in so much trouble, but your cablegram was later than your letters, and we gathered from it that the pressure was about to slack up. That was comfort. We were minded to cable you to send us no more money for a month or two, and we *wanted* to do that, but our expenses are so heavy that I didn't quite dare. The $200-check enclosed in your letter came mighty handy.

I sent to you an authorization for Whitmore to sign royalties for you, but I am not quite certain whether I said 20 or only 10. However, to make sure, I will cable you to-day to tell him he can sign 20 if required. If Woodford sells, place such immediate cash as results in the Mount Morris, reserving from it only such amount as you are obliged to have to meet your unavoidable necessities, and making a short note (3 months?) for said amount (in Mrs. Clemens' name), which you may send to Gen. Langdon. For, you see, I do not want to increase the firm's indebtedness a dollar if it can be helped. I am hoping you can sell me out to the Harpers or some good house, and to increase the debt would not increase the chance of selling. I am willing to sell on the terms I proposed, without payment of *any part of the capital sum,* but only interest, for *5 years,* if that will make a good house more willing to buy. I want to sell, for I am not made for business; the worry of it makes me old, and robs life of its zest. I wish you were able to buy me out yourself and reap the fruits of your hard work and excellent management.

I wish you'd cable me (through Drexel Harjes & Co.,) these several things if ever they have the luck to happen: Use these single words—I will understand:

1. *FINISHED* (meaning the first machine *is*.)
2. *TRACTION.* (meaning Traction deal consummated.) [2]
3. *CUSTOMER* (meaning somebody is talking of buying me out of the firm.)

I hope you will drop in on Frink every few days and tell me what he says in the way of machine-news. Your news that Webster is likely to run ahead of time on the machines is very acceptable indeed.[3] You know they were expecting to finish 10 by the end of the year and turn out the rest of the first 50 at the rate of 5 or 6 per month after that.

Also, the Conn. Co. were expecting to begin to build their big factory in July. That will not happen in these hard times I suppose —still, I should like to know the prospect.

I hope you are much more comfortable and less worried by this date, and I hope there is visible daylight ahead for us all.

Sincerely Yours

S L Clemens

[1] FJH's letters report that General Stewart L. Woodford had become interested in selling $40,000 of MT's Paige typesetter royalties. But on 16 June he advised MT that the national financial situation had so worsened that General Woodford "could do nothing whatever now" to sell them.

[2] On 2 June, FJH told MT that the "Traction Syndicate" had been interested in purchasing the stock of the Connecticut Company: "When the Traction Company and the Connecticut Company actually join hands and the stock is transferred . . . I can place [with Woodford] the entire amounts of royalties at the price mentioned by you." But, again, FJH reported on 16 June, "the Traction Company's stock had fallen nearly 40% and while there were millions behind them, at present they [the Connecticut Company] could not close any deal with them."

[3] The firm of T. K. Webster was constructing a Paige typesetter in Chicago; Frink was apparently both a member of that company and an investor in the machine through the Connecticut Company.

282. To Fred J. Hall

Munich
3 July 1893

Dear Mr. Hall:

You make a suggestion which has once or twice flitted dimly through my mind heretofore: to-wit, *sell L.A.L.*[1]

I like that better than the other scheme, for it is no doubt feasible, whereas the other is perhaps not. The *firm* is in debt, but L.A.L. is free—and not only free but has large money owing to it. A proposition to sell that by itself to a big house could be made without embarrassment—we merely confess that we cannot spare capital from the rest of the business to run it on the huge scale necessary to make it an opulent success.

It seems clear to me that it would take $200,000 to pay our debts and push it up to the turning-point—the point where it was bringing in more money than it was carrying out.[2] Therefore we would better sell, for we cannot raise that capital. With L.A.L. out of the way and the firm out of debt we could drive the trade business and make it profitable. I vote to sell L.A.L. Not now, of course, but in the fall, as soon as business freshens up and times are easier and less scary.

It will be selling a good thing—for somebody; and it will be getting rid of a load which we are clearly not able to carry. Whoever buys will have a noble good opening—a complete equipment, a well organized business, a capable and experienced manager, an enterprise not experimental but under full sail, and immediately able to pay 50 per cent a year on every dollar the publisher shall actually invest in it—I mean in *making* and *selling* the books.

Do not you think you would like to have that load removed from your shoulders and give your labor and attention to the more comfortable task of trade-publishing?

I am miserably sorry to be adding bothers and torments to the over-supply which you already have in these hideous times, but I feel so troubled, myself, considering the dreary fact that we are getting deeper and deeper in debt and the LAL getting to be a heavier and heavier burden all the time, that I must bestir myself and seek a way of relief.

It did not occur to me that in selling out I would injure you—for that I am not going to do. But to sell LAL will not injure you—it will put you in better shape.

Sincerely Yours,

S L Clemens

[1] On 16 June, FJH had written that "the one great mistake we have made and the mistake that has caused us all so much uneasiness is in trying to swing a book like the 'Library of American Literature.' Before we touched it we should have been in a position to lay aside at least two hundred thousand dollars and say—this is to be sunk in the manufacture and sale of the 'L.A.L.' on instalments." MT admired the logic so much that he borrowed it as his own (*MTE*, p. 191). FJH went to Elmira to consult with the Langdon family, and was advised to sell *LAL* (FJH to MT, 23 June).
[2] A financial statement of CLW & Co. of 1 July 1893 shows that the firm had over $62,000 in uncollected installment accounts and total liabilities of $197,089.75.

283. To Fred J. Hall

[Munich]
8 July [1893]

Dear Mr. Hall,—

I am sincerely glad you are going to sell L. A. L. I am glad you are shutting off the agents, and I hope the fatal book will be out of our hands before it will be time to put them on again.[1] With nothing but our non-existent capital to work with the book has no value for us, rich a prize as it will be to any competent house that gets it.

I hope you are making an effort to sell before you discharge too many agents, for I suppose the agents are a valuable part of the property.

We have been stopping in Munich for awhile, but we shall make a break for some country resort in a few days now.

Sincerely Yours

S. L. C.

July 8

P.S. No, I suppose I am wrong in suggesting that you wait a moment before discharging your L. A. L. agents—in fact I didn't mean that. I judge your only hope of salvation is in discharging them all at once, since it is their commissions that threaten to swamp us. It is they who have eaten up the $14,000 I left with you [2] in such a brief time, no doubt.

I feel panicky.

I think the sale might be made with better advantage, however, now, than later when the agents have got out of the purchaser's reach.[3]

S. L. C.

P.S. No monthly report for many months.

---

[1] On the advice of C. J. Langdon, FJH shut down sales of *LAL* and discharged all but a skeleton crew of agents and office help (FJH to MT, 23 June, 7 July). He succeeded in reducing office expenses $1,000 a week (FJH to C. J. Langdon, 11 July).

[2] On his trip to this country (3 April–13 May), MT withdrew $14,000 from the Halsey account (see letter 289 below). At any rate, the $14,000 which was to serve as the "emergency fund" (letter 276 above) was turned into the business immediately (FJH to MT, 24 July 1893).

[3] The text of the preceding three paragraphs is based on the original page, now at the University of Texas, rather than on the faulty transcription in *MTL*.

284. To FRED J. HALL

[Krankenheil]
18 July [1893]

Dear Mr. Hall:

Doubtless Mr. Walker is away on vacation, but please keep a

copy of the enclosed in your regular letter-book, and get the original to him as soon as you can.[1]

It is my ingenious scheme to protect the family against the almshouse for one more year—and after that . . . well, goodness knows! I have never felt so desperate in my life—and good reason, for I haven't got a penny to my name, and Mrs. Clemens hasn't enough laid up with Langdon to keep us two months.

It makes me quake to think that if Whitford should have to withdraw his protection, even my royalties might be seized before we got the Mount Morris bill paid.[2] Yet if the firm can be kept alive a while longer no doubt you can save yourself and me too by selling L.A.L.

As no letters arrive I am afraid it means that you have no hopeful news to give me about either our firm or the machine. It is now past the middle of July and no cablegram to say the machine is finished.[3] We are afraid you are having miserable days and worried nights, and we sincerely wish we could relieve you, but it's all black with us and we don't know any helpful thing to say or do. We have nothing in the world to offer but our deepest sympathies, but you have those.

Yours sincerely

S L Clemens

P.S. *July 22.*
Dear Mr. Hall: Please keep a copy of enclosed "PS" and send original to Brisbin Walker of Cosmopolitan.[4]

Got the $250-check. Mrs. Clemens's interest-money goes from you to Langdon—and stays there till such times as we are obliged to draw against it—which we don't do if we can help it, because it is now the only rainy-day money we have got left, in case of sudden disaster.

If they *do* get the machine done and set up in the Herald—which cannot be earlier than the middle of September [5]—I may

possibly want three or four royalties sold to live on, but I hope I
shan't have to part with more than 5.

Ys sincerely

S L C

¹ On 12 April, John Brisben Walker had written MT, "I can think of no
feature likely to attract so wide a circle of readers [to the *Cosmopolitan*] as a
series of humorous articles from the pen of 'Mark Twain.' Would you do me the
favor to prepare twelve articles of from 2,500 to 3,500 words each, to follow in
regular succession if convenient . . . the honorarium for the twelve articles to be
five thousand dollars." On the envelope, MT wrote, "12 articles of 2,500 to 3,500
words for $5,000? No." By mid-July, however, the offer seemed more attractive.
In Notebook 27, TS p. 23, he wrote:

Krankenheil, July 18. Wrote John Brisbin Walker and proposed that he
double words and money both—instead of an average of 3,000 words for 12
months, for $5,000, make it *double.*—and furnish him "The Innocents Adrift"
—on Rhone.

If he disapproves am to "whirl out something else now and then *if I can.*"
Told him have 20,000 words of "In. Adrift" already.

The proposed material was a record of a boating excursion MT made in the fall
of 1891. See *MTB*, pp. 924–928; the manuscript, Paine No. 138, is in MTP.

² Whitford continued to serve as the firm's protector. FJH had written on 23
June, "The only impending trouble I can foresee is from the Mount Morris Bank,
and Mr. Whitford thinks he will be able to protect us there."

³ On 14 July, FJH explained that "I have not cabled you as you requested
because none of the things you wished me to cable about have taken place, but I
have not forgotten your instructions" (in letter 281 above).

⁴ Notebook 27, TS p. 23, explains: "*July 22.* P.S. to Walker to say I spoke too
soon—probably have to cramp Rhone into much smaller space." Walker was
apparently not interested in MT's counterproposal, though he did print "Is He
Living, Or Is He Dead?," "The Esquimau Maiden's Romance," and "Travelling
with a Reformer" at the end of 1893. FJH approved the *Cosmopolitan* deal
because "it is going to be . . . absolutely impossible for us to send you money
with any regularity" (7 August).

⁵ The Paige typesetter was originally to be tested in the office of the Chicago
Herald; in 1894 it was finally placed in the offices of the *Times-Herald* where it
immediately disintegrated (see *MTB*, pp. 990–991).

285. To Fred J. Hall

[Krankenheil]
26 July 1893

Dear Mr. Hall:

If you could get the other man pledged to 3,000 sets the first year and not fewer than ⟨6,000⟩ 4,000 per year thereafter—yes, that would be a good thing.[1] You would not have to pledge him higher, I suppose—his self-interest would fix that—particularly if you allowed him better and still better terms the higher he carried his output.

But I should think you ought to try it on *now*. First, before there is a wide gap showing between your former considerable output and no output at all; and secondly, before your good canvassers get dispersed and snapped up by other people.

I hope the machine *will* be finished this month; but it took me four years and cost me $100,000 to finish the other machine *after* it was apparently entirely complete and setting type like a house-afire.

I wonder what they call "finished." After it is absolutely perfect it can't go into a printing-office until it has had a month's wear, running night and day, to get all the bearings smooth, I judge.

I may be able to run over about mid-October. Then if I find you relieved of LAL we will start a magazine—*inexpensive,* and of an entirely unique sort.[2] Arthur Steadman and his father editors of it. Arthur could do all the work, merely submitting it to his father for approval.

The first number should pay—and all subsequent ones. 25 cents a number. Cost of first number (20,000 copies) $2,000. Give most of them away, sell the rest. Advertising and other expenses—cost unknown. Send one to all newspapers—it would get a notice—favorable, too.

But we cannot undertake it until LAL is out of the way. With our hands free and some capital to spare, we could make it hum.

Where is the Shelley article?[3] If you have it on hand, keep it and I will presently tell you what to do with it. *Don't forget to tell me.*

Ys sincerely

S L C

---

[1] On 14 July, FJH had suggested that instead of selling *LAL* outright, "there is another plan . . . whereby we would share in the prosperity of the book and at

the same time run no risk whatever from any loss arising, that is, if we could get somebody to accept the sole general agency for the book, we merely to manufacture and sell the book to them at a certain discount." FJH attempted to make such an arrangement with Williams (see letter 237 above) and R. S. Peale & Co. of Chicago (FJH to MT, 7 August 1893). Ultimately, William E. Benjamin, H. H. Rogers' son-in-law, made an arrangement to take the *LAL* stock from the Company (FJH to MT, 18 October 1893; *MTB*, p. 971; *MTLM*, p. 12), and a "new edition" appeared under his imprint in 1894.

[2] "The Back Number," a magazine which would consist of articles from old issues of early newspapers and journals. MT's dummy title page and Editor's Preface are in the Morgan Library; Notebook 27 contains several references to the idea (TS pp. 24, 37, 46), including one to make Samuel Moffett editor (p. 39a).

[3] "In Defense of Harriet Shelley," published in the *North American Review* in 1894.

286. To Fred J. Hall

[Krankenheil]
30 July 1893

Dear Mr. Hall:

This time "Pudd'nhead Wilson" is a success! Even Mrs. Clemmens, the most difficult of critics, confesses it, and without reserves or qualifications. Formerly she would not consent that it be published either before or after my death. I have pulled the twins apart and made two individuals of them; I have sunk them out of sight, they are mere flitting shadows, now, and of no importance; *their* story has disappeared from the book. Aunt Betsy Hale has vanished wholly, leaving not a trace behind; aunt Patsy Cooper and her daughter Rowena have almost disappeared—they scarcely walk across the stage. The whole story is centred on the murder and the trial; from the first chapter the movement is straight ahead without divergence or side-play to the murder and the trial; everything that is done or said or that happens is a preparation for those events. Therefore, 3 people stand up high, from beginning to end, and only 3—Pudd'nhead, "Tom" Driscoll and his nigger mother Roxana; none of the others are important, or get in the way of the story or require the reader's attention. Consequently, the scenes and episodes which were the strength of the book formerly are stronger than ever, now.

When I began this final reconstruction the story contained 81,500 words; now it contains only 58,000. I have knocked out everything that delayed the march of the story—even the description of a Mississippi steamboat. There ain't any weather in, and there ain't any scenery—the story is stripped for flight!

Now, then, what is she worth? The amount of matter is but 3,000 words short of the American Claimant, for which the syndicate paid $12,500. There was nothing new in that story, but the finger-prints in this one is virgin ground—absolutely *fresh,* and mighty curious and interesting to everybody.

I don't want any more syndicating—nothing short of $20,000 anyway, and that I can't get—but won't you see how much the Cosmopolitan will stand? At the rate Walker paid for the little story he bought last spring, this one would be worth toward $9,000 —say $8,500. At the rate he offered me later for 12 contributions (on any subject) of 2,500 or 3,500 words each (an average of 3,000 each or 36,000 for the 12), the price would be—well, I don't quite know what. *But*—a 58,000-word story is worth a higher rate than random sketches and contributions, and maybe Walker will stand a raise. Now you just praise the thing up, and get his price and cable me *"Walker offers (so many) dollars."* I will cable *"Accept"* or *"Try elsewhere."*

If I cable the latter, go privately and try the Century. If they won't stand a raise, cable me thus: *"Gilder no better"* or *"Gilder offers (name sum)"* and I will return answer.

Do your best for me, for I do not sleep, these nights, for visions of the poor-house.

This in spite of the hopeful tone of yours of 11th to Langdon (just received from him with approving words)—for in me hope is very nearly expiring. Everything does look so blue, so dismally blue!

By and by I shall take up the Rhone open-boat voyage again, but not now—we are going to be moving around too much. I have torn up some of it, but I still have 15,000 words that Mrs. Clemens approves and that I like. I may go at it in Paris again next winter, but not unless I *know* I can write it to suit me.

Otherwise I shall tackle Adam once more, and do him in a kind of a friendly and respectful way that will commend him to the Sunday schools. I've been thinking out his first life-days to-day and framing his childish and ignorant impressions and opinions for him.

Will ship Pudd'nhead in a few days. When you get it, cable as fol—

Mark Twain,
Care Brownship, London
Received.

Or cable through Drexel Harjes if *they* have an inexpensive cable-address of one word—as no doubt they have.

Sincerely Yrs.

S. L. C.

P. S. I *may* run over in October, but it's only the merest *may*.

287. To FRED J. HALL

[Krankenheil]
6 August 1893

Dear Mr. Hall:

I am very sorry—it was thoughtless in me. Let the reports go.[1] Send me once a month two items, and two only:

Cash liabilities _____ (so-much)
    "   assets _____ (so-much).

I can perceive the condition of the business at a glance, then, and that will be sufficient.

Here we never see a newspaper, but even if we did I could not come anywhere near appreciating or correctly estimating the tempest you have been buffeting your way through—only the man who is in it can do that—but I have tried not to burden you

thoughtlessly or wantonly. I have been overwrought and unsettled
in mind by apprehensions, and that is a thing that is not helpable
when one is in a strange land and sees his resources melt down to a
two-months' supply and can't see any sure daylight beyond. The
bloody machine offered but a doubtful outlook—and will still offer
nothing much better for a long time to come; for when Davis's
"three weeks" are up there will be three months' tinkering to follow
I guess.[2] That is unquestionably the boss machine of this world,
but it is the toughest one on prophets, when it is in an incomplete
state, that has ever seen the light. Neither Davis nor any other man
can foretell with any considerable approach to certainty when it
will be ready to get right down to actual work in a printing office.

[Unsigned]

[1] In reply to MT's postscript to letter 283 above, FJH wrote on 24 July that "I
have cut the help down in all departments to one-quarter what it was, and the
financial troubles that we have been having kept me so occupied that I have not
had time nor in fact have I thought of the reports at all as there were so many
other things infinitely more important to attend to."
[2] FJH's 24 July letter relayed the opinion of Charles Davis, a shop foreman on
the construction of the typesetter, that "there is less than three weeks work on the
machine."

288. To FRED J. HALL

[Krankenheil]
9 August 1893

Dear Mr. Hall:

Won't you have the enclosed brief Romance very *very* carefully
type-written (you carefully correcting it afterward yourself)?[1]

I enclose a non-committal letter for you to type-write and sign
and send to Mr. Rush—as a feeler (after speaking to Walker).
Rush probably won't want any literature at that figure. He'll not
answer the letter, I guess. But if he *should* want it I think it a good
idea to trade with him, for his magazine is obscure and I don't want
to appear in print in the full glare of the big magazines too
often.[2]

Of course *Walker* can take this Romance if he wants it, but I am traveling on the idea that if he takes Pudd'nhead he can't take this too, because he won't have any room for it. But you can ask him, if you will be so good.

Great Scott but it's a long year—for you and me! I never knew the almanac to drag so. At least not since I was finishing that *other* machine.

I watch for your letters hungrily—and I used to watch for the cablegram saying the machine's finished—but when "next week *certainly*" suddenly swelled into "three weeks *sure*" I recognized the old familiar tune I used to hear so much. *Ward* [3] don't know what sick-heartedness is—but he is in a way to find out.

Ys sincerely

S L C

[1] Notebook 27, TS p. 25: "*Aug. 9.* Sent Esquimaux to Hall—told him to tell ⟨Louisville⟩ his man my price is $150 per 1000 words."

[2] Mr. Rush, perhaps the "Louisville" man, and his obscure magazine have resisted identification.

[3] Ward was another of the Paige typesetter group, whose progress reports FJH had been forwarding to MT during the summer (FJH to MT, 2, 16 June; 7, 14, 24, 31 July; 7 August 1893).

289. To FRED J. HALL

[Krankenheil]
14 August 1893

Dear Mr. Hall:

I am very glad indeed if you and Mr. Langdon are able to see any daylight ahead.[1] To me none is visible. I strongly advise that every penny that comes in shall be applied to paying off debts. I may be in error about this, but it seems to me that we have no other course open. We can pay a part of the debts owing to outsiders— none to the Clemenses. In very prosperous times we might regard our stock and copyrights as assets sufficient, with the money owing to us, to square up and quit even, but I suppose we may not hope for such luck in the present condition of things.

What I am mainly hoping for, is to save my royalties. If they come into danger I hope you will cable me, so that I can come over and try to save them, for if they go I am a beggar.

I would sail to-day if I had anybody to take charge of my family and help them through the difficult journeys commanded by the doctors. I may be able to sail ten days hence; I hope so, and expect so.[2]

We can never resurrect the L.A.L. I would not spend any more money on that book. You spoke, a while back, of trying to start it up again as a preparation to disposing of it, but we are not in a shape to venture that, I think. It would require more borrowing, and we must not do that.

S L C.

Ys sincerely

Yes, I got the £50 check and it came exceedingly handy.

I mean to ship *"Pudd'nhead Wilson"* to you—say, tomorrow. It'll furnish me hash for a while I reckon. I am almost sorry it is finished; it was good entertainment to work at it, and kept my mind away from things.

We leave here in about ten days, but the doctors have changed our plans again. I think we shall be in Bohemia and thereabouts till near the end of September, then go to Paris and take a rest.

Yours sincerely

S L C.

I shall not forget Whitford—he has done for us what few men would have done.[3]

P.S. Mrs. Clemens has come in since, and read your letter and is deeply distressed. She thinks that in some letter of mine I must have reproached you. She says it is wonderful that you have kept the ship afloat in this storm that has seen fleets and fleets go down; that from what she learns of the American business-situation from her home letters you have accomplished a marvel in the circumstances, and that she cannot bear to have a word said to you that shall voice anything but praise and the heartiest appreciation—and not the shadow of a reproach will she allow.

I tell her I *didn't* reproach you, and never thought of such a thing. And I said I would break open my letter and say so.

Mrs. Clemens says I must tell you not to send us any money for a month or two—so that you may be afforded what little relief is in our power. All right—I'm willing; (this is honest); but I wish Brer Chatto would send along his little yearly contribution. I dropped him a line about another matter a week ago—asked him to subscribe for the Daily News for me—you see I wanted to remind him in a covert way that it was pay-up time—but doubtless I directed the letter to you or some one else, for I don't hear from him and don't get any Daily News either.[4]

Aug. 16.[5] I have thought, and thought, but I don't seem to arrive in any very definite place. Of course you will not have an instant's safety until the bank debts are paid. There is nothing to be thought of but to hand over every penny as fast as it comes in—and that will be slow enough! Or could you secure them by pledging part of our cash assets and—

I am coming over, just as soon as I can get the family moved and settled.

S L C

The Pudd'nhead and Esquimaux Romance belong to Mrs. Clemens, in part pay for her $14,000 which I took out of Halsey's hands and lent to the firm. Please sell them, and take notes (if desired) extending over several months, (drawn in her name), so-much payable monthly, and send the notes to Mr. Langdon.

I am grateful to him for trying to save us, but heaven knows I am sorry we had to ask him.

[1] FJH had advised on 31 July that "the crisis has come and I hope that we have successfully passed it." The Mount Morris Bank "met with some very heavy losses through one or two large failures and for that reason had to call in their discounts. They refuse to renew our discounts and even Mr. Whitford's influence

was useless." Finally Langdon "agreed to take up the two notes of $3,000.00 each, due August 6th and August 11th, and also to endorse notes to the extent of $15,000.00, provided the bank agrees to renew them."

² In Notebook 27, TS p. 26, right after an entry dated 16 August, "I start in a week for America," MT added, "Wrote Charley [Davis] and Hall I am coming." He sailed from Bremen on 29 August, and remained in the United States seven months.

³ After Langdon agreed to endorse a $15,000 note, Whitford was confident he could "persuade the bank people to carry us along." In addition, Whitford may have loaned CLW & Co. $1,100. On the July 1893 statement of the Company's situation, MT wrote a list of funds turned back into the organization, including Langdon's $6,000 and "Whitford 1,100."

⁴ The letter to Chatto & Windus, dated 5 August, is in the Lilly Collection, Indiana University. On 15 August, Chatto & Windus replied advising they had deposited £722 royalties with Drexel Harjes in MT's name. MT acknowledged the money elatedly (18 August, TS in MTP).

⁵ Beginning with this date, the text of the letter is based upon a fragment in MTP.

290. To Fred J. Hall

[New York]
6 January 1894

Dear Mr. Hall:

I think I will go to Elmira tomorrow and distribute some stock to people who are anxious to get it.¹ I expect to get back Monday night. If I don't and the bank is stubborn, go to Mr. Rogers and ask him if he can't tell those people to hold on a bit and give me a chance.²

Ys

S L C

Get promptly to work in arranging a partnership with Mr. Barrows and getting in some new capital.³ I may not be here long, now.

S L C

¹ Perhaps to Susan Crane, who had offered MT $5,000 in stocks and bonds the preceding fall; see *LLMT*, p. 270.
² FJH wrote on 3 January,
We have paid since the Benjamin deal $10,500. to the Mount Morris

Bank. . . . At the United States Bank they have accepted, as shown on the statement sent you, the Benjamin notes, as collateral security for money [$5000] loaned us. . . . If they should happen to get cranky and Benjamin should make any trouble about paying his notes, we might, within the next six weeks or two months, have some trouble with them.

Although William E. Benjamin was interested in *LAL*, his present investment and main interest in CLW & Co. was in a uniform edition of MT's works. Watson Gill's old exclusive contract to sell *Life on the Mississippi* required some negotiation (MT to H. H. Rogers, [Paris], 9 December, 1894; *ibid.*, Paris, 3 January 1895), and Bliss was required to deal with Benjamin regarding *Pudd'nhead Wilson* and the possible publication of an edition by the American Publishing Company (MT to H. H. Rogers, "At Sea, Wednesday" [1894]; *ibid.*, Paris, 3 January 1895). MT also suggested that Benjamin approach Harpers about the edition ("Bliss is an ass. It would be a mistake to publish with him on any terms" [MT to H. H. Rogers, Paris, 14 April 1895].) Ultimately, of course, Rogers negotiated the agreements whereby Bliss issued subscription editions and Harpers published trade editions.

[3] This may be the George Barrow who had loaned FJH $15,000. MT wrote H. H. Rogers on 14 September 1894 from Etretat, "Barrows' offer of $9,000 was not very gaudy, still it proved something—proved that Mr. Hall's poor old literary ash-pile is worth *something*, anyway—a thing not easily believable." FJH also mentioned "A long and pleasant talk with Mr. Scott—there were no new developments" (3 January 1894). A "Scott" is mentioned in Notebook 27 (TS pp. 33, 38, 40), but it appears more likely he was involved with typesetter affairs (MT to H. H. Rogers, Etretat, 14 September, and Rouen, 13 October 1894).

The Epitaph

(1894)

For seven months in late 1893 and early 1894, Mark Twain set up residence at The Players Club in New York and attempted, with the constant advice and assistance of Henry H. Rogers, to untangle the complex affairs of the Paige typesetter. The problems of Charles L. Webster & Co. seemed less important, though they intruded when Mount Morris Bank notes came due (see *LLMT*, pp. 270, 274). Twain worked on *Tom Sawyer, Detective* (*ibid.*, p. 277); and he contemplated, simultaneously, paying "Websterco's bank debt so it can't jump on my back in some sudden panic" and having "terms . . . arranged for getting me out of Websterco. If satisfactory, I will accept and sign" (MT to Olivia Clemens, [New York], 7 or 8 February [1894]).

Finally, in the midst of the power plays over the typesetter, he "laid Webster's disastrous condition before Mr. Rogers" on 15 February. "We discussed it from various standpoints, and found it a sufficiently difficult problem to solve; but he thinks that after he has slept upon it and thought it over he will know what to suggest" (MT to Olivia Clemens, New York, 15 February 1894).

The earliest plan was apparently to reorganize the Company with Mark Twain's name in the title but with only a limited partnership and therefore a limited liability; Orion pointed out, however, with citations from his eternal law books, that a partner who lends his name to a firm is legally a general partner (Orion Clemens to MT, Keokuk, 2, 3 February 1894). Next there were schemes for the Century Company to purchase Twain's books from the Company and for Frank Bliss to issue *Pudd'nhead Wilson* by subscription (MT to Olivia Clemens, New York, [20 February 1894]; *LLMT*, pp. 296–297; MT to Olivia Clemens, New York, 2 March 1894). As the affairs of the Company came more and more to light, Mark Twain's temper boiled. After explaining to his sympathetic sister (Charles Webster's mother-in-law) that plans for the typesetter were running smoothly, Mark Twain added,

> But Webster & Co—*that* is another matter! It was insanely managed from the day it got the Grant book till now. That terrible book! which made money for everybody concerned but me. *Privately,* I will confide to you that I am trying to wind up that hated concern. It owes me a hundred and ten thousand dollars, it owes Livy about sixty thousand, and it owes banks and printers eighty-three thousand —and has assets which I *hope* are marketable for sixty thousand, but I sort of doubt it. It is barely possible that assets are marketable for eighty thousand—but no, they're not. But I am going to get out at *whatever* loss. Webster—however, the blatherskite is dead, let him ⟨rot⟩ in peace (To Pamela Moffett, New York, 25 February 1894).

The situation hung fire, however, during the entire month of March.

On 16 April, after a three-week reunion with his family in Europe, Mark Twain wrote a cheerful letter back to Mrs. Clemens from New York:

> Mr. Rogers feels so much encouraged about Websterco's probable ability to pull through alive, that he suggested, without my saying anything, that we hold on and try to work out, paying a hundred cents on the dollar and finally closing the concern without any stain upon its name. Mr. Rogers has been at Websterco's several times and kept close watch upon its affairs, and has kept it out of financial trouble by the strength of his name—and with his money, too, the other day where two or three thousand dollars were immediately necessary.

Ironically, later the same day Hall appeared to announce that a new president and board of directors of the Mount Morris Bank had decided to refuse to renew two $5,000 notes that came due that day (*MTB*, p. 983; "Fred J. Hall Tells the Story of His Connection With Charles L. Webster & Co.," *The Twainian*, VI [November–December 1947], 1–3). Hall and Mark Twain completed assignments papers, and discovered that Dan Whitford—who may have been elevated to the board of directors of the Bank—rapidly lost all appearances of guardian angel: Whitford laughed when told of the assignment (*LLMT*, p. 300), and "began to bluster and threaten" at a creditors' meeting (*ibid.*) Bainbridge Colby, of the law firm of Alexander & Colby, was appointed the receiver (Colby to Miss Katherine I. Harrison, New York, 2 November 1896), and Mark Twain hoped "the assignee will put things on a stringent basis and we shall have no more of Mr. Hall's stupid and extravagant mismanagement" (MT to Olivia Clemens, New York, 22 April 1894).

Mark Twain hoped that "the creditors are going to allow us to resume business; and if they do we shall pull through and pay the debt" (*ibid.*), but the Mount Morris Bank refused to allow the business to continue: "I cannot understand their attitude. To go on a year would not injure their chance to 'go for' me in accordance with that profound Whitford's desire, and might profit them somewhat during the year" (MT to H. H. Rogers, La Bourboule, 25 June 1894). Hall was suspicious that the assignment was a premeditated takeover of the Company (perhaps by Whitford?), and Mark Twain wrote him on 1 June, "I have no authority and can do nothing. If the assignment was a put-up job I knew nothing of it, and never in the least suspected it" (TS fragment in MTP).

Altogether, 101 creditors filed claims for a total of $79,704.80 against the Company—excluding Mrs. Clemens, who received as preferred creditor the assignment of royalties on Mark Twain's books. Twain disputed the claim of the Mount Morris Bank (*LLMT*, pp. 300–301) and apparently attempted to repudiate the $15,000 personal loan to Hall from the Barrow family and the claims of the Grant family (MT to H. H. Rogers, Port Elizabeth,

19 June 1896, TS in MTP); but by 1898 all claims were settled and all creditors apparently satisfied. Mark Twain continued to write books—and occasionally to write his publishers, but the great majority of his letters concerning his publications went through H. H. Rogers, who served as intermediary and informal business agent. Not only was Mark Twain badly scarred from his close contact with the publishing of his own books—in addition, the era of the single subscription book was dead. The big edition, the round-the-clock printing schedule, the monumental royalty check were all parts of the past, along with the "submerged" audience on whom subscription-book success depended. Like Mark Twain, the firm of Harper and Brothers with whom he aligned himself was becoming too old, too respectable, too august to indulge in the wildcat operations which had provided the real spice of Twain's relationships with Bliss, Osgood, Webster, and Hall.

A Calendar of Letters

THE FOLLOWING list catalogs the letters in the present text. Of the 290 letters, twenty-eight are based upon previously published texts. The other 262 are either previously unpublished or are reedited at the present time from holograph originals. The assembling and publishing of these has been dependent on the assistance and permission of ten library collections (and the Samuel C. Webster Collection, represented by typescripts in MTP), as follows:

Berg
: Henry W. and Albert A. Berg Collection
New York Public Library

Buffalo
: Lockwood Memorial Library
State University of New York at Buffalo

Columbia
: Columbia University Library
New York City

CWB
: Clifton Waller Barrett Library
University of Virginia Library

Harvard
: Rogers Theater Collection
Houghton Mifflin Collection
Harvard College Library

Huntington
: Henry E. Huntington Library and Art Gallery
San Marino, California

Morgan
: Pierpont Morgan Library
New York City

MTP	Mark Twain Papers University of California Library Berkeley
Newberry	The Newberry Library Chicago
Princeton	Princeton University Library Princeton
Yale	Mark Twain Collections Yale University Library

The "authority" for present texts is the location of the original letter, except when the abbreviations TS (typescript) and PH (photocopy) indicate that the location of the original is unknown or that it is inaccessible for scholarly research.

I. 1867–1871

No.	To	Location	Date	Authority
1.	Charles H. Webb	St. Louis	19 March 1867	CWB
2.	Frank Fuller	New York	1 June 1867	Hartford Memorial
3.	EB	Washington	2 December 1867	MTP
4.	EB	New York	27 January 1868	MTP
5.	EB	Washington	4 February 1868	MTP
6.	EB	San Francisco	28 May 1868	CWB
7.	Frank Bliss	Chicago	7 January 1869	Yale
8.	EB	Elmira	30 March 1869	MTP
9.	EB	Elmira	12 April 1869	MTP
10.	EB	Elmira	20 April 1869	MTP
11.	EB	Elmira	April Something 1869	TS, MTP
12.	EB	Elmira	29 April 1869	MTP
13.	EB	Elmira	22 July 1869	Yale
14.	EB	Elmira	1 August 1869	TS, MTP
15.	EB	Buffalo	12 August 1869	MTP
16.	EB	Buffalo	15 August 1869	TS, MTP
17.	EB	Buffalo	3 September 1869	MTP
18.	EB	Buffalo	27 September 1869	MTP
19.	EB	Elmira	22 January 1870	MTP

20. EB	Elmira	28 January 1870	MTP
21. EB	Buffalo	23 February 1870	MTP
22. EB	Buffalo	23 April 1870	MTP
23. EB	Elmira	7 May 1870	MTP
24. EB	Buffalo	20 May 1870	TS, MTP
25. EB	Elmira	4 July 1870	TS, MTP
26. EB	Elmira	2 August 1870	PH, MTP
27. EB	Elmira	11 August 1870	PH, MTP
28. EB	Buffalo	4 September 1870	MTP
29. EB	Buffalo	22 September 1870	MTP
30. EB	Buffalo	13 October 1870	TS, MTP
31. EB	Buffalo	5 November 1870	Berg
32. EB	Buffalo	28 November 1870	MTP
33. EB	Buffalo	2 December 1870	MTP
34. James H. Riley	Buffalo	2 December 1870	MTP; Berg
35. EB	Buffalo	22 December 1870	Yale
36. EB	Buffalo	3 January 1871	MTP
37. EB	Buffalo	24 January 1871	TS, MTP
38. EB	Buffalo	27 January 1871	MTP
39. EB	Buffalo	15 February 1871	MTP
40. Orion Clemens	Buffalo	11 March 1871	TS, MTP
41. EB	Buffalo	17 March 1871	Berg
42. EB	Elmira	20 March 1871	MTP
43. Orion Clemens	Elmira	4 April 1871	MTP
44. Orion Clemens	Elmira	8 April 1871	MTP
45. Orion Clemens	Elmira	18 April 1871	MTP
46. EB	Elmira	3 May 1871	MTP
47. EB	Elmira	June 1871	MTP
48. Orion Clemens	Elmira	2 July 1871	MTP
49. EB	Wilkes-Barre	19 October 1871	TS, MTP

II. 1872–1880

50. EB	Elmira	20 March 1872	MTP
51. EB	Elmira	21 March 1872	Yale

52. JRO	Elmira	Sunday, 1872	TS, MTP
53. EB	Saybrook	7 August 1872	Yale
54. EB	Hartford	4 March 1873	CWB
55. EB	Hartford	3 May 1873	TS, MTP
56. Charles Dudley Warner	"Under Way"	May 1873	TS, MTP
57. EB	London	16 July 1873	Yale
58. Charles Dudley Warner	London	16 July 1873	Yale
59. T. B. Pugh	Edinburgh	27 July 1873	Yale
60. EB	Edinburgh	27 July 1873	Yale
61. Thomas Bailey Aldrich	Hartford	24 March 1874	Harvard
62. Charles Dudley Warner	Elmira	5 May 1874	MTP
63. H. O. Houghton	Hartford	12 February 1875	Harvard
64. JRO	Hartford	12 February 1875	Harvard
65. EB	Hartford	26 February 1875	MTP
66. Charles H. Webb	Hartford	8 April 1875	Buffalo
67. William F. Gill	Hartford	31 May 1875	CWB
68. William F. Gill	Hartford	8 June 1875	Harvard
69. JRO	Hartford	13 July 1875	Harvard
70. JRO	Hartford	20 July 1875	Yale
71. JRO	Hartford	23 July 1875	TS, MTP
72. EB	Hartford	5 November 1875	MTP
73. JRO	Hartford	17 January 1876	Harvard
74. JRO	Hartford	25 January 1876	Harvard
75. EB	Hartford	19 March 1876	Yale
76. Moncure D. Conway	Hartford	9 April 1876	Columbia
77. Moncure D. Conway	Hartford	16 April 1876	Columbia
78. EB	Elmira	24 June 1876	Yale

79. EB	Elmira	22 July 1876	MTP
80. Moncure D. Conway	Elmira	1 August 1876	TS, MTP
81. EB	Elmira	8 August 1876	MTP
82. Moncure D. Conway	Hartford	2 November 1876	Columbia
83. Moncure D. Conway	Hartford	13 December 1876	Columbia
84. Frank Bliss	Heidelberg	13 July 1878	TS, MTP
85. Frank Bliss	Lucerne	20 August 1878	Berg
86. Joe Twichell	Munich	23 January 1879	Yale
87. Frank Bliss	Paris	15 April 1879	Berg
88. Frank Bliss	Paris	10 May 1879	Princeton
89. Frank Bliss	Paris	10 June 1879	TS, MTP
90. Frank Bliss	Paris	10 June 1879	TS, MTP
91. Frank Bliss	Paris	13 June 1879	TS, MTP
92. Frank Bliss	Paris	17 June 1879	TS, MTP
93. Frank Bliss	Elmira	8 September 1879	TS, MTP
94. Frank Bliss	Elmira	9 September 1879	TS, MTP
95. Moncure D. Conway	Elmira	19 January 1880	Columbia
96. EB	Hartford	20 March 1880	Berg
97. Moncure D. Conway	Hartford	20 April 1880	Columbia
98. Orion Clemens	Hartford	24 October 1880	MTP
99. Chatto & Windus	Hartford	1 December 1880	PH, MTP

III. 1881–1884

100. JRO	Hartford	Sunday, 1881	Harvard
101. JRO	Hartford	12 February 1881	Harvard
102. JRO	Hartford	7 March 1881	Harvard
103. JRO	Hartford	26 March 1881	Harvard
104. JRO	Hartford	30 March 1881	Berg
105. JRO	Hartford	23 May 1881	CWB
106. JRO	Hartford	30 May 1881	MTP
107. Frank Bliss	Hartford	30 May 1881	TS, MTP
108. Benjamin Ticknor	Branford	1 August 1881	Yale
109. Benjamin Ticknor	Elmira	14 August 1881	Yale
110. Benjamin Ticknor	Elmira	9 September 1881	Yale
111. JRO	Hartford	2 October 1881	TS, MTP
112. JRO	Hartford	24 October 1881	MTP
113. JRO	Hartford	27 October 1881	PH, MTP
114. JRO	Hartford	28 October 1881	Berg
115. JRO	Hartford	1 November 1881	Harvard
116. JRO	Montreal	28 November 1881	Harvard
117. JRO	Hartford	28 December 1881	Harvard
118. JRO	Hartford	29 December 1881	Berg
119. JRO	Hartford	31 December 1881	Harvard
120. JRO	Hartford	4 January 1882	CWB
121. JRO	Hartford	7 January 1882	Harvard
122. JRO	Hartford	12 February 1882	Harvard
123. JRO	Hartford	4 March 1882	Berg
124. JRO	Hartford	7 April 1882	Harvard
125. JRO	Hartford	Friday, 1882	CWB
126. JRO	Hartford	3 June 1882	Berg
127. JRO	Hartford	19 July 1882	Yale
128. JRO	Elmira	18 September 1882	TS, MTP
129. JRO	Hartford	18 October 1882	CWB
130. JRO	Hartford	29 December 1882	Morgan
131. JRO & Co.	Hartford	6 January 1883	TS, Newberry
132. JRO	Hartford	15 January 1883	Yale

133. JRO	Hartford	17 April 1883	Harvard
134. JRO	Hartford	21 December 1883	Harvard
135. JRO	Hartford	17 January 1884	Harvard
136. JRO	Hartford	20 March 1884	Harvard
137. JRO	Hartford	24 May 1884	Princeton

IV. 1884–1887

138. CLW	Hartford	29 February 1884	*MTBus*, pp. 239–240
139. CLW	Hartford	14 April 1884	*MTBus*, pp. 248–249
140. CLW	Hartford	7 May 1884	*MTBus*, p. 253
141. CLW	Hartford	23 May 1884	*MTBus*, pp. 254–255
142. CLW	Hartford	18 July 1884	Webster; TS, MTP
143. CLW & Co.	Elmira	August 1884	Webster; TS, MTP
144. CLW	Elmira	1 September 1884	*MTBus*, pp. 273–274
145. CLW	Janesville	19 January 1885	*MTBus*, pp. 293–294
146. CLW	Minneapolis	25 January 1885	*MTBus*, p. 296–297
147. CLW	Columbus	10 February 1885	*MTBus*, p. 300
148. CLW	Hartford	16 March 1885	*MTBus*, p. 307
149. CLW	Hartford	4 April 1885	*MTBus*, pp. 307–309
150. CLW	Hartford	4 April 1885	Webster; TS, MTP
151. CLW	Hartford	8 April 1885	Webster; TS, MTP
152. CLW	Hartford	17 June 1885	Webster; TS, MTP
153. CLW	Elmira	28 July 1885	*MTBus.*, pp. 329–330

154.	CLW	Hartford	30 October 1885	*MTBus.*, p. 337
155.	CLW	Hartford	11 November 1885	*MTBus.*, pp. 341–342
156.	CLW	Hartford	20 December 1885	*MTBus.*, p. 347
157.	CLW	Hartford	19 March 1886	*MTBus.*, pp. 356–357
158.	CLW	Hartford	6 June 1886	*MTBus.*, pp. 360–361
159.	FJH	Elmira	12 July 1886	Berg
160.	FJH	Elmira	14 July 1886	PH, MTP
161.	FJH	Elmira	16 July 1886	Berg
162.	FJH	Elmira	21 July 1886	Berg
163.	FJH	Elmira	17 August 1886	Berg
164.	FJH	Elmira	19 August 1886	Berg
165.	FJH	Elmira	25 August 1886	Webster; TS, MTP
166.	FJH	Elmira	28 August 1886	Berg
167.	FJH	Elmira	4 September 1886	Berg
168.	FJH	Elmira	11 September 1886	Berg
169.	FJH	Hartford	30 September 1886	Berg
170.	CLW	Hartford	17 November 1886	*MTBus.*, pp. 367–368
171.	CLW	Hartford	6 December 1886	Webster; TS, MTP
172.	CLW	Hartford	14 December 1886	*MTBus.*, pp. 370–371
173.	CLW	Hartford	4 January 1887	*MTBus.*, p. 373
174.	CLW	Hartford	13 January 1887	*MTBus.*, p. 374
175.	CLW	Hartford	1 March 1887	*MTBus.*, p. 377
176.	CLW	Hartford	10 April 1887	Webster; TS, MTP
177.	CLW	Hartford	25 April 1887	Berg
178.	CLW	Hartford	28 May 1887	*MTBus.*, p. 383
179.	CLW	Hartford	16 June 1887	Berg
180.	FJH	Elmira	12 July 1887	Berg
181.	FJH	Elmira	15 July 1887	Berg

182. CLW	Elmira	3 August 1887	Berg
183. FJH and CLW	Elmira	15 August 1887	Berg
184. CLW	Elmira	16 August 1887	Berg
185. CLW & Co.	Elmira	23 August 1887	Berg
186. FJH	Hartford	2 September 1887	Berg
187. CLW and FJH	Elmira	5 September 1887	Berg
188. Orion Clemens	Elmira	7 September 1887	MTP
189. FJH	Elmira	8 September 1887	Berg
190. CLW & Co.	Hartford	18 September 1887	Berg
191. CLW & Co.	Hartford	14 October 1887	Berg
192. CLW & Co.	Hartford	17 October 1887	Berg
193. CLW & Co.	Hartford	19 October 1887	Webster; TS, MTP
194. CLW & Co.	Hartford	27 October 1887	Webster; TS, MTP
195. CLW & Co.	Hartford	13 November 1887	Webster; TS, MTP
196. CLW & Co.	Hartford	24 December 1887	Webster; TS, MTP
197. CLW	Hartford	28 December 1887	*MTBus,* pp. 389–390

V. 1888–1891

198. FJH	Hartford	7 May 1888	Berg
199. CLW & Co.	Elmira	15 July 1888	Berg
200. FJH	Hartford	12 November 1888	TS, MTP
201. FJH	Hartford	12 November 1888	Berg
202. FJH	Hartford	11 January 1889	TS, MTP
203. FJH	Elmira	2 July 1889	MTP
204. FJH	Elmira	24 July 1889	*MTL,* p. 511
205. FJH	Elmira	20 August 1889	CWB
206. FJH	Elmira	5 September 1889	Berg
207. FJH	Hartford	24 November 1889	MTP
208. FJH	Hartford	19 April 1890	Berg

209. FJH	Hartford	30 June 1890	Berg
210. FJH	Hartford	15 October 1890	Berg
211. FJH	Hartford	23 October 1890	Berg
212. FJH	Hartford	11 November 1890	MTP
213. FJH	Hartford	30 November 1890	Berg
214. FJH	Hartford	27 December 1890	PH, MTP
215. FJH	Hartford	3 February 1891	Berg
216. FJH	Hartford	13 February 1891	Berg
217. FJH	Hartford	13 February 1891	Berg
218. FJH	Hartford	15 February 1891	Berg
219. FJH	Hartford	27 February 1891	Berg
220. FJH	Hartford	10 March 1891	Berg
221. FJH	Hartford	29 March 1891	Berg
222. FJH	Hartford	9 April 1891	Berg
223. FJH	Hartford	4 May 1891	Berg
224. FJH	Hartford	13 May 1891	Berg
225. FJH	Hartford	13 May 1891	Berg
226. FJH	Hartford	20 May 1891	Berg
227. FJH	Paris	17 June 1891	Berg
228. FJH	Aix-les-Bains	10 July 1891	Berg
229. FJH	Aix-les-Bains	26 July 1891	Berg
230. FJH	Bayreuth	7 August 1891	Berg
231. FJH	Marienbad	24 August 1891	Berg
232. FJH	Geneva	15 September 1891	Berg
233. FJH	Berlin	16 October 1891	Berg
234. FJH	Berlin	20 October 1891	Berg
235. FJH	Berlin	27 October 1891	Huntington
236. FJH	Frankfurt	28 October 1891	Huntington
237. FJH	Berlin	7 November 1891	Berg
238. FJH	Berlin	8 November 1891	Berg
239. FJH	Berlin	19 November 1891	Berg
240. FJH	Berlin	22 November 1891	Berg
241. FJH	Berlin	27 November 1891	Berg
242. FJH	Berlin	1 December 1891	Berg
243. FJH	Berlin	22 December 1891	Berg

VI. 1892–1894

| 244. FJH | Ilsenburg | 6 January 1892 | Berg |
| 245. FJH | Berlin | 21 January 1892 | TS, MTP |

246. FJH	Berlin	25 January 1892	Berg
247. FJH	Berlin	2 February 1892	Berg
248. FJH	Berlin	5 February 1892	Berg
249. FJH	Berlin	12 February 1892	*MTL*, pp. 562–563
250. FJH	Mentone	8 March 1892	Berg
251. FJH	Rome	4 April 1892	Berg
252. FJH	Rome	24 April 1892	Berg
253. FJH	Venice	22 May 1892	Berg
254. FJH	Bad-Nauheim	22 July 1892	Berg
255. FJH	Bad-Nauheim	24 July 1892	Berg
256. FJH	Bad-Nauheim	10 August 1892	*MTL*, p. 565–566; **P.S.** from **Berg**
257. FJH	Bad-Nauheim	23 August 1892	Berg
258. FJH	Bad-Nauheim	4 September 1892	TS, MTP; P.S. from Berg
259. FJH	Lucerne	18 September 1892	Berg
260. FJH	Florence	5 October 1892	Berg
261. FJH	Florence	13 October 1892	Berg
262. FJH	Florence	31 October 1892	TS, MTP
263. Frank Bliss	Florence	31 October 1892	**Yale**
264. FJH	Florence	24 November 1892	Berg
265. FJH	Florence	7 December 1892	MTP
266. FJH	Florence	12 December 1892	Berg
267. FJH	Florence	26 December 1892	CWB
268. FJH	Florence	28 December 1892	Berg
269. FJH	Florence	1 January 1893	*MTL*, pp. 576–577
270. FJH	Florence	24 January 1893	Berg
271. FJH	Florence	28 January 1893	Berg
272. FJH	Florence	28 January 1893	Berg
273. FJH	Florence	3 February 1893	Berg
274. FJH	Florence	5 February 1893	Berg
275. FJH	Florence	25 February 1893	Berg
276. FJH	Florence	8 March 1893	Berg
277. Frank Bliss	Florence	8 March 1893	Berg
278. FJH	Florence	13 March 1893	Berg

279. FJH	Florence	2 June 1893	Berg
280. FJH	Florence	3 June 1893	TS, MTP
281. FJH	Munich	26 June 1893	Berg
282. FJH	Munich	3 July 1893	Berg
283. FJH	Munich	8 July 1893	*MTL*, p. 588
284. FJH	Krankenheil	18 July 1893	Berg
285. FJH	Krankenheil	26 July 1893	Berg
286. FJH	Krankenheil	30 July 1893	PH, Morgan
287. FJH	Krankenheil	6 August 1893	Berg
288. FJH	Krankenheil	9 August 1893	Berg
289. FJH	Krankenheil	14 August 1893	Berg; MTP
290. FJH	New York	6 January 1894	Berg

Index